THE BEST
AMERICAN
MAGAZINE
WRITING

2013

THE BEST
AMERICAN
MAGAZINE
WRITING
2013

**Compiled by
the American
Society of
Magazine
Editors**

Columbia University Press   New York

Columbia University Press
Publishers Since 1893
New York   Chichester, West Sussex
cup.columbia.edu
Copyright © 2013 Columbia University Press
All rights reserved

Library of Congress Cataloging-in-Publication Data
ISSN 1541-0978
ISBN 978-0-231-16225-8 (pbk.)

Columbia University Press books are printed on permanent and durable
acid-free paper.
This book is printed on paper with recycled content.
Printed in the United States of America

p 10 9 8 7 6 5 4 3 2 1

Cover Design: Catherine Casalino

References to websites (URLs) were accurate at the time of writing.
Neither the author nor Columbia University Press is responsible for URLs
that may have expired or changed since the manuscript was prepared.

Contents

James Bennet

Introduction

I have had it with long-form journalism. By which I mean—don't get me wrong—I'm fed up with the term *long-form* itself, a label that the people who create and sell magazines now invariably, and rather solemnly, apply to the work you will find in these pages. Reader, do you feel enticed to read a story by the distinction that it is long? Or does your heart not sink just a little? Would you feel drawn to a movie or a book simply because it is long? ("Oooh—you should really read *Moby-Dick*—it's *super* long.") Editors presumably care about words as much as anyone, so it is particularly mysterious that they would choose to promote their work by ballyhooing one of its less inherently appealing attributes. Do we call certain desserts "solid-fat-form food" or do we call them cakes and pies? Is baseball a long-form sport? Okay, sure—but would Major League Baseball ever promote it as that?

This choice of words matters, I think, not only because of the false note it sounds about stories like these but also because of the message it sends to the world about magazines' ambitions these days. The term *long-form* has come to stand for magazine journalism during the same period—over the past twenty years, and particularly the past ten—that magazines have had, as the politicians say, some challenges. I think this wrong turn in our taxonomy is a sign of, and may even contribute to, the continuing commercial upheaval and crisis in confidence. The story of the transition from an industry that was within memory so exuberant and ambitious—so grandiose, really, in its conception of its cultural and societal role—that it could declare itself to be inventing a "New Journalism," to an industry wringing its hands over preserving something called "long-form journalism," does not sound like a long-form story with a happy ending. It certainly doesn't sound like one I'd want read, much less live through. "New Journalism" is a stirring promise to the wider world; "long-form" is the mumbled incantation of a decaying priesthood.

And, in the digital age, making a virtue of mere length sends the wrong message to writers as well as readers. For when you don't have to print words on pages and then bundle the pages together and stick postage stamps on the result, you slip some of the constraints that have enforced excellence (and provided polite excuses for editors to trim fat) since Johannes Gutenberg began printing books. You no longer have to make that agonizing choice of the best example from among three or four—you can freely use them all. More adjectives? Why not? As a magazine writer, I used to complain that my editors would cut out all my great color, just to make the story fit; as an editor, I now realize that, yes, they had to make my stories fit and, no, that color wasn't so great. The editors were working to preserve the stuff that would make the story go, to make sure the story earned every incremental word, in service to the reader. *Long-form*, on the Web, is in danger of meaning merely "a lot of words."

This is a particularly ripe moment to rethink our terminology because deeply reported narrative and essayistic journalism is suddenly all the rage. Far from fading away, it shows signs of an energy and imagination not seen since the heyday of New Journalism. This was the year that the sports department of the *New York Times* pulled off the most digitally ambitious accomplishment in feature journalism, "Snow Fall," a narrative of skiers buried in an avalanche that was told through the layering of words, video, and graphics. The story brought in countless readers and a Pulitzer Prize. (Actually, you can count the readers—the *Times* said "Snowfall" generated 3.5 million page views in one week alone.) This was also the year that digital upstarts like *Buzzfeed* and *The Verge* turned to "long-form" editors to create big features, and produced compelling work. Heralding "a coming renaissance of long-form journalism," the twitchy news site *Politico* hired away the editor in chief of *Foreign Policy* magazine to commission writerly, deeply reported stories. "High-impact, magazine-style journalism is not a throwback to the past," *Politico*'s editors declared in a memo that should chasten the hand-wringers. "It is a genre that is even more essential in today's hyperkinetic news environment. It is a style of reporting and a mindset about illuminating what matters most that has a brilliant future."

Is this just a fad, maybe even a fraud? Cynics would say that publishing a few big feature stories is a shortcut to respectability, and they'd be correct. But realists, I'm happy to say, would comment further that such features work: they draw in a lot of readers. As social networks of human beings displace search algorithms, digital editors are discovering that not just headlines but overall quality matters more and more, whether a story is short or long. If you hope to entice a real person to pass your story on to a friend, then reporting matters, writing matters, and design matters. As journalism and its distribution on the Web mature, the most meaningful distinction is turning out to be not short versus long but good versus bad.

All of which brings me, at last, to the journalistic triumph that is Brian Mockenhaupt's feature "The Living and the Dead," which appears in this volume. For a feature story, it is really, really long. But I defy you to find a wasted word among the 22,000 that Mockenhaupt assembled. Length here is not a virtue in itself; it is, like a notebook or a computer or curiosity, a writer's tool, one that Mockenhaupt deploys, as he does the others, to maximum effect. As we follow a marine platoon on its rounds in Helmand province in southern Afghanistan, details accrete, characters deepen, drama builds. We witness, over time, the shocking and more subtle consequences of abrupt twists in the action. (This is why length is so important in baseball, too, by the way). Few magazines these days could afford to devote the many pages that Mockenhaupt's story would have required. I say "would have" because this story was published by Byliner, a digital platform for what its creators have the wit to call "quick reads."

Among the paradoxes of this era, when commercial travails are menacing the most costly forms of reporting, is that we have coincidentally produced maybe the greatest generation of war correspondents in the country's history. You will encounter the work of several of them in this volume. It is instructive to read Mockenhaupt's piece against Dexter Filkins's haunting memoir of war, "Atonement," for the insights the comparison yields into storytelling technique and into the depth of experience these reporters have gained from so many years covering war. Mockenhaupt, an Iraq War veteran, vanishes into his story. His reporting is so precise, so knowing, that he never uses the first person to describe what he has witnessed. Filkins, by contrast, is central to his tale. Ten years ago he was there, in Baghdad, after Fox Company, Second Battalion, Twenty-Third Marine Regiment accidentally opened fire on a family fleeing a scene of fighting. Filkins chanced to meet the survivors, and he wrote about the family back then for the *New York Times*. So it was to Filkins, years later, that one of the guilt-wracked marines turned in hopes of finding the family, to explain himself and seek understanding, maybe forgiveness. Filkins ultimately helped arrange a meeting, and then, in *The New Yorker*, summed the costs of war by telling this story of one veteran's, and one family's, braided pain.

Here's a taxonomic riddle for you: How is that Stephen King's tale in this collection, though of comparable length to the "long-form" stories, is known as a "short story"? The King short story justifies its label's emphasis on relative brevity—and further underscores the obtuseness of that other label—by delivering many of the satisfactions of a novel in a fraction of the length. It is a marvel of compression. In "Batman and Robin Have an Altercation," we meet an ordinary, sad man on an ordinary, sad errand—taking his father out of his nursing home for lunch. With just a few brush strokes, King portrays a son feeling abandoned as his father slips away into dementia. And then this seemingly quiet tale takes a shocking turn that affirms the resilience of the father's love for his child. Too many short stories these days, I think, read like writing exercises. You can admire the craftsmanship without feeling moved; you can respect the psychological insight while wondering why it is that nothing ever seems to happen. King's story—comic, dramatic, poignant, revelatory—is a reminder of the potential power of this form to entertain and provoke.

Length is hardly the quality that most meaningfully classifies these stories. Yet there is a legitimate conundrum here: If *long-form* doesn't fit, what term is elastic enough to encompass the varied journalism in this anthology, from the war stories to Mimi Swartz's lacerating examination of the assault on family planning in Texas, for *Texas Monthly*, to Charles Graeber's rollicking profile, for *Wired*, of the digital pioneer and accused criminal Kim Dotcom? How do you link a cinematic narrative, like Chris Heath's account for *GQ* of what happened when dozens of animals escaped a private zoo in Ohio, to a crystalline marvel of thinking and writing like Charles C. Mann's essay, for *Orion*, on the nature and fate of our own species?

And how do you account for the blurring of boundaries also evident here, as work from the digital realm energizes and reshapes traditional forms of journalism? For the first time, a purely digital magazine, *Slate*, won a National Magazine Award in head-to-head competition with print magazines, for the crisp authority of Dahlia Lithwick's commentary on the Supreme

Court. Consider, also, *The Atlantic*'s Ta-Nehisi Coates, who won the award for one of the oldest forms of magazine writing, the essay. That may have looked like a straightforward old-school triumph, but it wasn't. The morning after he won, Coates wrote a blog post thanking his commenters for their help over the years as, on our website, he worked through the ideas that ultimately cohered to form the essay. Noting that *The Atlantic* had also won the National Magazine Award for best website, Coates wrote, "In my mind, these awards are linked. Writing for the Web site has fundamentally changed how I write in print."

The magazine industry is moving past lazy dichotomies of print versus digital to a fusion of old values, ambitions, and techniques with new ways and means of reporting and storytelling. This is a hard transition, obviously, but, equally obviously, there's no going back. As journalists—people whose job it has always been to go out and learn something new every day—we should be on the attack, not in a defensive crouch. We should be talking about what we do in terms that help us look forward as well as back. So what can we call this emerging fusion? It seems to me that one might quite reasonably take a page from the last period of great creative ferment in our business and call it, simply, new journalism. What journalism could be newer? But there's another perfectly good, honorable name for this kind of work—the one on the cover of this anthology. You might just call it all magazine writing. And get on with it.

Acknowledgments

The American Society of Magazine Editors was founded fifty years ago, in September 1963. From the beginning, one of ASME's goals—really, its main goal—was to establish the National Magazine Awards. It didn't take long to get things going. ASME and its cosponsor, the Columbia Journalism School, presented the first National Magazine Award to *Look* magazine in 1966 for work published in 1965 (which is something you may want to remember as you read this book—it's the 2013 National Magazine Awards for stories published in 2012), along with Certificates of Special Recognition to *Ebony*, *The New Yorker* (for Truman Capote's *In Cold Blood*), and *Scientific American*.

Since that first award was presented (1966 was the year John Lennon said the Beatles were "more popular then Jesus now"—which presumably had nothing to do with the publication of *Time* magazine's "Is God Dead?" cover one month later), the National Magazine Awards have grown far beyond what the founders of ASME could have expected. There were fewer than one hundred entries in those early years and a handful of judges (based on the photographic evidence, they were generally tweed-wearing, pipe-smoking men except for one or two shirtdress-wearing, cigarette-smoking women).

Nowadays there are thousands of entries and hundreds of judges—330 this year—and an addiction to tobacco products has been replaced by a fixation on tiny screens. But the quality of the work endures. In fact, as James Bennet suggests in his introduction to this anthology, at a time when the relevance of magazine media is sometimes questioned, magazine journalism has never been better, and the enthusiasm readers show for it has never been greater. That goes not only for the kinds of long-form stories collected in this latest iteration of *Best American Magazine Writing* but also for the service journalism, celebrity profiles, fashion photography, graphic design, websites, and tablet editions that the members of ASME also celebrate when they gather every year at the National Magazine Awards Dinner in May to find out who won what.

Months before that happens, though, magazines by the truckload begin to arrive at the ASME offices for eventual distribution to the judges. This year nearly 260 publications entered the National Magazine Awards, submitting 1,636 entries in 24 categories, including 5 categories for digital content. The magazines that enter the awards every year range from literary journals that count their readers in the thousands to mass-market publications with audiences numbering in the tens of millions.

The judges are an equally diverse lot. Most work in New York for major publishers, but a quarter of the judges live and work outside the metropolitan area, many at smaller regional magazines. The majority are editors, some are writers, but there are also dozens of art directors and photography editors as well as journalism educators from around the country. What they all have in common is patience and dedication, at least when it comes to the National Magazine Awards. They have to, since each judge has to read hundreds of pages in preparation for the judging then sit in sometimes cramped conference rooms in downtown Manhattan for hours of deliberation before choosing finalists and winners.

The judges pick five finalists in most categories—seven in some with an especially large number of entries, such as Reporting and Feature Writing—then they pick the winner. It is those finalists and winners that are represented in this volume. And what do the winners get? A reproduction of Alexander Calder's stabile "Elephant" (which is the reason the National Magazine Awards are sometimes called Ellies, though a lot of editors just call them the ASMEs). These miniature mastodons are distributed at the aforementioned dinner, which this year was attended by 600 editors and publishers and hosted by Willie Geist of MSNBC's *Morning Joe* and NBC's *Today*.

Many of the winners and finalists are inside this book. Not all of them, of course—there's no way to include every piece. And some of them just won't fit, like *Mother Jones* magazine's election-changing "Full Secret Video of Private Romney Fundraiser," a.k.a. "the 47-percent video" (proving, as the judges said, the enduring influence of magazines, whether in print or digital form). You can watch it on YouTube along with the rest of the dinner. To find out more, visit magazine.org/asme to see the categories, finalists, winners, and judges for this year's awards. There's also a searchable database of past finalists and winners—a guide to a half century of extraordinary journalism.

The success of the awards depends on the judges—for their commitment and, of course, their impartiality—but the administration of the National Magazine Awards, including the judging and the dinner, is overseen by the ASME board of directors. ASME members are thankful for the hard work of both the judges and the board. Special thanks are due to the president of ASME, Lucy Schulte Danziger, the editor in chief of *Self*, for her selfless enthusiasm and electrifying energy.

The Columbia School of Journalism still sponsors the National Magazine Awards with ASME. I want to thank the dean of the school and Henry R. Luce Professor, Nicholas Lemann—who is leaving Columbia after a decade—and the associate dean of programs and prizes, Arlene Notoro Morgan, for their contributions to the awards.

I am especially grateful to James Bennet, the editor in chief of *The Atlantic*, for writing the introduction to this edition of *Best American Magazine Writing*. Congratulations are in order as well—*The Atlantic* won two National Magazine Awards this year, for Essays and Criticism (the piece opens this book) and Website (another winner that won't fit in this volume). It's also worth pointing out that *The Atlantic* is the most honored monthly in the history of the awards.

The members of ASME are thankful to our agent, David McCormick of McCormick & Williams, for his skillful representation of our interests. As always, I am thankful for the talent and enthusiasm of our editors at the Columbia University Press, Philip Leventhal and Michael Haskell.

On behalf of ASME, I want to thank our colleagues at MPA— the Association of Magazine Media, especially the chair of the board of directors, Michael Clinton of Hearst Magazines. I also want to thank Mary G. Berner, the president and CEO of MPA, as well as Cristina Dinozo, Sarah Hansen, Caitlin Cheney, John DeFrancesco and, of course, ASME's Nina Fortuna, whose hard work and common sense make the National Magazine Awards go.

And finally, ASME thanks the writers, editors, and magazines that permitted their stories to be published in *Best American Magazine Writing 2013*. Whatever you call what they do—long-form journalism, narrative journalism, literary journalism—there can be little doubt that we owe them more than thanks for their work.

THE BEST AMERICAN MAGAZINE WRITING

2013

The Atlantic

WINNER—ESSAYS AND
CRITICISM

This anthology opens with two essays about the 2012 presidential candidates, yet neither piece feels like old news. Both in fact tackle issues of enduring importance. The Atlantic *won the National Magazine Award for Essays and Criticism for Ta-Nehisi Coates's "Fear of a Black President"—a piece the judges called "politically and morally insightful." Here Coates argues that although race is, in Barack Obama's own words, an issue "this nation cannot afford to ignore," it is also a subject our first African American president cannot directly address.* The Atlantic *has long wrestled with the issue of race in America—the magazine was founded in support of abolition—and more than 150 years later it continues to shape the way magazine readers think about the future of our republic.*

Ta-Nehisi Coates

Fear of a Black President

The irony of President Barack Obama is best captured in his comments on the death of Trayvon Martin and the ensuing fray. Obama has pitched his presidency as a monument to moderation. He peppers his speeches with nods to ideas originally held by conservatives. He routinely cites Ronald Reagan. He effusively praises the enduring wisdom of the American people, and believes that the height of insight lies in the town square. Despite his sloganeering for change and progress, Obama is a conservative revolutionary, and nowhere is his conservative character revealed more than in the very sphere where he holds singular gravity—race.

Part of that conservatism about race has been reflected in his reticence: for most of his term in office, Obama has declined to talk about the ways in which race complicates the American present and, in particular, his own presidency. But then, last February, George Zimmerman, a twenty-eight-year-old insurance underwriter, shot and killed a black teenager, Trayvon Martin, in Sanford, Florida. Zimmerman, armed with a 9 mm handgun, believed himself to be tracking the movements of a possible intruder. The possible intruder turned out to be a boy in a hoodie, bearing nothing but candy and iced tea. The local authorities at first declined to make an arrest, citing Zimmerman's claim of self-defense. Protests exploded nationally. Skittles and Arizona

Iced Tea assumed totemic power. Celebrities—the actor Jamie Foxx, the former Michigan governor Jennifer Granholm, members of the Miami Heat—were photographed wearing hoodies. When Representative Bobby Rush of Chicago took to the House floor to denounce racial profiling, he was removed from the chamber after donning a hoodie midspeech.

The reaction to the tragedy was, at first, trans-partisan. Conservatives either said nothing or offered tepid support for a full investigation—and in fact it was the Republican governor of Florida, Rick Scott, who appointed the special prosecutor who ultimately charged Zimmerman with second-degree murder. As civil-rights activists descended on Florida, *National Review*, a magazine that once opposed integration, ran a column proclaiming "Al Sharpton Is Right." The belief that a young man should be able to go to the store for Skittles and an iced tea and not be killed by a neighborhood-watch patroller seemed uncontroversial.

By the time reporters began asking the White House for comment, the president likely had already given the matter considerable thought. Obama is not simply America's first black president—he is the first president who could credibly teach a black-studies class. He is fully versed in the works of Richard Wright and James Baldwin, Frederick Douglass and Malcolm X. Obama's two autobiographies are deeply concerned with race, and in front of black audiences he is apt to cite important but obscure political figures such as George Henry White, who served from 1897 to 1901 and was the last African American congressman to be elected from the South until 1970. But with just a few notable exceptions, the president had, for the first three years of his presidency, strenuously avoided talk of race. And yet, when Trayvon Martin died, talk Obama did:

> When I think about this boy, I think about my own kids, and I think every parent in America should be able to understand why it is absolutely imperative that we investigate every aspect

of this, and that everybody pulls together—federal, state, and local—to figure out exactly how this tragedy happened . . .

But my main message is to the parents of Trayvon Martin. If I had a son, he'd look like Trayvon. I think they are right to expect that all of us as Americans are going to take this with the seriousness it deserves, and that we're going to get to the bottom of exactly what happened.

The moment Obama spoke, the case of Trayvon Martin passed out of its national-mourning phase and lapsed into something darker and more familiar—racialized political fodder. The illusion of consensus crumbled. Rush Limbaugh denounced Obama's claim of empathy. *The Daily Caller,* a conservative website, broadcast all of Martin's tweets, the most loutish of which revealed him to have committed the unpardonable sin of speaking like a seventeen-year-old boy. A white-supremacist site called Stormfront produced a photo of Martin with pants sagging, flipping the bird. *Business Insider* posted the photograph and took it down without apology when it was revealed to be a fake.

Newt Gingrich pounced on Obama's comments: "Is the president suggesting that if it had been a white who had been shot, that would be okay because it wouldn't look like him?" Reverting to form, *National Review* decided the real problem was that we were interested in the deaths of black youths only when nonblacks pulled the trigger. John Derbyshire, writing for *Taki's Magazine,* an iconoclastic libertarian publication, composed a racist advice column for his children inspired by the Martin affair. (Among Derbyshire's tips: never help black people in any kind of distress; avoid large gatherings of black people; cultivate black friends to shield yourself from charges of racism.)

The notion that Zimmerman might be the real victim began seeping out into the country, aided by PR efforts by his family and legal team, as well as by various acts of stupidity—Spike Lee tweeting Zimmerman's address (an act made all the more repugnant by the fact that he had the wrong Zimmerman), NBC misleadingly editing a tape of Zimmerman's phone conversation with a police dispatcher to make Zimmerman seem to be racially profiling Martin. In April, when Zimmerman set up a website to collect donations for his defense, he raised more than $200,000 in two weeks, before his lawyer asked that he close the site and launched a new, independently managed legal-defense fund. Although the trial date has yet to be set, as of July the fund was still raking in up to $1,000 in donations daily.

But it would be wrong to attribute the burgeoning support for Zimmerman to the blunders of Spike Lee or an NBC producer. Before President Obama spoke, the death of Trayvon Martin was generally regarded as a national tragedy. After Obama spoke, Martin became material for an Internet vendor flogging paper gun-range targets that mimicked his hoodie and his bag of Skittles. (The vendor sold out within a week.) Before the president spoke, George Zimmerman was arguably the most reviled man in America. After the president spoke, Zimmerman became the patron saint of those who believe that an apt history of racism begins with Tawana Brawley and ends with the Duke lacrosse team.

The irony of Barack Obama is this: he has become the most successful black politician in American history by avoiding the radioactive racial issues of yesteryear, by being "clean" (as Joe Biden once labeled him)—and yet his indelible blackness irradiates everything he touches. This irony is rooted in the greater ironies of the country he leads. For most of American history, our political system was premised on two conflicting facts— one, an oft-stated love of democracy; the other, an undemocratic white supremacy inscribed at every level of government. In warring against that paradox, African Americans have historically been restricted to the realm of protest and agitation. But when President Barack Obama pledged to "get to the bottom of exactly what happened," he was not protesting or agitating. He was not appealing to federal power—he was employing it. The power was black—and, in certain quarters, was received as such.

No amount of rhetorical moderation could change this. It did not matter that the president addressed himself to "every parent in America." His insistence that "everybody [pull] together" was irrelevant. It meant nothing that he declined to cast aspersions on the investigating authorities, or to speculate on events. Even the fact that Obama expressed his own connection to Martin in the quietest way imaginable—"If I had a son, he'd look like Trayvon"—would not mollify his opposition. It is, after all, one thing to hear "I am Trayvon Martin" from the usual placard-waving rabble-rousers. Hearing it from the commander of the greatest military machine in human history is another.

By virtue of his background—the son of a black man and a white woman, someone who grew up in multiethnic communities around the world—Obama has enjoyed a distinctive vantage point on race relations in America. Beyond that, he has displayed enviable dexterity at navigating between black and white America, and at finding a language that speaks to a critical mass in both communities. He emerged into national view at the Democratic National Convention in 2004, with a speech heralding a nation uncolored by old prejudices and shameful history. There was no talk of the effects of racism. Instead Obama stressed the power of parenting, and condemned those who would say that a black child carrying a book was "acting white." He cast himself as the child of a father from Kenya and a mother from Kansas and asserted, "In no other country on Earth is my story even possible." When, as a senator, he was asked if the response to Hurricane Katrina evidenced racism, Obama responded by calling the "ineptitude" of the response "color-blind."

Racism is not merely a simplistic hatred. It is, more often, broad sympathy toward some and broader skepticism toward others. Black America ever lives under that skeptical eye. Hence the old admonishments to be "twice as good." Hence the need for a special "talk" administered to black boys about how to be extra careful when relating to the police. And hence Barack Obama's insisting that there was no racial component to Katrina's effects; that name-calling among children somehow has the same import as one of the oldest guiding principles of American policy—white supremacy. The election of an African American to our highest political office was alleged to demonstrate a triumph of integration. But when President Obama addressed the tragedy of Trayvon Martin, he demonstrated integration's great limitation—that acceptance depends not just on being twice as good but on being half as black. And even then, full acceptance is still withheld. The larger effects of this withholding constrict Obama's presidential potential in areas affected tangentially—or seemingly not at all—by race. Meanwhile, across the country, the community in which Obama is rooted sees this fraudulent equality, and quietly seethes.

Obama's first term has coincided with a strategy of massive resistance on the part of his Republican opposition in the House, and a record number of filibuster threats in the Senate. It would be nice if this were merely a reaction to Obama's politics or his policies—if this resistance truly were, as it is generally described, merely one more sign of our growing "polarization" as a nation. But the greatest abiding challenge to Obama's national political standing has always rested on the existential fact that if he had a son, he'd look like Trayvon Martin. As a candidate, Barack Obama understood this.

"The thing is, a *black man* can't be president in America, given the racial aversion and history that's still out there," Cornell Belcher, a pollster for Obama, told the journalist Gwen Ifill after the 2008 election. "However, an extraordinary, gifted, and talented young man who happens to be black can be president."

Belcher's formulation grants the power of antiblack racism, and proposes to defeat it by not acknowledging it. His is the per-

fect statement of the Obama era, a time marked by a revolution
that must never announce itself, by a democracy that must never
acknowledge the weight of race, even while being shaped by it.
Barack Obama governs a nation enlightened enough to send an
African American to the White House, but not enlightened
enough to accept a black man as its president.

·　　　·　　　·

Before Barack Obama, the "black president" lived in the African
American imagination as a kind of cosmic joke, a phantom of
all that could never be. White folks, whatever their talk of freedom and liberty, would not allow a black president. They could
not tolerate Emmett's boyish gaze. Dr. King turned the other
cheek, and they blew it off. White folks shot Lincoln over "nigger
equality," ran Ida Wells out of Memphis, beat Freedom Riders
over bus seats, slaughtered Medgar in his driveway like a dog. The
comedian Dave Chappelle joked that the first black president
would need a "Vice President Santiago"—because the only thing
that would ensure his life in the White House was a Hispanic
president-in-waiting. A black president signing a bill into law
might as well sign his own death certificate.

And even if white folks could moderate their own penchant
for violence, we could not moderate our own. A long-suffering
life on the wrong side of the color line had denuded black people
of the delicacy necessary to lead the free world. In a skit on his
1977 TV comedy show, Richard Pryor, as a black president, conceded that he was "courting an awful lot of white women" and
held a press conference that erupted into a riot after a reporter
requested that the president's momma clean his house. More recently, the comedian Cedric the Entertainer joked that a black
president would never have made it through Monicagate without
turning a press conference into a battle royal. When Chappelle

tried to imagine how a black George W. Bush would have justified the war against Saddam Hussein, his character ("Black
Bush") simply yelled, "The nigger tried to kill my father!"

Thus, in hard jest, the paradoxes and problems of a theoreti-
cal black presidency were given voice. Racism would not allow
a black president. Nor would a blackness, forged by America's
democratic double-talk, that was too ghetto and raw for the re-
finement of the Oval Office. Just beneath the humor lurked a
resonant pain, the scars of history, an aching doubt rooted in the
belief that "they" would never accept us. And so in our Harlems
and Paradise Valleys, we invoked a black presidency the way a
legion of five-foot point guards might invoke the dunk—as evidence of some great cosmic injustice, weighty in its import, out
of reach.

And yet Spud Webb lives.

When presidential candidate Barack Obama presented himself to the black community, he was not to be believed. It strained
credulity to think that a man sporting the same rigorously managed haircut as Jay-Z, a man who was a hard-core pickup basketball player, and who was married to a dark-skinned black woman
from the South Side, could coax large numbers of white voters
into the booth. Obama's blackness quotient is often a subject of
debate. (He himself once joked, while speaking to the National
Association of Black Journalists in 2007, "I want to apologize for
being a little bit late, but you guys keep on asking whether I'm
black enough.") But despite Obama's postelection reluctance to
talk about race, he has always displayed both an obvious affinity
for black culture and a distinct ability to defy black America's
worst self-conceptions.

The crude communal myth about black men is that we are in
some manner unavailable to black women—either jailed, dead,
gay, or married to white women. A corollary myth posits a direct
and negative relationship between success and black culture.
Before we actually had one, we could not imagine a black presi-

dent who loved being black. In *The Audacity of Hope,* Obama describes his first kiss with the woman who would become his wife as tasting "of chocolate." The line sounds ripped from *Essence* magazine. That's the point.

These cultural cues became important during Obama's presidential run and beyond. Obama doesn't merely evince blackness; he uses his blackness to signal and court African Americans, semaphoring in a cultural dialect of our creation—crooning Al Green at the Apollo, name-checking Young Jeezy, regularly appearing on the cover of black magazines, weighing the merits of Jay-Z versus Kanye West, being photographed in the White House with a little black boy touching his hair. There is often something mawkish about this signaling—like a Virginia politico thickening his Southern accent when talking to certain audiences. If you've often been the butt of political signaling (Sister Souljah, Willie Horton), and rarely the recipient, these displays of cultural affinity are powerful. And they are all the more powerful because Obama has been successful. Whole sections of America that we had assumed to be negrophobic turned out in support of him in 2008. Whatever Obama's other triumphs, arguably his greatest has been an expansion of the black imagination to encompass this: the idea that a man can be culturally black and many other things also—biracial, Ivy League, intellectual, cosmopolitan, temperamentally conservative, presidential.

It is often said that Obama's presidency has given black parents the right to tell their kids with a straight face that they can do anything. This is a function not only of Obama's election to the White House but of the way his presidency broadcasts an easy, almost mystic blackness to the world. The Obama family represents our ideal imagining of ourselves—an ideal we so rarely see on any kind of national stage.

What black people are experiencing right now is a kind of privilege previously withheld—seeing our most sacred cultural practices and tropes validated in the world's highest office.

Throughout the whole of American history, this kind of cultural power was wielded solely by whites, and with such ubiquity that it was not even commented upon. The expansion of this cultural power beyond the private province of whites has been a tremendous advance for black America. Conversely, for those who've long treasured white exclusivity, the existence of a President Barack Obama is discombobulating, even terrifying. For as surely as the iconic picture of the young black boy reaching out to touch the president's curly hair sends one message to black America, it sends another to those who have enjoyed the power of whiteness.

· · ·

In America, the rights to own property, to serve on a jury, to vote, to hold public office, to rise to the presidency have historically been seen as belonging only to those people who showed particular integrity. Citizenship was a social contract in which persons of moral standing were transformed into stakeholders who swore to defend the state against threats external and internal. Until a century and a half ago, slave rebellion ranked high in the fevered American imagination of threats necessitating such an internal defense.

In the early years of our republic, when democracy was still an unproven experiment, the Founders were not even clear that all white people should be entrusted with this fragile venture, much less the bestial African. Thus Congress, in 1790, declared the following:

> All free white persons who have, or shall migrate into the United States, and shall give satisfactory proof, before a magistrate, by oath, that they intend to reside therein, and shall take an oath of allegiance, and shall have resided in the United

States for one whole year, shall be entitled to all the rights of citizenship.

In such ways was the tie between citizenship and whiteness in America made plain from the very beginning. By the nineteenth century, there was, as Matthew Jacobson, a professor of history and American studies at Yale, has put it, "an unquestioned acceptance of whiteness as a prerequisite for naturalized citizenship." Debating Abraham Lincoln during the race for a U.S. Senate seat in Illinois in 1858, Stephen Douglas asserted that "this government was made on the white basis" and that the Framers had made "no reference either to the Negro, the savage Indians, the Feejee, the Malay, or an other inferior and degraded race, when they spoke of the equality of men."

After the Civil War, Andrew Johnson, Lincoln's successor as president and a unionist, scoffed at awarding the Negro the franchise:

The peculiar qualities which should characterize any people who are fit to decide upon the management of public affairs for a great state have seldom been combined. It is the glory of white men to know that they have had these qualities in sufficient measure to build upon this continent a great political fabric and to preserve its stability for more than ninety years, while in every other part of the world all similar experiments have failed. But if anything can be proved by known facts, if all reasoning upon evidence is not abandoned, it must be acknowledged that in the progress of nations Negroes have shown less capacity for government than any other race of people. No independent government of any form has ever been successful in their hands. On the contrary, wherever they have been left to their own devices they have shown a constant tendency to relapse into barbarism.

The notion of blacks as particularly unfit for political equality persisted well into the twentieth century. As the nation began considering integrating its military, a young West Virginian wrote to a senator in 1944:

> I am a typical American, a southerner, and 27 years of age . . . I am loyal to my country and know but reverence to her flag, BUT I shall never submit to fight beneath that banner with a negro by my side. Rather I should die a thousand times, and see Old Glory trampled in the dirt never to rise again, than to see this beloved land of ours become degraded by race mongrels, a throw back to the blackest specimen from the wilds.

The writer—who never joined the military, but did join the Ku Klux Klan—was Robert Byrd, who died in 2010 as the longest-serving U.S. senator in history. Byrd's rejection of political equality was echoed in 1957 by William F. Buckley Jr., who addressed the moral disgrace of segregation by endorsing disenfranchisement strictly based on skin color:

> The central question that emerges—and it is not a parliamentary question or a question that is answered by merely consulting a catalog of the rights of American citizens, born Equal—is whether the White community in the South is entitled to take such measures as are necessary to prevail, politically and culturally, in areas in which it does not predominate numerically? The sobering answer is Yes—the White community is so entitled because, for the time being, it is the advanced race.

Buckley, the founder of *National Review*, went on to assert, "The great majority of the Negroes of the South who do not vote do not care to vote and would not know for what to vote if they could."

The idea that blacks should hold no place of consequence in the American political future has affected every sector of American society, transforming whiteness itself into a monopoly on American possibilities. White people like Byrd and Buckley were raised in a time when, by law, they were assured of never having to compete with black people for the best of anything. Blacks used inferior public pools and inferior washrooms, attended inferior schools. The nicest restaurants turned them away. In large swaths of the country, blacks paid taxes but could neither attend the best universities nor exercise the right to vote. The best jobs, the richest neighborhoods, were giant set-asides for whites—universal affirmative action, with no pretense of restitution.

Slavery, Jim Crow, segregation: these bonded white people into a broad aristocracy united by the salient fact of unblackness. What Byrd saw in an integrated military was the crumbling of the ideal of whiteness, and thus the crumbling of an entire society built around it. Whatever the saintly nonviolent rhetoric used to herald it, racial integration was a brutal assault on whiteness. The American presidency, an unbroken streak of nonblack men, was, until 2008, the greatest symbol of that old order.

Watching Obama rack up victories in states like Virginia, New Mexico, Ohio, and North Carolina on Election Night in 2008, anyone could easily conclude that racism, as a national force, had been defeated. The thought should not be easily dismissed: Obama's victory demonstrates the incredible distance this country has traveled. (Indeed, William F. Buckley Jr. later revised his early positions on race; Robert Byrd spent decades in Congress atoning for his.) That a country that once took whiteness as the foundation of citizenship would elect a black president is a victory. But to view this victory as racism's defeat is to forget the precise terms on which it was secured, and to ignore the quaking ground beneath Obama's feet.

During the 2008 primary, *The New Yorker*'s George Packer journeyed to Kentucky and was shocked by the brazen declarations of white identity. "I think he would put too many minorities in positions over the white race," one voter told Packer. "That's my opinion." That voter was hardly alone. In 2010, Michael Tesler, a political scientist at Brown University, and David Sears, a professor of psychology and political science at UCLA, were able to assess the impact of race in the 2008 primary by comparing data from two 2008 campaign and election studies with previous surveys of racial resentment and voter choice. As they wrote in *Obama's Race: The 2008 Election and the Dream of a Post-Racial America*:

> No other factor, in fact, came close to dividing the Democratic primary electorate as powerfully as their feelings about African Americans. The impact of racial attitudes on individual vote decisions . . . was so strong that it appears to have even outstripped the substantive impact of racial attitudes on Jesse Jackson's more racially charged campaign for the nomination in 1988.

Seth Stephens-Davidowitz, a doctoral candidate in economics at Harvard, is studying how racial animus may have cost Obama votes in 2008. First, Stephens-Davidowitz ranked areas of the country according to how often people there typed racist search terms into Google. (The areas with the highest rates of racially charged search terms were West Virginia, western Pennsylvania, eastern Ohio, upstate New York, and southern Mississippi.) Then he compared Obama's voting results in those areas with John Kerry's four years earlier. So, for instance, in 2004 Kerry received 50 percent of the vote in the media markets of both Denver and Wheeling (which straddles the Ohio–West Virginia border). Based on the Democratic groundswell in 2008, Obama should have received about 57 percent of the popular vote in both regions. But that's not what happened. In the Denver area, which had one of the nation's lowest rates of racially charged Google searching, Obama received the predicted 57 percent. But in Wheeling, which had a high rate of racially charged Google searching, Obama's share of the popular vote was only 48 percent. Of course, Obama also picked up some votes because he is black. But, aggregating his findings nationally, Stephens-Davidowitz has concluded that Obama lost between 3 and 5 percentage points of the popular vote to racism.

After Obama won, the longed-for postracial moment did not arrive; on the contrary, racism intensified. At rallies for the nascent Tea Party, people held signs saying things like OBAMA PLANS WHITE SLAVERY. Steve King, an Iowa congressman and Tea Party favorite, complained that Obama "favors the black person." In 2009, Rush Limbaugh, bard of white decline, called Obama's presidency a time when "the white kids now get beat up, with the black kids cheering 'Yeah, right on, right on, right on.' And of course everybody says the white kid deserved it—he was born a racist, he's white." On *Fox & Friends*, Glenn Beck asserted that Obama had exposed himself as a guy "who has a deep-seated hatred for white people or the white culture. . . . This guy is, I believe, a racist." Beck later said he was wrong to call Obama a racist. That same week he also called the president's health-care plan "reparations."

One possible retort to this pattern of racial paranoia is to cite the Clinton years, when an ideological fever drove the right wing to derangement, inspiring militia movements and accusations that the president had conspired to murder his own lawyer, Vince Foster. The upshot, by this logic, is that Obama is experiencing run-of-the-mill political opposition in which race is but a minor factor among much larger ones, such as party affiliation. But the argument assumes that party affiliation itself is unconnected to race. It pretends that only Toni Morrison took note of Clinton's particular appeal to black voters. It forgets that Clinton felt compelled to attack Sister Souljah. It forgets that whatever ignoble labels the right wing pinned on Clinton's health-care plan, "reparations" did not rank among them.

Michael Tesler, following up on his research with David Sears on the role of race in the 2008 campaign, recently published a study assessing the impact of race on opposition to and support for health-care reform. The findings are bracing. Obama's election effectively racialized white Americans' views, even of health-care policy. As Tesler writes in a paper published in July in *The American Journal of Political Science*, "Racial attitudes had a significantly greater impact on health care opinions when framed as part of President Obama's plan than they had when the exact same policies were attributed to President Clinton's 1993 health care initiative."

While Beck and Limbaugh have chosen direct racial assault, others choose simply to deny that a black president actually exists. One in four Americans (and more than half of all Republicans) believe Obama was not born in this country, and thus is an illegitimate president. More than a dozen state legislatures have introduced "birther bills" demanding proof of Obama's citizenship as a condition for putting him on the 2012 ballot. Eighteen percent of Republicans believe Obama to be a Muslim. The goal of all this is to delegitimize Obama's presidency. If Obama is not truly American, then America has still never had a black president.

White resentment has not cooled as the Obama presidency has proceeded. Indeed, the GOP presidential-primary race featured candidates asserting that the black family was better off under slavery (Michele Bachmann, Rick Santorum); claiming that Obama, as a black man, should oppose abortion (Santorum again); or denouncing Obama as a "food-stamp president" (Newt Gingrich).

The resentment is not confined to Republicans. Earlier this year, West Virginia gave 41 percent of the popular vote during the Democratic primary to Keith Judd, a white incarcerated felon

(Judd actually defeated Obama in ten counties). Joe Manchin, one of West Virginia's senators, and Earl Ray Tomblin, its governor, are declining to attend this year's Democratic convention, and will not commit to voting for Obama.

It is often claimed that Obama's unpopularity in coal-dependent West Virginia stems from his environmental policies. But recall that no state ranked higher on Seth Stephens-Davidowitz's racism scale than West Virginia. Moreover, Obama was unpopular in West Virginia before he became president: even at the tail end of the Democratic primaries in 2008, Hillary Clinton walloped Obama by 41 points. A fifth of West Virginia Democrats openly professed that race played a role in their vote.

What we are now witnessing is not some new and complicated expression of white racism—rather, it's the dying embers of the same old racism that once rendered the best pickings of America the exclusive province of unblackness. Confronted by the thoroughly racialized backlash to Obama's presidency, a stranger to American politics might conclude that Obama provoked the response by relentlessly pushing an agenda of radical racial reform. Hardly. Daniel Gillion, a political scientist at the University of Pennsylvania who studies race and politics, examined the *Public Papers of the Presidents*, a compilation of nearly all public presidential utterances—proclamations, news-conference remarks, executive orders—and found that in his first two years as president, Obama talked less about race than any other Democratic president since 1961. Obama's racial strategy has been, if anything, the opposite of radical: he declines to use his bully pulpit to address racism, using it instead to engage in the time-honored tradition of black self-hectoring, railing against the perceived failings of black culture.

His approach is not new. It is the approach of Booker T. Washington, who, amid a sea of white terrorists during the era of Jim Crow, endorsed segregation and proclaimed the South to be a land of black opportunity. It is the approach of L. Douglas Wilder, who, in 1986, not long before he became Virginia's first black governor, kept his distance from Jesse Jackson and told an NAACP audience: "Yes, dear Brutus, the fault is not in our stars, but in ourselves. . . . Some blacks don't particularly care for me to say these things, to speak to values. . . . Somebody's got to. We've been too excusing." It was even, at times, the approach of Jesse Jackson himself, who railed against "the rising use of drugs, and babies making babies, and violence . . . cutting away our opportunity."

The strategy can work. Booker T.'s Tuskegee University still stands. Wilder became the first black governor in America since Reconstruction. Jackson's campaign moved the Democratic nominating process toward proportional allocation of delegates, a shift that Obama exploited in the 2008 Democratic primaries by staying competitive enough in big states to rack up delegates even where he was losing, and rolling up huge vote margins (and delegate-count victories) in smaller ones.

And yet what are we to make of an integration premised, first, on the entire black community's emulating the Huxtables? An equality that requires blacks to be twice as good is not equality—it's a double standard. That double standard haunts and constrains the Obama presidency, warning him away from candor about America's sordid birthmark.

.   .   .

Another political tradition in black America, running counter to the one publicly embraced by Obama and Booker T. Washington, casts its skepticism not simply upon black culture but upon the entire American project. This tradition stretches back to Frederick Douglass, who, in 1852, said of his native country, "There is not a nation on the earth guilty of practices more shocking and bloody than are the people of the United States at this very hour." It extends through Martin Delany, through Booker T.'s nemesis W. E. B. Du Bois, and through Malcolm X. It includes Martin

Luther King Jr., who at the height of the Vietnam War called America "the greatest purveyor of violence in the world today." And it includes Obama's former pastor, he of the famous "God Damn America" sermon, Jeremiah Wright.

The Harvard Law professor Randall Kennedy, in his 2011 book, *The Persistence of the Color Line: Racial Politics and the Obama Presidency*, examines this tradition by looking at his own father and Reverend Wright in the context of black America's sense of patriotism. Like Wright, the elder Kennedy was a veteran of the U.S. military, a man seared and radicalized by American racism, forever remade as a vociferous critic of his native country: in virtually any American conflict, Kennedy's father rooted for the foreign country.

The deep skepticism about the American project that Kennedy's father and Reverend Wright evince is an old tradition in black America. Before Frederick Douglass worked, during the Civil War, for the preservation of the Union, he called for his country's destruction. "I have no love for America," he declaimed in a lecture to the American Anti-Slavery Society in 1847. "I have no patriotism . . . I desire to see [the government] overthrown as speedily as possible and its Constitution shivered in a thousand fragments."

Kennedy notes that Douglass's denunciations were the words of a man who not only had endured slavery but was living in a country where whites often selected the Fourth of July as a special day to prosecute a campaign of racial terror:

On July 4, 1805, whites in Philadelphia drove blacks out of the square facing Independence Hall. For years thereafter, blacks attended Fourth of July festivities in that city at their peril. On July 4, 1834, a white mob in New York City burned down the Broadway Tabernacle because of the antislavery and antiracist views of the church's leaders. Firefighters in sympathy with the arsonists refused to douse the conflagration. On

July 4, 1835, a white mob in Canaan, New Hampshire, destroyed a school open to blacks that was run by an abolitionist. The antebellum years were liberally dotted with such episodes.

Jeremiah Wright was born into an America of segregation—overt in the South and covert in the North, but wounding wherever. He joined the Marines, vowing service to his country, at a time when he wouldn't have been allowed to vote in some states. He built his ministry in a community reeling from decades of job and housing discrimination and heaving under the weight of drugs, gun violence, and broken families. Wright's world is emblematic of the African Americans he ministered to, people reared on the anti-black-citizenship tradition—poll taxes, states pushing stringent voter-ID laws—of Stephen Douglas and Andrew Johnson and William F. Buckley Jr. The message is "You are not American." The countermessage—God damn America—is an old one, and is surprising only to people unfamiliar with the politics of black life in this country. Unfortunately, that is an apt description of large swaths of America.

Whatever the context for Wright's speech, the surfacing of his remarks in 2008 was utterly inconvenient not just for the Obama campaign but for much of black America. One truism holds that black people are always anxious to talk about race, eager to lecture white people at every juncture about how wrong they are and about the price they must pay for past and ongoing sins. But one reason Obama rose so quickly was that African Americans are war-weary. It was not simply the country at large that was tired of the old Baby Boomer debates. Blacks, too, were sick of talking about affirmative action and school busing. There was a broad sense that integration had failed us, and a growing disenchantment with our appointed spokespeople. Obama's primary triumphs in predominantly white states gave rise to rumors of a new peace, one many blacks were anxious to achieve.

And even those black Americans who embrace the tradition of God Damn America do so not with glee but with deep pain and anguish. Both Kennedy's father and Wright were military men. My own father went to Vietnam dreaming of John Wayne but came back quoting Malcolm X. The poet Lucille Clifton once put it succinctly:

> They act like they don't love their country
> No
> what it is
> is they found out
> their country don't love them.

In 2008, as Obama's election became imaginable, it seemed possible that our country had indeed, at long last, come to love us. We did not need our Jeremiah Wrights, our Jesse Jacksons, our products of the polarized sixties getting in the way. Indeed, after distancing himself from Wright, Obama lost almost no black support.

Obama offered black America a convenient narrative that could be meshed with the larger American story. It was a narrative premised on Crispus Attucks, not the black slaves who escaped plantations and fought for the British; on the Fifty-Fourth Massachusetts, not Nat Turner; on stoic and saintly Rosa Parks, not young and pregnant Claudette Colvin; on a Christlike Martin Luther King Jr., not an avenging Malcolm X. Jeremiah Wright's presence threatened to rupture that comfortable narrative by symbolizing that which makes integration impossible—black rage.

From the "inadequate black male" diatribe of the Hillary Clinton supporter Harriet Christian in 2008, to Rick Santelli's 2009 rant on CNBC against subsidizing "losers' mortgages," to Representative Joe Wilson's "You lie!" outburst during Obama's September 2009 address to Congress, to John Boehner's screaming "Hell no!" on the House floor about Obamacare in 2010, politicized rage has marked the opposition to Obama. But the rules of our racial politics require that Obama never respond in like fashion. So frightening is the prospect of black rage given voice and power that when Obama was a freshman senator, he was asked, on national television, to denounce the rage of Harry Belafonte. This fear continued with demands that he keep his distance from Louis Farrakhan and culminated with Reverend Wright and a presidency that must never betray any sign of rage toward its white opposition.

Thus the myth of "twice as good" that makes Barack Obama possible also smothers him. It holds that African Americans—enslaved, tortured, raped, discriminated against, and subjected to the most lethal homegrown terrorist movement in American history—feel no anger toward their tormentors. Of course, very little in our history argues that those who seek to tell bold truths about race will be rewarded. But it was Obama himself, as a presidential candidate in 2008, who called for such truths to be spoken. "Race is an issue that I believe this nation cannot afford to ignore right now," he said in his "More Perfect Union" speech, which he delivered after a furor erupted over Reverend Wright's "God Damn America" remarks. And yet, since taking office, Obama has virtually ignored race.

Whatever the political intelligence of this calculus, it has broad and deep consequences. The most obvious result is that it prevents Obama from directly addressing America's racial history, or saying anything meaningful about present issues tinged by race, such as mass incarceration or the drug war. There have been calls for Obama to take a softer line on state-level legalization of marijuana or even to stand for legalization himself. Indeed, there is no small amount of inconsistency in our black president's either ignoring or upholding harsh drug laws that every day injure the prospects of young black men—laws that could have ended his own, had he been of another social class and arrested for the marijuana use he openly discusses. But the intellectual argument doubles as the counterargument. If the fact of a black president is enough to racialize the wonkish world of health-care reform, what havoc would the Obama touch wreak upon the already racialized world of drug policy?

The political consequences of race extend beyond the domestic. I am, like many liberals, horrified by Obama's embrace of a secretive drone policy, and particularly the killing of American citizens without any restraints. A president aware of black America's tenuous hold on citizenship, of how the government has at times secretly conspired against its advancement—a black president with a broad sense of the world—should know better. Except a black president with Obama's past is the perfect target for right-wing attacks depicting him as weak on terrorism. The president's inability to speak candidly on race cannot be bracketed off from his inability to speak candidly on everything. Race is not simply a portion of the Obama story. It is the lens through which many Americans view all his politics.

But whatever the politics, a total submission to them is a disservice to the country. No one knows this better than Obama himself, who once described patriotism as more than pageantry and the scarfing of hot dogs. "When our laws, our leaders, or our government are out of alignment with our ideals, then the dissent of ordinary Americans may prove to be one of the truest expressions of patriotism," Obama said in Independence, Missouri, in June 2008. Love of country, like all other forms of love, requires that you tell those you care about not simply what they want to hear but what they need to hear.

But in the age of the Obama presidency, expressing that kind of patriotism is presumably best done quietly, politely, and with great deference.

•   •   •

This spring I flew down to Albany, Georgia, and spent the day with Shirley Sherrod, a longtime civil-rights activist who embodies exactly the kind of patriotism that Obama esteems. Albany is in Dougherty County, where the poverty rate hangs around 30 percent—double that of the rest of the state. On the drive in from the airport, the selection of vendors—payday loans, title loans, and car dealers promising no credit check—evidenced the statistic.

When I met Sherrod at her office, she was working to get a birthday card out to Roger Spooner, whose farm she'd once fought to save. In July 2010, the conservative commentator Andrew Breitbart posted video clips on his website of a speech Sherrod had delivered to the NAACP the previous March. The video was edited so that Sherrod, then an official at the U.S. Department of Agriculture, appeared to be bragging about discriminating against a white farmer and thus enacting a fantasy of racial revenge. The point was to tie Obama to the kind of black rage his fevered enemies often impute to him. Fearing exactly that, Sherrod's supervisors at the USDA called her in the middle of a long drive and had her submit her resignation via BlackBerry, telling her, "You're going to be on *Glenn Beck* tonight."

Glenn Beck did eventually do a segment on Sherrod—one in which he attacked the administration for forcing her out. As it turned out, the full context showed that Sherrod was actually documenting her own turn *away* from racial anger. The farmer who was the subject of the story came forward, along with his wife, and explained that Sherrod had worked tirelessly to help the family. The farmer was Roger Spooner.

Sherrod's career as an activist, first in civil rights and then later in the world of small farmers like Roger Spooner, was not chosen so much as thrust upon her. Her cousin had been lynched in 1943. Her father was shot and killed by a white relative in a dispute over some cows. There were three witnesses, but the grand jury in her native Baker County did not indict the suspect. Sherrod became an activist with the Student Nonviolent Coordinating Committee, registering voters near her hometown. Her husband, Charles Sherrod, was instrumental in leading the Albany Movement, which attracted Martin Luther King Jr. to town. But when Stokely Carmichael rose to lead SNCC and took it in a black-nationalist direction, the Sherrods, committed to nonviolence and integration, faced a weighty choice. Carmichael himself had been committed to nonviolence, until the killings and beatings he encountered as a civil-rights activist took their toll. Sherrod, with a past haunted by racist violence, would have seemed ripe for recruitment to the nationalist line. But she, along with her husband, declined, leaving SNCC in order to continue in the tradition of King and nonviolence.

Her achievements from then on are significant. She helped pioneer the farm-collective movement in America, and cofounded New Communities—a sprawling 6,000-acre collective that did everything from growing crops to canning sugar cane and sorghum. New Communities folded in 1985, largely because Ronald Reagan's USDA refused to sign off on a loan, even as it was signing off on money for smaller-scale white farmers. Sherrod went on to work with Farm Aid. She befriended Willie Nelson, held a fellowship with the Kellogg Foundation, and was short-listed for a job in President Clinton's Agriculture Department. Still, she remained relatively unknown except to students of the civil-rights movement and activists who promoted the rights of small farmers. And unknown she would have remained, had she not been very publicly forced out of her position by the administration of the country's first black president.

Through most of her career as an agriculture activist, Sherrod had found the USDA to be a barrier to the success of black farmers. What hurt black farms the most were the discriminatory practices of local officials in granting loans. Sherrod spent years protesting these practices. But then, after the election of Barack Obama, she was hired by the USDA, where she would be supervising the very people she'd once fought. Now she would have a chance to ensure fair and nondiscriminatory lending practices. Her appointment represented the kind of unnoticed but significant changes Obama's election brought.

But then the administration, intimidated by a resurgent right wing specializing in whipping up racial resentment, compelled Sherrod to resign on the basis of the misleading clips. When the full tape emerged, the administration was left looking ridiculous.

And cowardly. An e-mail chain later surfaced in which the White House congratulated Agriculture Secretary Tom Vilsack's staff for getting ahead of the news cycle. None of them had yet seen the full tape. That the Obama administration would fold so easily gives some sense of how frightened it was of a protracted fight with any kind of racial subtext, particularly one that had a subtext of black rage. Its enemies understood this, and when no black rage could be found, they concocted some. And the administration, in a panic, knuckled under.

Violence at the hands of whites robbed Shirley Sherrod of a cousin and a father. White rage outlined the substantive rules of her life: Don't quarrel with white people. Don't look them in the eye. Avoid Route 91 after dark. White racism destroyed New Communities, a fact validated by the nearly $13 million the organization received in the class-action suit it joined alleging racial discrimination by the local USDA officials granting loan applications. (Which means that her being forced out by Vilsack was the second time the USDA had wronged her directly.) And yet through it all, Sherrod has hewed to the rule of "twice as good." She has preached nonviolence and integration. The very video that led to her dismissal was of a speech aimed at black people, warning them against the dangers of succumbing to rage.

Driving down a sparse country road, Sherrod and I pulled over to a grassy footpath and stepped out at the spot where her father had been shot and killed in 1965. We then drove a few miles into Newton, and stopped at a large brick building that used to be the courthouse where Sherrod had tried to register to vote a few months after her father's death but had been violently turned back by the sheriff; where a year later Sherrod's mother pursued a civil case against her husband's killer. (She lost.) For this, Sherrod's mother enjoyed routine visits from white terrorists, which abated only after she, pregnant with her dead husband's son, appeared in the doorway with a gun and began calling out names of men in the mob.

When we got back into the car, I asked Sherrod why she hadn't given in to rage against her father's killers and sided with Stokely Carmichael. "It was simple for me," she said. "I really wanted to work. I wanted to win."

I asked Sherrod if she thought the president had a grasp of the specific history of the region and of the fights waged and the sacrifices made in order to make his political journey possible. "I don't think he does," Sherrod said. "When he called me [shortly after the incident], he kept saying he understood our struggle and all we'd fought for. He said, 'Read my book and you'll see.' But I *had* read his book."

In 2009, Sergeant James Crowley arrested Henry Louis Gates Jr., the eminent professor of African American studies at Harvard, at his front door in Cambridge, for, essentially, sassing him. When President Obama publicly asserted the stupidity of Crowley's action, he was so besieged that the controversy threatened to derail what he hoped would be his signature achievement—health-care reform. Obama, an African American male who had risen through the ranks of the American elite, was no doubt sensitive to untoward treatment at the hands of the police. But his expounding upon it so provoked right-wing rage that he was forced away from doing the kind of truth telling he'd once lauded. "I don't know if you've noticed," Obama said at the time, "but nobody's been paying much attention to health care."

Shirley Sherrod has worked all her life to make a world where the rise of a black president born of a biracial marriage is both conceivable and legal. She has endured the killing of relatives, the ruination of enterprises, and the defaming of her reputation. Crowley, for his actions, was feted in the halls of American power, honored by being invited to a "beer summit" with the man he had arrested and the leader of the free world. Shirley Sherrod, unjustly fired and defamed, was treated to a brief phone call from a man whose career, in some profound way, she had made possible. Sherrod herself is not immune to this point. She talked to me about crying with her husband while watching Obama's Election Night speech. In her new memoir, *The Courage to Hope*, she writes about a different kind of tears: when she discussed her firing with her family, her mother, who'd spent her life facing down racism at its most lethal, simply wept. "What will my babies say?" Sherrod cried to her husband, referring to their four small granddaughters. "How can I explain to my children that I got fired by the first black president?"

•   •   •

In 2000, an undercover police officer followed a young man named Prince Jones from suburban Maryland through Washington, D.C., into northern Virginia and shot him dead, near the home of his girlfriend and eleven-month-old daughter. Jones was a student at Howard University. His mother was a radiologist. He was also my friend. The officer tracking Prince thought he was on the trail of a drug dealer. But the dealer he was after was short and wore dreadlocks—Prince was tall and wore his hair cropped close. The officer was black. He wore dreadlocks and a T-shirt, in an attempt to look like a drug dealer. The ruse likely worked. He claimed that after Prince got out of his car and confronted him, he drew his gun and said "Police"; Prince returned to his car and repeatedly rammed the officer's unmarked car with his own vehicle. The story sounded wildly at odds with the young man I knew. But even if it was accurate, I could easily see myself frightened by a strange car following me for miles, and then reacting wildly when a man in civilian clothes pulled out a gun and claimed to be a cop. (The officer never showed a badge.)

No criminal charges were ever brought against Carlton Jones, the officer who killed my friend and rendered a little girl father-less. It was as if society barely blinked. A few months later, I moved to New York. When 9/11 happened, I wanted nothing to do with any kind of patriotism, with the broad national ceremony of mourning. I had no sympathy for the firefighters, and some-thing bordering on hatred for the police officers who had died. I lived in a country where my friend—twice as good—could be shot down mere footsteps from his family by agents of the state. God damn America, indeed.

I grew. I became a New Yorker. I came to understand the lim-its of anger. Watching Barack Obama crisscross the country to roaring white crowds, and then get elected president, I became convinced that the country really had changed—that time and events had altered the nation, and that progress had come in places I'd never imagined it could. When Osama bin Laden was killed, I cheered like everyone else. God damn al-Qaeda.

When trans-partisan mourning erupted around Trayvon Martin, it reinforced my conviction that the world had changed since the death of Prince Jones. Like Prince, Trayvon was sus-pected of being a criminal chiefly because of the color of his skin. Like Prince's, Trayvon's killer claimed self-defense. Again, with little effort, I could see myself in the shoes of the dead man. But this time, society's response seemed so very different, so much more heartening.

Then the first black president spoke, and the Internet bloomed. Young people began "Trayvoning"—mocking the death of a black boy by photographing themselves in hoodies, with Skittles and iced tea, in a death pose.

In a democracy, so the saying goes, the people get the govern-ment they deserve. Part of Obama's genius is a remarkable ability to soothe race consciousness among whites. Any black person who's worked in the professional world is well acquainted with this trick. But never has it been practiced at such a high level, and never have its limits been so obviously exposed. This need to talk in dulcet tones, to never be angry regardless of the offense, bespeaks a strange and compromised integration indeed, revealing a country so infantile that it can countenance white acceptance of blacks only when they meet an Al Roker standard.

And yet this is the uncertain foundation of Obama's historic victory—a victory that I, and my community, hold in the highest esteem. Who would truly deny the possibility of a black presidency in all its power and symbolism? Who would rob that little black boy of the right to feel himself affirmed by touching the kinky black hair of his president?

I think back to the first time I wrote Shirley Sherrod, requesting an interview. Here was a black woman with every reason in the world to bear considerable animosity toward Barack Obama. But she agreed to meet me only with great trepidation. She said she didn't "want to do anything to hurt" the president.

New York

FINALIST—COLUMNS AND
COMMENTARY

This piece was written in January 2012, yet even that early in the campaign for the Republican nomination, Frank Rich correctly identified the problem Mitt Romney would pose for voters in the primaries and later in the general election—the sense of unease about the man. More impressive is the way Rich located the source of the problem: Romney's unwillingness to talk about his faith—and this in a nation where religion remains central. The National Magazine Award judges described this piece and the two others by Rich that were nominated with it for the National Magazine Award for Columns and Commentary— "Mayberry RIP," about Americans' willful amnesia toward our past, and "Nora's Secret," about the death of his friend Nora Ephron— as "precise, powerful, and sometimes prescient."

Frank Rich

Who in God's Name Is Mitt Romney?

Back in the thick of the 2008 Republican presidential race, I asked a captain of American finance what he had made of Mitt Romney when they were young colleagues at Bain & Company. "Mitt was a nice guy, a smart businessman, and an excellent team player," he responded without missing a beat. Then came the CEO's one footnote, delivered with bemusement, not pique: "Still, whenever the rest of us would go out at the end of the day, we'd always find ourselves having the same conversation: None of us had any idea who this guy was."

Here we are in 2012, and nothing has changed. What Romney's former colleague observed of the young Mitt at close range decades ago could stand as the judgment of most Americans watching him at a cable-news remove now. That's why his campaign has so often been on the ropes. That's why, in a highly polarized nation, the belief that Romney is a phony may be among the very last convictions still bringing left, right, and center together. As a focus-group participant evocatively told pollster Peter Hart in November, Romney reminded him of the "dad who's never home." Nonetheless, this phantom has spent most of the campaign as the "presumed" front-runner for his party's nomination. Amazingly, this conventional wisdom held up throughout 2011, even though 75 percent of Romney's own party was searching so frantically for an alternative that Donald Trump enjoyed a nanosecond bump in the polls.

Now much of the 75 percent has identified the non-Mitt candidate who really does express where the GOP is today. Newt Gingrich is proud to stir a dollop of race into the vitriol he hurls at Barack Obama, "the food-stamp president." He's a human Vesuvius at spewing populist anger at all elites; attacks by the press or by Republican establishment talking heads like Karl Rove and Joe Scarborough only make him stronger. And unlike any other GOP leader, he can boast that he actually realized the Tea Party's goal of shutting the government down. The morning after Newt shut Mitt down in South Carolina, Rich Lowry, the editor of the pro-Mitt, anti-Newt *National Review*, channeled the horror of GOP grandees everywhere. "If Romney can't right himself," he wrote, then "every major elected Republican in the country will panic" and "every unlikely scenario to get another candidate in the race will be explored." The names once again being floated—Mitch Daniels! Jeb Bush! Paul Ryan! Bobby Jindal!—have not been known to raise the pulse rate of anyone beyond the 25 percent of the GOP embodied by elite conservative pundits in Washington and New York.

What's more likely is that the party's panicked establishment, and its Wall Street empire, will succeed in their push to crush Gingrich and prop up Romney in any way they can. They still see Mitt as the best available front man for the radical party the Republicans have become—the dutiful Eagle Scout who can hold down the fort as the right's self-styled revolutionary rabble threaten to overwhelm today's GOP elites the way the Goldwater insurgents once did Nelson Rockefeller and Romney's father, George. Some of the same Beltway types who have reinforced Mitt's presumed victory march since last summer believe he can be rebooted for the fall merely with some stern course correction.

As this narrative has it, Americans are at least comfortable with old, familiar Mitt—heaven knows he's been running long enough. He may be a bore and a flip-flopper, but he doesn't frighten the horses. His steady sobriety will win the day once the lunatic Newt has finished blowing himself up. As one prominent Romney surrogate, the Utah congressman Jason Chaffetz, has it, Romney is "the most vetted candidate out there." Maybe—if you assume there will be no more questions about Bain, the Cayman Islands, the expunged internal records from Romney's term as governor, or his pre-2010 tax returns. Or about the big dog that has yet to bark, and surely will by October: Romney's long career as a donor to and lay official of the Church of Jesus Christ of Latter-day Saints. But you can also construct an alternative narrative—that the vetting has barely even begun, and that the "Mitt Romney" we've been sold since 2008 is a lazy media construct, a fictional creation, or maybe even a hoax.

·   ·   ·

For four years now, Republicans have been demonizing Barack Obama for his alleged "otherness"—trashing him as a less-than-real American pushing "anticolonial," socialist, and possibly Islamist ideas gleaned from a rogue's gallery of subversive influences led by his Kenyan father, Saul Alinsky, and the Reverend Jeremiah Wright. And yet Romney is in some ways more exotic and more removed from "real America" than Obama ever was, his gleaming white camouflage notwithstanding. Romney is white, all right, but he's a white shadow. He can come across like an android who's been computer-generated to be the perfect genial candidate. When forced to interact with actual people, he tries hard, but his small talk famously takes the form of guessing a voter's age or nationality (usually incorrectly) or offering a greeting of "Congratulations!" for no particular reason. Richard Nixon was epically awkward too, but he could pass (in Tom Wicker's phrase) as "one of us." Unlike Nixon's craggy face, or, for that matter, Gingrich's, Romney's does not look lived in. His eyes don't show the mileage of a veteran fighter's journey through triumphs and hard knocks—the profile that Americans prefer to immaculate perfection in a leader during tough times. Even at Mitt's most human, he resembles George Hamilton without the self-deprecating humor or the perma-tan.

That missing human core, that inauthenticity and inability to connect, has been a daily complaint about Romney. To flesh out the brief, critics usually turn to his blatant political opportunism and rarefied upbringing—his history of ideological about-faces and his cakewalk as the prep-school-burnished, Harvard-educated son of a fabled auto executive. But the hollowness of Romney is not merely a function of his craven surrender to the rightward tilt of the modern GOP or the patrician blind spots he acquired at too many fancy schools and palatial country clubs. If that were the case, he'd pass for another Bush and receive some of the love that Bush father and son earned from the party faithful in their salad days. Some think he can get there by learning better performance skills: As Chuck Todd of NBC News put it, he "has to learn how to connect, how to speak emotionally . . . more from the heart." If Nixon could learn how to sell himself in 1968 under the tutelage of Roger Ailes, and Bush 41 could receive coaching from the legendary acting teacher Stella Adler in 1980, there might still be hope for Romney under the instruction of, say, Kelsey Grammer. But Romney is too odd, too much a mystery man. We don't know his history the way we did Nixon's and Bush's. His otherness seems not a matter of style and pedigree but existential.

We don't know who Romney is for the simple reason that he never reveals who he is. Even when he is not lying about his history—whether purporting to have been "a hunter pretty much all my life" (in 2007) or to being a denizen of "the real streets of America" (in 2012)—he is incredibly secretive about almost everything that makes him tick. He has been in hiding throughout his stints in both the private and public sectors. While his career-long refusal to release his tax returns was damaging in itself, it resonated even more so as a proxy for all the other secrets he has kept and still keeps.

Just as Republican caucus votes were being (re-)counted in Iowa, the first serious and thorough Romney biography was published, to deservedly favorable reviews. The authors, Michael Kranish and Scott Helman, are *Boston Globe* investigative reporters who have tracked him for years. Their book, *The Real Romney*, is manifestly fair and nonpartisan, giving him full credit for his drive and smarts as a pioneer in the entrepreneurial realm of private equity. But it's a measure of how much voters view Romney as a nonentity that they have shown so little interest in reading it. Not even a rave in the *Times* the week before the South Carolina primary could catapult *The Real Romney* into the top 500 of the Amazon list, despite the serious possibility that its protagonist could be the next president of the United States.

The book has no bombshells, and the very lack of them is revealing. For all the encyclopedic detail its authors amassed, and all the sources they mined, their subject remains impenetrable. "A wall. A shell. A mask," they write at the outset, listing the terms used by many who "have known or worked with Romney" and view him as "a man who sometimes seems to be looking not into your eyes but past them." Former business and political colleagues are in agreement that he has scant interest in mingling with people in even casual social interactions (in a hallway, for instance) and displays "little desire to know who people are." He so "rarely went out with the guys in any social venue" that one business associate dubbed him the Tin Man for "his inability to bond." During his one term as governor of Massachusetts, Romney was inaccessible to legislators, with ropes and elevator settings often restricting access to his suite of offices. He was notorious, one lawmaker explained, for having "no idea what our names were—none." A longtime Republican, after watching Romney's vacuous, failed senatorial campaign against Teddy Kennedy in 1994, came to the early conclusion that Mitt's "main cause appeared to be himself." This was borne out in 2006, when Romney spent more than 200 days out of Massachusetts ginning up a presidential run rather than attending to his duties as the state's chief executive.

Aside from his ability to build Bain Capital and pile up profits there, Romney has remarkably few visible accomplishments to show for his sixty-four years. He can't prove that he actually generated any jobs as a venture capitalist (beyond those at Bain itself), which is why he constantly revises the number of jobs he claims to have created (or, as he carefully hedges it, "helped create"). His sole achievement as governor was the Massachusetts prototype for the Obama health-care law—a feat he now alternately fudges or runs away from. The state's record of job creation on his watch was the fourth worst of the fifty states.

Known for being frugal to a fault, Romney does not seem to particularly relish spending his fortune. He likes data, and his piles of dollars seem to be mainly markers to keep score of his success. Though he now tries to wrap himself in Main Street brands like Staples and Domino's Pizza that passed through Bain's clutches, he was not intellectually or managerially engaged in the businesses that Bain bought and sold; he didn't run any of them. He seems to have no cultural passions beyond his and his wife's first-date movie, *The Sound of Music*. He is not a sportsman or conspicuous sports fan. His only real, nonnumerical passions seem to be his photogenic, intact family, which he wields like a weapon whenever an opponent with multiple marriages like John McCain or Gingrich looms into view—and, of course, his faith.

That faith is key to the Romney mystery. Had the 2002 Winter Olympics not been held in Salt Lake City, and not been a major civic project of Mormon leaders there, it's unlikely Romney would have gotten involved. (Whether his involvement actually prompted a turnaround of that initially troubled enterprise, as he claims, is a subject of debate.) But Romney is even less forthcoming about his religion than he is about his tax returns. When the Evangelical view of Mormonism as a non-Christian cult threatened his 2008 run, Romney delivered what his campaign hyped as a JFK-inspired speech on "Faith in America." This otherwise forgotten oration was memorable only for the number of times it named Romney's own faith: once.

In the current campaign, Romney makes frequent reference to faith, God, and his fierce loyalty to "the same church." But whether in debates, or in the acres of official material on his campaign website, or in a flyer pitched at religious voters in South Carolina, he never names what that faith or church is. In Romneyland, Mormonism is the religion that dare not speak its name. Which leaves him unable to talk about the very subject he seems to care about most, a lifelong source of spiritual, familial, and intellectual sustenance. We're used to politicians who camouflage their real views about issues, or who practice fraud in their backroom financial and political deal making, but this is something else. Romney's very public persona feels like a hoax because it has been so elaborately contrived to keep his core identity under wraps.

His campaign is intent on enforcing the redaction of his religion, not least, one imagines, because a Gallup poll found that 22 percent in both parties say they would not vote for a Mormon for president. (Only 5 percent admit feeling that way about an African American.) A senior adviser explained the strategy of deflecting any discussion of Romney's Mormon life to *Politico*: "Someone takes a shot at the governor's faith, we put a scarlet letter on them, RB, religious bigot." Good luck with that. Like Romney's evasions about his private finances, his conspicuous cone of silence about this major pillar of his biography also leaves you wondering what he is trying to hide. That his faith can be as secretive as he is—Ann Romney's non-Mormon parents were not allowed to attend the religious ceremony consecrating her marriage to Mitt—only whets the curiosity among the 82 percent of Americans who tell pollsters they know little or nothing about Mormonism.

Weeks before his death, Christopher Hitchens, no more a fan of LDS than of any other denomination, wrote that "we are fully entitled" to ask Romney about the role of his religion in influencing his political formation. Of course we are. Romney is not merely a worshipper sitting in the pews but the scion of a family dynasty integral to the progress of an American-born faith that has played a large role in the public square. Since his youthful stint as a missionary, he has served LDS in a variety of significant posts. The answers to questions about Romney's career as a lay church official may tell us more about who he is than his record at Bain, his sparse tenure as governor, or his tax returns.

The questions are not theological. Nor are they about polygamy, the scandalous credo that earlier Romneys practiced even after the church banned it in 1890. Rather, the questions are about the Mormon church's political actions during Mitt Romney's lifetime—and about what role Romney, as both a leader and major donor, might have played or is still playing in those actions. To ask these questions is not to be a religious bigot but to vet a candidate for the nation's highest job. Given how often Romney himself cites his faith as a defining force in his life, voters have a right to know what role he played when his faith intersected with the secular lives of his fellow citizens.

As we learn in *The Real Romney*, Mitt Romney has performed many admirable acts of charity for members of his church in dire straits. But the flip side of this hands-on engagement is whether, in his various positions in the church, he countenanced or enforced its discriminatory treatment of blacks and women, practices it only started to end in earnest well after he had entered adulthood. It wasn't until 1978, when he was in his thirties, that blacks were given full status in his church—an embarrassing fact that Romney tried to finesse in his last campaign by speaking emotionally on *Meet the Press* of seeing his father join Martin Luther King on a civil-rights march. (The *Boston Phoenix* would soon report that this was another lie about his past.) In the seventies, Romney's church also applied its institutional muscle to battling the ratification of the Equal Rights Amendment for women. And these days, no major faith puts more money where its mouth is in battling civil rights for gay Americans. Its actions led Stuart Matis, a faithful graduate of Brigham Young University who'd completed his missionary service, to commit suicide on the steps of a Mormon chapel in 2000 in anguished protest of his dehumanized status within his religion. Unchastened, the Mormon church enlisted its congregants to put over Proposition 8 in California in 2008. Mormons contributed more than $20 million to the effort and constituted an estimated 80 to 90 percent of the campaign's original volunteers. Romney, who endorsed gay rights when running as a moderate against Kennedy in 1994, has swung so far in the other direction that he ridiculed gay couples when pandering to South Carolina Republicans a few years ago. ("Some are actually having children born to them!" he said with horror.) Did some of his yet undivulged Mormon philanthropy support the Prop 8 campaign?

Even if these questions yield benign answers, we know that Romney's faith has contributed to his self-segregation from the actual "real streets of America." His closest circle comes from within his faith, and while there's nothing wrong with that, the fact remains that today the American Mormon population is still only 1 percent black. (Those recent television promo spots marketing LDS as a fount of diversity are a smoke screen.) Much as the isolating cocoon of Romney's wealth can lead him to dismiss $347,327 in speaking fees as "not very much" (to take just one recent example of his cluelessness about how the other 99 percent lives), so the demographic isolation imposed by his religion takes its own political toll. When he's forced to interact with the America beyond his hermetically sealed Mormon orbit, we get instant YouTube classics like his attempt to get down and rap with black voters on Martin Luther King Day four years ago by quoting "Who Let the Dogs Out?"

·   ·   ·

Given Romney's maladroitness as a retail politician, the failure of even his own fans to convey any enthusiasm for him, and the 75 percent of his party that questions his conservatism, it's hard to fathom how he kept being judged inevitable by so many observers just as he was losing two of the first three election-year contests. Even a normally hardheaded, data-driven analyst like the *Times* poll maven Nate Silver couldn't resist being swept up by this narrative, going beyond the numbers to write in a January 16 post that the 90 percent odds given a Romney nomination by the betting market Intrade "may if anything be too conservative." (Six days later, after South Carolina, Silver wrote, "Perhaps, then, there is profound resistance among Republican voters to nominating Mr. Romney after all.") Much of the Romney inflation, naturally, has to do with his good fortune in having such a splintered and screwy scrum of opponents. Often we're told that he "looks like a president" (that would be a pre-Obama president). We also hear constantly about his message discipline, his organization, and his money—attributes that matter more to political consultants and the pundits who pal around with them than to an angry electorate trying to dig out of a recession. To the political class, Romney is the most electable candidate because his mealy-mouthed blandness is what will lure that much-apotheosized yet indistinct band of moderates and independents to his side. But as Michael Kinsley long ago joked that Al Gore was an old person's idea of a young person, so Mitt Romney is a political hack's idea of an electable conservative president. Voters may have another view, and certainly did in South Carolina, where exit polls found that those who most valued a candidate's electability rallied to Newt.

But if the power of Mitt's money and the power of pack journalism helped contribute to his status as indestructible, the power of denial at the higher reaches of the GOP did even more so. The Republican establishment has been adamant in insisting that economic populism and class warfare do not infect their own ranks and that economic inequality is strictly a lefty and Democratic gripe. If that's the case, then Romney's strong identification with the 1 percent stigmatized by Occupy Wall Street would indeed present no problem. But a January Pew poll found that a majority of both Republicans and Independents now join Democrats in feeling that there are "strong conflicts" between the rich and poor in America; a recent NBC News–*Wall Street Journal* survey found that Republican voters were just as likely as Democrats to blame "Wall Street bankers" most of all for the country's economic problems. It's hardly a stretch that some of that blame might attach itself to Romney, especially after Gingrich turned a spotlight on his Bain résumé.

When the battle over Bain broke out in New Hampshire, both the Romney campaign and the right were blindsided. "Perhaps the most striking thing about the current fight over Mitt Romney's career in private equity is how little we knew about it," wrote Byron York, the conservative columnist at the *Washington Examiner*, adding that Romney's "business experience has not been the topic of long and detailed public examination and debate." He, like many of his cohort in the Fox echo chamber, seemed unaware that Romney's Bain record has been debated for nearly two decades, starting with his 1994 battle with Kennedy (who engaged "truth squads" of downsized workers from a Midwestern Bain-owned company to stalk Romney). That record has been examined repeatedly by mainstream journalists ever since.

Even as the Republican establishment continues to prop up Mitt, it remains in denial about his long-term prospects. Romney rationalizers argue that Gingrich's blunderbuss assault on Bain was a blessing in disguise, for it will force Romney to come up with an airtight defense before the fall. But Romney has been trying since 1994 to formulate answers to questions about his Bain career, his vast wealth, and his leadership role in his church. If he hasn't found them by now, it's because he doesn't have them. And so his preferred route has been just to avoid tough questions altogether—and confrontation in general—by sticking to manicured campaign events as immaculate as his Brooks Brothers shirts. He tries to shun mainstream-news-organization interviews, and dropped the "Ask Mitt Anything" sessions with voters that were a staple of his 2008 campaign. Even straightforward interviews with sympathetic interlocutors like Fox News's Bret Baier and the radio talk-show host Laura Ingraham throw him into a tizzy, if not a hissy fit. Remarkably, he received high marks for months for his steady demeanor and discipline in the Republican debates, but as we now know, all it takes is a tough question about his own biography to prompt a stammering answer and robotic herky-jerky head movements suggestive of a human-size Pez dispenser. His belated efforts to go on the attack against Gingrich often make him sound like an adolescent tattletale. In Romney's best debate, last Thursday, he was still outshone by the also-ran Rick Santorum.

To escape the twin taints of Bain and his one-percenter's under–15 percent tax rate, some Republican elders are urging Romney to "stake his campaign on something larger and far more important than his own business expertise" (the *Wall Street Journal* editorial page) or, as Fred Barnes suggested more baldly, to find "a bigger idea to deflect attention from Bain." But even Mitt's own spokesman, Eric Fehrnstrom, once described him (to the *Des Moines Register*) as "not a very notional leader." Romney is incapable of an arresting turn of phrase, let alone a fresh idea. Running on empty, he resorts to filling out his canned campaign orations with lengthy recitations of the lyrics from patriotic anthems. ("Believe in America" is his campaign slogan.) Take away the bogus boasts about "job creation" at Bain and the disowned Romneycare, and what else is there to Mitt Romney? Mainly, his unspecified service to his church and his perfect marriage. That reduces him to the stature of the Republican presidential candidate he most resembles, Thomas Dewey—in both his smug and wooden campaign style and in the overrating of his prospects by the political culture. Even the famously dismissive description of Dewey popularized by the Washington socialite Alice Roosevelt Longworth—as "the little man on the wedding cake"—seems to fit Mitt.

No Republican has ever won the nomination after losing the South Carolina primary. No incumbent president since FDR has won reelection with an unemployment rate higher than 7.2 percent on Election Day, and ours currently stands at 8.5 percent. No candidate with a 58 percent disapproval rating—especially Newt—is likely to win a national election, even for dogcatcher. But surely someone has to be nominated by the Republicans, and someone has to win in November.

"This race is getting to be even more interesting," said Romney when conceding to Gingrich in South Carolina. As always, it's impossible to know whether he really meant what he said or not, but this much is certain: He will continue to be the least interesting thing about it.

Slate

WINNER—COLUMNS AND
COMMENTARY

*Writing with what the National
Magazine Award judges called
"wit, zeal, and occasional
outrage," Dahlia Lithwick explores
the state of mind of the U.S.
Supreme Court in the days before
and after its decision about the
Affordable Care Act, a.k.a.
Obamacare. Lithwick correctly
predicted that the court would
uphold the law (though she got
the point spread wrong), but,
more important, she explains what
the decision meant. In doing so,
she also demonstrates what sets
magazine journalism apart—the
power not only to place events in
context but to tell stories that
survive the news cycle. That
Lithwick was writing for* Slate—*a
digital-only magazine—is also
notable. In fact, this was the first
time an online magazine won a
National Magazine Award in
competition with print magazines.*

Dahlia Lithwick

It's Not About the Law, Stupid *and* The Supreme Court's Dark Vision of Freedom *and* Where Is the Liberal Outrage?

It's Not About the Law, Stupid

Next week the Supreme Court will hear arguments over the Affordable Care Act, what many people know as Obamacare. The mainstream opinion is that this is unquestionably the most important case of this term. That opinion is no doubt supported by the attention it will receive—six hours of argument over three days. But amid all the throat clearing, odds making, and curtain raising that surrounds next week's health-care case, it seems worth noting what is in dispute and what's not. So let's start by setting forth two uncontroversial propositions.

The first proposition is that the health-care law is constitutional. The second is that the court could strike it down anyway. Linda Greenhouse makes the first point more eloquently than I can. That the law is constitutional is best illustrated by the fact that—until recently—the Obama administration expended almost no energy defending it. Back when the bill passed Nancy Pelosi famously reacted to questions about its constitutionality with the words, "Are you serious?" And the fact that the Obama administration rushed the case to the Supreme Court in an election year is all the evidence you need to understand that they remain confident in their prospects. The law is a completely valid exercise of Congress's Commerce Clause power, and all the conservative longing for the good old days of the pre–New Deal courts won't put us back in those days as if by magic. Nor does it amount to much of an argument.

So that brings us to the really *interesting* question: Will the Court's five conservatives strike it down regardless? That's what we're really talking about next week, and that has almost nothing to do with law and everything to do with optics, politics, and public opinion. That means that Justice Antonin Scalia's opinion in the *Raich* medicinal marijuana case, and Chief Justice John Roberts's and Anthony Kennedy's opinions in *Comstock* only get us so far. Despite the fact that reading the entrails of those opinions suggest that they'd contribute to an easy fifth, sixth, and seventh vote to uphold the individual mandate as a legitimate exercise of Congressional power, the real question isn't whether those justices will be bound by seventy years of precedent or their own prior writings on federal power. The only question is whether they will ignore it all to deprive the Obama of one of his signature accomplishments.

Professor Randy Barnett, the intellectual power behind the entire health-care challenge, wrote recently that Justice Scalia could break from his previous opinions—freeing him to strike down the Affordable Care Act—"without breaking a sweat." I suspect that's right.

If that's true, we should stop fussing about old precedents. These old milestones of jurisprudence aren't what will give Scalia pause. What matters is whether the five conservative justices are so intent in striking down Obama'shealthcare law that they would risk a chilly and divisive 5–4 dip back into the waters of *Bush v. Gore* and *Citizens United*.

Oddly enough that turns more on what *we* think about the case than what they think.

The court likes to pretend it's completely above public opinion, inured to the momentary zigs and zags of the polls. But most of us know that nothing could be further from the truth.

Consider a couple of relevant data points:

We know that the court took a huge public opinion hit after *Bush v. Gore* and again after *Citizens United*. But that doesn't necessarily help the administration. Because in this case the American public believes the health-care law is unconstitutional. The most recent polling I have seen shows that over 50 percent of the American people—including many who benefit from popular provisions of the law—still believe it's unconstitutional.

Part of this goes back to the administration's abject failure in defending the constitutionality of the law over the past two years. Of course the public thinks the law is unconstitutional. They never heard a single word defending it. And I am willing to lay odds that if the public broadly supported ACA, we would not be having a six-hour conversation next week suggesting that the court would strike it down. The challengers' greatest weapon in this case was momentum: A series of lower courts, and then an appeals court, signed off on the argument that this was a fundamental incursion into basic liberty. Then, suddenly, the case seemed plausible.

On the other hand, I'd suggest that there is an equally powerful countervailing force at work on the justices. Because, as it happens, the current court is almost fanatically worried about its legitimacy and declining public confidence in the institution. For over a decade now, the justices have been united in signaling that they are moderate, temperate, and minimalist in their duties. From Chief Justice Robert's description of himself as just an "umpire" and his speeches about humility and the need for unanimity, to Stephen Breyer's latest book, *Making Our Democracy Work*—a meditation on all the ways the courts depend on public confidence. Roberts even nodded at that court-wide anxiety by devoting most of his 2011 State of the Judiciary report to issues of recusal and judicial integrity, and by reversing his own policy on same-day audio release, in order to allow the American public to listen in on the health care cases next week (albeit on a two-hour delay). That means that the court goes into this case knowing that the public is desperately interested in the case, desperately divided about the odds, and deeply worried about the neutrality of the court. (Greenhouse points to a Bloomberg News national poll showing that 75 percent of Americans expect the decision to be influenced by the justices' personal politics.) To hand down a 5–4, ideologically divided opinion just before the Republican and Democratic Party conventions, would—simply put—prove that 75 percent correct, and erode further the public esteem for the court. Justice Clarence Thomas doesn't worry much about things like that. I suspect Chief Justice Roberts and Justice Kennedy worry quite a lot.

If I am right about this, some justices may believe that this isn't a fight worth having. Not now and not over this issue. Recall, even absent the health-care case, the 2011 and 2012 terms will represent two of the most divisive and incendiary terms in recent memory. The court isn't just hearing the health-care case this year. It also heard a Texas redistricting case, and the Arizona immigration case. Next year it will hear the Texas affirmative-action case, and very likely a case that will question the entire existence of Section 5 of the Voting Rights Act. Oh, and next term, the court may well have to contend with a gay-marriage case, and at the rate state legislators are passing patently unconstitutional abortion regulations, it's not unlikely the court will be revisiting *Roe* soon thereafter.

Given that line-up of future cases, the five conservatives may want to keep their powder dry for now. I think they will. A poll released this week by the American Bar Association agrees, saying that most court watchers (85 percent) believe Obamacare will survive. And why is that? Not just the fact that—as I've said at the outset—the law is constitutional, well within the boundaries of Congress's Commerce Clause authority. It's because for the court to strike it down, the justices would have to pick a fight that wasn't theirs in the first place.

The challenges to Obama's health-care initiative didn't begin in the conservative legal academy. They didn't even really blossom in the conservative legal media or think tanks. The real energy of these challenges arose out of those Tea Party town halls throughout the summer of 2010, in response to a longing to return to constitutional values, states' rights, and ideas of individual liberty that have been dead for almost a century. That isn't to dismiss the validity of the passionate public opposition to this law, or even to denigrate the truly heroic efforts of Randy Barnett, the Cato Institute, or the millions of Americans who deeply believe that this is a case about liberty, broccoli, and the short hop from the individual mandate to federal tyranny. It's simply to say that it's no accident that these cases were filed by state attorneys general and governors swept up in political currents, willing to make novel arguments in the form of what was always a constitutional Hail Mary pass. It's no accident that until the lower district courts started striking down the act, none of the challengers really believed that they could succeed. And it's no accident that three of the most influential and well-respected conservative jurists in the land have ruled that of course the law is constitutional, even if they hate it as a policy matter. It's no accident, either, that Charles Fried, Reagan's solicitor general and Harvard conservative legend, said in an interview with *Dan Rather Reports* this week the case would be decided 8–1—in favor of the law. The conservative legal elites don't believe in the merits of this challenge, even if the public does.

Next week's health-care cases rocketed up from the district courts to the Supreme Court in less than two years, such that we are all still feeling the whiplash. Even so, they may in the end be too late. The political momentum that lit the visceral public fire under these challenges has already begun to falter. The Tea Party has plummeted in the polls. Ideas about getting back to the "Framers' constitution" seem to have stalled with Michele Bachmann's confusion of what the Framers really believed. The economic crisis has largely displaced the constitutional crisis that marked the 2010 election cycle. And the American public has started to see the tangible benefits of the law; a gradual process of understanding that this is less about mandating what we eat or buy and more about the (deeply conservative) notion that nobody should benefit from a system into which they are not willing to pay.

That brings me full circle to the court's five conservatives. Is it possible that they are sufficiently ideological and political that the grim joy of sticking it to the president and the Congress will lead them to strike down the law? Of course. But is it also possible that unlike Sandra Day O'Connor and William H. Rehnquist— who represented the high-water mark of states' rights activism at the Rehnquist court, the two new justices, Samuel Alito and John Roberts, cut their teeth on Ed Meese's conservatism instead. They were raised on Reagan-era opposition to abortion and affirmative action, to the perceived indignities of the Voting Rights Act, and objections to the wall erected between church and state. *Those* are the fights to which these men dedicated themselves as young lawyers. They didn't join the Reagan administration to return to the glory days before the court expanded the reach of the Commerce Clause to include even wheat grown for personal consumption in the 1942 case of *Wickard v. Filburn*. (Wickard: "When men were men and the wheat was scared.")

That's why the current fuss being made over the health-care cases has offered the court a perfect cover story. They will hear six hours of argument next week. They will pretend it is a fair fight with equally compelling arguments on each side. They will even reach out and debate the merits of the Medicaid expansion, although not a single court saw fit to question it. And then the justices will vote 6–3 or 7–2 to uphold the mandate, with the chief justice joining the majority so he can write a careful opinion that cabins the authority of the Congress to do anything more than regulate the health-insurance market. No mandatory gym memberships or forced broccoli consumption. And then—having been hailed as the John Marshall of the twenty-first century—he will proceed to oversee two years during which the remainder of the Warren Court revolution will be sent through the wood chipper.

Looked at on the merits, the Affordable Care Act isn't the "case of the century." It probably isn't even the "case of 2012." Next week we will all be glued to the political spectacle. But stay tuned. The real action in Roberts's court has yet to come.

The Supreme Court's Dark Vision of Freedom

The fight over Obamacare is about freedom. That's what we've been told since these lawsuits were filed two years ago, and that's what we heard both inside and outside the Supreme Court this morning. That's what Michele Bachmann and Rick Santorum have been saying for months. Even people who support President Obama's signature legislative achievement would agree that this debate is all about freedom—the freedom to never be one medical emergency away from economic ruin. What we have been waiting to hear is how members of the Supreme Court—especially the conservative majority—define that freedom. This morning, as the justices pondered whether the individual mandate—that part of the Affordable Care Act that requires most Americans to purchase health insurance or pay a penalty—is constitutional, we got a window into the freedom some of the justices long for. And it is a dark, dark place.

It's always a bit strange to hear people with government-funded single-payer health plans describe the need for other Americans to be free from health insurance. But after the aggressive battery of questions from the court's conservatives this morning, it's clear that we can only be truly free when the young are released from the obligation to subsidize the old and the ailing. Justice Samuel Alito appears to be particularly concerned about the young, healthy person who "on average consumes about $854 in health services each year" being saddled with helping pay for the sick or infirm—even though, one day that will describe all of us. Or as Justice Antonin Scalia later puts it: "These people are not stupid. They're going to buy insurance later. They're young and need the money now." (Does this mean that if you are young and you pay for insurance, Scalia finds you "stupid"?)

Freedom also seems to mean freedom from the obligation to treat those who show up at hospitals without health insurance, even if it means letting them bleed out on the curb. When Solicitor General Donald Verrilli tries to explain to Justice Scalia that the health-care market is unique because "getting health-care service . . . [is] a result of the social norms to which we've obligated ourselves so that people get health care." Scalia's response is a curt: "Well, don't obligate yourself to that."

Freedom is the freedom not to rescue. Justice Kennedy explains "the reason [the individual mandate] is concerning is because it requires the individual to do an affirmative act. In the law of torts, our tradition, our law has been that you don't have the duty to rescue someone if that person is in danger. The blind man is walking in front of a car and you do not have a duty to stop him, absent some relation between you. And there is some severe moral criticisms of that rule, but that's generally the rule."

Freedom is to be free from the telephone. Verrilli explains that "telephone rates in this country for a century were set via the exercise of the commerce power in a way in which some people paid rates that were much higher than their costs in order to subsidize." To which Justice Scalia is again ready with a quick retort: "Only if you make phone calls." Verrilli tries to point out that "to live in the modern world, everybody needs a telephone," but that assumes facts not in evidence.

Freedom is the freedom not to join a gym, not to be forced to eat broccoli. It's the freedom not to be compelled to buy wheat or milk. And it's the freedom to purchase your health insurance only at the "point of consumption"—i.e., when you're being medevaced to the ICU (assuming you have the cash).

Some of the members of the court find this notion of freedom troubling. Justice Ruth Bader Ginsburg notes that: "Congress, in the thirties, saw a real problem of people needing to have old age and survivor's insurance. And, yes, they did it through a tax, but they said everybody has got to be in it because if we don't have the healthy in it, there's not going to be the money to pay for the ones who become old or disabled or widowed. So, they required everyone to contribute. There was a big fuss about that in the beginning because a lot of people said—maybe some people still do today—I could do much better if the government left me alone. I'd go into the private market, I'd buy an annuity, I'd make a great investment, and they're forcing me to paying for this Social Security that I don't want. But that's constitutional."

Justice Sonia Sotomayor invokes government tax credits for "solar-powered homes and fuel-efficient cars." Paul Clement, representing the twenty-six states challenging the health-care law, replies to explain how the Framers would have thought about taxing carriages. The analogy of taxing carriages probably makes perfect sense to the court's conservatives, who likened GPS devices to tiny constables in this year's GPS case. We seem to be talking across the centuries once again in this room, and the days of leeches are looking pretty darn dreamy for some. Sotomayor says, "There is government compulsion in almost every economic decision because the government regulates so much. It's a condition of life." But one gets the sense that not everyone acknowledges the reality of that life, much less approves of it.

Sotomayor, again pondering whether hospitals could simply turn away the uninsured, finally asks: "What percentage of the American people who took their son or daughter to an emergency room and that child was turned away because the parent didn't have insurance—do you think there's a large percentage of the American population who would stand for the death of that child if they had an allergic reaction and a simple shot would have saved the child?"

But we seem to want to be free from that obligation as well. This morning in America's highest court, freedom seems to be less about the absence of constraint than about the absence of shared responsibility, community, or real concern for those who don't want anything so much as healthy children, or to be cared for when they are old. Until today, I couldn't really understand why this case was framed as a discussion of "liberty." This case isn't so much about freedom from government-mandated broccoli or gyms. It's about freedom from our obligations to one another, freedom from the modern world in which we live. It's about the freedom to ignore the injured, walk away from those in peril, to never pick up the phone or eat food that's been inspected. It's about the freedom to be left alone. And now we know the court is worried about freedom: the freedom to live like it's 1804.

Where Is the Liberal Outrage?

Depending on whether you generally prefer your vitriolic abuse from the left or the right, it's been a tough week for Chief Justice John Roberts. Having given conservatives the sun, the moon, and the stars for seven years, Roberts suddenly finds himself on the wrong side of everyone from the *Washington Post*'s Marc Thiessen, to the *Wall Street Journal*'s John Yoo, to presidential hopeful Mitt Romney, who not only returned the chief justice's class ring and football jacket yesterday but also vowed to only date future justices who are, well, a carbon copy of Mitt Romney.

In contrast to all the weeping and wailing that has accompanied what appears to be John Roberts's single significant defection since joining the court, liberals have been strangely silent—as they are always strangely silent—about the myriad ways in which the liberal justices have disappointed them this term. Oh sure, we get a little eye-roll from Elizabeth Warren over Justice Elena Kagan's vote in the Medicaid expansion part of the Affordable Care Act cases. But looked at in its entirety, the 2011 term was yet another festival of defections by assorted members of the so-called liberal wing.

Think about it: The court's liberals voted to find a ministerial exception to employment discrimination laws for religious schools and churches; ruled against the EPA in a wetlands case; and, as Adam Liptak points out, the court's liberals pretty much crushed the Obama administration again this term. Yet you don't find liberals burning their Stephen Breyer Pokémon cards, in part because liberals don't have Stephen Breyer Pokémon cards in the first place. We can't really be bothered.

Yesterday at *Politico*, Josh Gerstein wondered why the left had ignored Kagan, the liberal "turncoat," and her massive defection on the Medicaid expansion. He singles out Kagan—as opposed to Justice Breyer, who also voted with the conservatives on the Medicaid issue—because everyone always assumed Kagan was in the tank for the Obama administration. Or as Gerstein put it, "The absence of public outrage toward Kagan is particularly notable since she wasn't parting company just with her liberal ideological counterparts, but with the president who appointed her to the court and with the administration she served as Solicitor General immediately prior to taking the bench." Gerstein proposes several explanations for the left's silence on Kagan, including the fact that her Medicaid vote may ultimately have limited practical impact and that liberals are giving her a pass for a possibly strategic decision to trade her Medicaid vote for Roberts's vote on the individual mandate. I don't think any of his conclusions are wrong, but I do think they paint only part of the picture.

The truth is that liberals have been forgiving the liberal justices their defections for decades. The notion of liberal commentators rising up en masse with threats to impeach and impale a justice for a single decision, as conservatives have done with Justice Anthony Kennedy, Justice Sandra Day O'Connor, and now Chief Justice Roberts, is beyond imagining. When Justice John Paul Stevens voted with the court's conservatives on upholding a voter ID requirement a few years back—indeed, Stevens went so far as to write the opinion—liberals just chalked it up to his jaunty bow tie.

Why is that? For one thing, the court's left wing has always been more fractured than the right, and the sense that the four liberals should be acting in perfect lockstep has never really gained any force on the left. Again this term, the pairs that agreed most frequently were Alito and Roberts, and Thomas and Scalia. The court's liberals tend to be more inclined to flop around, so much so that it no longer surprises anyone when it happens in a single case. For another thing, conservative commentators are quick to use even one-off defections by the conservative justices as ammunition for the next confirmation fight. See for instance Thiessen and Yoo arguing that the *real* lesson of the ACA challenges is that the next nominee will need to be both further to the right than John Roberts and also far more thoroughly vetted. This isn't about the right's anger at Roberts so much as a warning shot about the next justice to be named. Liberals don't think that way about the court, much less talk that way out loud.

The relative silence from the left also betrays a longstanding confusion from the left about what precisely it expects from a liberal justice. The fact is that conservative constitutional thought is so much more crisply expressed, and so much more broadly accepted, than liberal thought—an argument expressed forcefully today in the *New York Times* by Professor William E. Forbath of the University of Texas. He explains that there is a long tradition of liberal counter-argument to the laissez-faire constitutional vision put forth by the court's five conservatives. Sadly, he says, "liberals have largely forgotten how to think, talk and fight along these lines." In other words, it's much harder to break up with your justice for doing something you dislike if you have no idea what you wanted him to do in the first place.

One wants to be careful what one wishes for here: The day candidate Obama tells the mainstream media that he would never confirm a justice to the Supreme Court that disagrees with him about anything, ever, I'd start to feel very, very nervous about the meaning of an independent judiciary. And certainly, the idea that liberals are a little bit more, well, liberal in the bandwidth they've created for acceptable judicial behavior cannot be called a bad thing. But instead of smugly chuckling at the ways conservatives have turned on their chief justice this week, liberals might also want to take a page from their playbook. The courts matter. How we talk about the courts matters. And who is on the courts matters as well. John Roberts's critics may be unreasonably vengeful this week. But the alternative to their unbending vision of judicial good behavior is to have a compelling competing vision as opposed to the fuzzy conviction that being lucky will always be enough.

Texas Monthly

WINNER—FEATURE WRITING
INCORPORATING PROFILE
WRITING

The National Magazine Award judges described this twenty-five-year saga of a man falsely imprisoned for the murder of his wife as "a true-crime story, a human drama, an argument for legal reform—and a vivid reminder of the enduring power of magazine storytelling." Pamela Colloff was already familiar to the judges—two of her stories had been nominated in previous years, 2001 and 2011, and her article "Hannah and Andrew," about a Texas homemaker found guilty of murdering her five-year-old foster son by force-feeding him salt, was also a finalist in Reporting this year—but this was the first time her work for Texas Monthly, *where she is executive editor, won an award. The explanation is easy: this is long-form journalism at its finest.*

Pamela Colloff

The Innocent Man

Part I

I.

On April 12, 1987, Michael Morton sat down to write a letter. "Your Honor," he began, "I'm sure you remember me. I was convicted of murder, in your court, in February of this year." He wrote each word carefully, sitting cross-legged on the top bunk in his cell at the Wynne prison unit, in Huntsville. "I have been told that you are to decide if I am ever to see my son, Eric, again. I haven't seen him since the morning that I was convicted. I miss him terribly and I know that he has been asking about me." Referring to the declarations of innocence he had made during his trial, he continued, "I must reiterate my innocence. I did NOT kill my wife. You cannot imagine what it is like to lose your wife the way I did, then to be falsely accused and convicted of this terrible crime. First, my wife and now possibly, my son! Sooner or later, the truth will come out. The killer will be caught and this nightmare will be over. I pray that the sheriff's office keeps an open mind. It is no sin to admit a mistake. No one is perfect in the performance of their job. I don't know what else to say except I swear to God that I did NOT kill my wife. Please don't take my son from me too."

His windowless concrete cell, which he shared with another inmate, measured five by nine feet. If he extended his arms, he could touch the walls on either side of him. A small metal locker that was bolted to the wall contained one of the few remnants he still possessed from his previous life: a photograph of Eric when he was three years old, taken shortly before the murder. The boy was standing in the backyard of their house in Austin, playing with a wind sock, grabbing the streamers that fluttered behind it in the breeze. There was a picture too of his late wife, Christine— a candid shot Michael had taken of her years earlier, with her hair pinned up, still wet from a bath. She was looking away from the camera, but she was smiling slightly, her fingers pressed against her mouth. The crime-scene photos were still fresh in Michael's mind, but if he focused on the snapshot, the horror of those images abated. Christine with damp hair, smiling—this was how he wanted to remember her.

The last time he had seen her was on the morning of August 13, 1986, the day after his thirty-second birthday. He had glanced at her as she lay in bed, asleep, before he left for work around five-thirty. He returned home that afternoon to find the house cordoned off with yellow crime-scene tape. Six weeks later, he was arrested for her murder. He had no criminal record, no history of violence, and no obvious motive, but the Williamson County Sheriff's Office, failing to pursue other leads, had zeroed in on him from the start. Although no physical evidence tied him to the crime, he was charged with first-degree murder. Prosecutors argued that he had become so enraged with Christine for not wanting to have sex with him on the night of his birthday that he had bludgeoned her to death. When the guilty verdict was read, Michael's legs buckled beneath him. District attorney Ken Anderson told reporters afterward, "Life in prison is a lot better than he deserves."

The conviction had triggered a bitter custody battle between Christine's family—who, like many people in Michael's life, came to believe that he was guilty—and Michael's parents. The question of who would be awarded custody of Eric was to be resolved by state district judge William Lott, who had also presided over Michael's trial. If Christine's family won custody, Michael was justifiably concerned that he would never see his son again.

Two weeks after sending his first entreaty to Lott, Michael penned another letter. "My son has lost his mother," he wrote. "Psychological good can come from [seeing] his one surviving parent." Ultimately, custody of the boy was awarded to Christine's younger sister, Marylee Kirkpatrick. But at the recommendation of a child psychiatrist who felt that Eric should know his father, Lott agreed to allow two supervised visits a year. Marylee drove Eric to Huntsville every six months to see his father. He was four when the visits began.

At first, Eric was oblivious to his surroundings. He raced his Matchbox cars along the plastic tabletops in the visitation area, mimicking the sounds of a revving engine. He talked about the things he loved: dinosaurs, comic books, astronomy, his dog. As he grew older, he described the merit badges he had earned in Boy Scouts and his Little League triumphs. Marylee always sat beside him, her impassive expression impossible to decipher. For Eric's sake, she seemed determined to make the mandated reunions—which she had strenuously opposed—as normal as possible. She flipped through magazines as Eric and his father spoke, sometimes glancing up to join in. Michael tried to pretend there was nothing unusual about the arrangement either, dispensing lemon drops he had purchased at the prison commissary and talking to his son about the Astros' ups and downs or the Oilers' failed attempts at a comeback. During the months that stretched between visits, he wrote letters to Eric, but Marylee did not encourage the correspondence, and it remained a one-way conversation.

Over the years, as Eric got older, Michael would try not to register surprise at each new haircut and growth spurt, but the changes always startled him. He was dumbstruck the first time he heard Eric call Marylee "Mom." The boy's memories of his mother had, by then, receded. "Of course, I have lost him," Michael wrote in his journal after one visit, when Eric was ten. "He knows little or nothing of me or the short time we spent together."

Around the time Eric turned thirteen, the tenor of their visits changed. Eric was distant and impatient to leave. Michael knew that the boy had started asking questions; during a trip to East Texas to see his paternal grandparents, he had asked if it was true that his father had killed his mother. Fearful of alienating Eric any further, Michael never tried to engage him in a conversation about the case or persuade him that he had been wrongfully convicted. He assumed that Marylee would contradict any argument he made, and he doubted Eric would believe him anyway.

The silences that stretched between them became so agonizing that Michael often found himself turning to Marylee to make conversation. Two hours were allotted for their visits, but that was an eternity. "Well . . . ," Marylee would say when they ran out of small talk.

"Yes," Michael would agree. "It's probably time."

Their last meeting was so brief that Eric and Marylee barely sat down. Eric, who was fifteen, was unable to look Michael in the eye. "I don't want to come here anymore," he choked out.

Michael considered thanking Marylee for turning his son against him or telling Eric that everything he had been led to believe was a lie. But as he looked at his son, who stared hard at the floor, he kept those thoughts to himself. "I'm not going to force you to come see me," Michael told him. "You can come back anytime if you change your mind." Before he walked away, he said to Marylee, "Take good care of my son for me."

II.

When Michael and Christine bought the house on Hazelhurst Drive, in 1985, northwest Austin had not yet been bisected by toll roads or swallowed up by miles of unbroken suburban sprawl. The real estate bust had brought construction to a standstill, and the half-built subdivision where they lived, east of Lake Travis, was a patchwork of new homes and uncleared, densely wooded lots. Although the Morton home had an Austin address, it sat just north of the Travis County line, in Williamson County—an area that, despite an incursion of new residents and rapid development, still retained the rural feel and traditional values of small-town Texas. Austin was seen as morally permissive, a refuge for dope smoking and liberal politics that Williamson County, which prided itself on its law-and-order reputation, stood against. In Georgetown, the county seat, bars and liquor stores were prohibited.

Their neighborhood was a place for newcomers, most of them young professionals with children. The Mortons arrived when Eric was a toddler, and Christine had quickly learned everyone's name on their street, often stopping in the driveway after work to visit with the neighbors. Friendly and unguarded, with long brown hair and bright-blue eyes, she had a disarming confidence; she might squeeze the arm of the person she was talking to as she spoke or punctuate conversation with a boisterous laugh. Michael was slower to warm to strangers, and his neighbors on Hazelhurst, whom he never got to know well, found him remote, even prickly. ("He would spend the whole morning working in the yard and never look up," one told me.) The Mortons' next-door neighbor Elizabeth Gee, a lawyer's wife and stay-at-home mother, often seemed taken aback by Michael's lack of social graces. He made no secret of the fact that he found her comically straitlaced; he and Christine had gone out to dinner with the Gees once, and Michael had rolled his eyes when she had demurely looked to her husband to answer for her after the waiter asked if she wanted a drink.

Christine had grown up in the suburbs south of Houston and attended Catholic school, where she was a popular student and member of the drill team. Michael was rougher around the edges. His father's job with an oil field service company had taken the family from Waco to a succession of small towns across Southern California before they finally settled in Kilgore, where Michael attended his last two years of high school. One day when Michael was sixteen, his father brought him along to an oil-drilling site, and Michael sat in the car and watched as his dad slogged through his work in an icy rain. The experience forever cured him of wanting to toil in the oil patch. He went to Stephen F. Austin State University, in Nacogdoches, where, in 1976, he met Christine in a psychology class. For their first date, he took her out in a borrowed Corvette, and not long afterward, she confided to her friend Margaret Permenter that she thought he might be "the one." "Mike was pretty reserved, but he was nice and handsome, with one of those Jimmy Connors haircuts," Permenter told me. "Chrissy was more committed than he was at first."

Christine followed Michael to Austin in 1977 after he dropped out of SFA. They had hoped to finish their degrees at the University of Texas, but the plan fizzled when they learned that many of their credits would not transfer. Instead, Michael landed a job stocking shelves at night at a Safeway and eventually became a manager, overseeing toiletries and housewares. (He would also later start a side business cleaning parking lots.) He and Christine spent their weekends at Lake Travis, waterskiing and buzzing around in the jet boat that Michael and several of his college buddies had pooled their money to buy. He became an avid scuba diver, and on his days off, he would explore Lake Travis for hours.

Michael and Christine were affectionate with each other but also voluble about their problems. "It was not *Who's Afraid of*

Virginia Woolf? but they had what I would call passionate conversations," Jay Gans, a former roommate of Michael's, told me. "There was nothing subtle about either one of them. They would argue very intensely, and eventually one of them would start cracking up, and not long after that, they would disappear into the bedroom." They married in 1979.

The candor with which they spoke to each other could unnerve even their closest friends. "When they argued, they were both very vocal," Christine's best friend, Holly Gersky, told me. "That's how their marriage worked. They got everything out in the open." They bickered constantly, and no subject was too inconsequential. After they bought the house on Hazelhurst, the topic of the landscaping spawned pitched battles over everything from the size of the deck that Michael was building to the prudence of Christine's decision to plant marigolds at the end of the driveway, beyond the sprinkler's reach. Michael also liked to rib Christine, and his sense of humor could be sarcastic and sometimes crude. A running gag between them involved Michael calling out, "Bitch, get me a beer!"—something they had once overheard a friend of a friend shout at his girlfriend. Christine would respond by telling Michael to go screw himself. "He teased her a lot, and he would go right up to the line of what was acceptable, and sometimes he went over it," Gersky said. Referring to an attractive friend of theirs who stopped by the house one day wearing shorts, he told Christine, "Now, *that's* the way you should look."

Yet the connection between them ran deep. They weathered a tragedy in the early years of their marriage, when Christine suffered a late miscarriage with her first pregnancy, in 1981. She had been four and a half months pregnant at the time. If not for Michael, she later wrote to his mother, she could not have survived the anguish of their loss. They were overjoyed when she became pregnant again less than two years later and elated when she reached her ninth month without any serious complications.

But within an hour of Eric's birth, in the summer of 1983, the Mortons were informed that their son had major health problems. Emergency surgery had to be performed that day to repair an abnormality in his esophagus. During the three-week stay in the neonatal unit that followed, doctors discovered that Eric also had a congenital heart defect. The condition prevented his blood from receiving the proper amount of oxygen. Doctors advised Michael and Christine that their son would not survive to adulthood unless he had open-heart surgery. But he could not undergo the procedure until he became bigger and hardier; he had to either reach his third birthday or weigh thirty pounds. Operating sooner carried too much risk. Until then, there was nothing that Michael and Christine could do but wait.

Together, they devoted themselves to caring for Eric. If he exerted himself, he turned blue, a symptom that only worsened as he got older. As a two-year-old, he would sit quietly and draw or leaf through picture books. He tired so easily that if he ran around the living room once or twice he would fall to the floor from exhaustion. Christine dropped him off on weekday mornings at a day care in Austin, an arrangement that allowed her to continue working full-time as a manager at Allstate, but in the evenings, she was reluctant to leave him with a babysitter. "Mike thought it was important to take a break and do something fun from time to time, but Chris felt she needed to stay close to home," Gersky said. "They were both so worried about Eric and keeping him healthy until his surgery, and that put a lot of stress on their marriage."

The strain on the relationship became obvious. Nothing stayed below the surface for long, and Michael's wisecracks began to have a harder edge to them. He openly complained to friends that he and Christine were not having enough sex and that she needed to lose weight. "His comments stung," Gersky said. "Chris shrugged them off—she would say, 'Just ignore him'—but they made other people uncomfortable. The bottom line was that Mike loved her, she loved him, and they adored Eric, and he was the most important thing to both of them, but they were definitely having a difficult time."

In June 1986, shortly before Eric's third birthday, the Mortons drove to Houston for his operation. Christine took a leave of absence and Michael used all of his vacation time so they could both be present for Eric's three-week hospital stay. They each took turns sleeping at his bedside so that he was never alone. The surgery went smoothly, and by the time he was discharged, he seemed to be a different child. The transformation was dramatic, even miraculous. For the first time in his life, his cheeks were pink and he was full of energy. When they returned home, Michael and Christine watched in amazement as he gleefully ran up and down the sidewalk outside their house, laughing.

•   •   •

Six weeks later, on the morning of Wednesday, August 13, Michael rose before dawn and dressed for work, quietly moving around the bedroom so as not to wake Christine. They had celebrated his birthday the night before, and it had been a fun evening at first. They brought Eric with them to the City Grill, a trendy restaurant in downtown Austin, for a rare night out. Michael and Christine smiled at each other as their son, now the picture of health, ate from his mother's plate and then dug into a bowl of ice cream. Eric nodded off in the car on the way home, and when they arrived, Michael carried him to his room and tucked him in. Once he and Christine were alone, Michael put on an adult video that he had rented for the occasion, hoping to spark some romance. But not long after they began watching the movie, Christine fell asleep on the living room floor. Hurt and angry, Michael retreated to the bedroom without her. Later, when she came to bed, she leaned over and kissed him. "Tomorrow night," she promised.

The episode had rankled Michael, and before he went to the kitchen that morning to fix himself something to eat, he glanced over at Christine; she lay sleeping in their water bed, in a pink nightgown she had put on for his birthday, her dark hair fanned out across her pillow. After he ate breakfast, he wrote her a note, which he propped up on the vanity in the bathroom so she would be sure to see it before she left for work:

> Chris, I know you didn't mean to, but you made me feel really unwanted last night. After a good meal, we came home, you binged on the rest of the cookies. Then, with your nightgown around your waist and while I was rubbing your hands and arms, you farted and fell asleep. I'm not mad or expecting a big production. I just wanted you to know how I feel without us getting into another fight about sex. Just think how you might have felt if you were left hanging on your birthday.

At the end, he scribbled "I L Y"—"I love you"—and signed it "M."

It was still dark outside when he pulled out of the driveway sometime after 5:30 that morning. When he arrived at the Safeway, he rapped his keys against the glass doors out front, and the produce manager, Mario Garcia, let him in. He punched his time card at 6:05 a.m. Throughout the morning, he and Garcia stopped to talk about their mutual interest in scuba diving. They made plans to go on a dive the next day, which they both had off from work. Michael agreed to call Garcia that evening so they could pick a place to meet.

He left work shortly after two o'clock that afternoon and stopped at the mall to run a few errands. Afterward, at around three-thirty, he went to pick up Eric. Mildred Redden, an older woman who looked after the boy in her home along with several other children, was surprised to see Michael. She told him that she had neither seen Eric nor heard from Christine all day. Alarmed, Michael reached for the phone and dialed home.

The phone rang several times and then a man whose voice he did not recognize picked up. For a moment, Michael thought it might be Christine's brother, who was in town. "Can I help you?" the man asked.

"Yeah, I'm calling my house," Michael said.

"Say, where are you?" the man asked.

"I'm over at the Reddens'," Michael replied.

"Over where? This is the sheriff."

"What's going on?" Michael said. "I live there."

"Well, we need to talk to you, Mike."

"I'll be there in ten minutes," he said, sounding panicky.

"Okay," the sheriff said. "Just take it easy though, okay?"

Michael bolted for the door so quickly that Redden, who had turned for a moment to place a baby in a swing, never saw him leave.

III.

To his admirers, Williamson County sheriff Jim Boutwell was larger than life; to his detractors, he was a walking cliché. The amiable, slow-talking former Texas Ranger wore a white Stetson, and he took his coffee black and his Lucky Strikes unfiltered. As a young pilot for the Department of Public Safety, he was famous for having flown a single-engine airplane around the University of Texas Tower in 1966 while sniper Charles Whitman took aim at bystanders below. (Boutwell succeeded in distracting Whitman and drawing his fire as police officers moved in, though he narrowly missed being shot himself.) Law enforcement was in his blood—his great-grandfather John Champion had briefly served as the Williamson County sheriff after the Civil War—and stories were often repeated about Boutwell's ability to win over almost anyone, even people he was about to lock up. More than once, he had defused a tense situation by simply walking up to a man wielding a gun and lifting the weapon right out of his hands. At election time, Boutwell always ran unopposed.

But Boutwell also played by his own rules, a tendency that had, in one notorious case, resulted in a botched investigation whose flawed conclusions reverberated through the cold-case files of police departments across the country. In 1983, three years before Christine's murder, Boutwell coaxed a confession from Henry Lee Lucas, a one-eyed drifter who would, within a year's time, be considered the most prolific serial killer in American history. Earlier that summer, Lucas had pleaded guilty to two murders—in Montague and Denton counties—and then boasted of committing at least a hundred more. At the invitation of the sheriff of Montague County, his old friend W. F. "Hound Dog" Conway, Boutwell had driven to Montague to question Lucas about an unsolved Williamson County case known as the Orange Socks murder. (The victim, who was never identified, was wearing only orange socks when her body was found in a culvert off Interstate 35 on Halloween in 1979.) After a productive initial interrogation, Boutwell brought Lucas back to Williamson County and elicited further details from him about the killing, but his methods were unethical at best. "He led Henry to the crime scene, showed him photos of the victim, and fed him information," reporter Hugh Aynesworth, whose 1985 exposé on Lucas for the *Dallas Times Herald* was nominated for a Pulitzer Prize, told me. "Henry didn't even get the way he killed her right on the first try: he said Orange Socks must have been stabbed, instead of strangled. His 'confession' was recorded four times so it could be refined."

Lucas, who was held at the Williamson County jail, seemed to like the attention. In subsequent interviews with Boutwell, the number of murders he claimed to have committed climbed to a staggering 360. Despite signs that Lucas was taking everyone for a ride, the Williamson County DA's office—which had nothing but his confession to connect him to the Orange Socks killing— charged him with capital murder. Among the many problems with the state's case was the fact that Lucas had cashed a paycheck in Jacksonville, Florida, nearly one thousand miles away, a day after the killing. When the case went to trial, in 1984, his job foreman testified that he had seen Lucas at least three times on the day the murder occurred. (Prosecutors countered by laying out a time line that allowed Lucas to kill his victim and return to Jacksonville without a second to spare.) During a break in the trial, Boutwell speculated that jurors would see past the case's myriad contradictions. "Even if they don't believe Henry did this one, they know he done a lot of them, and they'll want to see him put away for good," Boutwell observed. Lucas was found guilty and sentenced to death.

After his conviction, Lucas remained in the Williamson County jail, where he would eventually confess to committing more than 600 murders. He soon became a kind of macabre celebrity. Investigators from across the country traveled to Georgetown to interview him about their unsolved cases, but the integrity of Lucas's confessions was dubious. A task force manned by Boutwell and several Texas Rangers often briefed him before detectives arrived; one Ranger memo stated that in order to "refresh" Lucas's memory, he was furnished with crime-scene photos and information about his supposed victims. Provided with milk shakes, color TV, and assurances that he would not be transferred to death row as long as he kept talking, Lucas obliged. He gave visiting investigators enough lurid details that he was eventually indicted for 189 homicides. Not a single fingerprint, weapon, or eyewitness ever corroborated his claims. Even as his stories grew more and more outlandish—he declared that he had killed Jimmy Hoffa and delivered the poison for the 1978 Jonestown massacre in Guyana—Boutwell never washed his hands of him. The sheriff, who was interviewed by reporters from as far away as Japan, appeared to enjoy the limelight.

Years later, after Boutwell died of lymphatic cancer, Governor George W. Bush took the unusual step of commuting Lucas's death sentence to life in prison. "While Henry Lee Lucas is guilty of committing a number of horrible crimes, serious concerns have been raised about his guilt in this case," Bush announced in 1998, on the eve of Lucas's execution for the Orange Socks murder. By then, it was no secret that the investigation Boutwell had kick-started was a fiasco. Aynesworth's exhaustive *Times Herald* series had used work records, receipts, and a trail of documents to show that Lucas was likely responsible for no more than three of the slayings credited to him. In the spring of 1986 Texas attorney general Jim Mattox had issued a scathing report about the Lucas "hoax" and the investigators who had perpetuated it.

This was just a few months before the murder of Christine Morton, but when Boutwell arrived at the crime scene that day, Mattox's report probably wasn't weighing too heavily on his mind. It might have hurt his reputation in Austin, twenty-eight miles south, but in Georgetown he remained untarnished. "He'd go around town, boy, and everyone would clap him on the back," Aynesworth told me. "He was a hero."

·　　·　　·

The house on Hazelhurst was blocked off with crime-scene tape when Michael returned home. Despite the oppressive heat that August afternoon, many of his neighbors were standing outside in their yards; they stopped talking when they saw him pull up. Michael sprinted across the lawn and tried to push his way inside, past the sheriff's deputies and technicians from the DPS crime lab who were already on the scene, but several officers converged on him. "He's the husband," Boutwell called out, once Michael had identified himself.

Michael was breathing hard. "Is my son okay?" he asked.

"He's fine," Boutwell said. "He's at the neighbors'."

"How about my wife?"

The sheriff was matter-of-fact. "She's dead," he replied.

Boutwell led Michael into the kitchen and introduced him to Sergeant Don Wood, the case's lead investigator. "We have to ask you a few questions before we can get your son," Boutwell told him. Dazed, Michael took a seat at the kitchen table. He had shown no reaction to the news of Christine's death, and as he sat across from the two lawmen, he tried to make sense of what was happening around him. Sheriff's deputies brushed past him, opening drawers and rifling through cabinets. He could see the light of a camera flash exploding again and again in the master bedroom as a police photographer documented what Michael realized must have been the place where Christine was killed. He could hear officers entering and exiting his house, exchanging small talk. Someone dumped a bag of ice into the kitchen sink and stuck Cokes in it. Cigarette smoke hung in the air.

Bewildered, Michael looked to the two law enforcement officers for answers. "She was murdered?" he asked, incredulous. "Where was my son?" Boutwell was not forthcoming. The sheriff said only that Christine had been killed but that they did not yet know what had happened to her.

By then, Boutwell had been in the house for two and a half hours. Sheriff's deputies had arrived earlier that afternoon, responding to a panicked phone call from the Mortons' next-door neighbor Elizabeth Gee, who had spotted Eric wandering around the Mortons' front yard by himself, wearing only a shirt and a diaper. Alarmed, she let herself in to the Morton home and called out for her friend. Hearing nothing, she looked around the house. After searching the home several times, she finally discovered Christine's body lying on the water bed, with a comforter pulled up over her face. A blue suitcase and a wicker basket had been stacked on top of her. The wall and the ceiling were splattered with blood. Her head had been bludgeoned repeatedly with a blunt object.

From the start, Boutwell treated Michael not like a grieving husband but like a suspect. The sheriff had never tried to reach

Michael to notify him of Christine's death, and once he arrived, their conversation at the kitchen table began with Boutwell's reading Michael his Miranda rights. His opinion of Michael was informed by the note left in the bathroom for Christine, which established that Michael had been angry with her in the hours leading up to her murder. Boutwell had read it shortly after arriving at the house. Michael's lack of emotion at the news of her death did not help to dispel the sheriff's suspicion that the murder had been a domestic affair. Odd details about the crime scene only reinforced his hunch. There were no indications of a break-in, a fact that Boutwell would repeat to the media in the weeks to come. (Though it was true that there were no signs of forced entry, the sliding-glass door in the dining area was unlocked.) Robbery did not appear to have been the motive for the crime; Christine's purse was missing, but her engagement ring and wedding band were lying in plain sight on the nightstand. Other valuables, like a camera with a telephoto lens, had also gone untouched.

Michael, who did not request an attorney, was cooperative and candid during his conversation with Boutwell and Wood. When he was asked to account for his time, beginning with the previous morning, he described his day in painstaking detail, down to the particular kind of fish Christine had eaten for dinner and the color of socks he had worn to bed. As the afternoon wore on, they pressed him about tensions in his marriage and whether either of them had ever had an affair. Sensing the drift of the conversation, Michael said at one point, "I didn't do this, whatever it is." Boutwell, who had not examined Christine's injuries, had incorrectly surmised that she had been shot in the head at close range, and many of his questions focused on the guns that Michael kept in the house. Michael liked to hunt, and he had seven guns in all. As he spoke, he reeled off their makes and models according to caliber. When he listed his .45 automatic, Boutwell and Wood glanced up from their legal pads. "Is my .45

missing?" Michael asked. The pistol could not be accounted for—they had already searched his cache of firearms and hadn't seen it—but neither man answered him.

Growing more and more uneasy with their line of questioning, Michael finally erupted. "I didn't kill my wife," he insisted. "Are you fucking crazy?"

The conversation stretched on for the rest of the afternoon. Afterward, Wood escorted Michael to a neighbor's home, where Eric had been playing. Relieved to see his father, Eric ran to him. Michael fell to his knees and embraced the boy. For the first time since the ordeal had begun, he broke down and wept.

People would later remark on how strange it was that Michael did not go to a hotel or a friend's house that night, but in the fog of shock and grief, he and Eric went home. Michael did not ask what, if anything, the three-year-old had witnessed. (Wood had already tried to question the boy but was unable to get any information from him.) Instead, Michael offered his son assurances that everything would be all right. The house was in disarray; furniture was overturned, clothes were strewn across the bedroom floor, and the kitchen was littered with empty Coke cans and cigarette butts. Intent on reclaiming some sense of normalcy, Michael pulled down the yellow crime-scene tape outside and began to clean up. As it grew dark, he went from room to room, turning on lights. When exhaustion finally overtook him, he crawled into Eric's bed and lay beside him, holding the boy close. The lights stayed on all night.

· · ·

The next morning, Orin Holland, who lived one block north of the Mortons, on Adonis Drive, stopped a sheriff's deputy who was canvassing the neighborhood to share what he thought might be important information. Holland told the officer that his wife, Mary, and a neighbor, Joni St. Martin, had seen a man park a green van by the vacant, wooded lot behind the Morton home on several occasions. Holland went on to explain that his wife and St. Martin had also seen the man get out of the van and walk into the overgrown area that extended up to the Mortons' privacy fence. Shortly after Holland talked to the deputy—either that night or the next, Holland told me—a law-enforcement officer visited his home. "His purpose was not to ask us questions about what we had seen but to reassure us," Holland said. "Everyone was very unnerved at that time, and he came to say that we shouldn't worry and that we were not in any danger. He didn't overtly say, 'We know who did it,' but he implied that this was not a random event. I can't remember his exact words, but the suggestion was that the husband did it."

The St. Martins had also contacted the sheriff's office about the van. "Joni remembers me seeing the van early in the morning on the day Christine was killed, when I left to go to work," her ex-husband, David, told me. "I trust Joni's memory more than mine, but twenty-six years later, I can't say exactly when I saw it." Still, the van made an impression on both of them. "There were only two houses on our street: the Hollands' and ours," Joni explained. "People dumped trash in that area, so if we saw a vehicle we didn't know, we paid attention." After learning of Christine's murder, David called the sheriff's office. "We kept waiting for the police to come talk to us, but they never did," Joni told me. "Eventually, we figured the evidence led them in another direction." Like most people in the neighborhood, she and David did not know Michael particularly well. "We'd said hi at the mailbox before, but that was it—he pretty much kept to himself," Joni told me. "So when he was arrested, we thought, 'Well, what do we know? They must have something on him.'"

In fact, what little physical evidence had been recovered from the crime scene pointed away from Michael. Fingerprints lifted from the door frame of the sliding-glass door in the dining area did not match anyone in the Morton household. All told, there were approximately fifteen fingerprints found at the house—including one lifted from the blue suitcase that was left on top of Christine's body—but they were never identified. A fresh footprint was also discovered just inside the Mortons' fenced-in backyard. The most compelling piece of evidence was discovered by Christine's brother, John Kirkpatrick, who searched the property behind the house the day after her murder. Just east of the wooded lot where the man in the green van had been seen by the Mortons' neighbors, there was an abandoned construction site where work on a new home had come to a halt. John walked around the site, looking for anything that might help illuminate what had happened to his sister. As he examined the ground, he spotted a blue bandana lying by the curb. The bandana was stained with blood.

John immediately turned the bandana over to the sheriff's office, but its discovery did not spur law enforcement to comb the area behind the Morton home for additional evidence. Either the significance of the bandana was not understood, perhaps because investigators had failed to follow up on the green van lead, or, worse, it was simply ignored.

When John handed over the bandana that afternoon, Boutwell and Wood were already absorbed by another development in the case. Based on an analysis of partially digested food found in Christine's stomach, the medical examiner had estimated that she had been killed between one and six o'clock in the morning (Michael had, by his own account, been at home with her until five-thirty). The results did not necessarily implicate Michael, but they did not clear him of suspicion either. And neither did the medical examiner's finding that Christine had not been sexually assaulted. Neither rape nor robbery appeared to have motivated her killer, but the savage nature of the beating—eight crushing blows to the head—seemed to suggest that rage had played a part.

A few days later, Boutwell met with Michael, Marylee, and Christine's parents, Jack and Rita Kirkpatrick, to update them on the progress of the investigation. Michael had always enjoyed a cordial relationship with his wife's family, but the sheriff's comments that day quickly erased whatever goodwill existed between them. As Boutwell comforted the Kirkpatricks with the assurance that he would find Christine's killer, he made it clear that Michael had not yet been ruled out as a suspect. "I'd like to show you some photos and update you on the progress of the investigation," Boutwell said. "But I can't show you anything if he's"—the sheriff nodded at Michael—"in the room." By the time Christine's funeral was held later that week, in Houston, the uneasiness between Michael and the Kirkpatricks was obvious. "I noticed Mike standing off by himself afterward, and I could tell something wasn't right," a friend of the Mortons' told me. "Chris's brother, John, told me there were some questions about Mike. He said, 'I'm heading back to Austin to look into some things.'"

Over the next few weeks, dozens of people who had known Michael and Christine—from close friends to coworkers and passing acquaintances—were visited by Wood. A former truck driver and small-town police chief, he was hardly a seasoned homicide detective; he had been promoted to the position of investigator only seven months earlier. But he was diligent, sometimes producing as many as four reports a day, and he often reviewed his handwritten notes with the sheriff before typing up his findings. Boutwell's unwavering focus on Michael left Christine's best friend, Holly Gersky, who spent days on end being interrogated at the sheriff's office, deeply shaken. "I knew Chris's routine, I knew about her marriage, I knew everything they wanted to know about, so they had a lot of questions for me," she explained. "The whole time, I kept insisting that Mike could never have hurt Chris. I told them that he was incapable of abandoning Eric. One morning Sheriff Boutwell sat me down. He didn't raise his voice—he was to the point—but he had a very big, intimi-dating presence. He said, 'You're either lying or there's something you're not telling us.'"

Michael passed two lie detector tests in the weeks that fol-lowed and cooperated fully with the investigation, answering another round of questions from Boutwell and Wood without a lawyer present. He gave them consent to search his black Datsun pickup, and he provided them with samples of his hair, saliva, and blood. (Before the advent of DNA testing, in the nineties, forensic tools—such as blood-typing and hair analysis—were relatively primitive. They were effective at eliminating suspects, but they could not pinpoint a perpetrator's identity.) No physical evidence was ever found that tied Michael to the murder.

Still, Boutwell stuck to his theory of the case, telling a local newspaper, *Hill Country News,* that footprints found near the scene of the crime had been determined to have no connection to the killing and that blood stains discovered at a nearby work site—a reference to the blue bandana—were believed to have re-sulted from a minor construction accident. No doubt mindful of how an unsolved murder might unsettle the real estate devel-opers and new families who were moving in to Williamson County, the sheriff sought to allay concerns about the safety of the community. Above all, Boutwell emphasized, Christine's mur-der had not been random. "I feel confident to say there is no need for public alarm, because I seriously doubt that we have a serial murderer running loose in the area," he said.

. . .

Of all the nightmarish possibilities that Michael turned over in his mind about what might have happened on the day Christine was killed, he was the most preoccupied by the possibility that Eric had witnessed the attack or had been harmed in some way himself. Certain details about the crime scene—that the blinds, which Christine always opened when she woke up, remained closed; that she had still been wearing her nightgown—suggested to him that she had been murdered shortly after he left for work, and so he held out hope that Eric had slept through the ordeal. He was heartened when Jan Maclean, a child therapist he had arranged for Eric to talk to, told Michael that his son manifested the usual signs of separation anxiety that often follow the death of a parent, but nothing indicated that the boy had himself been victimized.

Then, several weeks after the funeral, Eric said something that knocked the breath out of him. Michael was on his hands and knees in the master bathroom, scrubbing the bathtub, when Eric walked up behind him. The boy stared at the tub and looked up at the shower, studying it. "Daddy," the three-year-old said, turning to him. "Do you know the man who was in the shower with his clothes on?"

Michael sat back, stunned. He had no doubt that Eric was speaking of the man who had killed Christine. The boy's question dovetailed with details from the crime scene; there had been blood on the bathroom door. Hesitant to say anything that might upset his son, Michael did not probe further. "I don't know him," Michael said finally. "But I think if you have any questions about him, you should ask Jan."

Maclean would never glean any more details from Eric, and Michael did not disclose the boy's statement to the sheriff's office. Given how aggressively Boutwell and Wood had questioned him, Michael did not want them anywhere near his son. At the urging of a friend, he retained two well-regarded Austin lawyers, Bill Allison and Bill White, who advised him to stop talking to law enforcement. By then, Michael had lost any confidence that Boutwell and his deputies would ever find Christine's killer.

Just before dinnertime on September 25, Michael heard the doorbell ring. He turned off the stove and grabbed Eric, hoisting the boy onto his hip. When he opened the door, he saw Boutwell and Wood standing on his front porch. Boutwell had a warrant for his arrest. Though the sheriff could have let Michael turn himself in at a prearranged time, giving him enough notice to make a plan for Eric's care, Boutwell had instead chosen to surprise him at home. "You've got to be kidding me," Michael said.

The last time Eric had seen police officers was the day his mother was killed, and as he was pulled from Michael's arms and handed to their neighbor Elizabeth Gee, he became hysterical. Boutwell put Michael in handcuffs and led him down the front walkway. Michael turned to see Eric, his arms outstretched, screaming for him.

IV.

"Perhaps no sheriff and district attorney had a closer working relationship than Jim [Boutwell] and I had," wrote Williamson County DA Ken Anderson in his 1997 book, *Crime in Texas: Your Complete Guide to the Criminal Justice System*. "We talked on the phone daily and, more often than not, drank a cup of coffee together." The two men frequently met at the L&M Cafe, a greasy spoon just down from the courthouse square in Georgetown. There, wrote Anderson, "we painstakingly pieced together circumstantial murder cases. We debated the next step of an investigation. . . . The downfall of more than one criminal doing life in the state prison system began with an investigation put together on a coffee-stained napkin at the L&M."

Anderson, whose family moved from the East Coast to Houston when he was a teenager, had formed his early impressions of the legal profession from watching Gregory Peck in *To Kill a Mockingbird* and Spencer Tracy in *Inherit the Wind*. He saw himself as one of the good guys. He had enrolled in UT Law School in the wake of the Watergate hearings, when his politics were left-leaning and his sympathies lay with defending people, not prosecuting them. After graduation, he worked as a staff attorney representing the ultimate underdogs: three-time offenders serving life sentences at a prison outside Huntsville. But the experience left him profoundly disillusioned; he often felt that he was being misled by his clients. "They were innocent, every one of them," he later told the *Austin American-Statesman*. "Even if you were wet behind the ears, liberal, fresh-graduated out of law school, you realized they were lying pretty quickly."

Anderson's ideology took a hard right turn in 1980, when he joined the Williamson County DA's office. He quickly became an indispensable first assistant to district attorney Ed Walsh, whose ascent had paralleled the county's rapid growth. Before Walsh was elected, in 1976, there had been no full-time district attorney; at the time, the county's population hovered at around 49,000 people, about one-tenth what it is today. Walsh had run on a tough-on-crime platform that promised convictions and jail time for drug dealing—a campaign pledge he made good on. But while Walsh was an amiable figure who enjoyed a good rapport with the defense bar, his first assistant quickly developed an unforgiving reputation, often taking a harder line on punishment than his boss did. Anderson routinely asked for, and won, harsh sentences and fought to keep offenders in prison long after they became eligible for parole. A prominent Austin defense attorney once quipped that Anderson had "one foot in each century—that being the nineteenth and the twentieth."

His view of the world, which would shape the modern-day Williamson County DA's office, was strictly black and white. "Ken did not see grays," said one attorney who practiced with him in the eighties. "He felt very strongly about the cases he was working on." Intense and driven, he poured himself into each case he prosecuted, preparing for trial with scrupulous attention to detail. By his own admission, he was not so much a brilliant lawyer as a meticulous one. He was also famously adversarial, sharing as little information with defense attorneys as possible through a firm "closed file" policy. His job, as he saw it, was to fight "the bad guys," and the struggle between the forces of good and evil was a common theme in his writing and courtroom oratory. "When you go home tonight, you will lock yourselves in your house," he often reminded jurors during closing arguments. "You will check to see that you locked your windows, that your dead-bolted doors are secure. Perhaps you will even turn on a security system. There is something very wrong with a society where the good people are locked up while the criminals are running free on the street."

Boutwell, who was a generation older than him, loomed large in the young prosecutor's imagination. The sheriff was "a lawman from the tip of his Stetson to the soles of his cowboy boots," Anderson rhapsodized in *Crime in Texas*. "I admire and respect all the Jim Boutwells of this world." Their meetings at the L&M Cafe had begun when Anderson, as a first assistant DA, would accompany Walsh whenever the district attorney sat down with Boutwell for one of their regular coffees. Among the topics at hand was no doubt the Lucas case, which Walsh and Anderson had prosecuted. When Walsh stepped down, in 1985, to run for higher office, Anderson was appointed district attorney by Governor Mark White. He had been DA for little more than a year when Christine was murdered. Just thirty-three, he had never run for public office before. Winning a conviction in the Morton case, which was front-page news, would become one of the new district attorney's signature achievements. In the decades that followed, Anderson often cited the case in interviews and in his own writing when he reflected back on the high points of his twenty-two-year career as a prosecutor.

Yet even with his strong allegiance to the sheriff, Anderson expressed reservations about the evidence early on. Boutwell had been ready to arrest Michael within a week of the murder, but it was Anderson who had held him off. ("I wanted to make sure, dadgum sure, everything was right on this case before we went out and arrested the guy," Anderson would later tell Judge Lott during the trial.) According to Kimberly Dufour Gardner, a prosecutor who worked in the DA's office in the mid-eighties, Anderson had voiced his doubts even after Michael's arrest. "Mr. Anderson made a remark relative to Sheriff Boutwell arresting Morton so soon," Gardner stated last year in a sworn affidavit. "I recall that he said he did not feel confident about the evidence against Mr. Morton at that time."

.   .   .

After his arrest, Michael spent a week in the county jail in George-town before he was finally released on bond in early October. He returned home and tried to resume a normal life with Eric, who had been cared for by both sets of grandparents in his absence. Normalcy, of course, was impossible: in less than five months, he would be standing trial for the murder of his wife. Still, Michael continued working forty hours a week at the Safeway (the grocery chain's union held that members could not be fired unless they were actually convicted of a crime), and he attended to the innu-merable responsibilities of single parenthood, driving Eric to ther-apy sessions and cardiologist appointments. He knew that some of his coworkers didn't know what to make of him, but others, like Mario Garcia, welcomed him back. The two men had not known each other particularly well before Michael's arrest—they had never socialized outside of work before—but Garcia, who had let Michael into the Safeway on the day Christine was murdered, had always been certain that he was innocent. "That morning, he was the same as he always was," Garcia told me. "I never doubted him. After everything he did to make Eric well, why would he leave him at a crime scene? Why would he kill Christine and then say, 'And to hell with my son'? It didn't add up."

The notoriety of the crime followed Michael wherever he went. Strangers who had read about the case in the newspaper slowed down as they drove past the house. Teenagers cruised by at night, sometimes whistling and honking and making a scene. Michael had decided to sell the house shortly after the murder, and he put it on the market for a song, but there were no takers. One day, a customer approached him in the Safeway. "Hey, I heard that that guy who killed his wife works here," the man said, lowering his voice. "Which one is he?"

During those months leading up to Michael's trial, sheriff's deputies regularly stopped by the Gee house to speak to Elizabeth, who was still recovering from having discovered Christine's body. Her husband, Christopher, became accustomed to returning home from work to find a squad car parked out front. "She was home all day, next to where the murder happened, and she was scared to death," he told me. (The Gees are now divorced, and Elizabeth did not respond to requests for an interview.) "Sheriff's deputies would stop by our house while they were patrolling the neighborhood, and they would fill her head with these whacked-out theories about Mike dealing drugs and stuff that was way out in the ozone," he said. "They scared the tar out of her. They kept telling her, 'You need to be careful. You don't know what this guy is going to do.'" By then, Christopher told me, it was clear that Elizabeth's testimony would be part of the prosecution's case; she not only had discovered Christine's body but also had overheard some of Michael's less charitable comments to his wife. Kept on edge by frequent visits from sheriff's deputies, she would prove to be a powerful witness.

Though Michael had never been a demonstrative person, his stoicism and his apparent lack of sentimentality for Christine only fed Elizabeth's anxiety. She was astonished to see him two days after Christine's funeral using a Weed Eater to cut down the marigolds at the end of his driveway, which she knew Christine had planted over his objections. It did not matter that the flowers had already withered in the summer heat or that Michael had been sprucing up the landscaping to attract prospective home buyers; within the context of a murder investigation, cutting down the marigolds took on a sinister dimension. So did another, far stranger thing he did. After a friend who worked in construction cleaned and repainted the master bedroom, Michael resumed sleeping there, on the water bed where Christine was killed. ("I have happy memories of this bed too," he told a horrified Marylee.) He was clearly still in a state of shock; he had also started keeping a pistol-grip shotgun beside him while he slept. But taken together, the marigolds, the bed, and the caustic remarks he used to make to Christine all hardened perceptions that he was callous and unrepentant and no doubt capable of murder.

Cementing that view was the decision of Travis County medical examiner Roberto Bayardo, who had performed Christine's autopsy, to change the estimated time of death. (Bayardo had previously worked with Boutwell and Anderson on the Orange Socks case.) Originally, based on his belief that she had eaten dinner as late as 11 p.m., Bayardo had found that Christine could have died as late as 6 a.m., a half hour after Michael left for work. But the medical examiner would later testify that he made that determination when "I didn't know all the facts. I didn't know when she had her last meal." Bayardo changed his estimate shortly after Boutwell and Anderson visited the City Grill and retrieved a credit card receipt showing that Michael had paid for their meal at 9:21 p.m. According to Bayardo's revised time of death, Christine could not have died after 1:30 a.m.

This conclusion was based on an examination of her partially digested stomach contents, a notoriously imprecise method for determining the time of death that was not recognized, even twenty-six years ago, as sound science. Bayardo's math also defied logic; although the time that the Mortons' dinner ended had been revised by less than two hours, he had adjusted the estimated time of death more dramatically, by nearly five hours. Still, his conclusion was crucial to the state's case: besides Eric, the only person who had been with Christine between 9:30 p.m. and 1:30 a.m. was Michael.

Years later, Bayardo testified in the cases of two wrongfully accused defendants outside Williamson County who were eventually freed after evidence pointed to their innocence: Anthony Graves, who was sentenced to death in 1994 for murdering six people in Somerville, and Lacresha Murray, who was convicted of the 1996 fatal beating of a two-year-old girl in Austin. A 2004 assessment on appeal of Bayardo's methodology in the Morton case by noted forensic pathologist Michael Baden, the former chief medical examiner of New York City and a preeminent expert in his field, would indicate that the medical examiner's work was deeply flawed in this instance as well. According to Baden, Bayardo did not have critical data that would have allowed him to make a more reliable evaluation. "My review reveals a number of serious mistakes in the methodology used by the medical examiner," wrote Baden in a sworn affidavit. "No proper observations were made at the scene of death of rigor mortis, livor mortis, or algor mortis—the stiffening of the body, the settling of the blood, or the body's change in temperature—which are the traditional measures that assist forensic pathologists in determining time of death."

Just weeks after Bayardo changed his time-of-death estimate, Anderson, who had expressed reservations about the strength of the state's evidence, felt confident enough about the case to present it to a grand jury. And when the hearing was convened, Boutwell was the only witness he called. Based on his testimony, the grand jury indicted Michael for first-degree murder. At trial, Anderson would lean heavily on Bayardo's conclusions to bolster the state's case. The district attorney would even go so far as to have Christine's last meal prepared and delivered to the courtroom for the jury's inspection.

Bill Allison, one of Michael's attorneys, told me that until Bayardo's revision, "the evidence was weak. His finding changed everything."

.　　　.　　　.

On February 10, 1987, the morning that *The State of Texas v. Michael W. Morton* got under way, Michael put on a suit, kissed his son on the forehead, and handed the boy to his mother, Patricia, who had come from Kilgore with his father, Billy, to help out during the trial. Michael had not boxed up any of the belongings that filled the four-bedroom house or made arrangements for Eric's care in the event that he was convicted; given the lack of evidence against him, he felt cautiously optimistic that twelve people would not be able to find him guilty beyond a reasonable doubt. He drove his pickup to the home of Allison's law partner, Bill White, an ex-navy man and former prosecutor. White's blunt, outspoken style complemented the more cerebral Allison, a clinical law professor at UT. When Michael arrived, White—who was busy poring through his notes—tossed him the keys to his Porsche and told him to drive. A quiet scene greeted them when they arrived at the Greek Revival courthouse on Georgetown's main square. The crush of media attention would come later; on the first day, only a few reporters showed up.

In preparation for trial, Ken Anderson had immersed himself in the details of the case. The district attorney knew he was up against formidable opponents: both defense attorneys had impressive track records, and Allison had been one of Anderson's own law professors. Addressing the five-man, seven-woman jury that morning, the district attorney laid out the state's theory of the case, arguing that on the night of his birthday, Michael had worked himself into a rage after Christine rejected his advances. "He had rented a videotape, a very sexually explicit videotape, and he viewed that sexually explicit videotape, and he got madder and madder," Anderson said. "He got some sort of blunt object, probably a club, and he took that club and he went into the bedroom . . . and he beat his wife repeatedly to death." Anderson went on to explain that Michael had staged a burglary afterward to cover his tracks, though he had done a poor job of it, pulling out only four dresser drawers and emptying them. "He also decided he would write a note as if his wife was still alive," Anderson continued. "So he wrote a note, pretending she was still alive, and left that in the bathroom." The motive was a stretch—how often do husbands bludgeon their wives to death for not wanting to have sex?—but Anderson pressed on, telling the jury that Michael had taken Christine's purse, his .45, and the murder weapon and disposed of them before showing up to work.

In the absence of any concrete evidence, Anderson relied on his most emotional material, calling as his first witness Rita Kirkpatrick, who haltingly provided a few facts about her daughter's life. She was followed by Elizabeth Gee, who painted a portrait of an unhappy marriage. She told the jury of the Mortons' frequent arguments and how she once heard Michael bark, "Bitch, go get me a beer." She vividly described finding Christine's body and how aloof Michael had been in the weeks that followed. When Anderson asked her to recount what he had done two days after Christine's funeral, Elizabeth became emotional; she paused for a moment to collect herself, then looked at Michael. "Weed-Eating her marigolds," she said, enunciating each word. Though much of Elizabeth's testimony had felt "almost rehearsed," jury foreman Mark Landrum told me, her disgust for Michael in that moment had been palpable. "From that moment on, I didn't like Michael Morton," Landrum said. "I'm assuming the entire jury felt that way too. Whether he was a murderer or not was still to be determined, but I knew that I did not like him."

Building on the idea that Michael hated his wife, Anderson also cast him as sexually deviant. Over the protests of the defense, Judge Lott allowed the district attorney to show jurors the first two minutes of *Handful of Diamonds*, the adult video that Michael had rented, under the pretext that it established his state of mind before the murder. Though tame by today's standards, the film did not curry favor with a Williamson County jury. "I was repulsed," Lou Bryan, a now-retired schoolteacher who served on the jury, told me. "I kept thinking, 'What kind of person would watch this?'"

Anderson's portrait of Michael only darkened after DPS serologist Donna Stanley testified that a stain on the Mortons' bedsheet contained semen that was consistent with Michael's blood type. (In fact, later analysis detected both semen and vaginal fluid, corroborating Michael's account to Boutwell that he and Christine had had sex the week before she was killed.) Anderson used Stanley's testimony to suggest an appalling scenario: that after beating his wife to death, Michael had masturbated over her lifeless body.

The burden on the state to prove beyond a reasonable doubt that Michael had killed Christine was arguably lessened once he was cast as a sadist. Viewed through that lens, Michael was doomed. When he broke down as Anderson held up a succession of grisly crime-scene photos, his reaction was seen not as an outpouring of grief but as the remorse of a guilty man. "I felt like he was crying over what he had done," Landrum told me. In fact, as he sat at the defense table weeping, Michael was grasping the full horror of what had happened to his wife.

Though the case remained entirely circumstantial, Anderson provided enough details to make Michael appear culpable. William Dayhuff, the husband of Christine's boss at Allstate, took the stand to say that he remembered Michael carrying a billy club in his pickup for protection when he worked nights cleaning parking lots after-hours. Having introduced the existence of a potential murder weapon, Anderson then called Bayardo to the stand to provide testimony that would, in effect, place Michael at the scene of the crime. Bayardo told the jury that Christine had died within four hours of eating her last meal, though he added that his estimated time of death was an opinion based on his experience and "not a scientific statement." (When Bayardo was asked in 2011 to clarify what he had meant by this, he said under oath that his estimate was "not based on science, real science.") It was a subtle distinction lost on the jury, who naturally viewed Travis County's chief medical examiner as a credible source for scientific testimony.

At lunchtime each day, when the courtroom emptied for an hour-long recess, Michael hung back, too unsettled to eat. The windows of the old, drafty courtroom afforded a view of Georgetown's main square, and he often stood by them, staring down at the people below who casually went about their business. He marveled as they walked to their lunch appointments or waved at friends, unencumbered by anything like the terror that had begun to creep into his mind that he might actually be found guilty.

His attorneys also seemed more anxious, often forgoing lunch to study documents in preparation for the afternoon's witnesses. But they were hampered by what they did not know. During the discovery phase that preceded the trial, Anderson had disclosed only the most rudimentary information about the investigation. He had turned over the autopsy report and crime-scene photos but fought to keep back virtually everything else, even the comments Michael had made to Boutwell and Wood on the day of the murder. "I'd never heard of a prosecutor withholding a defendant's oral statements from his own attorneys," Allison told me. "This was a degree of hardball that Bill and I had never encountered before."

What Allison and White did have on their side was a Texas statute that required law-enforcement officers to turn over all their reports and notes once they took the stand. However, when Boutwell climbed into the witness box on the third day of the trial, he produced fewer than seven pages of handwritten notes—notes which represented, he said, along with a brief report he failed to bring with him, all of his documentation on the case. "This was a major homicide investigation, and there was nothing there," White told me.

Stranger still, Boutwell would be the state's final witness. Anderson never called Wood—who had identified himself at a pretrial hearing as the case's lead investigator—to the stand. It was a mystifying decision by the prosecution. "We smelled a rat, but we didn't know what the nature of the rat was," White said. "There were lots of reasons why Anderson might have decided not to put Wood on. Maybe he was a lousy witness who would get tripped up on cross-examination, or maybe Anderson was setting us up, trying to get us to call Wood, even though he was an adverse witness."

There was another possibility as well. By not asking Wood to testify, the state was not obligated to turn over his reports or notes (though by law, the state was required to disclose any exculpatory evidence). With the limited information they did have, Allison and White mounted a vigorous defense, calling expert witnesses who cast serious doubts on Bayardo's time-of-death estimate. But unlike the prosecution, they did not have a cohesive story to tell. As for who had killed Christine, Allison admitted to the jury, "We can't answer that question because we don't know." He and White wove together the available facts they had—the unidentified fingerprints, the unlocked sliding-glass door, the footprint in the backyard—to suggest that an unknown intruder had attacked Christine. But without access to Wood's notes, they were unable to see the whole picture. They did not know about the reports of a mysterious green van behind the Morton home, and they failed to understand the importance of the discarded bandana with a blood stain on it that had been recovered approximately one hundred yards away from the crime scene. Ultimately, neither Allison nor White would make mention of it during the trial. Nor did they bring up the frightening question that Eric had asked Michael about the man in the shower. The two attorneys knew that Eric had been home at the time of the crime and might have seen something, but they also knew the chances that Lott would allow a three-year-old to testify were slim, and they worried that Michael would object. "Michael was very protective of Eric," Allison told me. "We were not allowed to talk to him about the case."

When Michael himself took the stand on the fifth day of the trial, he calmly and steadily answered the questions that were posed to him, but he did not betray the sense of personal devastation that might have moved the twelve people who would render a verdict. "During this whole ordeal, he never fell apart," Allison told me. "He wanted people to see him as strong. And I think in the end, that very trait worked against him." Jurors were put off by his perceived woodenness on the stand. Landrum explained, "I would have been screaming, 'I could never have done this! I love my wife!'" Bryan was not persuaded by his testimony either. "He just did not come off as genuine, because there was no emotion there," she said.

Instead, it was Anderson who turned in the histrionic performance. At one point tears streamed down his face as he addressed the jury, and he shouted so loudly during his cross-examination that people waiting in the hallway outside the courtroom could hear him.

"Isn't it a fact that you . . . took that club and you beat her?" Anderson cried.

"No," Michael replied.

"And you *beat* her?" Anderson said, bringing his arms down forcefully as if he were using a bat to strike Christine.

"No."

"And you *beat* her?" said Anderson, again bringing his arms down.

"No," Michael insisted.

"When you were done beating her, what were you wearing to bed?"

"I didn't beat her."

"What were you wearing to bed?"

"Nothing."

"Nothing on? And when you got done beating her, you masturbated?"

"No."

". . . And you took your dead wife's blood while you were beating her and splattered it on your little boy's picture, didn't you?"

"No," Michael said, his voice breaking.

During closing arguments, Anderson recast some of his shakiest evidence as ironclad proof of Michael's guilt. Echoing his cross-examination of Michael, Anderson suggested that the billy club was not just a weapon he had once owned but the instrument he had used to "beat her and beat her and beat her." Bayardo's time of death—which the medical examiner had qualified as an opinion, not scientific fact—became incontrovertible truth. "Medical science shows this defendant killed his wife," Anderson told the jury, referring to Bayardo's testimony. "The best [that] medical science can bring us shows this defendant is a killer." (He used the term "medical science" a total of seven times.) Allison and White gave impassioned closing arguments that sought to persuade jurors that the state had not proved its case, but in the end, it was Anderson's view of Michael—"He is remorseless. He is amoral. He is beyond any hope," the district attorney would say—that overshadowed the slightness of the evidence against him. The jurors deliberated for less than two hours, though eleven of them were ready to convict at the start. "I was certain of his guilt," Landrum told me.

As the guilty verdict was read, Michael's legs went weak, and he had to be supported by one of his attorneys. Finally, he fell back into his chair, rested his head on the defense table, and wept.

"Your Honor, I didn't do this," he insisted before he was sentenced to life in prison. "That's all I can say. I did not do this."

The trial had lasted six days. Allison—who would be haunted by the verdict for years to come and eventually go on to found the Center for Actual Innocence at UT Law School—lingered after Michael was led away in handcuffs. Both he and prosecutor Mike Davis, who had assisted Anderson during the trial, stayed behind to ask the jurors about their views of the case. It was during their discussions in the jury room that Allison says he overheard Davis make an astonishing statement, telling several jurors that if Michael's attorneys had been able to obtain Wood's reports, they could have raised more doubt than they did. (Davis has said under oath that he has no recollection of making such a statement.) What, Allison wondered, was in Wood's reports?

.   .   .

With his hands shackled in his lap, Michael looked out the window of the squad car and watched as the rolling farmland east of Georgetown gradually gave way to the piney woods of East Texas. Two Williamson County sheriff's deputies sat in the front seat, exchanging small talk as they sped down the two-lane roads that led to Huntsville. Michael had, by then, spent a little more than a month in the county jail waiting to be transferred to state custody. During that time, he had gotten to know several county inmates who were well acquainted with the Texas Department of Corrections. They had given him advice he never forgot: keep your mouth shut and your eyes open, and always fight back. In prison, it didn't matter if you won or lost. In the long run, getting the hell beaten out of you was better than showing that you were too scared to fight.

When they reached Huntsville, the deputies deposited him at the Diagnostic Unit, the intake facility where he would spend the next several weeks before being assigned to a prison. Once inside, he was ordered to strip naked. His hair was sheared and his mustache was shaved off, leaving a pale white stripe above his upper lip. He was issued boxer shorts and ordered to get in line to pick up his work boots. As he waited, Michael studied the man in front of him, whose back was crisscrossed with scars—stab wounds, he realized, as he counted thirteen of them in all. Michael was herded along with the other inmates into the communal showers and then to the mess hall, where they gulped down food as a prison guard shouted at them to eat faster. At last, when the lights shut off at ten-thirty, Michael lay down in his bunk, a thin mattress atop an unforgiving metal frame. Sporadically during the night, he could hear inmates calling out to one another, imitating different animal sounds—a rooster crowing, a dog baying—that reverberated through the cell block.

Even then, as he lay in the dark listening to the cacophony of voices around him, Michael felt that he would be vindicated someday. He just didn't know how or when that day would come.

Part II

I.

"Even though I asked to be transferred here for the master's program, coming here was a shock," Michael Morton wrote on January 22, 2002, from his cell in the Ramsey I prison unit, south of Houston. He was replying to a letter he had recently received from Mario Garcia, a former coworker at the Safeway in Austin where he had worked before being sent to prison fifteen years earlier. Besides his parents and his younger sister—who made the five-hundred-mile round-trip from East Texas to visit when they could—Garcia was the only person from Michael's previous life who had stayed in contact with him. Virtually everyone else believed that he was guilty. Throughout the fall and winter of 1986, his case had been splashed across the front pages of Central Texas newspapers, earning him a grisly notoriety. "Victim's Husband Held in Murder Investigation," the *Hill Country News* announced in the fall of 1986. "Killing Linked to Sexual Rage," trumpeted an *Austin American-Statesman* headline just before he was sentenced to life in prison, in February 1987. The *Williamson County Sun* announced, "He's Guilty." Michael had become a pariah—a "murderous pervert," as he would ironically refer to himself.

"When I got here, they used to put all new arrivals in the field force," Michael wrote, referring to inmates who were assigned to work on the prison farm. That had been three years earlier. Now forty-seven, he was too old to be doing hard physical labor all day long, he told Garcia. His face had settled into the softer contours of middle age, and his sandy blond hair was going gray. "Try to imagine twenty to forty men," he continued, "shoulder to shoulder, hip to hip, swinging their [hoes] in unison and chopping weeds that are, I swear to God, six to ten feet high. Or, on the bad days, working in a huge irrigation ditch, skinning the banks down to bare earth and then dragging the chopped-up vegetation back up the banks. It's long, hard, backbreaking work. Sometimes guys pass out and have to be carried to the hospital. (Fakers are found out by being dragged onto a fire ant mound. Either way, the consequences suck.) During all this, armed, hard-ass guards are riding around on horseback, shouting Christian-hearted encouragement. Added to the natural camaraderie and high spirits of working outdoors are more snakes, rats, poison ivy, and biting, stinging, and pinching insects than I like to remember. The first few weeks damn near killed me."

During his fifteen years in prison, Michael had already survived sweltering summers with no air-conditioning, when temperatures inside the old red-brick penitentiary reached into the triple digits for weeks on end. He had fought off the unwanted attention of a hulking inmate, an enforcer for a prison gang who later died of AIDS, by inviting him into his cell and slamming a makeshift tabletop against his throat. He had been kept awake by inmates who cried at night and by his own longing for his son, Eric, and his wife, Christine, whose absences he felt only more acutely as the years wore on. But in his letters to Garcia, Michael tried to strike an upbeat note. "I have fallen in with a tolerable collection of half-witted misfits," he wrote in one letter. "Despite it all, I am okay," he assured Garcia in another. "Honest."

When he did allude to the indignities of his daily life, he added a heavy dose of gallows humor, as when he dubbed a stomach flu that swept through the prison population one winter "the Brown Storm." ("I live on a dorm with 56 guys and four toilets," he wrote. "Do the math. It wasn't pretty.") He proudly described working toward his master's degree in literature—he had already earned his bachelor's degree in psychology during the early years of his incarceration—and he expressed how much he enjoyed reading Homer and Dante. He casually mentioned that he was at work on a novel.

Eric was a recurrent subject in his letters to Garcia. The boy was being raised by Christine's sister, Marylee, who, along with the rest of her family, had come to believe he was guilty. "It seems hard to believe, but he's eighteen years old," Michael wrote that January. "This spring, he'll graduate from a private Catholic high school in Houston. The Jesuits are supposed to be good at cramming info into the heads of teenagers, so I hope he's ready for college. I say 'I hope he's ready' because I don't know. We've drifted apart. A few years ago, he reached the age where coming to visit his old man wasn't at the top of his to-do list." In fact, Eric—when he was fifteen—had cut off all contact with his father.

Michael never failed to express his gratitude to Garcia for taking the time to correspond with him. "No matter how my train wreck of a life ends up, I will always think of you as one of the best," Michael signed off one letter. "Adiós for now, my friend."

.   .   .

Amid the jumble of holiday mail that arrived at Bill Allison's house every December, there was always one envelope that stood out, distinguished by the return address from prison and Michael's familiar handwriting. The Christmas card inside—in which Michael thanked Allison for defending him so forcefully during his trial—left him flooded with emotion. He had always felt certain that Michael was innocent, and he was filled with regret that he had not been able to convince the jury of this. "I've practiced law for forty-one years," he told me. "In terms of the psychological toll that cases have taken on me, Michael's was the worst." In the aftermath of the guilty verdict, he said, "I couldn't get over it. I went into a three-year tailspin."

In Allison's opinion, something had gone very wrong during the six-day trial at the Williamson County courthouse in George-town. On the afternoon that Michael was convicted, Allison and one of the prosecutors in the case, Mike Davis, had lingered after the trial to talk with jurors. As they discussed the case, Allison overheard what he believed to be a shocking admission. According to Allison, Davis told several jurors that if Michael's attorneys had been able to obtain the reports of the case's lead investigator, Sergeant Don Wood, they could have raised more doubt than they did. (Davis has said under oath that he has no recollection of making such a statement.)

Allison had immediately hurried back to his office in Austin to write down Davis's comments. While he puzzled over what the prosecutor might have meant, he thought back to an argument he'd had with Davis's boss, Williamson County district attorney Ken Anderson, who had led the prosecution's effort.

During two pretrial hearings, the lawyers had clashed over what evidence the state should, or should not, have to turn over. As Allison remembered it, state district judge William Lott had ordered Anderson to provide him with all of Wood's reports and notes before the trial so he could determine whether they contained any "Brady material." (The term refers to the landmark 1963 U.S. Supreme Court ruling in *Brady v. Maryland,* which holds that prosecutors are required to turn over any evidence that is favorable to the accused. Failure to do so is considered to be a "Brady violation," or a breach of a defendant's constitutional right to due process.)

Judge Lott had examined everything Anderson had given him and ruled that no Brady material was present. Afterward, as is the protocol in such a situation, the judge had placed the papers in a sealed file that could be opened only by the appellate courts to review at a later date. Thinking back on that series of events, Allison had a terrible thought: What if Anderson had not, in fact, given Lott all of Wood's reports and notes?

It was this idea that prompted Allison's motion for new trial, which was denied, and his first appeal, which he filed in 1988, one year after Michael was found guilty. That December, the Third Court of Appeals upheld Michael's conviction and denied Allison's claim that Brady material had been withheld from the defense. The language of the decision also made it clear that the court believed that Lott's sealed file—which its justices had taken the time to open and examine themselves—contained the entirety of Wood's notes. Still, Allison remained convinced that something was amiss. He appealed the ruling to the Court of Criminal Appeals, but the following year, its justices declined to reconsider the lower court's decision. This was a major blow to Allison's efforts. "I can't say that I ever completely gave up," Allison told me, "but I was pretty close." Despairing, he called an old friend, noted criminal defense attorney Barry Scheck. "Bill told me that he was haunted by this case," Scheck recalled. "He felt that Michael was innocent and that Anderson was hiding something. He smelled a rat from the very, very beginning."

Scheck was an early proponent of DNA testing, a new forensic technology that was just emerging in the late eighties. Though the science was first used to match perpetrators to their crimes, Scheck and his law partner, Peter Neufeld, had become convinced that DNA testing could be used for another purpose: to exonerate the falsely accused. In 1992 the two attorneys founded a nonprofit legal organization in New York called the Innocence Project and began to take on cases in which biological material from the crime scenes could still be tested. In time this practice would transform the landscape for the wrongfully convicted, but litigating these cases was difficult at first. The technology was still in its infancy and required large quantities of DNA material, which were often unavailable. Despite these hurdles, Scheck and Neufeld managed to win numerous exonerations, and as news of their success spread, they were inundated with requests for help from across the country. "I badgered Barry and the people who worked for him for years to take on Michael's case, but they were swamped," Allison told me. "Barry would say, 'We'll get to it,' but it took a long time."

In prison, Michael had become well versed in the science of DNA analysis from the many magazine articles he had read on the subject. While he waited for Scheck to get to his case, he secured a court order, with the help of Allison and another lawyer, to permit DNA testing of a semen stain found on the sheet of the bed where Christine had been murdered. Michael still knew next to nothing about what had happened to his wife. He had returned home from work on the day she was killed to find their house overrun with law enforcement. The walls and ceiling of their bedroom were spattered with blood. Because she had been in bed at the time of the killing, in her nightgown, with the blinds closed, Michael believed that she had been attacked shortly after he left for work early that morning. But who had broken into his house and savagely beaten her was still a mystery, one he was determined to solve.

The technology proved to be too primitive to yield a result on such a small sample, however, and two rounds of testing—first in 1991 and then in 1994—were inconclusive. Over the next few years, the process grew more sophisticated as it became possible to "amplify" DNA, or duplicate even minute amounts of genetic material so there would be a large enough sample to analyze. Michael obtained another court order to have the sheet retested. The results, which he received in 2000, did not identify Christine's killer, but they did directly contradict a sinister theory of the prosecution's—that, after murdering Christine, Michael had masturbated over her dead body. It was a sadistic image that district attorney Anderson had repeatedly asserted during the trial, and it had helped turn jurors' opinions against Michael. But the stain, it turned out, was not composed of semen alone; it was a combination of Michael's semen and Christine's vaginal fluid, indicating that something much more mundane had taken place: in the days or weeks leading up to the murder, the Mortons had had sex.

In 2002 the Innocence Project was ready to take on Michael's case. Staff attorney Nina Morrison—who, to date, has secured no fewer than twenty DNA exonerations—headed up the effort in New York; she tapped a Houston attorney named John Raley to serve pro bono as her co-counsel. At first glance, Raley was an unusual choice: he was a civil attorney—his specialty had long been medical-malpractice defense—and he had never practiced criminal law before. But he came highly recommended by a former colleague at Fulbright & Jaworski, in part for his facility with scientific testimony. He and Morrison would push for DNA testing on a wide range of evidence that had been gathered during the investigation: fingernail clippings; vaginal, anal, and oral swabs taken at Christine's autopsy; her nightgown; stray hairs found on her hand; and a bloody bandana that had been discovered approximately one hundred yards behind the Morton home. Raley, a six-foot-three former University of Oklahoma offensive guard, had an optimistic, almost wide-eyed view of how Williamson County would respond to the request for DNA testing. "Had the murder happened in the present day, there's no doubt that law enforcement would have tested the evidence to try and find Christine's killer, so initially I didn't think they would oppose us," Raley told me.

By then Anderson had left the district attorney's office—in 2001 Governor Rick Perry named him district judge—but he kept in close communication with his successor, district attorney John Bradley. For eleven years, Bradley had been Anderson's loyal first assistant, and when Anderson was appointed to the bench, Bradley became his replacement. The Houston native was well suited to carry on Anderson's tough-on-crime legacy. A brash and sometimes polarizing figure who had cut his teeth as a young prosecutor in the Harris County DA's office, Bradley had honed his hard-boiled approach under the legendary Johnny Holmes, who had won more death sentences than any district attorney in Texas history. After becoming Williamson County DA, Bradley issued press releases he drafted himself that publicized the numerous convictions and often draconian sentences that his prosecutors won. He was notorious for bullying defense attorneys into taking pre-indictment plea bargains for their clients, which often required people who had been accused of crimes to enter guilty pleas before knowing how strong or weak the state's evidence was against them. His unusually combative stance toward defendants was an easy fit in an office molded by Anderson. "John was Ken's protégé," Allison told me. "Every policy, every strategy, got handed down from Ken to John. The only difference between them is that John's louder. He likes to be onstage more. That was never really Ken's forte."

While Raley hoped for cooperation, Morrison cautioned that they would probably meet resistance on their motion for DNA testing. Lawyers from outside Williamson County had never been made to feel particularly welcome in Georgetown, and a request for DNA testing—which by its very nature implied that Bradley's mentor may have made a grievous error in prosecuting Michael—was certain to get a chilly reception. Though Anderson was no longer DA, his presence in the courthouse was still keenly felt. The motion would have to be filed with the original trial court where Michael had been sentenced, just down the hall from the courtroom where Anderson, now a judge, presided.

Before filing the motion, Raley called the DA to introduce himself. He let Bradley know that he came from a law enforcement family—his father, John Wesley Raley Jr., served as U.S. attorney for the eastern district of Oklahoma under two presidents, and his brother, Robert, is a federal prosecutor in Tulsa. "I said that I hoped he would agree to the motion or, at a minimum, not oppose it," Raley told me, explaining that his overtures were rebuffed. "He was polite at first, but after we filed the motion, he made it clear that he would fight us. I couldn't understand why he was opposing testing that we were paying for, that would cost the county nothing, especially if he was so certain that Michael was guilty."

In fact, Bradley was generally skeptical of post-conviction testing, in part because it could undermine the finality of the legal process. One telling indication of his view on the matter came years later, in 2007, in a now-redacted thread on an online forum for prosecutors that was discovered by Scott Henson, of the criminal-justice blog *Grits for Breakfast*. Posting on the forum, Bradley had advocated a troubling strategy: that when obtaining guilty pleas, prosecutors should also secure agreements that would ensure that all physical evidence could be subsequently destroyed, so as to preclude the possibility of endless appeals. "Then there is nothing to test or retest," Bradley wrote. (Bradley declined to be interviewed for this article.)

Unsurprisingly, when Morrison and Raley filed their motion in 2005, Bradley opposed it. As the DA stonewalled, Raley's conversations with him became increasingly antagonistic. "At one point I asked him, 'Why won't you just agree to this? What harm can it cause?'" Raley said. "And he told me, 'It would muddy the waters.'" (This phrase had previously been used in a 2002 Court of Criminal Appeals ruling that denied DNA testing to a death row inmate, holding that such testing could not definitively prove the defendant's innocence and would "merely muddy the waters.") Bradley's response left Raley stupefied. "I said, 'Mr. Bradley, truth clarifies,'" Raley recalled.

Yet despite Bradley's resistance, a decision handed down by district court judge Billy Ray Stubblefield in 2006 gave Morrison and Raley a partial victory. The judge agreed to allow DNA testing to go forward on the evidence collected from the Morton home, but he denied the request to test the bandana. Bradley had made the case that the bandana's connection to the murder could not be proved because it had been found too far from the crime scene. "They fought us the hardest on the bandana," Raley told me, adding that Bradley had been willing to have only the hair sample that was found on Christine's hand tested and nothing else. "We argued that the fingerprints on the sliding-glass door and the footprint in the backyard established that the bandana had dropped along the killer's escape route. I could picture it—him wiping the blood from his hands and face on the bandana, sticking it in his back pocket, and running." But Stubblefield did not see it the same way.

When DNA testing on the fingernail clippings, swabs, nightgown, and hair was completed, the results were discouraging. Only Christine's DNA was detected, and Michael could not be excluded as the donor of one of the hairs.

Bradley would later scoff to reporters that Michael and his attorneys were "grasping at straws" in their search for a "mystery killer." He used a similarly contemptuous tone when Michael came up for parole in 2007, having served the first third of his sixty-year sentence. "I am writing to protest parole and request that you put off reconsideration of parole for as long as the law permits," Bradley wrote to the Texas Board of Pardons and Paroles. "Michael Morton has never accepted responsibility for murdering his wife." (In an aside Bradley added, "His nickname for Christine was 'Bitch.'") The district attorney was correct that Michael appeared to be unrepentant; Michael had been told by other inmates that he would be eligible for early release only if he showed remorse for his crime, but he emphatically refused to do so. He would not lie to get out, he told his parents. His innocence, he said, was all he had.

When the DA's office received notice that Michael had been denied parole, someone—it's unclear who—scrawled a note on the letter from the Texas Department of Criminal Justice. In small, blocky letters, it read, "Victory."

．　　　．　　　．

Six years earlier, Michael had hit rock bottom. In 2001 a letter had arrived for him at the Ramsey I Unit informing him that his son had decided to change his name. Eric was eighteen at the time. He had recently been adopted by his aunt, Marylee, and her husband, whom she married when Eric was twelve. That the boy had rejected his own name was too much for Michael to bear. Before Eric was born, Christine had wanted to name him Michael Morton Jr., but Michael had balked, telling her that he would rather their son have his own distinct identity. And so they had compromised on Eric Michael Morton. Now Eric Michael Morton no longer existed.

"That's when I finally broke," Michael told me. "Nothing before then did it—not Chris's murder, not my arrest, not my trial, not my conviction. Not getting a life sentence. Not the failed appeals, not the lab results that led nowhere. Eric was what I had been holding on to. He was the reason I was trying to prove my innocence. Once I found out that he had changed his name, I knew that reconciliation was not a possibility anymore. We weren't going to be able to put this back together. That was a hollow, empty feeling, because getting out had never been the goal. It was getting out so that I could tell Eric, 'Look, see? I didn't do this.'

"I can't remember if it was Marylee or Eric who wrote to tell me, but I remember being nearly catatonic for at least a week. It was like the bottom fell out. This wasn't just another difficult thing to overcome, this was the end. This was a death. I literally cried out to God, 'Are you there? Show me something. Give me a sign.' I had nothing. I was spent, I was bankrupt. It was the most sincere plea I have ever made in my life. And I got nothing. A couple weeks went by and . . . nothing. No response.

"I was lying in my bunk one night listening to the radio on my headphones, and I ran across a classical station. I heard something you rarely ever hear: a harp. There was no slow buildup, no preamble to what happened next. I was just engulfed in this very warm, very comforting blinding light. I don't know what to call it—an ecstatic experience? a revelation?—because it was indescribable. Any words I use to explain it will fall short. I had this incredible feeling of joy. There was an overwhelming sense of this unlimited compassion aimed right at me. Then I heard my alarm go off and it was over, and I sat up in bed. Outwardly, everything was still the same. But I knew that I had been in the presence of God.

"My life didn't change right away. Everything didn't instantly fall into place. I was in prison for another decade, so it wasn't like God knocked open the doors for me. Becoming a believer was a slow, organic process that I had to grow into. But I was different after that. You can't buy inner peace, but I had it."

II.

During the five years that Michael and his attorneys sought to have the bandana tested and Bradley tried mightily to resist their efforts, the bandana itself sat within the Williamson County Sheriff's Office. It didn't look like anything extraordinary. The deep-blue Western-themed handkerchief was bordered by a white lariat pattern that repeatedly spelled, in loopy script, the word "Wrangler." Scattered across the fabric, which was deeply creased, were a number of small brown bloodstains.

Whose blood was it? On January 8, 2010, the Third Court of Appeals reversed Stubblefield's decision and allowed testing on the bandana to go forward. Justice G. Alan Waldrop noted in his decision that the unidentified fingerprints on the sliding-glass door of the Morton home and the footprint in the backyard did, in fact, suggest that there was a trail of evidence connecting the bandana to the crime scene. Further, he suggested that DNA testing could definitively determine whether or not there was a link. "If the bandana contains Christine's blood, it is sufficient by itself to establish a trail."

Still, the bandana was seen as a long shot. "I did not have high hopes," Morrison told me. She and Raley had requested that the bandana be shipped from Williamson County to a private lab in Dallas that could amplify small amounts of DNA using the most cutting-edge technology available. But Bradley insisted that the bandana instead be submitted to the Department of Public Safety crime lab for analysis, even though the lab was not equipped to amplify DNA. In a letter to Stubblefield, Raley, who had grown increasingly impatient, wondered if Bradley's insistence on using the DPS crime lab stemmed from "a desire to cause additional delays, or to minimize the odds that interpretable DNA results will be obtained." Finally, after five months, Stubblefield ruled that the bandana, as well as a single strand of hair that was found on it, be shipped to the lab that the Innocence Project had initially requested. By then the dried blood on the bandana was nearly twenty-four years old.

Testing small quantities of degraded evidence takes time, and private firms that specialize in the process are in high demand. For a full year, the blue bandana sat in the lab in Dallas. It was stored carefully, folded into a neat square, its secrets held within. In May 2011, it was submitted for testing, which was completed the following month. The results, which Morrison was informed of by a phone call from the lab, were breathtaking. Both the blood and the strand of hair matched Christine's DNA profile. The DNA profile of an unknown man was also recovered, intermingled with Christine's blood and hair. Michael's DNA was absent.

·   ·   ·

Morrison, who already had plans to be in Dallas that week to work on another wrongful conviction case, met Raley at DFW Airport so they could tell Michael the news together. The mood in Morrison's rental car that morning was "euphoric," Raley told me. "I don't think the wheels ever actually touched the ground." It was the first time during the eight years they had worked together that Raley had seen Morrison allow herself to be confident about their chances of getting Michael out. The dauntless Yale graduate had always met Raley's enthusiasm with the cautious pragmatism she had developed after years of dealing with lost evidence, recalcitrant prosecutors, and a slow-moving justice system. That morning, she beamed as they headed east into the Piney Woods, toward Palestine, where Michael had been transferred to another prison— the Michael Unit—after earning his master's degree.

Michael suspected that the news was good when he learned that Morrison was coming. Although he had spoken on the phone with her for years, he had never actually met her in person before. "I knew this wasn't just a grip and grin," Michael told me. When Morrison and Raley were escorted into the cramped visitation booth where he sat waiting for them, he could see that they were elated. He pressed his hand against the glass that separated them in greeting and picked up the phone on his side of the partition. His attorneys talked animatedly, passing the phone receiver back and forth between them. "I don't remember the exact words they said, but we were all bouncing off the walls," he told me. "After a while Nina said, 'Okay, sit down and take a deep breath. They've fought us all this way, and they're going to keep fighting. This isn't over.'"

Proving a DNA-based innocence claim requires showing that a jury would not have found the defendant guilty had the DNA results been known at the time of trial. Doing so, however, can take years. Michael's lawyers understood that Bradley would almost certainly oppose any innocence claim and that years of appeals could follow. Even if Michael's conviction were eventually overturned by a higher court, the DA's office could still choose to retry him. The quickest way to clear his name would be to learn if the unknown man's DNA profile matched any one of the millions of individuals with prior convictions that are stored in the FBI's national DNA database, CODIS.

"Then there would be no question of Michael's innocence," Morrison told me. "When you have a name and a face to put to the DNA, it usually removes any possible hypotheses about contamination or tampering or accomplices." Initially, though, it was unknown whether the DNA profile, which had been extracted from bloodstains that were old and fragile, was detailed enough to be compared with those in CODIS. "Among the many miracles in this case is that had the DNA profile on the bandana been missing just one more marker it would not have been eligible for a national search," Morrison said.

The DNA profile was entered into CODIS, and on August 9 Morrison was informed that there had been a match. His name was Mark Alan Norwood, a drifter with a long criminal record, including arrests in Texas, California, and Tennessee for aggravated assault with intent to kill, arson, breaking and entering residences, drug possession, and resisting arrest. Old mug shots revealed a man with a large, drooping mustache, his chin tilted upward, looking down at the camera with a cold-eyed stare.

Almost twenty-five years to the day after Christine was murdered, Morrison and Raley called Michael to tell him that the man whose DNA was found on the bandana had been identified. "I remember Michael was quiet for a while after we told him," Raley said. "There was just silence on the other end of the line. And I said, 'Michael, are you there?' I thought he might have fainted or something. And he said, 'Yes, I'm here. I'm just letting this all wash over me.'"

.   .   .

As dramatic as the DNA results were, the Williamson County district attorney's office was not ready to admit that Michael had been wrongly convicted. No sooner did the news break that another man's DNA had been identified than Bradley began to discount the significance of the bandana, pointing out that it had been found roughly one hundred yards from the crime scene, not in the Morton home. "I don't think, on its face, that a DNA result [on] . . . a piece of evidence away from the crime scene immediately proves innocence," he told the *Austin American-Statesman*. "It does raise some good issues that are worthy of investigation, and we will do that." As Morrison had predicted, Michael was in for a fight.

By then, he was accustomed to the stubbornness of the system that had put him away, and he knew better than to expect it to yield. He understood that the district attorney's office was deeply invested in maintaining that he was guilty. Yet he did not fully fathom how singularly obsessed Williamson County had been in its pursuit of him until he was able to see portions of Sergeant Wood's reports and notes. This material, which the Innocence

Project had, after years of litigation with the DA's office, acquired through a public records request, was nothing short of astounding.

The stack of old documents contained critical clues that might have helped identify Christine's killer had they ever been followed up on. Michael learned from a 1986 sheriff's deputy's report that several of his neighbors had seen a green van parked by the vacant, wooded lot behind his home around the time of the murder and had observed its driver walking into the overgrown area that extended up to his privacy fence. He read an internal memo to Wood about a call received from one of Christine's relatives in Phoenix who reported that a check his father-in-law had made out to her had been cashed after her death with what appeared to be a forged signature. (On later inspection, Michael would realize the signature was actually his own.) The internal memo, which was unsigned, included a telling note to Wood: "They seem to think that Chris' purse was stolen, course, we know better than that." Though Christine's purse was missing from the crime scene, Anderson had brushed aside this detail by telling the jury that Michael had staged a burglary to deflect attention away from himself.

It was this sense of certainty that appeared to have blinded investigators to what was surely the most incredible missed clue in the entire case: a handwritten phone message for Wood reporting that Christine's credit card had apparently been used at a store in San Antonio two days after her murder. "Larry Miller can ID the woman," stated the message, which included a number to call. Wood did not appear to have ever investigated the lead.

As he sifted through the papers, Michael felt "no anger, just bewilderment," he told me. "By that time, I had been pummeled with so much, for so long, that I recall just staring at the pages, stunned." For the first time in almost twenty-five years, he began to have a sense of clarity about what had happened. Michael

carefully turned the pages and came across an eight-page transcript of a phone call that had taken place between Wood and
Michael's mother-in-law, Rita Kirkpatrick, less than two weeks
after Christine's murder. As he studied each typewritten word,
Michael could feel his throat tightening.

"Eric and I were alone at my house . . . , which was the first
time he and I had been alone since his mother's death," Rita told
Wood. "I was putting on makeup in the bathroom. Eric layed [*sic*]
his blanket on the floor of my bedroom. He said, 'Mommie is
sleeping in the flowers.' His dad had told him that last week at the
cemetery. Then he kicked the blanket and said, 'Mommie, get
up.'" Rita explained to Wood that at Marylee's suggestion she had
written down everything her grandson had then said. She read
her exchange with the boy back to the investigator:

Eric: Mommie's crying. She's—stop it. Go away.
Grandmother: Why is she crying?
Eric: 'Cause, the monster's there.
Grandmother: What's he doing?
Eric: He hit Mommie. He broke the bed.
Grandmother: Is Mommie still crying?
Eric: No, Mommie stopped.
[Grandmother:] Then what happened? . . .
Eric: The monster throw a blue suitcase on the bed. He's
    mad . . .
    Was he big?
    Yeah.
    Did he have on gloves?
    Yeah, red.
    What did he carry in his red gloves?
    Basket.
    What was in the basket?
    Wood.

The boy's account perfectly matched the crime scene. Christine had been bludgeoned in her bed. Wood chips had been found in her hair, suggesting that she had been beaten with a log or a piece of lumber. A blue suitcase and a wicker basket had been stacked on top of her body. But it was the last part of Rita's conversation with Eric that Michael found the most astonishing:

Where was Daddy, Eric? . . . Was Daddy there?
No. Mommie and Eric was there.

Rita had then added, "So, Sgt. Wood, I'd get off the . . . domestic thing now and look for the monster and I have no more suspicions in my mind that Mike did it."

Just as Allison had suspected more than two decades earlier, there had been critical evidence in Wood's reports—evidence that would have changed the outcome of Michael's trial had the jury ever learned of it. But the transcript did not end there. Michael read along with disbelief as, over the course of the next six pages, Wood failed to ask a single pertinent question or inquire about a time when he could question Eric. Wood sought instead to convince Rita of a bizarre theory that the "big monster with the big mustache," as she referred to the killer—a reference, presumably, to a description that Eric had given her—had actually been Michael wearing his scuba-diving gear.

When I asked Michael to describe what he had felt after reading the transcript, he bowed his head and searched for the right words for a long time. "The magnitude of the tragedy felt more profound," he said finally. "I had no idea that Eric had seen anything as catastrophic as his mother's murder." After reading the transcript, he told me, "I was doubled over." He was incredulous that his wife's family had known that Eric had said that a stranger killed Christine. "The betrayal by my in-laws became magnified," he said. Why did he think the Kirkpatricks never told him of Eric's account? "The police said I did it, so I did it," Michael told me.

Soon after the results of the DNA testing became front-page news, Michael received a letter from Margaret Permenter, a friend of Christine's. Permenter apologized for having believed the worst about him and asked for his forgiveness. (Her mistaken assumption that Michael was guilty, she told me, was based on a single conversation she'd had with a woman at the Williamson County courthouse in 1987. "I called the court to order a transcript, because I hadn't been able to attend the trial," she told me. "The woman I spoke with told me that the medical examiner testified that Chrissy had died at a time when she could only have been with Mike. And that was enough for me.") Michael sent a gracious letter back, absolving her of blame. He reserved his anger for the Williamson County authorities who he believed were responsible for his wrongful conviction. "To this day, I wrestle with what might have been—and what continues to be—their motivations," Michael wrote. "I still wonder, why? Careerism? Peer pressure? Hubris? Misplaced duty? A warped longing to 'get' the bad guys? I don't know. I only know what they did."

III.

At first the whereabouts of Mark Alan Norwood—the convicted felon whose DNA had been detected on the bandana—were unknown. To prevent his name from being publicized, he was referred to only as John Doe in court documents. "We were very concerned about what he might do if he saw his name in print, because we felt he was a flight risk," Raley told me. Locating him was of paramount importance to Michael's attorneys, but they did not believe that the district attorney's office felt the same sense of urgency. Even after Williamson County opened an investigation on Norwood in August 2011, Bradley and his staff continued to question the importance of the DNA results, casting doubt on the bandana's "chain of evidence." (Strict protocols now dictate how law enforcement collects and transports evidence; in Michael's case, the bandana had been recovered not by a police officer but by Christine's brother, John Kirkpatrick, who had picked it up, placed it in a plastic bag, and driven it to the sheriff's office.) "There could be many innocent explanations for why DNA is on that bandana," assistant DA Kristen Jernigan asserted during a hearing late last summer.

To debunk that hypothesis, Morrison launched her own parallel investigation. The first step would be determining whether Norwood *could* have committed the murder; if he had been living out of state at the time or if he had been in jail on an unrelated charge, then Morrison would have to pursue other possibilities. ("Sometimes a CODIS hit leads you right to the killer," she told me. "And sometimes it leads you there indirectly, by identifying someone who is closely connected to the killer, like a crime partner or a roommate.") Though she lacked the resources law enforcement has to conduct a nationwide search, she was able to draw on a network of volunteers who had worked with the Innocence Project on other wrongful conviction cases. "We don't have much money, but we do have a lot of people who want to help us for free, so we had private investigators and lawyers across the country—everywhere that Norwood had a criminal record—volunteering to go to the nearest courthouse and pull his files for us," she said. Based on information culled from these sources, she was able to assemble a detailed time line that plotted out where Norwood had previously resided. "We figured out pretty quickly that he had been living in the Austin area at the time of the murder, and that he was out of custody"—not behind bars—"on the day that Christine was killed," she said.

It was while looking over this time line that Raley's longtime paralegal, Kay Kanaby, made a revelatory discovery. Like everyone who worked at Raley's close-knit, six-attorney law firm, Raley & Bowick, Kanaby had become preoccupied with Michael's case. A former oncology nurse who had spent the early part of her career caring for leukemia patients at M.D. Anderson, Kanaby had seen her share of tragedy, but she was particularly struck by the injustice of Michael's odyssey through the criminal justice system. As she studied the time line and Norwood's lengthy rap sheet, she noticed that the serial criminal had never been charged with murder—a curious omission, she thought, if he actually was the man who had killed Christine. "I didn't think someone would commit a crime like that once," she told me. She searched the Internet for any mention of unsolved murders in the places where Norwood had passed through—Davidson County, Tennessee; Broward County, Florida; Riverside County, California—but little information was available online. She was relieved when she found that the Austin Police Department maintained a webpage devoted to cold cases. As she scrolled through photographs of the victims in those cases, one photo, of a woman named Debra Baker, gave her pause. "She looked like Christine Morton—dark hair, early thirties, attractive," Kanaby said. "The resemblance was striking."

Kanaby read the case summary beside the photo. It stated, "Debra Baker was last seen the night of January 12, 1988. She failed to report for work at Elliot Systems on January 13. She was found deceased in bed by a family member who went to the residence to check on her. She had been beaten multiple times with a blunt object and there was evidence of possible forced entry into the residence."

Kanaby was floored. Whoever had murdered Baker had used the same MO—bludgeoning her in her bed—as Christine's killer, just seventeen months after Christine's death.

Kanaby saw that the address of Baker's home was listed, and she plugged it into GoogleMaps. As the satellite image of the North Austin neighborhood materialized before her on her computer screen, she noticed that the street where Baker had lived, Dwyce Drive, ran parallel to Justin Lane, where Norwood had lived at the time. "I got chills," Kanaby said. "I didn't have his exact address yet, but I could see that Justin Lane and Dwyce Drive were about two hundred feet apart. The homes on Justin Lane backed up to the homes on Dwyce. Their proximity seemed like more than just a coincidence."

She hastily wrote an e-mail to Morrison asking if her investigators could pinpoint Norwood's old residence on Justin Lane. As she waited for a reply, she continued looking online for information about Baker. She soon stumbled across a criminal-justice blog on which Baker's daughter, Caitlin, had written several long posts. "There were pleas from her from 2005 begging for any information that anyone might have about who had killed her mother," Kanaby said. "She had clearly done this out of desperation. She said that the police had not adequately investigated the murder and that detectives had told the family they were working on it, but she didn't believe they were." Kanaby read on as Caitlin explained that she had barely known her mother because the murder had happened when she was three. "It was heart-wrenching," Kanaby said. So too was the realization that Caitlin and Eric had been the same age when they lost their mothers.

Were the Morton and Baker cases linked? she wondered. As she studied the map, she had the "steadily escalating sense," she told me, that they were. "I couldn't stop thinking that if Norwood had been arrested and convicted of Christine's murder, Debra might still be here, and Caitlin's story, like Eric's, would have been so different," she said.

Morrison was not able to obtain the information until five days later. On August 23 she e-mailed Kanaby, telling her that investigators had verified which house Norwood had lived in on Justin Lane. Kanaby typed his address, and then Baker's, into GoogleMaps and looked at the image that appeared on her screen. "He basically lived around the corner from her," she told me. "I kept staring at the blue line that traced the path from his house to hers."

·   ·   ·

Morrison was already in Texas when she learned of Kanaby's findings, having flown in from New York to attend a hearing in Georgetown that afternoon. The hearing would take up a request made by the defense that was almost certainly doomed: that Judge Stubblefield recuse Bradley from the case and appoint a special prosecutor to review the evidence with fresh eyes. Stubblefield—who had consistently sided with the state since the battle over DNA testing had begun—was not swayed. "It would be truly an extraordinary act for this court to disqualify or recuse Mr. Bradley," he observed, expressing his confidence that the two prosecutors who were present—Jernigan and first assistant DA Lindsey Roberts—would handle the case in an unbiased manner.

Stubblefield then turned his attention to another request from the defense. Citing the materials uncovered by the Innocence Project's public records request, Raley had made a strenuous case for Judge Lott's sealed file to be unsealed. He argued that the transcript of Wood's phone conversation with Rita Kirkpatrick was so plainly favorable to Michael—it conveyed an eyewitness account of the murder in which an unknown intruder, not Michael, was identified as the killer—that Lott would have undoubtedly disclosed it to the defense had he known of its existence. That he hadn't, Raley insisted, proved that Anderson had never produced the transcript to the judge. "The way to find that out is to unseal the file," Raley argued. Confident that everything had been above board, Jernigan did not object. "There's nothing to suggest that this transcript wasn't in that Court of Appeals' file," she said.

Stubblefield ordered that the file be retrieved from the appellate court in Austin—a process that would take a few days—so he could open it and review it with attorneys from both sides. "I personally am curious and would like to see it," the judge added. He paused for a moment before concluding the hearing, which was taking place just down the hall from Anderson's courtroom.

"We must all have the courage to learn the facts and to let them lead us where they may, regardless where that might be," he said.

The following morning, as the heat wave that gripped Texas broke all records, marking the seventieth consecutive day when the temperature soared over one hundred degrees, Morrison and Raley made their way to the Austin Police Department for a meeting they had requested with its cold-case unit. The two lawyers were met by detectives and a prosecutor from the Travis County DA's office, who listened intently as Morrison and Raley laid out the pieces of their case, from Norwood's DNA on the bandana to Kanaby's findings. The warm reception stood in contrast to the way they had been greeted over the years in Georgetown. "Everyone was very interested in what we had to say," Raley recalled. "They told us they would look into the possibility of comparing the DNA from the Baker crime scene to the recent Norwood evidence." As Morrison and Raley left the police department that morning, they were buoyed by the hope, however remote, that a link might be found between the two cases—a link that would erase any doubts about Michael's innocence. Raley's excitement was tempered by his frustration. "We were having to conduct our own investigation," he said. "We were doing the work of law enforcement. I kept thinking, 'Why isn't anyone in Georgetown trying to figure this out?'"

Two days later, on August 26, Jeffrey Kyle—the clerk for the Third Court of Appeals—drove from Austin to Georgetown to hand-deliver Lott's sealed file to Stubblefield. By then Morrison and Raley had returned home, and so Patricia Cummings, a local criminal defense attorney who had become a member of Michael's legal team, served as a witness to the unsealing. As she and the two prosecutors, Jernigan and Roberts, waited for the judge, Kyle stood with them, holding the small brown envelope that contained Lott's file.

"I think the expectation, at least from the DA's office, was that there was going to be a lot of material in there," Cummings told me. "But we could all see that the envelope was very thin." Stubblefield finally summoned them into the foyer of his chambers, where they remained standing while he opened the envelope. He pulled out six pages. All that was inside the file was a report of Wood's, written on the day that Christine was killed, and a one-page form that Michael had signed, allowing deputies to search his pickup. "No one said much afterward, but it was very, very awkward," Cummings said. After Stubblefield had copies of the file's contents made for everyone, Cummings excused herself, then raced to her car and pulled out her cell phone to call Morrison. "There's nothing there," she said.

Stubblefield recused himself from the case the following week when Morrison and Raley stated in court filings that the absence of Wood's reports and notes from Lott's file raised the "specter of official misconduct." (Stubblefield did not provide a reason for exiting the case, but he would have likely faced criticism had he not, given that Anderson was a fellow judge and longtime colleague.) In his absence, the Texas Supreme Court named a neutral party from outside Williamson County, state district judge Sid Harle, of San Antonio, to preside over the case.

Soon after, Travis County DA Rosemary Lehmberg contacted Harle to request an appointment. The judge—who was in the midst of a capital-murder trial in his home district—elected to speak to her by phone instead, but he had a court reporter transcribe the exchange, which took place on September 16. During a hearing in Georgetown ten days later, he provided a sealed transcript of the conversation to Morrison, Raley, Jernigan, and Roberts and called a recess during which the attorneys could read it. The transcript contained an earth-shattering bit of information: a pubic hair that had been recovered from Debra Baker's bed in 1988 did, in fact, match Norwood's DNA profile.

"I remember screaming a lot as we read that transcript," Morrison told me. "I said to John, 'The case is over! We are done! This is it!'" Why, I asked her, was she so certain? "There was no argument that could be made with a straight face that it was a coincidence that Norwood's DNA was found at the scene of both crimes," she said.

The Williamson County DA's office did not see things the same way. When attorneys from both sides of the case reconvened in the courtroom as reporters looked on, Raley—still shaking his head in amazement—stated what by then seemed obvious. "I would imagine that in light of this new information, the state should be prepared to agree to relief for Michael Morton immediately," he said firmly. "*Right now.*" But when Harle moved the hearing into chambers so they could speak freely about Norwood, whose name was still being withheld from the public, the two prosecutors dug in their heels.

Roberts told the judge that the bandana should undergo further DNA testing, and Jernigan brought up a report from the files of the late Williamson County sheriff Jim Boutwell, who had overseen the investigation into Christine's murder, that seemed to cast doubt on the importance of the bandana. The report had been written by a sheriff's deputy the day after John Kirkpatrick had turned the bandana over to investigators. In the report, the deputy stated that he too had seen the bandana while earlier canvassing the area, but he justified not gathering it as evidence by explaining that he had not noticed any blood on it. (The stains were small and easy to overlook.) Based on that report, the DA's office put forth a far-fetched theory: that Christine's blood had gotten onto the bandana *after* John picked it up, when he returned to the Morton home. (How, exactly, John had managed to get whatever dried blood remained at the house onto the bandana was not explained—nor was it explained how a hair of Christine's had come to be found on the bandana.) In other words, even if Norwood had dropped the bandana, that did not make him Christine's killer.

But the position that the DA's office had taken was untenable. By then both Morrison's investigators and Williamson County sheriff's deputies had managed to locate Norwood—he was found living with his mother thirty miles east of Austin in the town of Bastrop—lending the reinvestigation of the case a new urgency. With local media reporting that evidence in the Morton killing had been linked to an unnamed suspect in a Travis County murder, Bradley folded. Four days after the hearing, he called Barry Scheck.

This was a remarkable turn of events; just two years earlier, Bradley and Scheck had famously clashed over the state's reinvestigation of the troubled case of Cameron Todd Willingham, who was executed in 2004 for the deaths of his three daughters in an East Texas house fire. (Bradley, who was appointed by Governor Perry to head the Texas Forensic Science Commission, had openly disparaged Scheck's efforts to examine whether Willingham had been wrongly convicted using flawed forensic science.) But during an intense weekend of phone calls back and forth, Bradley finally relented to Scheck's terms. Bradley agreed not only to release Michael on bond while the Court of Criminal Appeals considered his claim of actual innocence but also to allow Michael's attorneys, during that time, to conduct a court-supervised investigation into possible misconduct in the case. The unusual arrangement would allow them to question Anderson, Wood, and others under oath.

"I didn't just want to get out," Michael told me. "I wanted to know exactly how this had happened to me."

· · ·

Monday, October 3, 2011, was Michael's 8,995th day in prison. It would be his last. He spent the morning giving away the few items he had that had made life more tolerable—a radio, an oscillating fan, a pair of sneakers—and took his final walk around the yard. That afternoon he was led from his dorm to a holding cell where he would spend the night before being transported back to Georgetown for his release. As a guard walked him through the dorm, he heard the rumble of applause. Over the years, Michael had earned the respect of his fellow inmates. He was known as a generous person who, along with two other prisoners with whom he attended Bible study, had routinely performed small acts of kindness for those who were the worst off—the men who never received any visitors or money in the mail with which to buy creature comforts. During the dog days of summer, Michael had used the commissary money his parents sent him to buy ice cream for some of them, earning himself the nickname the Ice Cream Man. Now, as he walked down the concrete hallway for the last time, he looked up and saw scores of inmates standing on the second tier, clapping and whistling and cheering for him.

Michael carried a Bible that his sister had given him, a few photos, and a toothbrush. Filled with the anticipation of what was to come the next day, he managed to sleep for just a few hours. Early in the morning, two Williamson County sheriff's deputies arrived to bring him back to Georgetown. The protocol for transporting an inmate—even a man who was about to be freed on grounds of actual innocence—required that he be handcuffed and put in leg irons, but one of the deputies hesitated before reaching for his cuffs. "Now, Mr. Morton," he said, "if you start having bad thoughts, I want you to remember that when all of this happened to you, I was only twelve years old." Michael smiled and assured the deputy that he had nothing to worry about. He held his wrists out to be shackled, eager to get on the road.

The drive took three hours. Staring out the window of the squad car, Michael studied the brown, desiccated landscape that stretched westward from the Piney Woods. Leaning forward, he asked the deputies if there had been a fire in the rolling farmland and was told that the devastation was a result of the state's historic drought. He had read about the drought, but he had not yet seen the toll it had taken and was amazed by the sight of the parched and brittle fields. There were other details that startled him too, like the peculiar metal spires he saw in the distance every now and then, which he soon understood were cell-phone towers. When one of the deputies pulled over at a gas station, he studied the self-service pump with its digital display and credit card reader. The last time he had seen the outside world was seven years earlier, when he had been transferred to the Michael Unit. He had not driven a car since midway through Ronald Reagan's second term.

When they arrived in Georgetown late on the morning of October 4, Michael could see that it too had undergone a trans-formation. Though still a small town, it thrummed with traffic that poured off the interstate, and the subdivisions that ringed it seemed to stretch on forever. No longer a sleepy, rural area, it had been overtaken by the northernmost edge of greater Austin. The century-old Greek Revival courthouse at the center of town where he had been convicted was shuttered. Michael was taken to the new jail, next to the Williamson County Justice Center—the spacious, modern courthouse where his bond hearing was to be held. In his cell, he found a tidy pile of clothes that his mother had hurriedly bought for him the previous day. Having worn only loose-fitting prison whites for as long as he could remember, he stared at them as he was unshackled: a white button-down shirt, khakis, boxers, and a pair of socks. Unac-customed to buttons, he fumbled them as he dressed himself. As he slid on the khakis, which felt impossibly soft, he began to cry.

A sea of faces greeted him in the courtroom: Morrison, Raley, and Scheck were there, as was Bill Allison, who embraced him. His mother, Patricia, and his father, Billy—who had asked the members of their church to pray for their son's release for nearly twenty-five years—sat behind him with his younger sister, Patti, beaming. Reporters crammed into the courtroom, craning for a better view. As Michael scanned the room, he saw a young woman who he would later learn was Caitlin Baker, Debra Baker's daughter. She sat quietly by herself, observing the proceedings.

He spotted Mario Garcia at the back of the courtroom and motioned to his friend to step forward, enveloping him in a long, silent bear hug.

The hearing lasted just a few minutes, during which Harle apologized to Michael from the bench. "We do not have a perfect system of justice, but we have the best system of justice in the world," the judge observed before agreeing to the terms of his release. For several minutes, everyone stood and applauded as Michael smiled broadly, his face electrified by the joy of the moment. "I thank God this wasn't a capital case," he told the crowd of reporters and TV cameramen. They trailed after him as he took his first steps out of the courthouse, his face upturned toward the sun.

Michael was already in his parents' SUV, beginning to pull away, when Raley motioned for them to stop. A dark-haired woman in her sixties stood next to him, looking distraught. Raley explained that she was Lou Bryan, one of the jurors from the 1987 trial. She had learned only that morning, when she picked up the newspaper, that DNA tests had proved Michael to be innocent. "I'm—I'm so sorry," she managed to say as she stared at Michael in disbelief.

He reached out to squeeze her hand. "I understand," he said.

IV.

By the time Michael walked out of prison a free man, Ken Anderson had long been a respected member of his community. He was a Sunday school teacher and Boy Scout volunteer who cast himself, in his rulings, as a champion of both crime victims and children. A father of two, the fifty-nine-year-old jurist held a regular mock trial for fifth graders that he called "The Great Stolen Peanut Butter and Jelly Caper," and he frequently made appearances at local schools to talk about the dangers of drugs and alcohol. He was a prolific writer, and of the eight books he had written, his most impressive work was a biography of Dan Moody, a Williamson County DA from the twenties whose prosecution of the Ku Klux Klan helped win him statewide acclaim and put him in the governor's mansion. Like Moody's, Anderson's ambition reached beyond Williamson County. At the courthouse, rumor held that he had his sights set on obtaining an appointment to the Court of Criminal Appeals, the state's highest court for criminal cases.

So it was a sudden reversal of fortune for Anderson when, eight days after Michael's release, the CCA overturned Michael's conviction on grounds of actual innocence. The ruling meant that Anderson had secured a guilty verdict against an indisputably innocent man. Yet whether he, or anyone else involved in the case, would ever be held accountable for the wrongful conviction remained an open question.

Immediately after his release, Michael's legal team began digging for answers. Thanks to Scheck's negotiations with Bradley, the lawyers—who now numbered six, including Morrison, Raley, and Scheck—were able to depose Anderson, Mike Davis (the former assistant DA who helped prosecute the case), and Wood and take affidavits from many others. The testimony was revealing. During his deposition, Anderson said that he had likely informed Allison and his co-counsel, Bill White, of the transcript in which Rita Kirkpatrick told Wood what Eric had seen but admitted that he had no recollection of what he had actually done.

"There's no way on God's green earth, if that was in my file, I wouldn't have told them that Eric said that the monster killed his mother," Anderson testified. Allison and White are both emphatic that he never did so. "If we had known what Eric told his grandmother, we would have fought hard to have the jury hear that evidence," Allison told me. "Eric's account would have been critical, because it supported the theory we presented at trial that an unknown intruder killed Christine."

Shortly after the investigation concluded in November, Anderson made what still remains his only public statement about the case. Standing outside the old courthouse on the town square in Georgetown, the white-haired judge looked down at his prepared remarks as he told reporters that he had behaved ethically—"In my heart, I know there was no misconduct whatsoever"—and that he had no plans to step down from the bench. Caitlin Baker, who stood in attendance, was unimpressed, telling reporters afterward that Anderson should resign. She held Anderson partially responsible for her mother's murder, she said, because his single-minded pursuit of Michael had allowed the real killer to go unpunished. "She could be alive right now," she said. Her outrage was fueled by what was widely seen as Anderson's failure to take any personal responsibility for his role in a conviction that he had long trumpeted as one of the pinnacles of his prosecutorial career. "As district attorney at the time, and as woefully inadequate as I realize it is, I want to formally apologize for the system's failure to Mr. Morton and every other person who was affected by the verdict," he had said before fielding a few questions and walking away.

Many observers in Williamson County wondered if the matter would end there. Rarely have Texas prosecutors had to answer tough questions about their conduct, even in the wake of wrongful convictions. But in February, Judge Harle ruled that the investigation conducted by Michael's lawyers suggested that there was probable cause to believe Anderson had broken the law in failing to turn over evidence that was "highly favorable" to the defense. Harle recommended that the Texas Supreme Court launch a court of inquiry to look into the matter. A week later, the Supreme Court concurred with Harle's findings and ruled that an inquiry should proceed. Anderson would have to answer for his alleged misconduct.

There was no precedent for this decision. A court of inquiry is an arcane and extremely rare legal procedure, unique to Texas, that can be used to investigate wrongdoing, most often on the part of state officials. But as far as anyone can remember, it has never before been used to probe allegations of prosecutorial misconduct, much less when the subject of the investigation was a sitting district judge. Nevertheless, the decision was well received. "The pursuit of justice shouldn't end with an innocent person's release from prison," the *Austin American-Statesman* concluded in an editorial extolling Harle's recommendation.

By then the tide of public opinion had turned against Anderson and Bradley. As the face of the Williamson County DA's office, Bradley—who had devoted untold time and taxpayer money to opposing Michael's requests for DNA testing—was excoriated in the local press. "Adjust the facts as needed, feign respectability, stick to the talking points, and, above all else, protect your friends and associates," wrote local legal blogger Lou Ann Anderson, suggesting that Williamson County was less tough on crime than "light on justice." Though Bradley had long been considered bulletproof politically in Williamson County, he soon found himself in a hard-fought race against a primary challenger. Despite support from Governor Perry, who sent letters to the county's registered Republicans exhorting them to vote for Bradley, the DA was defeated by a stunning ten-point margin. The race had become a referendum on his handling of the Morton case; in the months leading up to primary day, his critics had tied bandanas to his political signs.

This fall, attention turned back to Anderson. On October 4, the first anniversary of Michael's release, the state bar issued a withering report on Anderson's conduct. Sixteen years earlier, the agency had named him "Prosecutor of the Year"; now it filed disciplinary charges against the judge. After a ten-month investigation, it had concluded that Anderson had deliberately withheld evidence. A judge appointed by the Texas Supreme Court will hear evidence at an upcoming disciplinary hearing, which has not yet been scheduled. If the judge determines that Anderson withheld evidence, he could be reprimanded, have his law license suspended, or be disbarred.

As devastating as these penalties would be to a sitting judge, Anderson is no doubt far more concerned about the possible outcome of the court of inquiry, which is slated to begin on December 10. Fort Worth district judge Louis Sturns will preside over the inquiry, with legendary Houston criminal defense attorney Rusty Hardin—once a top prosecutor in the Harris County DA's office—serving as special prosecutor. The unusual legal proceeding will be held in Georgetown, at the Williamson County Justice Center, just down the hall from Anderson's courtroom. The irony of the situation will not be lost on anyone; the former DA—who subjected Michael to a ruthless cross-examination in 1987—could himself be called to testify while Michael looks on. If Sturns finds that Anderson violated the law, he could refer the case to the Texas attorney general's office, even though Anderson's attorneys have argued that the statute of limitations has long since expired on any offenses that he might be charged with. Michael's lawyers, however, argue that the four-year window during which a prosecutor can be charged for violations such as suppression of evidence has not yet closed because Anderson committed an ongoing act of "fraudulent concealment" that did not end until August 2011, when Judge Lott's file was unsealed.

Anderson is also expected to put on a vigorous defense that will draw on a narrow reading of what his legal obligations were to turn over evidence. He did not provide Wood's reports and notes to Lott, explained Anderson's attorney, Eric Nichols, "because it should be abundantly clear to any objective reader of the record that what the state agreed to produce was only a report from the day on which Christine Morton's body was found." The strategy of Anderson's legal team will presumably involve trying to shift blame onto the late Sheriff Boutwell, whose mishandling of the investigation into Christine's murder cast a long shadow on the case. They have pointed to the fact that several pieces of evidence, such as the phone message about Christine's credit card, were found only in the sheriff's office's files, not the former prosecutor's. Regardless, Allison told me he believed it was implausible that Anderson had not seen all the documents in the case, irrespective of where they were stored. "As the DA, Ken would have had complete access to the sheriff's office's records," he said. "Quite frankly, I can't imagine him stepping anywhere near the courtroom before going through every piece of paper first. He's very meticulous." No one knows exactly how long the court of inquiry will last; it could well be concluded before Christmas.

The denouement of the Morton case will come in January when Mark Alan Norwood, who was arrested last fall in Bastrop, will stand trial for Christine's murder. Given Williamson County's obvious conflict of interest—its own prosecutors, while fighting Michael's efforts to prove his innocence, discounted the very same DNA evidence that implicated Norwood—the case will be tried by special prosecutor Lisa Tanner of the attorney general's office. Because there is a gag order in the case, it is unknown if state investigators have been able to connect Norwood back to the green van, the contents of Christine's purse, or Michael's .45 automatic, which was also stolen from the Morton home. It also remains to be seen whether the DNA hit in the Baker case will be admissible.

For Michael, the experience will be surreal. He will essentially be watching his original trial replayed, featuring evidence that his jury never heard, with another man sitting behind the defense table. In recent court appearances, Norwood has appeared unkempt, his dark, greasy hair pulled back into a ponytail, his expression blasé as he surveys the bank of TV cameras in the courtroom. (Because of publicity surrounding the case, the trial has been moved to San Angelo on a change of venue.) "I won't do anything to jeopardize the trial, of course," Michael told me, "but I've wondered if I will be able to control myself when I see him face-to-face." Yet Michael has already shown Norwood mercy.

At his request, as well as that of the entire Kirkpatrick family, Tanner will not seek a death sentence.

.   .   .

Eric's memories of childhood begin with playing T-ball in the suburbs of Houston. He is five years old, a cheerful kid with blond hair and a wide, unclouded smile. Try as he might, he is incapable of drawing any earlier images to the surface; everything that took place before he was five is a blank. A photograph he has seen of himself with his mother, which was taken shortly after he underwent open-heart surgery when he was three, has evoked only a few unsatisfying details; he can recall the Hot Wheels set that he is playing with in the picture, but he has never been able to summon up an actual memory of the smiling woman with dark hair who is looking at him adoringly. His mother is lost to him.

The few recollections he has of his father start after Michael was already incarcerated. He can remember the lemon drops that Michael used to give him during their twice-a-year court-mandated visits at the Wynne Unit, in Huntsville. And he can remember the hand-drawn mazes that would arrive in the mail every so often, which his dad had carefully penciled onto graph paper before finishing in ink, each one more intricate than the last.

Those innocent details were overwhelmed, as Eric grew older, by the anguish of understanding why his father was in prison. That his father had been convicted of murdering his mother was a closely held family secret. Marylee had warned him not to tell his friends at school for fear that the stigma would rub off on him. "She and my grandmother wanted to protect me," Eric told me. "Everything they did was to shield me from what had happened. Obviously I was told my dad had been found guilty, but it wasn't something we talked about." When they did have to confront the past by making the two-hour drive to see Michael, Marylee attempted to make each visit as positive an experience as possible; the day would begin with a stop at McDonald's and a coloring book for Eric to fill in on the way to the prison. "I'm sure those visits were torture for her," he told me, "but she always put on a good face for me." Marylee was intent on moving forward, past the tragedy that had engulfed them, and Eric helped her, in his own way, by revising the family history. When friends asked about his mother, he said that she had died of cancer or that she had been killed in a car accident. He told people that his father had taken off not long after he was born and now lived in California.

And so for Eric, life moved on. He had a doting aunt and grandmother, a top education at a private Catholic school, friends from the many sports teams he played on, and a beloved mixed-breed collie named Shelby. "Everything was picture-perfect," he told me. "It was *Leave It to Beaver*, only with a single mom." When he was twelve, Marylee married a friend of hers from junior high school, and her new husband would play a large and positive role in Eric's life; Eric would later take his name—Olson—when he was preparing to apply to college. His decision had less to do with cutting ties to Michael, he explained, than with wanting to become part of the Olson family, which by then included not only Marylee and her husband but the son they'd had three years earlier, whom Eric thought of as his little brother.

Eric went on to attend Texas State University, where he became the president of a small Catholic fraternity. When he returned home to Houston, he went to work in the campus ministry at his old high school. He met his future wife, Maggie, while volunteering at a local church. A year before they married, he told her on a drive through the Hill Country, as he stared straight ahead at the two-lane highway, that his father had killed his mother. He asked her not to tell anyone. "It wasn't something that ate away at me or that I really dwelled on," Eric told me. "I put it out of my mind so I didn't have to deal with it. I just wanted to live a normal life."

In June 2011, three months after he and Maggie married, Eric received an e-mail from John Raley. After trying fruitlessly for weeks to track Eric down, Raley's wife, Kelly, who is also an attorney at Raley & Bowick, had finally come across his wedding announcement on the website of a small local newspaper; using the details that were provided, she had figured out where Eric worked, and she passed along his contact information to her husband. "I have called you a couple of times recently, and I want you to know who I am and why I called," John Raley's email explained. "I am part of a team of lawyers who, for many years, have been volunteering our time on behalf of your biological father." Raley then laid out what had not yet been disclosed to the public: DNA testing had provided "powerful new evidence" of Michael's innocence.

Eric did not respond for seven weeks. He was twenty-eight years old and had lived almost his entire life believing that his father had killed his mother. The e-mail rattled him so much that two days went by before he even mentioned it to his wife. "I wasn't sure if it was real at first," Eric told me. "There had never been any question that he did it, so this came totally out of the blue." When Eric failed to answer, the Raleys enlisted their pastor to help, asking him to contact the priest who oversees the private school where Eric works. Only after he received a visit from the priest did Eric answer Raley's e-mail, sending a curt note acknowledging that he had received it. By then the hit to Norwood had been made, and Raley replied with a more detailed accounting of the facts surrounding the case. "The most important thing I can tell you," he wrote in conclusion, "is that your father loves you."

The following day, Eric wrote back: "My family does not have any desire to reenter this discussion or to relive what happened

25 years ago. Please do not contact my place of work or my family again."

Eric's first instinct, he told me, was not to shut his father out but to protect the woman who had raised him and prevent her from ever having to dredge up her grief over her sister's murder. He did not tell Marylee about his exchange with Raley until weeks later. When he did, he found that she remained extremely skeptical that Michael could be innocent, even though she had, by then, read media coverage of recent developments in the case. Based on her communications with the Williamson County DA's office, which was still trying to discount the relevance of the bandana, she continued to trust that Michael was guilty. Still, Eric kept educating himself about his father's case, of which he knew little. He had never even been aware of Michael's long fight to have the bandana tested. Encouraged by Maggie, Eric began to form a different view of his father.

Marylee, however, did not do the same. As she had always done, she accepted the DA's office's view of the case—that the DNA results did not exonerate Michael. No one at the DA's office informed her of the deal that Bradley had brokered with Scheck, so she was blindsided when she learned of Michael's impending release. She found out when *Austin American-Statesman* reporter Chuck Lindell e-mailed her to ask for comment on the afternoon before Michael walked free.

Eric had, by then, come to accept that his father was likely innocent, but he felt fiercely protective of Marylee, who was struggling to understand how everything she had been told was rapidly unraveling. And so, on October 4, the day of Michael's release, Eric kept his distance. He was not present at the courthouse to hear Judge Harle's apology or the crowd's applause. When classes let out that afternoon, Eric closed the door to his office and sat down in front of his computer. On the website of an Austin TV news station, he was able to find a live-streaming video of the press conference that was being held nearly two hundred miles away in Georgetown. He leaned in closer, looking on in wonder as his father—older and grayer, wearing an exuberant grin—spoke to reporters. Eric did not have the urge to be there with him, but neither did he have the impulse to turn away.

Two days later, he wrote to Raley. "I want to begin by sharing my appreciation for your hard work," he typed. "I hope that you continue the work you have done by pursuing the true murderer." His family, he went on, was having "difficulty processing this new information." He described the preceding weeks as "a bit uncomfortable." Despite that tension, he wrote, "I feel the need to begin to reconcile the situation. I cannot imagine the pain everyone has felt, and I know that I was blessed with a childhood in which I was sheltered from most of that suffering. However, I would like to slowly establish contact again with my father."

·   ·   ·

Immediately after his release, Michael returned to East Texas with his parents and settled into their spare bedroom. In time he would assume a high profile—speaking at universities about the lack of oversight for prosecutors, meeting with lawmakers to discuss legislative reforms—but in those early days, he was intensely private. He was unaccustomed to the everyday things he had once taken for granted: using metal silverware, or carrying a wallet, or being able to push open a door. The tactile experience of being touched by another human being was foreign to him, and he was taken aback whenever his mother or his sister threw their arms around him. Though the Innocence Project made sure that a social worker who had previously worked with exonerees was present on the day he was freed and available to help him in the months that followed, he did not seek out her counsel. "It was a blessed, easy transition," he told me. "I had my family to help me and a roof over my head. Honestly, my return to the free world was not overwhelming compared to everything I'd been through up until then." He delighted in mundane indulgences like taking off his shoes and walking barefoot across the carpet. Even doing the laundry, he told me, was its own pleasure. "Sorting socks and folding underwear may be work for some folks," he said, "but you approach it from a radically different perspective if you haven't been able to wear your own clothes for twenty-five years."

The process of reconnecting with Eric was less straightforward. Michael tried to be patient as days and then weeks went by with no further word from him. It would take until shortly before Thanksgiving for Eric to agree to meet, and he did so without telling Marylee, who was still coming to grips with the revelations of the previous few months. John and Kelly Raley had offered their home in West Houston as a neutral location for the meeting. So one Saturday afternoon in November 2011, Eric and Michael set out to meet again.

Michael paced the floor as he waited for Eric, who was running late. After a while, Kelly began to worry that Eric might not come after all, and so she was relieved when she finally saw a car pull up outside. Eric and Maggie got out and approached the house, where Michael waited in the foyer with Raley. "This grown man was standing there," Michael told me of his surprise when Eric appeared at the door. "That was him, that was my little boy. I would have walked right past him if I had seen him on the street."

They shook hands. Then Michael reached out for Eric, and they embraced for a long time. "He was emotional, more than I was," Eric remembered. "I didn't know how to react, because I didn't know him. I kept thinking, 'Should I be crying? What should I be feeling?' I was just kind of stunned."

Eric was quiet for most of the evening as he took everything in. But his father, who had yearned in the solitude of his cell for this moment, could not hide his eagerness for them to be close again. "Michael was so excited that he was almost manic," Raley told me. "It was the fastest I'd ever seen him talk. I think he wanted to cram everything they had missed into that first hour together. Eric was respectful and courteous, but he did not engage." Raley and his wife watched with growing concern through dinner as Eric said little, and when the conversation stalled, Kelly talked to Maggie about the baby that she and Eric were expecting. Finally, Raley steered Michael and Eric outside to the back patio with mugs of coffee, where they could talk by themselves. It was the first time they had been alone together in twenty-five years.

They sat in the darkness, in a white garden swing that overlooked the yard, and it was only then that Eric opened up. "I told him that I was extremely freaked out," Eric recalled. "I said, 'I'm not mad. I don't hate you. I just feel weird, and I don't know how to act around you. Part of me feels like I'm betraying the Kirkpatricks right now. I know you're excited to be out, but this is hard.'" Michael relaxed and listened as his son explained his mixed emotions. Slowly, the conversation eased into subjects that Eric had always wondered about: his mother, whose adult life he knew little about, and the three years they had all spent together as a family. "There was an organic, natural cadence we fell into," Michael told me. "It just started going so well. We were alone, and it was good."

Michael would see his son twice more that winter. In January he visited Houston shortly after the birth of Eric and Maggie's daughter, and in February Eric came to East Texas to visit the extended Morton family. By then Eric had told Marylee about meeting his father, and he had been both surprised and relieved to discover that she was supportive of his desire to reconnect with Michael. But the Kirkpatricks themselves—having been conditioned for more than two decades to trust the sadistic portrayal presented of Michael at his trial—were more hesitant. (The conversation between three-year-old Eric and his grandmother, in which he described the murderer as a "monster," had ultimately not persuaded the Kirkpatricks that Michael was above suspicion; encouraged by the sheriff's office, they had always believed that Eric had simply made up the story after overhearing family members discussing details of the case.) When the entire family convened in April for the christening of Eric and Maggie's baby girl, Michael received what he felt was a lukewarm reception—first at a dinner with Marylee and in particular at the baptism itself. "We greeted each other, but there were few words spoken," Michael said. Even John Kirkpatrick, who was responsible for finding the bloody bandana that helped to free Michael, was cordial but distant. "I sensed that none of them had accepted or internalized my innocence," Michael told me. "But I also know that they were lied to, manipulated, and kept in the dark about the most important aspects of the investigation, so in the end, I have to forgive them."

By then Michael had received compensation for the time he served; in accordance with state law, which requires that exonerees be paid $80,000 for each year of wrongful imprisonment, he received just short of $2 million. He contributed some of the funds to a prison ministry that had buoyed him during his time behind bars and bought a piece of lakefront property, where he plans to build a house. He will remain close enough to his elderly parents that he can help them, having already shepherded them through several health crises since his release; not long after he returned home, his father had a stroke and his mother broke her arm. "I feel like I got home right in time," he told me.

He has toyed with the idea of moving out West someday, but too many ties bind him to East Texas. One is his relationship with a divorcée and mother of three grown children who attends the same church as Michael's parents. "We're like an old married couple because we're in our fifties," Michael said. "We have our reading night, when we lie around her living room and read our respective books. Another night is movie night, and we'll watch something I missed while I was away." Christine will never be far from his mind, he added. "I think of her, but she is not the overriding influence she used to be," he said. "It's a bittersweet thing to realize that. But maybe, in the end, healthy."

Michael tries not to overwhelm Eric by going to Houston too often, though he told me there were few things that made him happier than seeing his son holding his granddaughter. When he does visit, he usually stays with the Raleys and stops by Eric and Maggie's home to say hello. On a recent visit, he and Eric went to an Astros game. It was the first time they had ever gone to a ball game together. "We haven't had much one-on-one time, so I figured the game was the easiest way to do that," Eric told me. "It was nice. Of course, it was weird too."

It was on the heels of this visit, the night after the ball game, that I met Eric and Maggie for the first time. As we talked in the living room of their small, ranch-style house on the western edge of Houston, Maggie explained that Eric had become much more receptive to welcoming Michael back into his life since the birth of their daughter. She looked at her husband. "When you were turned off to the whole thing and you didn't want to meet Mike, I just said, 'You're going to understand his feelings as soon as this little girl's born,'" she reminded him. "I knew you were going to understand what a father's love was and that it doesn't just go away."

Eric nodded. "That little girl has been my saving grace," he told me. "The whole family has come a long way this year, and I think she's helped with that." I asked him about Marylee and how she was coping with the situation. He thought for a moment. "I think it's difficult for her to share how much confusion she's felt in the process of forgiving my father," he said. "She's come a long way from where she was when she seemed so resistant and angry. Now her anger and frustration is focused on the system and on Ken Anderson. She doesn't believe my father is to blame anymore." He was hopeful, he said, that there would be greater reconciliation when they all attended the Norwood trial together. Eric told me that he had less interest in the outcome of the court of inquiry than in seeing justice served in the Norwood case. "If he's convicted, then life can go on with my father and the Kirkpatricks and we can be normal," he said.

We heard the baby cry in the next room, and Maggie went to get her. A few minutes later she returned, holding the seven-month-old. The baby was tiny and alert, her expression placid as she stared at us. Her blue eyes were as bright as her late grandmother's, who would be fifty-seven were she still alive. We all stared back at the baby as she studied us, watchful and serene, unaware of all the pain and suffering that had come before her. Her name, of course, is Christine.

GQ

Chris Heath began his career writing about music for British magazines like Smash Hits and The Face and later wrote for Details and Rolling Stone in the United States before joining GQ. He has also long been associated with Pet Shop Boys—accompanying them on tour, writing liner notes for their albums, editing their fan club magazine. Which is all by way of saying that his winning the National Magazine Award for Reporting may come as a surprise—but only to those unlucky readers encountering his work for the first time. As the National Magazine Award judges explained: "Heath has the courage to think deeply, and this sharply written story—a faithful re-creation of the carnage that left fifty animals and their owner dead—is simply unforgettable."

Chris Heath

18 Tigers, 17 Lions, 8 Bears, 3 Cougars, 2 Wolves, 1 Baboon, 1 Macaque, and 1 Man Dead in Ohio

Part 1: Fifty-One Deaths

A little before five o'clock on the evening of October 18, 2011, as the day began to ebb away, a retired schoolteacher named Sam Kopchak left the home he shared with his eighty-four-year-old mother and headed into the paddock behind their house to attend to the horse he'd bought nine days earlier. Red, a half-Arabian pinto, was acting skittish and had moved toward the far corner of the field. On the other side of the flimsy fence separating them from his neighbor Terry Thompson's property, Kopchak noticed that Thompson's horses seemed even more agitated. They were circling, and in the center of their troubled orbit there was some kind of dark shape. Only when the shape broke out of the circle could Kopchak see that it was a black bear.

Kopchak wasn't overly alarmed by this sight, unexpected as it was, maybe because the bear wasn't too big as black bears go, and maybe because it was running away from him. He knew what he'd do: put Red in the barn, go back to the house, report what he'd seen. This plan soon had to be revised. He and Red had taken only a few steps toward the barn when Kopchak saw something else, close by, just ahead of them on the other side of the fence. Just sitting there on the ground, facing their way. A fully grown male African lion.

Kopchak had lived around here all of his life. The road his and Thompson's properties abutted was named Kopchak Road after his great-uncle. Before he retired four years ago, he used to teach seventh-grade science. He didn't know too much about lions, but he had heard that it was unwise to challenge them by looking them in the eye, and that if you ran away they had a tendency to chase you. So he settled on what he considered a brisk walking pace for himself and Red. He only looked back once, when they were about a third of the way to the barn. The lion was in the same place as a moment ago, still on the other side of the fence, though it was quite obvious that the animal could get over the fence anytime it wanted to.

Inside the barn Kopchak locked the doors, then telephoned his mother, sitting in front of the TV about a hundred yards away back in the house. There was, he told her, "a major problem." They'd long known that there were strange and unusual animals kept out of sight over the brow of the hill around Thompson's house—often they could hear lions bellow and roar. "We didn't have any idea how many there were," Mrs. Kopchak would later reflect. But they assumed that these two runaways must have come from there, so the first thing Mrs. Kopchak did was to dial her neighbor's number.

No answer.

Only then did she call 911 and alert the world. She sounded calm when she reported what her son had seen, as though there was really nothing too strange or alarming about a lion and a bear running loose on an October afternoon in Ohio. But maybe she was a little rattled. When the 911 operator asked for her first name, Mrs. Kopchak answered "Dolores," the name on her birth certificate but one she never uses: "I've been called Dolly for eighty-four years."

Her son remained trapped in the barn. From there, looking through a north-facing window, he watched the menagerie grow. Along came a wolf. And a second bear, this one much larger than the first. And there was the lion he had seen before, now pacing back and forth. And also a lioness, anxiously scuttering around. "And then," he says, "I saw a tiger. I'm telling you, the lion is bad enough, and the lioness is bad enough, and the wolf is bad, and the bear, but . . . don't be around the tiger. The tigers are actually bigger than the lions if they're fully grown. He started snarling, and went after the horses."

·   ·   ·

Deputy Jonathan Merry was two hours into his shift, serving a court summons a couple of miles away in Zanesville, when the call came through about a lion and a bear on the loose. When he arrived, he could see, just inside Thompson's fence, a tiger, a black bear, and two lionesses. While he was waiting for Mrs. Kopchak to answer the door, he saw a large gray wolf running southward along the road behind him. He set down his clipboard on the porch, where it would remain for the next few hours, ran to his patrol car, and followed the wolf. When it turned up toward a house, Merry got his rifle from the trunk and followed on foot. By now the order had come over the radio: Put the animal down. It was about eighty yards away from him, but it fell at the first shot.

After the wolf went down, Merry fired a few more times to make sure. He was inspecting the body when word came over the radio that some colleagues had a lion cornered near the Thompson residence. He hurried back. He knew that his colleagues would only have the two standard-issue weapons—the .40 caliber Glock 22 they wear at their side and the shotgun that is locked above their heads in the patrol cars—and that he was the only one with a rifle.

Merry drove back up the hill, until he came across a deputy running back and forth near Thompson's driveway. Merry didn't know what was going on, so he stopped. As he got out of the car, he grabbed for his rifle on the passenger seat, but it snagged on the computer stand so he left it. That was when he saw the black bear, at first facing him and then running straight toward him. Now he only had his Glock. Not the weapon you'd want when you're facing down 350 pounds of charging bear. He got off one shot.

The black bear fell about seven feet in front of Merry. He wouldn't ever know where the bullet went, though he assumed he must have hit the brain. All he remembered was the sight of the bear's head coming at him, and he also remembered what had been drilled into him at weapons training: *Shoot what you see.*

After that, Merry went back for his rifle. An African lioness crawled under the livestock fence and ran south down the road then headed toward someone's home, so he shot her before she could go farther. Then he turned back, intending to deal with a black bear and a tiger along the roadway, but he was distracted by a cougar heading south, so he followed the cougar into another driveway where he met a male African lion coming the other way. He shot the lion while some other deputies shot the cougar. Soon he was instructed to patrol the border between the Thompson property and Interstate 70, and over the evening he shot another wolf, two more lions, a tiger, and—later on, after its hiding place was revealed by a fireman's thermal-imaging camera—a grizzly bear. That's what it was like.

•   •   •

Sheriff Matt Lutz was settling into an evening in front of the TV. His son and wife were off to a literacy night so he was on his own. He'd already hung up his uniform and finished his dinner when, at around five-twenty p.m., he got the call reporting that Terry Thompson had an animal out. It didn't seem that big a deal— they all knew Thompson had animals and they'd been called out there again and again, mostly for loose horses. Occasionally there were reports of more unusual creatures running free but nothing too bad had ever happened. Still, Lutz said he wasn't busy and would drive over. In the fifteen minutes it took him to get to the scene, as the reports he was receiving over the radio escalated, the seriousness and strangeness became clear. Lutz instructed that if there were animals outside Thompson's property they needed to be shot. Never had to think twice about it. There was an apartment building just on the other side of the interstate that bordered Thompson's land. Maybe a mile away was a school soccer game—kids yelling and screaming in the open air. What if some of the cats were drawn toward them? By the time he got there, the culling had begun.

Nobody yet knew where Thompson was, and so there was concern for his safety. Maybe the animals had somehow busted out, and he was injured, in need of help. After Deputy Merry headed down the road in pursuit of a wolf, Sergeant Steve Blake, who'd been first on the scene, decided he should drive up to Thompson's house. As he neared the farm buildings he saw more animals. Their cages had either been cut through or left open. Blake sounded his horn outside Thompson's house, but there was no response, so he drove back, and at the foot of the drive he met John Moore, the caretaker who regularly fed the animals and had been alerted by a phone call from someone in the neighborhood. Together, they returned to the house, finding nothing but two monkeys and a dog in cages. But on their way back to the road, Moore spotted a body near the barn. A white tiger appeared to be eating it, and they couldn't get closer.

•   •   •

Forty miles away, at the Columbus Zoo, an event was being held for the International Rhino Foundation. Rhino experts from around the world had gathered, and the zoo was throwing a cocktail party on the grounds of the polar-bear exhibit. "One of our vets came into the cocktail area," says Tom Stalf, the zoo's chief operating officer, "and you could see the panic on her face. She said, 'We have to go—Terry Thompson's animals are out.'" Stalf, who had moved to Columbus only eighteen months earlier, didn't know who Thompson was, but others did. Dr. Michael Barrie, the zoo's director of animal health, had been up at Thompson's property to inspect his large private collection of animals in 2008, accompanying an ATF raid that eventually led to Thompson's imprisonment for a year on gun charges. Though ultimately no action was taken concerning the animals after Thompson moved to improve his facilities, Barrie had been horrified at what he saw up there in terms of security, cleanliness, and animal cruelty.

That evening, the zoo assembled its capture-and-recovery team, armed with both tranquilizer-dart guns and regular weapons, and set out for Zanesville. Meanwhile, at the gateway of Thompson's property, the police were wondering how many animals might be loose. John Moore mentally ran through the rows of cages he would feed. At first the number of animals he came up with was forty-eight, but then his fiancée arrived. She also helped with the feeding, and reminded him of some recent arrivals. The final total was fifty-six.

That's when Moore told Deputy Jeff LeCocq something that would later appear in the official police report and came to be taken as a kind of explanation for what had happened, albeit one that prompted many further questions. Moore said that he had last spoken with Thompson at nine o'clock the previous evening, and that Thompson, who was sixty-two, had told him about a letter he'd received from an unnamed author saying that his wife, Marian, had been unfaithful. Thompson had only returned from his prison sentence three weeks before. "That's when Terry actually goes to [Moore] and asks him about Marian having cheated on him while he was in prison," says Deputy LeCocq. "And his answer, to the way I recall, was he didn't know whether she did or she didn't. And then Terry makes this statement back to him: 'Well, I have a plan to find out, and you will know it when it happens.'"

. . .

When Deputy Todd Kanavel, who normally heads up the drug squad, arrived at the scene, Sergeant Blake told him about the body that they had spotted. "I think it's Terry," he said. "I don't know." They needed to find out for sure, and to see whether the person might still be alive. By now they had also decided that they would need to neutralize all of the animals that were loose, even those still on Thompson's property, so they formed a shooting party. Blake drove Kanavel's Silverado crew cab, and four others sat on the bed of the truck behind him so that they wouldn't have to fire out of windows. Deputy Tony Angelo, a sniper on their SWAT team, had a bolt-action rifle, Deputy Ryan Paisley had a nine-millimeter H&K MP5 submachine gun, Deputy Jay Lawhorne and Kanavel had assault rifles. As they pulled up between the barn and a row of cages, two tigers started out of the barn toward them. The animals were only about ten or twelve feet away. "It kind of took us by surprise," says Kanavel. "So those animals were put down." From where they were, they could see the man's body, flat on its back. The white tiger was atop him. "It stood up," says Kanavel, "and was standing there." He reported back to the sheriff that, whether the body was Thompson's or someone else's, it was deceased. (At 6:04 p.m.,

Lutz shared this information on the police radio: "Okay, we have located the owner. Code 16 [dead on arrival], possible 58 [suicide]. Unknown for sure on that. Here in the field.")

That was all the five of them could learn for now because they were urgently redeployed to the southern end of the property where some cats had been spotted readying to cross the boundary fence. First they had to deal with a male African lion that managed to run between some junk cars after the first shot—there were dozens and dozens of old cars and RVs and tractors parked in clumps of rusted metal around the hillside, weeds growing around them. As they moved toward other escapees spread over the hillside, they used the truck to give themselves elevation, trying to engage the animals from seventy to a hundred yards away, firing on them two at a time until they went down. Kanavel's tactic was to shoot for the head a couple of times, and then move on to the body and keep putting rounds into it. "I was sick, shooting these animals, because they didn't ask to be there," he says. "And, you know, I'm a cat person."

After a while the four shooters ran low on ammo and called for more, and eventually they headed back toward where the body was. The white tiger had gone. Nearby, they found bolt cutters and a stainless-steel Ruger .357 magnum revolver. The cause of death seemed to be a gunshot to the head.

One detail Sheriff Lutz chose to release to the press at the time was that there was a sizable laceration on Thompson's head that was consistent with a big cat's bite. Deliberately or not, he seemed to imply that Thompson's body was, aside from the gunshot wound suggesting a barrel placed in the mouth, otherwise fairly untouched. It wasn't quite that straightforward. "He had been dragged," says Kanavel. "You were able to tell that he had laid at one spot for a while and then he was dragged, it looked like by an arm, and his pants and stuff had been pulled down, and he had been chewed on."

There were also pieces of raw chicken scattered around near the body. "Apparently," Tom Stalf theorizes, "he wanted the animals to eat him."

•   •   •

"No other law-enforcement agency in the world has faced this—it's not like there was a manual," says Deputy LeCocq. "Other things will happen, but this is never going to happen again."

All evening it went on, the slaughter. Encounters with animals that would normally have been remembered for a lifetime were forgotten moments later as the next came along. Somehow, no one was hurt. (Even Mr. Kopchak, forgotten in his barn, safely managed to make his way unescorted back to his house at nightfall.) Given the situation—fifty animals, mostly large and potentially aggressive carnivores set loose toward the day's end—things could have gone so much worse.

Up near the house, where no media could see them, the officers laid the dead animals out in rows, by species, to ease the counting. That's where the famous, heartbreaking photo was taken—it remains unclear who took it—of all the bodies together in the early-morning light, the one that went round the world. Whatever people knew of the real situation, and of the hard decisions that had to be made, when you saw that image all you could think was: This is a photo of a place where dozens of big beautiful animals were massacred.

•   •   •

By the time the Columbus Zoo team had arrived at the holding area, it was dark. They were told that it wasn't safe for them to try to tranquilize anything because so many animals were circulating and others were scattering outward. Even when a tranquilizer dose is successfully administered it needs about ten minutes to take effect, and great care is required to establish that it has done so—impossible with so many animals running around.

When the zoo people returned to the site at five-thirty the next morning, they had been joined by Jack Hanna. Hanna—famous for his TV shows and his appearances on shows like Letterman—established his career at the Columbus Zoo and remains its director emeritus. (If you visit the Columbus Zoo, his face is everywhere—even on the Pepsi machines.) The previous day he was doing an event at Penn State, and although he'd just had knee surgery, he drove straight here "a hundred miles an hour." Zanesville held a special significance for him—he went to school near here, enlisted in the army here, spent his honeymoon night here.

After the sheriff spoke with Hanna and talked him through what happened, he gave interview after interview. It probably made all the difference. Hanna was a trusted animal advocate, and as he emotively articulated his pain at the deaths that had taken place, his unequivocal insistence that the sheriff's department had no other option than to act as they did served as a powerful antidote to the other obvious narrative—that a thoughtless small-town law-enforcement brigade had murdered dozens of noble beasts because they were too dumb and trigger-happy to think of a better alternative. "It's like Noah's Ark wrecking," he proclaimed, "right here in Zanesville, Ohio."

Forty-nine animals would be confirmed dead. There was now only one unaccounted for—a macaque. Though no trace would be found of it, dead or alive, it was eventually decided that it had most likely been eaten by one of the cats.

Six of Terry Thompson's animals survived. Three were leopards, still in their cages. Two more were the macaques kept in the living room of the house in two small birdcages. And finally, out back near the empty swimming pool, was a small grizzly bear, also in a birdcage. The house itself was disgusting. "It was the most horrific smells," says Stalf. "Garbage, and feces. Garbage bags filled with garbage that were knocked over, and the filth. I saw a pair of pants on the ground and the belt was twine. It was very sad to see—how someone clearly had lost their mind. There are no sane people that would live in those conditions."

Thompson's wife, Marian, arrived around lunchtime. She had to be convinced that the survivors should be taken to the zoo for safekeeping. "She was saying, 'Please, Mr. Hanna, don't take my children,'" says Hanna. Marian insisted on removing the macaques from their cages herself, waving off the zoo personnel's advice about the risk she was taking. She would explain that she had spent $30,000 buying them, and that she used to sleep with the young female. Her bond with them certainly seemed real. Before she opened the cage, she sang to them a lullaby, and they clung to her as she took them one by one to their carriers.

It was decided that the dead animals be buried, there and then, on the property. Mrs. Thompson chose the spot. A big digger was brought in and a hole was dug maybe thirty feet deep. The animals were scooped by the bucketload, placed in the hole, and earth backhoed over them. "Our role in life is to care for animals and to educate and inspire people about these great creatures," says Stalf, "and to see them piled in the mud . . . it was just a bad day, you know."

Thompson's body was taken from the scene for an autopsy at the Licking County Coroner's, where it revealed a few of its secrets. At death Terry William Thompson was five feet five inches tall and weighed 174 pounds. He had been wearing a black T-shirt, blue jeans, and white briefs. His gallbladder had been removed earlier in life, and he was suffering from severe atherosclerotic cardiovascular disease. The only notable substance in his blood was Benadryl. There was gray powder residue on his left hand that appeared to be from a gun being fired. The wounds mentioned in the autopsy report, aside from the gunshot wound, begin with "a 2¼ inch vertical laceration on the right lower forehead and along the spine of the nose." Twenty-one other injuries, or clusters of injuries, were detailed just on the head and neck, the site of the most widespread damage. Others were noted on his torso and his legs.

And then there was what the coroner described like this: "a 5 3/4 x 4 inch gaping laceration involving the pubic region and bilateral medial thighs with the absence of genitalia, exposure of the pubic bones and adjacent soft tissue." Or, to spell it out: By the time the body was recovered, no part of his external genitalia remained. Where they should have been, there was nothing but a raw gap. That was Terry Thompson's final grotesque parting gift—a last meal for one of his animals, sometime before it, too, met its death by bullet on the sad night of October 18, 2011, near Zanesville, Ohio.

Part 2: The Animals Among Us

For the majority of Americans who know little about the world of exotic animals, the astonishing events in Zanesville raised some obvious questions. How could a private citizen have amassed a collection of so many unusual and potentially dangerous animals in the first place? Surely he must have broken every law that prevents your next-door neighbor from secretly housing an ambush of tigers?

The answer to that first question: It's surprisingly easy. The answer to the second question is: What laws?

Though Ohio legislators are now scrambling to rectify this, the state where Terry Thompson lived is one of a handful where the regulations on exotic-animal ownership have historically been very light. Your neighbor could buy as many tigers, lions, cougars, and other exotic animals as he so desired and would be under no obligation to tell anyone. To breed or exhibit or commercially transport animals across state lines he would need a USDA license, requiring that his facilities be inspected periodically to check that they met some basic standards—but other than that there are no special checks or controls.

I will hear confident estimates of the number of big cats—tigers, lions, and so on—in Ohio that vary from the low hundreds to the low thousands. The strange truth is: *Nobody knows.* No one is sure how many there are, or where they are.

I set out to find some of them. These days many exotic-animal owners have learned to keep what they do to themselves, to avoid the unwanted attention of unhappy neighbors, animal-rights activists, and journalists who treat them as scary eccentrics or worse. But I find a few. Partly, I think, they talk because they're proud of what they do and the way they do it, but it's also because their way of life is under attack. They need people to know that not everybody who has a tiger or three tucked away behind their house is a Terry Thompson.

Over the days I spend visiting them I become strangely accustomed to the fact that, just around the back of an otherwise perfectly normal home in Ohio suburbia, there can be a tiger or a cougar—or, in some cases, many of each. ("Ever been this close to a tiger?" one owner nonchalantly inquires, as it nestles up against the fencing inches away from me in his garage.) I hear many tales of devotion and care that try to emphasize the ordinariness of what is being done ("We live a very normal life," one mother tells me, "besides the fact that I have alternative animals"); I hear from a man who had a bear escape and only averted disaster by luring it back into its cage with a trail of vanilla-cream cookies; I hear from a man who shared his house and bed with a leopard for nineteen years ("I know certainly if I would have done the wrong thing when she was getting possessive about things, she would have certainly killed me"); I hear from a couple who have not been on holiday for seven years because they won't abandon their six bobcats and who are planning to leave the state rather than be separated from their animals; I hear from a woman who says she will do absolutely *anything*—"shoveling shit in hell, sucking cock for fifty bucks"— to feed and protect her cats.

Most seem to have stumbled into it, impulsively buying a bear or lion cub without thinking through how, as one puts it, "a year from now, it's not going to be so cuddly." One of the surprising facts about owning animals like these in America right now is that while keeping them may not be cheap, buying them frequently is. Tom Stalf at the Columbus Zoo suggests to me that you can buy a lion for $300—cheaper than many pedigree dogs. Even that statistic slightly obscures the situation. There may still be a market for baby lions and tigers (the consensus seems to be that realistic prices are a little higher than Stalf's figure), but there is virtually no market at all for adult tigers and lions. They are effectively worthless, because there are usually more people trying to unload them than wanting to purchase them, which is also why across America there are a surprising number of sizable big-cat sanctuaries, several with over a hundred animals.

At the second-largest of these, the Exotic Feline Rescue Center in rural Indiana east of Terre Haute, where most of the 230 cats seem to come with their own tale of horror, the center's founder, Joe Taft, tells me an incidental story that won't leave my mind, because it seems to encapsulate, this time in a rather beautiful way, what people will do in the elusive pursuit of accord and communion between man and animal.

Though sanctuaries try to avoid pregnancies, sometimes new arrivals are pregnant and occasionally accidents happen, and when there are baby cubs they are hand-raised by humans. Ten years ago, after a heart attack, Taft had a quintuple-bypass operation. At the time there was a young tiger cub living with him and when Taft returned from the hospital he was unwilling to displace it. Nonetheless it was clearly impossible to allow a boisterous feline to clamber freely over someone who has just had major heart surgery. The solution was elegant, if unusual. In Taft's living room, a fence was built around his couch, and that is where he spent most of his time as he recuperated: safely inside a cage inside his own house, man looking out, tiger looking in.

•   •   •

The common assumption after the catastrophe at Zanesville was that when it came to Terry Thompson and his animals, he must have been a terrible man doing a terrible thing. But it isn't easy to work out what is right when it comes to animals like these, either morally or practically, which may be why there are so many shades of opinion. Just as "good" private owners explain why they should exist and why "bad" private owners should not, sanctuaries may suggest that they should endure while private owners are phased out, and zoos can loftily assume there are clear reasons that they should be cherished while most kinds of non-zoo ownership should be frowned upon. I can see a logic in some kind of extreme libertarian position (people should be able to do what they want with animals unless they are clearly shown to be doing harm) and, conversely, in a hard-core animal-rights position (no animals should be used for any human purpose whatsoever), but the arguments for everything in between seem murky. Frequently these are based on a confident assessment of the animals' happiness (a thorny notion), and on the pragmatic need to save animals from a place worse than where they are. (Everyone knows somewhere else worse.)

Likewise, there is wide disagreement about what kind of human intervention or interaction can be beneficial or justified. Perhaps it is obvious to you that removing a monkey's teeth and dressing it up in pseudo-human-children's clothing (Hanna "Monk"tana two-piece panne velvet dress, $38) and diapers (infant starter pack, $35) is wrong? But what about declawing cats, something considered quite acceptable in parts of the exotic owners' world? (Thompson was not unusual in routinely taking his cats to the vet for declawing.) What about giving primates

TV to watch? Or taking them to the McDonald's drive-thru? What about neutering, which is now considered not merely acceptable but responsible behavior when it comes to many nonexotic pets? What, then, about the way that male tigers are usually neutered in sanctuaries, but male lions are not, because when neutered they lose their manes? (Whose feelings, exactly, are being taken into account there?) What, too, of this practice of removing cubs from their big-cat mothers soon after birth and hand-rearing them by humans?

Only once you slide up and down these slippery moral slopes can you see how much easier it is for all of these owners to believe that they are acting with kindness to animals that they love, and that their love is on some level reciprocated. Maybe something went very astray with Terry Thompson, and so of course it is now in the interests of the other owners to draw a firm line between what he did and what they do, but my hunch is that if one had visited him a few years ago, he would have expressed the same love and care and concern for his animals, and done so with conviction. The truth is that while, on a practical level, we may feel as though we can distinguish between better and worse owners, it is logically impossible to know for certain what the animals are thinking or experiencing. Every human who interacts with an animal and then makes claims about what that interaction means to the animal—in back yards or zoos or even on the plains of Africa—is making a claim neither they nor anyone else can verify.

When the owners I meet with talk about the proposed new laws (which, in their most inflexible draft versions, would effectively close down everyone in Ohio whom I speak with, and so would inevitably lead to massive animal euthanization), there is one other common target of their ire, aside from Terry Thompson: Jack Hanna. They see hypocrisy in much of what he now says, particularly given his past use of animals from private owners as props on TV shows.

"He forgets where he came from," says one owner, Michael Stapleton (five tigers, four bears). "Jack needs to step back, take a breath, and look at Jack's history. Okay? Jack doesn't need to be telling me anything."

"He would not have his position now," echoes another, Evelyn Shaw (one cougar, two servals, one lemur, one macaw, one skunk), "if he had not started out as a private owner. He made mistakes, big mistakes, that the rest of us haven't made."

Hanna acknowledges that he is not universally popular for supporting what happened that night, and for supporting the laws being drafted. "I got death threats and everything else," he says. I wonder how I might bring up the dark moment that the exotic-animal owners think of as his great never-mentioned dirty secret, but I don't need to. "I've had three bad things happen in my life," he says, and proceeds to describe them. The first involves his daughter and cancer. The third is what happened that night in Zanesville. And the second occurred when he was a young private owner exhibiting his exotic animals.

"A little boy loses his arm to an African lion, 1972 or 1973, Tennessee," he remembers. Jack Hanna's lion, at Jack Hanna's animal farm. "My animals were raised in a magnificent setting, creeks going through the place and everything was gorgeous. But an accident happened. And I had to go and pick up the arm. It was beyond anything that you would ever want to experience."

I reiterate how angry animal owners are with him. "Yes, they have every right to be angry with me, but do they know that I lost everything I had?" he says. "Remember, 1973 was much different than 2011. And they have every right to think, 'Oh, here's Jack, he had his fun with animals—now we can't have our fun.' I can see that. And I have no problem with that. I just know that I learned the lesson the hard way, that's all."

•   •   •

There is a belief that unites the exotic-animal owners of Ohio: If only the right people had listened, what happened with Terry Thompson—and all the trouble now following in its wake—could have been avoided. The exotic-animal world is a close-knit one, and in the year before Thompson's death, after he was sent to prison, word spread that there were problems with his animals.

I hear different versions of what was being said: dead cats—a white tiger and a cougar—observed lying on the property; animals getting loose; a two-year-old lion being allowed to run around in the open; multiple animals in such bad health that they would have to be euthanized. Some owners took food down to Thompson's property themselves, some say they contacted the sheriff's department. "They told me," says one owner, Cindy Huntsman, "there were no laws on the books that would allow him to confiscate."

As for what actually happened on that day in October, I hear all kinds of theories, though most of them sound recklessly far-fetched. Thompson was involved with bad people and had fallen out with them. He was caught up in dangerously illegal black-market animal sales, dead or alive. (Tigers are reputedly worth as much as $20,000 dead when their body parts are illegally sold off.) Drug smuggling. Secret plane trips. The Mexican cartel. His death was part of a twenty-five-year plot to rid America of exotic animals. He was actually found with a pillowcase over his head and a gunshot wound to his stomach. Nearly all of the exotic-animal owners I speak with, deeply skeptical of the official account, identify the same "true" culprit: animal-rights activists.

I hear nothing to substantiate any of this, and the multitude and variety of the tales alone is enough to make one doubt any of them in particular. The craziest, most tangentially related rumor that I hear in Zanesville: Jack Hanna was supplying Charlie Sheen's tiger blood.

·   ·   ·

There are two mysteries about what happened along the driveway of 270 Kopchak Road that nobody has been able to explain. The first is why Thompson seems to have cut open so many of the cages when he simply could have opened them. The only reason I can think of is that it made it harder to undo what he had done, and so made it more of an act of irreversible destruction. Maybe. But while it seems foolish to expect someone's actions on the verge of suicide to be consistent with their behavior before then, this action—the cutting of the cages—does puzzle some for a different reason. People insist that the Terry Thompson they knew was too lazy to go to that kind of trouble.

The second, bigger mystery is how Thompson managed to let loose fifty animals without being seriously injured by any of them. Even if many of the animals were confused or scared, and not bloodthirsty for human flesh, some of the friendliest might have been expected to want to "play" with Thompson—and when a cat this big decides to play with you, you are in little less peril than when it decides to attack you.

This riddle hardly bolsters any of the conspiracy theories—if someone did this to Thompson, they too would have had to find a way of releasing the animals without coming to immediate harm (never mind to have escaped from the scene without being spotted). But people will believe what they need to believe. When a life explodes like this, in a shower of sparks and shrapnel, people pick through the remains and see what suits them best. That's what happens when your death defines you. The bigger the bang that takes someone out, the more likely it is that the person at its center will be obscured. Terry Thompson's story went round the world, but it was also barely told at all. Whether he was a daredevil hero or an idiot or an animal lover or an animal hater or a victim or a recluse or a good man betrayed, he was assumed to be a cartoon of a man whose whole life could be extrapolated from its final minutes. Almost from the moment Mrs. Kopchak picked up her telephone and reported that wild animals were on the loose, it was taken for granted that the manner of Terry Thompson's death explained all anyone needed to know about the life that came before it.

It seems worth taking at least a moment to wonder whether it might be the other way around.

Part 3: A Man Called Terry Thompson

In Vietnam we were so much more interested in lightweight because we were on the move a lot. I was in a helicopter so I was a machine gunner with an M60—that was on a bipod. I always had an M16 with me. . . . I've been to Southeast Asia for a year in a hole in the ground. . . . I've shot more rounds through a machine gun than all the cops in Zanesville put together, but I had to stay alive so it wasn't a fun thing. That's when you sleep with a machine gun. And it's the only thing that keeps you warm. . . . When you've been through a fire-fight and you've got that warm machine gun, that's all you got. You don't have anything else. . . . I'm not an expert. I guess I am an expert in the military. . . . Yeah, I am. But so what does that mean anything? . . . See, the guys who shot expert got killed in Vietnam.

—Terry Thompson, secretly recorded in his home by a government informant, April and May 2008

Terry William Thompson grew up just east of Zanesville on his parents' farm, close to the airport. "He'd ride his bicycle over, watch the airplanes, and wanted to fly," says Dr. Ralph Smith, a local vet who now lives on a lake where Terry used to go camping as a Boy Scout. Thompson's sounds like an idyllic small-town-America sixties childhood: bicycles, Boy Scouts, loving parents, sporting triumphs, souped-up cars, girls. "Beautiful blues eyes— that's what you noticed first," says Christine Perone, who dated him for some time in high school. "His eyes were just beautiful." Not that she was the only one who noticed. "There was never just one girl in his life," she remembers. "He would sometimes step on other guys' girlfriends. And he was like, 'You know, I'm a lover, not a fighter.' I always thought that was pretty funny." He had his pilot's license before he was sixteen. "He used to buzz my house," she says. "My dad really loved him, but I remember sitting at the dinner table and he buzzed our house and my dad said, 'I'm going to shoot that [she mumbles wordlessly] out of the sky.'"

And then, as Thompson would tell it, everything changed.

"He couldn't understand," says his friend Phil Cress, "why he got taken away from his life here to be drafted to go to Vietnam."

Many of Thompson's friends believe that his time in Vietnam was the defining experience of his life. Mike Marshall, who later flew civilian planes with him, says Thompson brought it up frequently. "He wanted people to know that he was there. He was upset with the army because he saw some horrible, ugly things." Thompson was a door gunner on a Huey helicopter; he told Marshall they had to soften up landing zones, drop soldiers off and pick them up under hostile fire, make emergency medical evacuations: "Dragged both bodies and wounded and maimed soldiers into the helicopter," Marshall says. "Many of them I'm sure died right there in his arms." On the worst days, there were more people to be rescued than they possibly could. "They could only get so many on the helicopter," says Cress, "and they actually had to pry their fingers off the helicopter so they could get off the ground." As for the enemy: "He said he just had to keep mowing them down. It was so bad one time, he ran out of bullets."

"He never really got over it," says Marshall.

"He had no reason why he was spared," says Cress. "Why him? And the guys that had a wife and children are in Arlington?"

"He wrestled with the biblical thing: 'I guess I'll never go to heaven because I killed people,'" says Chuck Spires, his friend and guitar teacher.

Fred Polk, a farmer and scrap dealer who was one of Thompson's neighbors and sometimes tangled with him, also knew him before and after he went away to war. "He always laughed and would be real pleasant before," says Polk. "He smiled a lot. When he came back . . . he had a funny look. You know what I mean? He was kind of a loner. He was just a bit different from the other ones. I think he had a little touch of Agent Orange. I said that he never left Vietnam. I'm going to put it that way. He never left it."

·   ·   ·

Now, the thing is, you know when everyone says this guy went into a schoolyard and kills a bunch of kids and he had an automatic rifle? Well, let me tell you, if you want to kill a bunch of kids you take that camper and run into a schoolyard full of kids, you'll kill about a hundred of them. You'll never kill one hundred with an AR because the gun will jam or you'll run out of ammo or someone will shoot you before.
—Terry Thompson, secretly recorded in his home by a
government informant, April 2008

On his way home from Vietnam, Thompson found himself in Columbus, Ohio. From there, he walked the fifty or so miles east to his parents' house. He wanted to clear his head. Soon after, he bought himself a brand-new Corvette. His wife-to-be, Marian Sharp, came from what was considered a good local family and was an accomplished barrel racer and horsewoman. "Kind of classy—you know," says Jim Stilwell, a longtime friend of Thompson's who went to school with Sharp. "Kind of uppity. Carried herself gracefully. A nice girl." The general impression seems to have been that it was a case of the good girl drawn to the wild boy. As one friend puts it: "Who is the guy who would piss my dad off the most?" Apparently it worked.

Whatever the dynamic that drew them together, for the next four decades they presented themselves as a formidable partnership. Marian became a well-respected local schoolteacher and a prizewinning rider. Thompson opened a bike shop in town. He became the local Harley dealer and also got a license to sell guns. Already, he did things differently from other people. "Back in the seventies," says Stilwell, "if you saw him with a toothbrush in his back pocket, you'd know he was going to go somewhere. Because he wouldn't take any clothes with him." For a while there was a plane on the shop's roof. Inside the shop, along with the bikes and guns, were the kind of animals he favored in those early days. "He raised Dobermans back then," says Stilwell. "There would be dog shit all over the showroom. You had to watch where you stepped." One time Thompson offered Dr. Smith a boat for half price. Smith asked why it was only half price. "It's only half a boat," Thompson explained.

Thompson did things his own way even when it led him into trouble. He once told Spires about someone repeatedly breaking the windows of his shop and vandalizing the place, and how he'd waited for three nights to catch the culprit. "On the third night," says Spires, "this guy showed up, started beating windows out. And [Terry] just really beat him up so bad. He kicked into the mode of what they taught him in Vietnam—beat people up, kill people. He said he didn't have any control over it. The guy was able to stumble to his feet and try to run, and Terry caught up to him, so at that moment he took off to run it was no longer self-defense." The charge didn't stick.

He eventually sold his bike shop and, for the rest of Thompson's life, his hobbies and whatever he did to make a living seemed to mingle in ways that were sometimes ill-defined. For a while he raced drag boats, and is said to have set a world record in his boat

Master Blaster by going from zero to 158 miles per hour on a quarter-mile course in an open cockpit. "Like riding on the end of a pencil, sitting on the hood ornament of your car as it accelerates from zero to 158 miles an hour," says Marshall. And there were always planes. "Everything he had was fast," says Marshall. "Fast motorcycles. Fast boats. Fast airplanes. He liked speed." (Nearly everything. He and his wife liked to drive a decommissioned fireman's truck around town until one night he wrecked it.)

Thompson flew regularly for a local millionaire, including a vintage World War II–era Stearman biplane, and also kept some of his own planes on the Kopchak Road property—he had the electric company move the power lines so that he could take off and land there. There are plenty of colorful stories about his exploits. "Some of them were true," says Marshall. "Some of them were untrue. And he never differentiated between them—he kind of liked the notoriety." One was that he had gone under the interstate bridge where it crosses the Muskingum River in the middle of Zanesville. There is little doubt at all that he once landed an ultralight on the county fairgrounds. Bo Keck, an officer who was there, told him he couldn't pull such a stunt. "Well," Thompson retorted, "find someone to file a complaint on me." Thompson clearly meant this as a testament to his popularity, though Keck wonders. "I think people were afraid of Terry. I mean, he was a gun man. He had these wild animals. He was the type of person, you weren't real sure what he would do. I think that was a lot of it. Some people just said, 'Oh, that's T.'"

His friends, and there do seem to be many of them, talk of Thompson with a deep devotion and testify at length to his goodness, generosity, and freeness of spirit, though they concede that he was certainly no lover of authority, and would maybe even go out of his way to rub up against it. When a state patrolman stopped him for having a taillight out, this is how Thompson described to Spires what happened next:

PATROLMAN: Oh, by the way, you don't have your seat belt
fastened—I've got to ticket you for that.

THOMPSON: Well, where were you when I was in Vietnam in
a foxhole, people shooting at me, if you're trying to
protect me? Where were you then?

PATROLMAN: Well, sir, this is not personal.

THOMPSON: It'd better not be—I'd be out of the truck by
now. How many tickets do you have in that book?

PATROLMAN: I don't know—probably seventy-five.

THOMPSON: You might as well keep writing, because when
I leave here I'm not fastening my seat belt.

"See," says Spires, "that's the way he was." (And continued to
be—county records show at least seven citations for failing
to wear a seat belt.)

Spires is one of the best-known guitar teachers in this part of
the country and was Thompson's teacher in his other great passion of these years. "He loved blues more than anything," says
Spires. "His favorite song was 'House of the Rising Sun.' It had a
special meaning." In the song, the house in question is a New
Orleans brothel, and the name was borrowed for similar estab-
lishments in Vietnam. Thompson told Spires of a visit on the day
a friend of his had been killed. "When he would go into the
house another buddy would hold an M16 out, protecting him,
and then when he came out he would hold the M16, protecting
his buddy. His friend got killed and I guess they're thinking,
'That could be me tomorrow.'"

• • •

Informant: You're crazy.

Thompson: That's what they all say. You know, I'm crazy,
but I live in the big house on the hill with the biggest horse

and the fastest boat, fastest bike. But, see, I just don't have that stuff, I've got the guts to use it.

—Terry Thompson and a government informant in conversation at his home, secretly recorded in May 2008

In 1977, Thompson went to an auction for exotic animals and bought his wife a baby tiger cub called Simba for her birthday. That was how it started. As time passed, people got used to the way he might turn up at the local airfield, say, with a baby bear or lion. Friends talk of driving to Columbus, a baby bear with them in the front cab, or having naps at his house with baby lions asleep on them. I also hear about how Thompson would tell people he had slept together with his big white tiger—the same one, presumably, that was with him at the end. And of the time when he and Marian—she seems to have been a full and enthusiastic participant in many of these adventures—turned up with a baby bear at a friend's fiftieth birthday party, held in their friend's newly decorated basement where everything—carpet, walls, furniture—was white, and seemed quite unperturbed by the upset caused when the bear did what bears tend to do on the nearest white rug.

He seems to have lived as though there weren't a rule invented that didn't deserve a little bending. Without a USDA license, he wasn't allowed to supply animals for photo shoots and commercial events, though he sometimes got around it by using fellow owner Cindy Huntsman's animals and accreditation. After his death, footage emerged showing Thompson handing one of his lion cubs to Heidi Klum on a fashion shoot, and in 2008 he appeared on the Rachael Ray show as an animal handler. His friends refer to other such outings—a shoot with Newt Gingrich, for instance—and say that he took animals on two different occasions to a Bloomberg corporate summer picnic in New York. Thompson also used to insist that he never sold exotic animals, but many in the animal world are scornful at this suggestion. "I was at an auction and he had a tiger that had ringworm and he had a baby monkey," says Nancy Wider, another owner. "He sold the monkey outside of the auction, because it wasn't legal to sell inside, for $3,500."

The first big public warning sign that, when it came to Thompson's animals, all might not be as it should came in 2005. He was charged with animal cruelty relating to some livestock he kept on his parents' old property on the other side of town after three cows and a buffalo were said to have died of starvation and was sentenced to six months' house arrest. In this era there were also numerous complaints of loose animals. His neighbor Fred Polk relates how two of Thompson's Rottweilers got out and killed a couple of Polk's calves. Thompson apologized and told Polk that he'd never see those dogs again, but three days later they were back and killed two more calves. "So we shot them," says Polk. He remembers Thompson picking up the bodies. "Oh, he didn't like it at all," Polk remembers.

.   .   .

This is a [Mannlicher-Schoenauer]—see the twists in the barrel.

I do see that.

Okay, hand built in Austria. Okay, this is a .308, so I could have killed you when you came in the front gate. But of course I've never killed anyone in civilian life.

I understand.

I don't even kill flies.

    —Terry Thompson and a government informant in conversation at his home, secretly recorded in April 2008

It's hard to tell whether Thompson pushed his luck more as he got older, or whether he couldn't (or wouldn't) adapt as the looser times of his youth tightened up, or whether his luck just ran out.

Friends say that Thompson loved having something that no-body else had, and he industriously accumulated objects that might fit the bill. "He always bragged," says Marshall, "that when he sold his business he had 138 motorcycles, 138 cars, and 138 guns." It was the guns that eventually landed him in real trouble. When the ATF raided his home in 2008, they took away 133 firearms and 36 rounds of ammunition. In the end, as his friends point out, Thompson was only convicted for ownership of a gun without a serial number (he said it was too old to have one) and the possession of a single machine gun. "My father's gun," he told a government interviewer, "brought home from World War II in Germany, never been shot, never been cleaned, never been handled." Spires says Thompson told him that he only pleaded guilty because otherwise they were also going to charge his wife as a co-owner of the property; Thompson told the judge that he pleaded guilty because he and his wife couldn't afford further legal fees.

It was this ATF raid that also forced real scrutiny for the first time on his exotic animals. Thompson would speak of his grand plans for what he liked to call T's Wild Kingdom: a large octagonal building, a pond for the bears. But for now most of the animals were kept in connected rows of cages along the driveway leading to his house, and to feed them he would often illegally collect road-kill deer. If there is a line that divides the avid collector from the hoarder, at some point Thompson seems to have crossed it.

"He would never sell anything," says Marshall. "If he liked it, he kept it. And none of it was taken care of. It just broke my heart. He'd have a beautiful '57 or '55 Chevrolet and they'd be sitting there with half an inch of dust and chicken manure all over the top of it." One time Marshall discovered that Thompson had some convertibles in the barn next to two kangaroos: "a boat-tailed roadster, a Duesenberg or something like that, covered with dust and crap. It broke my heart."

"He had an ego that you wouldn't believe," says Stilwell. "You couldn't buy nothing off of him. He would rather say he owned it. Sitting up there, rusting away, is a brand-new '34 Ford steel body."

Toward the end, according to Cindy Huntsman, he seemed to treat his collection of animals in the same way. "He was tops in everything he did. You know, Terry always had to be number one—that was Terry," she says. "For Terry, it started out as a love. In the later years it became very overwhelming because Terry went a little off the deep end. He really became a hoarder of the animals. He would have no sense of 'Okay, this is too many.' It was all about Terry after that. I asked, 'Why, Terry? Why do you need so many?' 'Because I can. Because I can.' Terry was Terry. He had a heart of gold. He just couldn't keep his brain on the right track."

•   •   •

Thompson went to the Federal Correctional Institution in Morgantown, West Virginia, on November 17, 2010. "I asked him what he was going to do when they turned the key on him," says Spires. "He hesitated. Usually he never hesitated. And he said, 'Well, I got through Vietnam . . .'"

When John Moore told the police about a letter accusing Marian Thompson of adultery that Thompson had received on the day before his death, the implication seemed to be that he had received some fresh, devastating news about his marriage. Whatever the exact truth, it wasn't that simple, though different people suggest different time frames. "They had split before he actually went to prison," says Huntsman. "He had accused her of turning him in for the guns. How could you blame a woman you have spent forty years of your life with for that, if you were sane? He was just going off the deep end. Terry became so verbally abusive to Marian. He didn't trust anybody after that. He didn't even trust his own wife."

A bond that tied two people for so long can take time to break completely. Spires mentions that one morning he found a note from Marian in his mailbox, with a stamped addressed envelope, asking if he would write to Terry in prison. And sometime in this period, Marian told Sam Kopchak that Terry was giving guitar lessons behind bars. But if afterward Thompson would try to present his year of incarceration with the same old bravado, telling people that he was voted "Most Interesting Person in prison," the events in his marriage clearly had taken a toll. "He said, you stand in line for two hours to get to the phone," remembers Stilwell, "and then you call home and there's no answer. Day after day. Week after week. Month after month. You finally just stop."

In August, Thompson was moved to a halfway house in Columbus. He was released, forty pounds lighter than a year before, on the day of September 30. Perhaps it was the first of many telltale signs that Thompson, man of so many friends, didn't call anyone. Instead, he walked over to Walmart, bought a Schwinn cruiser bicycle and rode nearly fifty miles through the rainy night along the old Route 40 until he reached his home.

•   •   •

[Talking about the property on which he lived and died] It's the high ground. It's what the Indians wanted.
—Terry Thompson, secretly recorded in his home by a government informant, May 2008

Jim Stilwell only found out that Thompson was back by accident when he drove up to the house in early October, expecting Marian to be there. She wasn't, but Terry was. "He was pretty dejected. He was pretty distraught." A lot of things seemed to be missing from the property and it was a mess: "The weeds were up over the cages— he couldn't even get in his house when he got home." Thompson seemed to need help, so Stilwell took up his Echo Weed Eater, and his lopper for the thicker growths, and his portable air compressor to pump up the flat tires of Thompson's Dually truck.

Thompson did speak to other friends in those days. "He was a broken individual," says Phil Cress. "Very depressed. It took his heart. The government stole his heart. How he was treated. What did he ever do to his country?" His probation officer also visited, and Thompson told him how distraught he was at the prospect of being hooked up for a year's electronic home confinement.

Three days before Thompson died, Chuck Spires, the guitar instructor, spoke with him for about twenty minutes. He told Spires that he was broke, that all he had was sixty horses, but Spires reassured him that he'd made money before and he could make money again. When Thompson said that as soon as he had some in his pocket he'd be back for more guitar lessons, Spires told him not to worry about that.

On one of his last visits, Stilwell walked around the animal cages with Thompson. The cats looked healthy enough, apart from one who had ribs showing, and they were rubbing their heads against the fences. "That means they're happy," Stilwell says. But Thompson explained how upset he was that he used to be able to go around his own private zoo and call his animals by name but could no longer do so. "When he came back, they had been changed around in the cages. He didn't know who was who."

As they passed by the lion cages Thompson talked about the split. "He threw up his arms," says Stilwell, "and said, 'She can just have it all.' And that's when he then said, 'I'm gonna die.'"

"Terry, are you *sick?*" asked Stilwell. "You got cancer or something?"

"No," he replied. "But you'll know when I go."

•   •   •

[From a court deposition Thompson gave while incarcerated on March 28, 2011] *Okay. Where do you plan to live when you are released . . . ?*

At my house.

Okay. And you've not spoken to your wife since her deposition [five weeks earlier]?

No. Now, I may have talked to her a couple times on the phone. We didn't talk about the deposition.

Okay. So, she hasn't told you that during her deposition, she told me that you weren't going to be living with her, you two were not going to be living together when you got out?

No. I don't know that.

Okay. You've had no conversation with her about that at all?

No.

Naturally, they try to make sense of it.

"He felt betrayed by the government, by the army, by society in general," claims Marshall. "Betrayed by his family. And the straw that broke the camel's back was, when he went to jail, he came back and his wife had abandoned him. This was his high school sweetheart. And it just broke his heart—this is what I think. I think it was the only way he felt that he could really punish Marian was to take something that she loved, too. Because she loved the animals as much as he did. They'd never had kids. So these animals were like her children. In the bottom of my heart, I think Terry was thumbing his nose at everybody, and he wanted to destroy that which Marian loved the most. I don't know how else to explain it." "I actually think that he expected this when he got home and kind of planned it," says Stilwell. "That's what happens when they send a guy to prison that don't deserve to go there."

Since Thompson died, Chuck Spires has been told by two people that Thompson had told them the same thing, and that he said it to the first of them before he even went to prison: "Basically, 'I should kill my wife and then me.'"

"I think he knew when he did what he did that he was going to put himself and Zanesville, Ohio, on the map," Stilwell says. "And he did it. I think he would say, 'That's just what I expect.'"

After it happened, one thing everyone wanted to understand was how a man who had loved animals enough to have gathered so many grand creatures could then have condemned them to what he had to know was certain death. Their assumption was that he had been thinking about the animals, and they couldn't work out his train of thought. Maybe there's a letter or a note that explains it all. Maybe Marian understands. But I lean toward another theory—that in the end the animals were just what they've usually been in human history: incidental collateral damage. The sentences that go round my brain are ones that were said to me by one of the animal owners I spoke to, Nancy Wider. "My father didn't like animals," she told me. "And he always used to say, 'I don't like animals but I would never hurt one. The animal lovers are the ones that hurt them.'"

But for those who'd prefer a Rosebud moment, here's one more story from forty years earlier, from the time when an Ohio youth with beautiful blue eyes found himself forsaken and lost, deep in the kind of darkness and damage that some never completely escape. There are all kinds of ways that tragedy and fate can reach across decades to taunt us and trap us.

"When he was in Vietnam," says Mike Marshall, "he told me that he was befriended by a little monkey. He lived in a hardback tent—you know, a wood frame and a wood floor—and apparently a monkey kinda befriended him. And it planted the seed of caring for wild animals for the rest of his life. He took care of that monkey most of the time he was over there. It kept him sane while he was there. I don't know what happened to it when he left."

New York Times Magazine

FINALIST—REPORTING

A staff writer for the New York Times Magazine, Robert F. Worth has been reporting on the Middle East since 2003. In the spring of 2012, Worth traveled to Libya with what his editors described as "the broadest mandate: to try to understand the country now that Muammar Qaddafi was gone." What happened next sounds like a Hollywood thriller. Worth talked his way into a makeshift prison run by one of the dozens of militias that now controlled the country. There he found eleven supporters of the old regime— men who had once tortured those who now held them captive. In the days that followed, Worth watched and listened then brought back a story that the National Magazine Award judges described as "bravely reported and brilliantly written."

Robert F. Worth

Did You Think About the Six People You Executed?

One night last September, a prisoner named Naji Najjar was brought, blindfolded and handcuffed, to an abandoned military base on the outskirts of Tripoli. A group of young men in camouflage pushed him into a dimly lit interrogation room and forced him to his knees. The commander of the militia, a big man with disheveled hair and sleepy eyes, stood behind Najjar. "What do you want?" the commander said, clutching a length of industrial pipe.

"What do you mean?" the prisoner said.

"*What do you want?*" the commander repeated. He paused. "Don't you remember?"

Of course Najjar remembered. Until a few weeks earlier, he was a notorious guard at one of Col. Muammar el-Qaddafi's prisons. Then Tripoli fell, and the same men he'd beaten for so long tracked him down at his sister's house and dragged him to their base. Now they were mimicking his own sadistic ritual. Every day, Najjar greeted the prisoners with the words *What do you want?* forcing them to beg for the pipe—known in the prison by its industrial term, PPR—or be beaten twice as badly. The militia commander now standing behind him, Jalal Ragai, had been one of his favorite victims.

"What do you want?" Jalal said for the last time. He held the very same pipe that had so often been used on him.

"PPR!" Najjar howled, and his former victim brought the rod down on his back.

I heard this story in early April from Naji Najjar himself. He was still being held captive by the militia, living with eleven other men who had killed and tortured for Qaddafi in a large room with a single barred window and mattresses piled on the floor. The rebels had attached a white metal plate onto the door and a couple of big bolts, to make it look more like a prison. Najjar's old PPR pipe and *falga*, a wooden stick used to raise prisoners' legs in order to beat them on the soles of the feet, rested on a table upstairs. They had gotten some use in the first months of his confinement, when former victims and their relatives came to the base to deliver revenge beatings. One rebel laughed as he told me about a woman whose brother had his finger cut off in prison: when she found the man who did it, she beat him with a broom until it broke. Now, though, the instruments of torture were mostly museum pieces. After six months in captivity, Najjar—Naji to everyone here—had come to seem more clown than villain, and the militiamen had appointed him their cook. Slouching in an armchair among a group of rebels who smoked and chatted casually, Najjar recounted his strange journey from guard to prisoner. "One of the visitors once broke the PPR on me," he told me.

"Naji, that wasn't a PPR; it was plastic," one rebel shot back. "You could beat a pig with a PPR all day, and it wouldn't break." Besides, he said, the visitor in question had a ruptured disc from one of Naji's own beatings, so it was only fair. The men then got into a friendly argument about Naji's favorite tactics for beating and whether he had used a pipe or a hose when he gashed Jalal's forehead back in July.

The militia's deputy commander strolled into the room and gave Najjar's palm a friendly slap. "Hey, Sheik Naji," he said. "You got a letter." The commander opened it and began to read. "It's from your brother," he said, and his face lit up with a derisive smile. "It says: 'Naji is being held by an illegal entity, being tortured on a daily basis, starved and forced to sign false statements.' Oh, and look at this—the letter is copied to the army and the Higher Security Committee!" This last detail elicited a burst of laughter from the men in the room. Even Naji seemed to find it funny. "We always tell the relatives the same thing," one man added, for my benefit: "There is no legal entity for us to hand the prisoners over to."

Libya has no army. It has no government. These things exist on paper, but in practice, Libya has yet to recover from the long maelstrom of Qaddafi's rule. The country's oil is being pumped again, but there are still no lawmakers, no provincial governors, no unions, and almost no police. Streetlights in Tripoli blink red and green and are universally ignored. Residents cart their garbage to Qaddafi's ruined stronghold, Bab al-Aziziya, and dump it on piles that have grown mountainous, their stench overpowering. Even such basic issues as property ownership are in a state of profound confusion. Qaddafi nationalized much of the private property in Libya starting in 1978, and now the old owners, some of them returning after decades abroad, are clamoring for the apartments and villas and factories that belonged to their grandparents. I met Libyans brandishing faded documents in Turkish and Italian, threatening to take up arms if their ancestral tracts of land were not returned.

What Libya does have is militias, more than sixty of them, manned by rebels who had little or no military or police training when the revolution broke out less than fifteen months ago. They prefer to be called *katibas*, or brigades, and their members are universally known as *thuwar*, or revolutionaries. Each brigade exercises unfettered authority over its turf, with "revolutionary legitimacy" as its only warrant. Inside their barracks—usually repurposed schools, police stations, or security centers—a vast experiment in role reversal is being carried out: the guards have become the prisoners and the prisoners have become the guards. There are no rules, and each *katiba* is left to deal in its own way with the captives, who range from common criminals to Seif al-Islam el-Qaddafi, the deposed leader's son and onetime heir apparent. Some have simply replicated the worst tortures that were carried out under the old regime. More have exercised restraint. Almost all of them have offered victims a chance to confront their former torturers face to face, to test their instincts, to balance the desire for revenge against the will to make Libya into something more than a madman's playground.

·　　　·　　　·

The first thing you see as you approach Jalal's base in the Tajoura neighborhood is a bullet-scarred bus—now almost a holy relic—that was used as a shield by rebels during the first protests in Tripoli in early 2011. Across a patch of wasted ground is an ugly, dilapidated military-training facility made mostly of cinder blocks. On its second floor is a long hallway, the walls of which are covered with images of prisoners at the Yarmouk military base, where perhaps the most notorious massacre of the Libyan war took place. On August 23, Qaddafi loyalists threw grenades and fired machine guns into a small hangar packed with prisoners. About one hundred were killed; most of their bodies were piled up and burned. Dozens more were executed nearby. Many of the brigade's current members are either former prisoners of Yarmouk or the relatives of men who were killed there. The victims' portraits line the hallway. One of them appears twice, a man with a youthful, sensitive face, framed by rimless glasses and pale gray hair. This is Omar Salhoba, a forty-two-year-old doctor who was shot and killed on August 24, more than two days after Tripoli fell. He was revered at Yarmouk for his insistence on treating injured fellow prisoners and for his brave, failed efforts to break the men free.

Omar's older brother Nasser is now the brigade's chief interrogator. He is lean and wiry, with a taut face and dark eyes that seem fixed in a wistful expression. When I met him, he was sitting in his office, a spare room with peeling paint and a battered desk with files stacked on it. He wore jeans and a blue-and-white button-down shirt, and he nervously chain-smoked. "I never left this place for the first three and a half months after we started," he told me just after we met. "It's only recently that I started sleeping at my apartment again."

Nasser Salhoba's grudge against Qaddafi goes back a long way. In 1996, he was in training to be a police investigator, his boyhood dream, when his brother Adel was gunned down in a Tripoli soccer stadium. The fans had dared to boo Saadi el-Qaddafi, the dictator's son and sponsor of a local team, and Saadi's guards opened fire, killing at least twenty people. When the Salhoba family was told they could not receive Adel's body unless they signed a form stating that he was a *mushaghib*, a hooligan, Nasser went straight to the Interior Ministry headquarters and confronted officials there, an unthinkable act of defiance. "I was furious," he told me. "I started waving my gun around and shouting." Guards quickly subdued him, and though they allowed him to go home that night, he soon got wind of his impending arrest. On his family's advice, Nasser fled to Malta, where he stayed for seven years, earning a meager living by smuggling cigarettes and falling into drinking and drugs. Even after he returned to Libya, his rampage at the Interior Ministry kept him blacklisted, and he could not find steady work. It was his little brother, Omar, now a successful pediatrician with two young daughters, who kept him going, lending him money and urging him to clean up his act.

Then came the revolution. While Nasser waited it out, cynical as ever, Omar—the family's frail idealist—risked his life by providing thousands of dollars' worth of medical supplies to the rebels. On June 7, Omar was operating on a child at his clinic in Tripoli when two intelligence agents arrived and bundled him into a car. No one knew where he was taken. More than two months later, on August 24, Nasser got a call telling him Omar had been shot in the Yarmouk prison. Gun battles were still raging in the streets, and Nasser searched for more than a day before a rebel showed him a picture of his brother's bloodied body. Muslim ritual requires bodies to be buried quickly, and Nasser drove to a military hospital and frantically held up the picture to anyone who might help, until a doctor told him that Omar's body had been sent to the local mosque to be buried. Nasser found the mosque and reached the graveyard just minutes after the body was sealed into a cement tomb. He reached out and touched the tomb: the mortar was still wet.

Nasser winced as he recalled that day. "I feel so bad I wasn't able to save him," he said more than once. "My brother was the special one in the family. I could never be compared to him."

The three men responsible for Omar's death were all now living one floor below us. The executioner was a twenty-eight-year-old named Marwan Gdoura. It was Marwan who insisted on speaking to the Yarmouk commander that morning, even though most of Tripoli had fallen to the rebels. It was Marwan who shot Omar and the other five victims first; the other two guards fired only after Marwan emptied two clips from his AK-47. I learned all this over the course of my conversations with them in the brigade jail. They were perfectly open about their roles at Yarmouk, though they spoke in soft, penitent tones, saying they had tortured and killed only on orders.

When I asked Nasser what it felt like to interrogate the man who murdered his brother, he got up from his office chair and walked out of the room. Scarcely a minute later, he reappeared with Marwan, who sat down and leaned forward, his hands clasped in front of him. He had small, narrow-set eyes, a thin beard and monkish, close-cropped dark hair. His gaze was direct but meek, and I could see nothing vicious in his face or manner. The rebels had already told me that Marwan was very devout, that he spent most of his time praying or reading the Koran. I asked about his background and then moved to the events of August 24, when he executed Omar and the other five men. Marwan spoke softly but without hesitation. "One thing is very clear," he said. "You're a soldier, you must obey orders. At that moment, if you say no, you will be considered a traitor and added to the victims. And if you don't do the execution, others will." Nasser smoked quietly as Marwan spoke, glancing at him now and then with a look of professional detachment.

Marwan explained that the Yarmouk prison commander, a man named Hamza Hirazi, ordered him by phone to execute six prisoners, including Omar and several officers who had been arrested for helping the rebels. "We brought them from the hangar and put them in a small room," he said when I pressed him for more details. "The killing happened with a light weapon. We closed the door and left." Marwan did not tell me—though I heard it from the other men who were present for the executions—that in the last moments before he was murdered, Omar Salhoba turned and made a final plea: "Marwan, fear God."

Hours after the execution, Marwan said, he fled with about 200 soldiers under the leadership of Khamis el-Qaddafi, another of the dictator's sons. The convoy ran into rebels, and Khamis was killed in a gun battle. The loyalists then fled to Bani Walid, where Seif al-Islam el-Qaddafi was receiving condolences for his brother's death in a military barracks. "I won't lie to you," Marwan said. "I shook his hand and kissed him." After camping out in an olive grove for a few days, a dwindling band of loyalists drove east to Sirte, Qaddafi's final stronghold, and then south to the city of Sabha. Every day, men were deserting and driving home, Marwan said. But he stayed until there were only five or six loyalists left, holed up in a farmhouse outside Sabha. Only when a truck full of rebels attacked the farmhouse did he flee into the desert. He hid until dark and then made his way to a nearby town, where he caught a minibus northward. A day later, he arrived in his hometown, Surman. I asked him why he stayed with Qaddafi's forces for so long. "I wanted to go home all along," he said, "but I had no car."

This was hard to believe. I was reminded of what some of Marwan's fellow prisoners had told me: that he was the true Qaddafi loyalist among the guards. They had all fled right after the execution. Naji Najjar left with another guard before it even started. But Marwan insisted on standing firm and carrying out Hamza Hirazi's orders to kill the six men. Some of the other prisoners now resented Marwan and blamed him for their fate. Naji once told me: "I have told Marwan, 'I wish I could be back in the prison, the first thing I would do is kill you.' Because if he'd listened to me, we would all have escaped on the day after Tripoli fell."

Marwan had stopped talking. Nasser was now staring at him through a cloud of cigarette smoke.

"During all that month after Tripoli fell, did you think about the six people you executed?" Nasser said.

"I did think about them and also about the prisoners who were killed and burned in the hangar."

"But this was different," Nasser said. "You executed these six people yourself. Did you talk about it with the other soldiers?"

"No," Marwan replied quietly.

There was a long pause. Nasser looked away, as if he felt he ought to stop, but then he turned back toward Marwan. "You say you followed orders," he said. "Suppose I get an order to do the same thing to you. Should I do it?"

Marwan stared down at the coffee table in front of him.

Later, after Marwan was taken back downstairs, Nasser said he still wanted to kill him. But more than that, he wanted to understand why. "I've asked him repeatedly why and how," he said. "I've talked to him alone and in groups. Once Marwan told me, 'One can't truly understand it unless one goes through the same experience.'"

I asked Nasser if he believed that Marwan felt remorse, as he says he does. Nasser shook his head slowly and grimaced. Not long ago, he said, Marwan went out of his way to avoid stepping on a Qaddafi-era flag that had been placed in a doorway (the rebels all relish stomping on it). He apparently thought no one was watching.

"I was furious," Nasser said. "I beat him with the *falga*. It was the only time I've ever done that. To think that he still feels that way after all this time, that he would kill all of us here if he could."

·   ·   ·

One evening at the brigade headquarters, Nasser and Jalal allowed me to sit with them as they looked through a packet of documents sent by someone urging them to arrest a Qaddafi loyalist. These kinds of letters still arrive at the rate of two or three a week, Jalal explained. "When there's something substantial on the person, we go and get them," he said. They sifted through the papers, and at one point, Jalal handed me a photocopied clipping, written in French, from a Burkina Faso newspaper. "Does it say anything bad about him?" Jalal asked. I looked at the story and translated its main points. As I did so, I had the uneasy feeling that my answer could decide whether they would go out into the night and grab this man from his home and put him into indefinite detention in the basement. "Nah," Jalal finally said. "I think this is just another person looking for revenge."

As far as I could tell, Jalal was more disciplined and less inclined to revenge than many of the commanders in Libya. In the early days after the fall of Tripoli, when I first met him, he had joined with a group of hard-core rebel fighters from Misurata, where some of the war's bloodiest battles took place. But the Misuratans began carrying out brutal reprisals on their newly acquired prisoners. One of the Yarmouk guards they captured, a man named Abdel Razaq al-Barouni, was actually viewed as a hero by some of the former prisoners, who told me Barouni unlocked the door of the hangar and urged them to escape just before the Yarmouk massacre began. After Jalal watched one of the Misuratans shoot Barouni in the foot during an interrogation, he decided to take his own fighters and leave, reluctantly allowing the Misuratans to cart off some of his prisoners to their city.

As for the prisoners still in their possession, Nasser and Jalal told me they were eager to hand them over as soon as there was a reliable government to take them. But they were keen to let me know that in a few cases, notorious killers had been turned over and promptly released. Jalal, who is starting to develop political ambitions, seemed especially eager to prove that he had solid reasons to hold onto his twelve prisoners. He had evidence that no one had seen, he said: torture tapes made by Qaddafi's jailers. He had taken them from the ransacked offices of Hamza Hirazi, the commander at Yarmouk.

One night Jalal drove me to his house in Tajoura, not far from the base. It was dark inside, a cluttered den crowded with black couches and tables and littered with cups and ashtrays. We sat on the floor with a couple of his friends sharing a bowl of spaghetti, and then Jalal set a dusty laptop on the edge of one of the couches. The screen lit up, revealing a small room with a brown leather desk chair. A man in a white blindfold appeared, arms tied behind his back, and was shoved into the chair. A voice behind the camera began interrogating him: "Who gave you the money? What were their names?" A cell phone rang in the background. The prisoner was taken off-camera, and then a horrifying electronic buzzing sound could be heard, accompanied by moans and screams of pain.

"They almost killed us in that room," Jalal said.

A slim, dark-skinned guard entered the torture room, carrying a tray of coffee. I recognized the face: This was Jumaa, one of the men now being held in the brigade's jail. The contrast with the man I had met—meek, apologetic, full of remorse—was alarming. In the video, Jumaa wore a look of bored arrogance. He sipped his coffee casually as the electric torture-prod buzzed and the prisoner screamed. Occasionally he joined in, kicking the prisoner in the ribs and calling him a dog. He came and went at random, apparently joining in the beatings for the sheer pleasure of it.

Jalal clicked on another video. In this one, Jumaa and two other guards were kicking and beating a blindfolded prisoner with extraordinary ferocity. "Kill me, Ibrahim, kill me!" the prisoner screamed repeatedly. "I don't want to live anymore! Kill me!" The man to whom he was pleading was Ibrahim Lousha, whom I already knew by reputation as the most notorious torturer at Yarmouk. "Do you love the leader?" Lousha said, and the prisoner replied frantically, "Yes, yes!"

Yet another video showed a handcuffed man, whose body looked twisted and broken, speaking in a shaky voice. Jalal then showed a photo of the same man, lying dead on the ground, facedown, his hands bound. And then another photo, this one of a blackened corpse: "This man was covered with oil, we think, and then burned," Jalal said.

On it went, a series of appalling scenes interrupted by Jalal's running commentary: "That guy survived and is living in Zliten," or "That guy died in the hangar." But Jalal and his friends, including one who had been in the prison with him, were so used to it that they spent half the time laughing at the videos. At one point, Jalal pointed to the wall behind a blindfolded prisoner's head, where a rack of keys could be seen. "Hey, look, on the end, those are the keys to my car!" he said. "I'm serious!" He and his friends cracked up and could not stop, the helpless peals of laughter filling the room. Later, Jumaa appeared on the screen grinning raucously and doing a mock-sensual dance behind the terrified prisoner. To an outsider like me, Jumaa's dance was sickeningly callous, but Jalal and his friends found it so funny that they replayed it again and again, clapping their hands and doubling over with laughter. It was a distinctive sound, and I came to think of it as Libyan laughter: a high-pitched, giddy surrender, which seemed to convey the absurdity and despair these men had lived with for so long. Driving home that night, a Libyan friend offered me an old expression that shed some light: *Sharr al baliyya ma yudhik*, which translates roughly as "It's the worst of the calamity that makes you laugh."

A few days later, I went to see Ibrahim Lousha, the torturer on the video. He was being held by one of the brigades in Misurata, about two hours from Tripoli, in a battered old government building. I was led to a big empty room and told to wait, and then suddenly there he was, looking like a mere child as he slumped in a chair. He wore gray sweat pants and a blue V-neck sweater and flip-flops. He had big eyes and a buzz cut, a morose expression on his face. He sat with his hands together in his lap, his left leg bouncing restlessly. The Misurata brigade had become infamous for the torture of Qaddafi loyalists in recent months, but Lousha said he was treated well. No one was monitoring us, aside from a bored-looking guard across the room.

He was twenty years old, he said, the son of a Tripoli policeman. When I asked him about the torture at Yarmouk, Lousha answered numbly: beatings, electricity, other methods. "We didn't give them water every day," he said. "We brought them piss." Whose? "Our piss. In bottles. Also we gave them a Muammar poster and made them pray on it." I asked if he was ordered to do these things. He said no, that he and the fellow guards came up with these ideas while drinking liquor and smoking hashish. Wasn't that an insult to Islam, to make people pray to Qaddafi, I asked. "We didn't think about it," he said. He told me that on the day of the massacre, a commander named Muhammad Mansour arrived late in the afternoon and ordered the guards to kill all the prisoners in the hangar. Then he left without saying anything about why they were to be killed or where the order originated.

"We looked at each other," Lousha said. "And then I got the grenades." He spoke in monosyllables, and I had to press him constantly for more details. "The other guards had the grenades. I told them, 'Give the grenades to me.'" He threw two into the hangar, one after the other, and the door blew open. He could hear the screams of the dying prisoners. I asked him what he thought about after he went home to his parents and siblings. He had made no effort to escape. "I was thinking about everything that happened," he said, his face as expressionless as ever. "The whole disaster, the killing. I was thinking between me and God."

.   .   .

The next time I saw Nasser, he proudly announced to me that their brigade was not just some freelance unit but officially recognized by the government. It turns out this is true of dozens of rebel bands in Libya, though all it means is that they have sent their names to the Interior Ministry, which has offered them the chance to apply for positions in the country's new security services. The recruits are mostly being directed to the National Guard, a newly formed body—free of the taint of Qaddafi's goon squads—that is housed in an old police academy building in Tripoli. I drove there on an April morning and found thousands of men standing outside in the sun. All of them were *thuwar,* and they were waiting to be paid. The transitional government decided in March to pay each rebel about $1,900 ($3,100 for married men). Anyone could sign up, and so 80,000 men registered as *thuwar* in Tripoli alone. One man waiting in line told me, "If we'd really had this many people fighting Qaddafi, the war would have lasted a week, not eight months." It is lucky for Libya that the oil fields did not burn and enough crude is being pumped and sold to keep the *thuwar* happy.

Inside the building, I was led into an upstairs room that resembled a hotel suite, with plush carpets and curtains and bright green walls. On the walls were old maps used by the border patrol during the Qaddafi era. After a few minutes, a middle-aged man named Ali Nayab sat down and introduced himself as the deputy head of the new National Guard. He was a fighter pilot in the old Libyan Air Force, he told me, but was jailed for seven years for his role in a 1988 coup plot (he had intended to fly his jet, Kamikaze-style, into Qaddafi's villa). "I really didn't want to die," Nayab said, "but I would have if that was the only way to get Qaddafi." When I asked about integrating the *thuwar* into the National Guard, he smiled apologetically and explained that the guard had not been able to do anything yet for the men who signed up. They were still waiting for the transitional government to make decisions. The men, meanwhile, were sitting at home or working with their brigades. "The result is a big void between the transitional government and the *thuwar*. They are starting to feel frustrated." Nayab also conceded that some brigade commanders were reluctant to give up the power they had acquired. Many were nobodies before the revolution, and now they command the respect due to a warlord. The longer the current vacuum lasts, the more entrenched these men may become, making it harder for a new national government to enforce its writ.

One of those commanders is now holding Hamza Hirazi, the officer who oversaw the massacre at the Yarmouk prison. I was eager to talk to him, because no one had yet been able to explain to me one of the central mysteries of the terrible massacres that took place in Yarmouk and other places in the last days of Qaddafi's regime. As Tripoli was clearly falling to the rebels, the loyalists killed Omar Salhoba and the others on August 23 and 24. Why? And who gave the orders?

The man guarding Hirazi runs a large brigade of men from the Nafusah Mountains, three hours southwest of Tripoli. His name is Eissa Gliza, and his brigade is based in one of Tripoli's wealthiest neighborhoods, in a flamboyant villa that used to belong to Qaddafi's sons. Before the revolution, Gliza was a construction contractor, he told me. Now he commands 1,100 men. When I arrived on a Tuesday morning, he was sitting at his desk in an opulent office, watching a gigantic TV screen. A warm breeze blew in from the Mediterranean, which glittered in the sun a few hundred yards away. Gliza is a powerfully built man of fifty, with thick greasy hair and a stubbly beard. He looked sweaty and tired. As we made small talk, the guards outside got into a screaming match, and then one of them threw a punch and the others pinned him down. Gliza ignored it. He held out his cell phone, showing me a series of sickening videos of men being beaten and tortured by Qaddafi loyalists. "It's a shame they're still alive, after what they did," he said. I asked about a meeting with Hirazi. Gliza said he would try to arrange something, but it wasn't easy. There had been two attempts on Hirazi's life already, he said. He was moving Hirazi around constantly. I asked if the government had expressed any interest in Hirazi, given his prominent role under Qaddafi. "The government?" Gliza said with contempt. "They are interested in business and oil. They are the sons of Qatar. They are being directed by Sheika Mozah"—a wife of the emir of Qatar. "They have not seen the front line."

On the television, there was an announcement that the head of Libya's Transitional National Council, Mustafa Abdel-Jalil, had threatened to use force to quell a battle going on between two towns in western Libya. Gliza laughed dismissively. "Who? Who will use force?" he said. "Three days ago they went to Zuwarah and said, 'We're the national army, we want to go to the front line.' They didn't stay one hour. One of them pissed his pants. They say 35,000 men have joined the national army. I tell you, if all 35,000 came here, they could not get past our 200 men. Until there's a true government, no one will give up power."

Not long afterward, an old man walked into the office, dressed in a djellaba, with a long white beard and a skullcap on his head, holding a cane. He began complaining that Gliza and his men were behaving as if they owned the entire neighborhood. They were giving out brigade ID cards to Africans and letting them wander all over the place, demanding money for cleaning people's cars. The old man's voice rose to a shout, and his thin arms shook with rage. "What gives you the right to issue IDs?" he went on. "These are not even Libyans!" Gliza shouted right back at him, saying the neighbors should be grateful. It went on for twenty minutes at earsplitting volume, each accusing the other of not showing proper respect, until finally the old man seemed to deflate and hobbled out the door.

Perhaps the most potent evidence of Libya's power vacuum is at the borders. In early April, fighting broke out between two bands of *thuwar* near the western town Zuwarah. The smuggling trade is lucrative, and a similar fight over the country's southern borders had left about 150 people dead the previous week. When I arrived in Zuwarah, two days after my visit with Gliza, it was a war zone. The earth shook with mortar blasts, and I recognized the rapid-fire thumping of antiaircraft guns. A man who called himself the spokesman of the local military council offered to drive me to the front line. He said 14 people from Zuwarah had been killed that day, and another 126 wounded. We drove along Zuwarah's main street, where the buildings were pocked with bullet holes. At the edge of town, the road was clustered with cars and pickup trucks mounted with guns. Two shipping containers marked the start of no-man's land. Beyond it, the road rose to a dusty hilltop and disappeared from sight. One rebel, a handsome twenty-three-year-old named Ayoub Sufyan who carried a rifle over his shoulder, shouted into my ear in English over the din of the guns: "The government says they sent the national army. Have you seen one of them? After they kidnapped twenty-five of our men, we said that's enough. We told the government: 'If you want to help us, fine. If not, we go alone.' As youngsters, we don't believe this is our government anymore."

A few hundred yards away, just beyond artillery range, I found some of Libya's best-known rebel commanders standing by the roadside in a state of confusion. Some said they represented the Interior Ministry, others the Defense Ministry, still others the Libya Shield border patrol. Among them was Mokhtar al-Akhdar, the famous leader of the Zintan brigade, which until recently controlled Tripoli's airport. He seemed born to play the part of a rebel, with chiseled features and a stoic expression, a scarf wrapped elegantly around his head. I asked him what he was doing here. "We're not fighting," he said. "We are the revolutionaries of Libya. We want to solve the problem. Both sides here are accusing each other, and we are determined to solve the problem."

The violence continued, and the following day, Jalal drove out to a town near Zuwarah to attend a meeting of a group called the Wise Men's Council. It was held in an old hotel on the seaside, in a conference room with a vast rectangular table set with miniature Libyan flags and bottles of water for each speaker. A series of older men wearing traditional white robes spoke about the lack of any government authority and the inability of any rebel leaders to stop the violence in Zuwarah. They reached no consensus, and after an hour, they began to get up and leave. "This council is useless," Jalal said as we drove back to Tripoli in his Land Cruiser. "The elders have no control over the street. Not like they used to. We need to speak to youth in language they understand. Some people are here for personal gain. I'm just here because my friends were burned and killed."

• • •

One morning in early April, Nasser told me, his frustration with Marwan reached a boiling point. He had spent months talking to him, asking him why he killed his brother, demanding more details about Omar's final days, trying to understand how, if the war was over, the execution of his brother had come to pass. "I see Marwan as such a cold person," Nasser told me later. "He was the head of the snake. Of all the guards, he insisted on following orders. The others didn't want to kill. He was so emotionless and still is. I wanted to see: Is he the same person when he sees his family?"

So Nasser called Marwan's father and invited him to come see his son. For the last six months, the family stayed away out of fear that the *thuwar* would take revenge on them all. On the following Friday, eight of them showed up at the base in Tajoura. Nasser greeted them at the door and led them downstairs. "It was a very emotional moment," Nasser said. "You can imagine how I felt when I saw my brother's killer embracing his brother." The two brothers hugged each other for a long time, sobbing, until finally Nasser pushed them apart, because he could not bear it anymore. Later, he took one of the cousins aside and asked him if he knew why Marwan was being held. The man said no. "I told him: 'Your cousin killed six very qualified people whom Libya will need, two doctors and four officers. One of them was my brother.' " The cousin listened, and then he hugged Nasser before the family left.

For Nasser, the family meeting was a revelation. "He was very emotional," he said of Marwan. "His sister loves him; his brother loves him. You see him with them, and it's such a contrast with this cold killer." He seemed comforted by this, less burdened, though he could not say exactly why. He told me that he now felt that he understood Marwan a little better, even if his crime remained a mystery.

On the following Friday, Marwan's father returned, this time with two relatives. Nasser helped them carry crates of food—yogurt, fruit, homebaked biscuits—down to Marwan's cell. When Nasser came back upstairs, Marwan's father was standing by the door. He went straight up to Nasser and looked him sorrowfully in the eye. "He embraced me and kissed me on the forehead," Nasser said. "So he must know."

Two days later, as we talked in his office, Nasser asked me: "What's the definition of revenge? To make the family of the person who did it feel what my family felt? I could have killed

Marwan at any time, nobody would have known. But I don't want to betray the blood of our martyrs. We want a country of laws." He picked up the files on his desk and put them into his cabinet. He seemed preoccupied, as though he were trying to convince himself of something. He rubbed out his cigarette in an ashtray and turned to me again. "Besides," he said, "where is the honor in taking revenge on a prisoner?"

I couldn't be sure exactly what was motivating Nasser in his long struggle with Marwan. Certainly, part of it was anger, which has not subsided and possibly never will. But the long months of interrogations had given him an unexpected solace, too, a chance to get to know his brother better and to sift through his own failings. "I keep asking the prisoners small details, like how many times he was beaten, what he talked about, how he seemed," Nasser told me. "How he used to get into fights, demanding proper medical attention for the other inmates. Whenever they were tortured, they would be brought to his cell so he could treat them." Nasser had been moved by the stories he heard of his brother's bravery. Once, Omar paid a guard to take a prescription notice to a pharmacy. He had written a plea for help on the note, in English. But the woman at the pharmacy simply translated the note for the guard, who went straight back to Yarmouk and beat Omar severely. Omar kept on trying, sending notes to colleagues who either could not, or would not, help.

One thing in particular was haunting Nasser. According to the prisoners, Omar had talked a lot about Nasser in jail, saying he was sure his brother would rescue him if he could. "I feel such remorse I wasn't able to help him," Nasser said again and again. He told a long story about a well-connected soldier he'd known, who might have been able to do something if he had pushed him hard enough. He said he hadn't seen Omar during the last days before the arrest, and now he chastised himself, imagining alternative endings. "I would've done anything, even gone to the front for Qaddafi's people, if that would have saved my brother,"

Nasser told me. "At the end of the day, it's what's inside you that counts." But he didn't sound convinced.

Nasser didn't stop with the recent past. He reviewed his whole life for me, trying to understand where he went wrong. He was always the family's bad angel, he said, a prodigal son. Omar was the conscientious one. He returned to Libya after a decade abroad in 2009, telling friends that he was ashamed of Libya's backwardness and eager to help out. He brought back books about Qaddafi written by dissidents and a conviction that the country needed to change. At the time, Nasser told me, he thought his brother was being naïve. Now he understood he was right. It was as if Omar had become a screen onto which Nasser's own failures were projected: the lies, the cowardly survival mechanisms that come with living under a dictatorship. I had the sense that Nasser was struggling to learn from his brother, and in an odd way, trying in turn to teach something to Marwan. After Marwan's family left, Nasser went downstairs and spoke to him. "I said, 'Look what I did, and look what you did,'" Nasser told me. "'You killed my brother, and I arranged for you to see your family.'"

Omar's life cast a similar shadow onto other people. One was his closest colleague, a doctor named Mahfoud Ghaddour. Omar's fellow prisoners from Yarmouk told me he was always trying to contact Ghaddour, whom he saw as a possible savior. In fact, Ghaddour was aware that Omar was being held in Yarmouk—one of the frantic messages Omar sent from the prison got through to him—and yet he did nothing. Ghaddour told me so himself, during a long talk in his office at the hospital. "I started looking in that place," he said, "using contacts with people in the government. But it was somewhat difficult. They started changing their mobile phones. I had difficulty getting help."

Ghaddour said this with a wincing half smile. I found it impossible to believe. I knew other people who got relatives out of Yarmouk. As a prominent doctor, Ghaddour had plenty of contacts he could have called on. And even if he failed, he could at least have told Omar's family, or his in-laws, who were desperate to know where he was being held. Ghaddour must have sensed my skepticism. He continued with a long, rambling narrative in which he tried to blame other people for not rescuing Omar from the prison and talked at length about how dangerous it was in Tripoli at that time. But there was something pained and apologetic about his manner, as if he were groping toward a confession. He cared about Omar but did not want to make trouble for his own family. He had done what so many others had done in Qaddafi's Libya—kept his head down and let others take the risks. These are the survivors in Libya, the ones who adapted to a place where fear was the only law. Most of the brave ones are dead.

·   ·   ·

One afternoon, Nasser drove me to see his brother's widow in Souq al-Jumaa, a middle-class neighborhood of Tripoli. Omar's daughter opened the door, a pretty ten-year-old with lots of orange and pink bracelets on her wrists. She greeted me in English and led us to a Western-style living room with a white shag carpet. Her name was Abrar, and her four-year-old sister, Ebaa, skipped across the room with us to the couch, where both girls sat beside me. After a minute their mother, Lubna, came downstairs and introduced herself. She launched right into a narrative about the family, their years living in Newcastle and Liverpool, their return to Libya and then her husband's disappearance. "We were so scared all during that time," she said. "Even now when I hear an airplane I am frightened." As Lubna spoke, her younger daughter toyed with my beard and stole my pen and notebook. Finally she cuddled up next to me, clutching my arm and pressing her head into my shoulder. "She has been like this ever since her father died," Lubna said. Abrar, the older girl, ran off to find a journal she kept about her father's death. It was a remarkable document, an account written in English on lined paper in a child's straightforward prose. "Then we got a phone call saying my daddy died, and my mama banged her head against the wall and screamed, and I cried," she wrote of the day they found out. This was followed by her descriptions of a series of dreams she had about her father. In all of them, he reassured her that he was in Paradise, and in two dreams he offered to introduce her to the Prophet Muhammad.

At one point Lubna mentioned that she had urged her husband to take them all to Tunisia, where it was safer. Abrar piped up, speaking in the same direct, poised tone as her writing: "We said, 'Take us out of Libya.' He said: 'Never, the hospital needs me. The kids need me. I will never leave. I will die in it.'"

Throughout our visit, Nasser quietly sat on the couch, now and then offering toys to the younger girl. On our way out, the girls offered to show us their father's home office. It was a small room, sparsely decorated, with his British medical degrees framed on the wall, and two big drawers full of toys for the girls. "This is what kills me," Nasser said. "All men love their children, but with him, it was even more."

We walked through the gathering dusk to the car, and I asked Nasser about his future. What would he do once the brigade no longer existed? He wants to become a police investigator, he said, but for a real department. Abrar got into the back seat, clutching a stuffed bear. Her uncle was taking her to the stationery store to buy school supplies. We drove toward Martyrs' Square, the new name given to the plaza where Qaddafi once urged Libyans to fight to the last man. Now there wasn't a single image of his face in the streets, and rebels had scrawled "Change the color" on any wall that was painted his signature green. There was a chill in the air, and I heard a single shot ring out over the Mediterranean as we wove through the traffic.

"I didn't always get along with my brother," Nasser said. "But only because he wanted me to be better."

New York

*There are only twenty-four
National Magazine Awards.
Some honor the kind of long-
form journalism collected in this
anthology; others recognize
editorial excellence in print
categories (such as Design and
Photography) or in digital media
(Multimedia and Video). One
award, simply called Magazine of
the Year, is given to publications
that do it all. This year* New York
*won that award, and Michael
Wolff's essay "A Life Worth
Ending" is one reason why. Wolff
is well known for his media
reporting, but in this piece, which
the National Magazine Award
judges called "brutally honest," he
describes his mother's final illness
and his own struggle with a
health-care system that prolongs
life even as it encourages human
folly. Wolff's mother, Van, died four
months after this piece was
published.*

Michael Wolff

A Life Worth Ending

On the way to visit my mother one recent rainy afternoon, I stopped in, after quite some constant prodding, to see my insurance salesman. He was pressing his efforts to sell me a long-term-care policy with a pitch about how much I'd save if I bought it now, before the rates were set to precipitously rise.

For $5,000 per year, I'd receive, when I needed it, a daily sum to cover my future nursing costs. With an annual inflation adjustment of 5 percent, I could get in my dotage (or the people caring for me would get) as much as $900 a day. My mother carries such a policy, and it pays, in 2012 dollars, $180 a day—a fair idea of where heath-care costs are going.

I am, as my insurance man pointed out, a "sweet spot" candidate. Not only do I have the cash (though not enough to self-finance my decline) but a realistic view: Like so many people in our fifties—in my experience almost everybody—I have a parent in an advanced stage of terminal breakdown.

It's what my peers talk about: our parents' horror show. From the outside—at the office, restaurants, cocktail parties—we all seem perfectly secure and substantial. But in a room somewhere, hidden from view, we occupy this other, unimaginable life.

I didn't need to be schooled in the realities of long-term care: The costs for my mother, who is eighty-six and who, for the past eighteen months, has not been able to walk, talk, or to address her most minimal needs and, to boot, is absent a short-term memory, come in at about $17,000 a month. And while her LTC insurance hardly covers all of that, I'm certainly grateful she had the foresight to carry such a policy. (Although John Hancock, the carrier, has never paid on time, and all payments involve hours of being on hold with its invariably unhelpful help-line operators—and please fax them, don't e-mail.) My three children deserve as much.

And yet, on the verge of writing the check (that is, the first LTC check), I backed up.

We make certain assumptions about the necessity of care. It's an individual and, depending on where you stand in the great health-care debate, a national responsibility. It is what's demanded of us, this extraordinary effort. For my mother, my siblings and I do what we are supposed to do. My children, I don't doubt, will do the same.

And yet, I will tell you, what I feel most intensely when I sit by my mother's bed is a crushing sense of guilt for keeping her alive. Who can accept such suffering—who can so conscientiously facilitate it?

"Why do we want to cure cancer? Why do we want everybody to stop smoking? For this?" wailed a friend of mine with two long-ailing and yet tenacious in-laws.

•   •   •

In 1990, there were slightly more than 3 million Americans over the age of eighty-five. Now there are almost 6 million. By 2050 there will be 19 million—approaching 5 percent of the population. There are various ways to look at this. If you are responsible for governmental budgets, it's a knotty policy issue. If you are in marketing, it suggests new opportunities (and not just Depends). If you are my age, it seems amazingly optimistic.

Age is one of the great modern adventures, a technological marvel—we're given several more youthful-ish decades if we take care of ourselves. Almost nobody, at least openly, sees this for its ultimate, dismaying, unintended consequence: By promoting longevity and technologically inhibiting death, we have created a new biological status held by an ever-growing part of the nation, a no-exit state that persists longer and longer, one that is nearly as remote from life as death, but which, unlike death, requires vast service, indentured servitude really, and resources.

This is not anomalous; this is the norm.

The traditional exits, of a sudden heart attack, of dying in one's sleep, of unreasonably dropping dead in the street, of even a terminal illness, are now exotic ways of going. The longer you live the longer it will take to die. The better you have lived the worse you may die. The healthier you are—through careful diet, diligent exercise, and attentive medical scrutiny—the harder it is to die. Part of the advance in life expectancy is that we have technologically inhibited the ultimate event. We have fought natural causes to almost a draw. If you eliminate smokers, drinkers, other substance abusers, the obese, and the fatally ill, you are left with a rapidly growing demographic segment peculiarly resistant to death's appointment—though far, far, far from healthy.

Sometimes we comb my mother's hair in silly dos, or photograph her in funny hats—a gallows but helpful humor: Contrary to the comedian's maxim, comedy is easy, dying hard. Better plan on two years minimum, my insurance agent says, of this stub period of life—and possibly much more.

Mike Wallace, that indefatigable network newsman, died last month in a burst of stories about his accomplishments and character. I focused, though, on a lesser element in the *Times* obituary, that traditional wave-away line: "He had been ill for several years."

"What does that mean?" I tweeted the young reporter whose byline was on the obit. Someone else responded that it meant Wallace was old. Duh! But then I was pointed to a *Washington*

Post story mentioning dementia. The *Times* shortly provided an update: Wallace had had bypass surgery four years ago and had been at a facility in Connecticut ever since.

This is not just a drawn-out, stoic, and heroic long good-bye. This is human carnage. Seventy percent of those older than eighty have a chronic disability, according to one study; 53 percent in this group have at least one severe disability; and 36 percent have moderate to severe cognitive impairments; you definitely don't want to know what's considered to be a moderate impairment.

From a young and healthy perspective, we tend to look at dementia as merely Alzheimer's—a cancerlike bullet, an unfortunate genetic fate, which, with luck, we'll avoid. In fact, Alzheimer's is just one form—not, as it happens, my mother's—of the ever-more-encompassing conditions of cognitive collapse that are the partners and the price of longevity.

There are now more than 5 million demented Americans. By 2050, upward of 15 million of us will have lost our minds.

Speaking of price: This year, the costs of dementia care will be $200 billion. By 2050, $1 trillion.

Make no mistake, the purpose of long-term-care insurance is to help finance some of the greatest misery and suffering human beings have yet devised.

•   •   •

I hesitate to give my mother a personality here. It is the argument I have with myself every day—she is not who she was; do not force her to endure because of what she once was. Do not sentimentalize. And yet . . . that's the bind: She remains my mother.

She graduated from high school in 1942 and went to work for the *Paterson Evening News*, a daily newspaper in New Jersey. In a newsroom with many of its men off to war, Marguerite Vander Werf—nicknamed "Van" in the newsroom and forevermore—shortly became the paper's military reporter. Her job was to keep track of the local casualties. At eighteen, a lanky ninety-five pounds in bobby socks, my mother would often show up at a soldier's parent's front door before the War Department's telegraph and have to tell these souls their son was dead. Many decades later, she would still go pensive at this memory. She married my father, Lew Wolff, an adman, and left the paper after eleven years to have me—then my sister, Nancy, and brother, David. She did freelance journalism and part-time PR work (publicity, it was called then). She was a restless and compelling personality who became a civic power in our town, elected to the board of education and taking charge of the public library, organizing and raising the money for its new building and expansion. She was the Pied Piper, the charismatic mom, a talker of great wit and passion—holding the attention of children and dinner-party drunks alike.

My father, whose ad agency had wide swings of fortune, died, suddenly, in that old-fashioned way, of a heart attack at sixty-three, during one of the downswings. My mother was fifty-eight—the age I am now—and left with small resources. She applied her charm and guile to a breathtaking reinvention and personal economic revival, becoming a marketing executive at first one and then another pharmaceutical company. At seventy-two, headed to retirement but still restless, she capped off her career as the marketing head of an online-game company.

For twenty-five years, she lived in an apartment building in Ridgewood, New Jersey, in a sitcom mode of sociability and gossip. Once a week, every week, she drove into Manhattan to cook dinner for my family and help my three children with their homework—I am not sure how I would have managed my life and raised children without her.

This is the woman, or what is left of this woman, who now resides in a studio apartment in one of those new boxy buildings that dot the Upper West Side—a kind of pre-coffin, if you will. It is even, thanks to my sister's diligence, my mother's LTC insurance and savings, and the contributions of my two siblings and me, what we might think of as an ideal place to be in her condition. It is a spacious room with a large picture window that, from the ninth floor and my mother's bed, has an uninterrupted view across town. The light pours in. The weather performs. The seasons change. A painting from 1960 by March Avery, from the collection she and my father assembled—an Adirondack chair facing a blue sea—hangs in front of her. Below the painting is the flat-screen TV where she watches cooking shows with a strange intensity. She is attended 24/7 by two daily shifts of devoted caregivers.

It is peaceful and serene.

Except for my mother's disquiet. She stares in mute reprimand. Her bewilderment and resignation somehow don't mitigate her anger. She often tries to talk—desperate guttural pleas. She strains for cognition and, shockingly, sometimes bursts forward, reaching it—"Nice suit," she said to me, out of the blue, a few months ago—before falling back.

That is the thing that you begin to terrifyingly appreciate: Dementia is not absence; it is not a nonstate; it actually could be a condition of more rather than less feeling, one that, with its lack of clarity and logic, must be a kind of constant nightmare.

"Old age," says one of Philip Roth's protagonists, "isn't a battle, it's a massacre." I'd add, it's a holocaust. Circumstances have conspired to rob the human person—a mass of humanity—of all hope and dignity and comfort.

When my mother's diaper is changed she makes noises of harrowing despair—for a time, before she lost all language, you could if you concentrated make out what she was saying, repeated over and over and over again: "It's a violation. It's a violation. It's a violation."

·　　·　　·

The numbing thing is that you see this all coming—you see it, but purposely and stubbornly don't see it.

As it started with my mother, it was already advanced for a college friend and close colleague. As an only child, he had less room to hide. I looked on with mild concern at his helplessness. I kept thinking my situation could never get as bad as his—he spoke actually, not comically, of murder. But we all catch up with each other. All train wrecks occur on a time line.

For my mother, it began with her feet. Her complaint, which no doctor could put a useful name to or offer much respite from, was that she felt the skin on her feet was too tight. One evening, almost three years ago, getting into the shower, she caught her lagging foot on the rail of the shower door and went down into the tub. She lay there, shivering in the tepid water until morning, when her neighbor became alarmed. There is a precept here, which no doctor quite spells out: Once it has begun, it has begun; decline follows decline; incident precedes incident. Here's the medical language: "A decrement in capacity occurs."

But we'll cope, of course. My mother's shower was equipped with special chairs (the furniture of aging is its own horrid story), grab-bars and easy-reach phones installed and I-can't-get-up beepers subscribed to. She actually learned how to fall (not falling not being an option). At the least sign of a tumble, she would sink almost elegantly to the ground, and then, not being able to get up, she'd beep the police, the affable police, who would come and hoist her to her feet, whereupon she'd fix them coffee and all would be sort of well.

And then a holiday—those unfailing barometers of family health. Thanksgiving 2009 was already a weird one. My wife and I had split earlier in the year. The woman I was seeing—and had moved in with—was coming. My children were boycotting. It was my mother who was trying to be the strong and constant pillar. She insisted she could do the job. Her neighbor—a man who had been squiring her around for many years—would load the turkey, too heavy for my mother to lift, into the oven. My sister and I would arrive before the handful of other guests to do the finishes. All was in order when we got there—the potatoes boiled and ready to be mashed in one pot, the carrots roasted, the onion custard baked—all in order except that my mother had done these preparations a week before. Every pot yielded an alarming odor. What was worse was her lack of comprehension—and lack of alarm.

Plans, obviously, had to begin in earnest. Her three children—my sister and I in New York, my brother, a software consultant, in Maui—conferred. An independent life goes into receivership—and you think, *How did we miss all the failing indicators?* My mother, like a rogue accountant, had been hiding much of the evidence: She could no longer tell time, nor count, nor keep track of dates.

Anyway, this is what assisted living is for, no?

We would move her to Manhattan, and, we managed to convince her and ourselves, she'd begin a great new adventure.

She was game—and relieved. The place, the Atria on West Eighty-Sixth Street, was just a few blocks from where my sister, an artist, lives and works. A national chain of residences for the elderly, the Atria is more a real-estate business than a health-care enterprise, providing, at hefty cost—the apartments are in the $8,000-a-month range—quite a pleasant one-bedroom apartment in a prewar building, full of amenities (terraces and hairdressers) and gradations of assistance. But it is important to understand—and there is no reason why one would—that assistance in an assisted-living facility, even as you increase it and pay more for it, is really not much more than kind words and attendance, opened doors, a bit of laundry, and your medications delivered to you. If there is a need for real assistance of almost any kind that involves any sort of calibration of concern, of dealing with the real complications and existential issues of aging people, then 911 is invariably called. This is quite a brilliant business model: All responsibility and liability is posthaste shifted to public emergency services and the health-care system.

The rate of hospitalization for all other age groups is declining or holding steady, but for people over sixty-five it's skyrocketed. The elderly use 50 percent of all hospital days, according to one study. Emergency rooms, the last stop for gangbangers and the rootless, at least in the television version, are really the land of the elderly, and their first step into the hospital system—where, as Medscape matter-of-factly explains, the "inability to recognize normal aging changes . . . raises the chances of iatrogenic illness." Iatrogenic illnesses being the ones caused by hospitals or doctors.

My mother went to the Atria's after-dinner movie—*The African Queen*, as I recall—one evening in May and then told someone she was short of breath. My sister got to the emergency room first—St. Luke's Roosevelt—and called me to say I ought to come.

·　　·　　·

Everybody would manage his or her parent's decline differently. Nobody is proud of himself. We all mess it up. This is partly because there is no good outcome. And it is partly because modern medicine is a random process without a real point of view and without anyone ultimately being in charge. The buck is relentlessly passed. Down this rabbit hole, we all become ineffective and pitiful.

My mother's cardiologist, Dr. Barbara Lipton, a peppy younger woman who, annoyingly, called my mom "Mom," had been for many years monitoring her for a condition called aortic stenosis— a narrowing of the aortic valve. The advice was do nothing until something had to be done. If it ever had to be done.

This was good advice insofar as she had lived with this condition uneventfully for fifteen years. But now that she was showing symptoms that might suddenly kill her, why not operate and reach for another few good years? What's to lose? That was the sudden reasoning and scenario.

My siblings and I must take the blame here. It did not once occur to us to say: "You want to do major heart surgery on an eighty-four-year-old woman showing progressive signs of dementia? What are you, nuts?"

This is not quite true: My brother expressed doubts, but since he was off in Maui, and therefore unable to appreciate the reality of, well, the reality of being near, we discounted his view. And my mother protested. Her wishes have always been properly expressed, volubly and in writing: She urgently did not want to end up where she ultimately has ended up. She had enough sense left to resist—sitting in the hospital writing panicky, beseeching, Herzog-like notes, to anyone who might listen—but of course who listens to a woman who scribbles such notes?

The truth is you're so relieved that someone else has a plan, and that the professionals with the plan seem matter-of-fact and unconcerned, that you disregard even obvious fallacies of logic: that the choice is between life as it was before the operation and death, instead of between life after the operation and death.

Here's what the surgeon said, defending himself, in perfect Catch-22-ese, against the recriminations that followed the stark and dramatic postoperative decline in my mother's "quality-of-life baseline": "I visited your mom before the procedure and fully informed her of the risks of such a surgery to someone showing signs of dementia."

You fully informed my demented mom?

The operation absolutely repaired my mother's heart—"She can live for years," according to the surgeon (who we were never to see again)—but left us longing for her level of muddle before the valve job. Where before she had been gently sinking, now we were in free fall.

She was reduced to a terrified creature—losing language skills by the minute. "She certainly appears agitated," the psychiatrist sent to administer antipsychotic drugs told me, "and so do you."

Six weeks and something like $250,000 in hospital bills later (paid by Medicare—or, that is, by you), she was returned, a shadow being, to Eighty-Sixth Street and her assisted-living apartment.

Unmoored in time, she began to wander the halls and was returned on regular occasions to the emergency room: Each return, each ambulance, each set of restraints, each catheter, dealt her another psychic blow.

And then we were evicted. I had been pleasantly surprised when my mother moved in that only a month-to-month lease was required. Now I learned why. Dying is a series of stops, of way stations, of signposts. Home. Assisted living. Nursing care. Hospice. You are always moving on.

But before we were evicted, there was another Thanksgiving— this one at my house, my mother collected and transported, my children reassembled—and then the next day, the "event." The big one.

We had reached, I gratefully believed, her end.

·   ·   ·

EMS arrived, and once more, we were back in the St. Luke's emergency cubicles. My mother's "presentation" could not have seemed bleaker. The young resident was clearly appalled that we might have strayed outside the time frame for administering the drug that could slow the effects of what surely seemed to be a stroke. Of course, they were yet game to try. But we held our ground: We elected to do nothing here (prompting much renewed scrutiny of the health-care proxy). And please note the DNR. Hours passed. I left and came back. My sister left and came back. One of my mother's aides left and came back.

And then those words, which turn out, in some instances, not to be a relief at all: "She seems to be out of the woods."

What? How?

She had not had a stroke. She'd had a massive seizure. The differences between which being not exactly clear. And, if she had more seizures, which she likely would, this would kill her, an explanation and urgency that somehow resulted—"Did you agree to this?" I said to my sister. "I don't think I did, did you?" "I don't think so"—in my mother getting vast amounts of antiseizure drugs, as well as being moved, once again, into more or less long-term hospital residence.

Coherence was completely gone. All that was left was a jumble of words and incredible anger.

Oh, yes, and here was the thing: The anti-seizure drugs were preventing further devastating and probably lethal seizures but, in themselves, were frying her brain even more.

And too, within a few weeks of lying in bed and resisting this final cataclysm, what abilities she had to walk, what slow and shambling remnant of walking, were gone.

This is where we were: immobile and incoherent. And filled with rage.

And so the first effort to directly talk about the elephant.

It happened in an interior room at the hospital, too small for much, and filled with cast-off furniture, into which fit her doctor, her neurologist, her social worker, and my sister and me. It seemed like the adult thing for us to do, to face up to where we were, and to not make these people have to tiptoe around the obvious.

I thanked everybody for what they had done, and then said reasonably: "How do we get from here . . . to there?"

An awkward number of beats.

NEUROLOGIST (shifting in his chair): "I think we want to define *here* and *there*"—and tossing to the doctor.
DOCTOR: "Your mom is quite agitated. So we don't really know what her less-agitated state will be."
MY SISTER: "What are the chances that she will come back to anything like where she was before the seizure?"

SOCIAL WORKER: "We always have to deal with a variety of
possible outcomes."

ME: "Maybe you could outline the steps you think we might
take."

DOCTOR: "Wait and see."

NEUROLOGIST: "Monitor."

DOCTOR: "Change the drugs we're using."

MY SISTER: "Can we at least try to get a physical therapist,
someone who can work her legs, at least. I mean . . . if she
does improve, she's left without being able to walk."

NEUROLOGIST: "They'll have to see if she's a candidate."

ME: "So . . . okay . . . where can you reasonably see this
ending up?"

NEUROLOGIST: "We can help you look at the options."

ME: "The options?"

SOCIAL WORKER (to my sister): "Where she might live. We
can go over several possibilities."

ME: "Live?"

It was my Maui brother who, with marked impatience, suggested
that I obviously had no idea how the real world works. Such a conversation, treading on legal fine lines and professional practices,
must be conducted in a strict code—keep saying, he advised,
"quality of life."

A week later, same uncomfortable room:

ME: "Obviously we are concerned on a quality-of-life basis."

MY SISTER: "She is completely transformed. Nothing is as it
was. She's suffering so much."

DOCTOR: "The baseline has clearly dropped."

NEUROLOGIST: "The risk is that the levels of medication that
the agitation might respond to could depress her breathing."

ME: "Again, this is a quality-of-life issue, right?"

Doctor: "Of course."

Me: "The agitation seems extreme enough to warrant I
would think going some distance, considering the
quality-of-life issues. Even if that—"

Neurologist: "I'm not sure I'd be comfortable . . ."

Me (with a sudden brainstorm): "Or what happens if you just
discontinue the drugs? Just cut them out."

Neurologist: "Cold turkey could precipitate a massive seizure."

Me: "And death?"

Neurologist: "And death. Possibly. Yes."

Me: "Is this an option?"

Neurologist: "You have to make that decision. We can't force
her to take medication."

ME: "Hum."

Discontinuing the medication felt like both a solemn and giddy
occasion. A week passed, and then the doctors began to report in
a chipper way that she was doing well, all things considered. She
had withstood the shock to the system. She was stable.

And then the social worker came around to say we were coming threateningly close to the maximum number of hospital days
for which Medicare would pay. (We'd heaped another few hundred thousand in cost on the American taxpayer.)

"Now," said my sister taking the straight-man role, "what do
we do?"

My mother—infuriating us with her primal stubbornness—
was transferred to the locked-floor dementia ward at the Atria
facility in Riverdale, where the only caveat to patient behavior
seemed to be a strict rule against hitting. Nine days later, after
my mother socked a locked-floor aide, we were back in our room
at St. Luke's, where—because of her brief discharge, she could
begin her Medicaid hospital-stay allotment from day one—she
was happily received (for another couple of hundred grand).

•   •   •

What do you do with your mom when she can't do anything—anything at all—for herself? This is not, first and foremost, about how you address her needs but about where you put her. No, it is first about who or what facility will take her.

No, it is first about what member of the family will actually sort through the incredibly byzantine and deadening options—or lack of options.

It is at this point that I became unreasonably mad at my Maui brother. In a way I understood the basis of his excuse: It was not a coincidence that he was living in Maui—his twenty years in paradise were in part an exercise of the modern right to distance himself from his family, a point which he was militantly maintaining now. He lived in Maui precisely to be far from all this. It was notable that among the people with whom I shared my tales-of-mother crisis, many, with far-flung ailing parents, identified themselves as the Maui brother. Of all things to escape, this might be the big one. And, too, in my Maui brother's defense, all responsibility is relative: If he was doing less than I was doing, I was doing by a significant leap less than my sister was doing.

It is among the most reductive facts in this story: Women take care of the old. They can't shake it because they are left with it. In the end, it is a game of musical chairs. The girl is the one almost invariably caught out.

My sister assembled the list of potential nursing homes, special elder-need facilities, and palliative-care centers in commutable distance. I grudgingly went along to the best after she'd eliminated the worst. Medicare grades each of these institutions on a five-star scale. Four stars were already charnel houses. One star therefore unimaginable. Just about the only five-star facilities in Manhattan are for HIV-positive patients.

Finely tuned into my mother's profound fear of virtually all strange presences, touches, and noises, and yet her need for constant attention and reassurance, my sister found fault with every place. This might have finally annoyed me, except for the fact that each of these places wanted you to pay prodigiously for its de-pressing indifference, and, what's more, many either excluded my mother's condition or had waiting lists that would, it seemed reasonable to assume, outlast my mother.

Hospice was the best alternative. But while my mother was surely dying—with her doctors gladly willing to certify her in this regard—hospice, we so learned, was not for the certainly dying but the promptly dying.

Curiously, and unhelpfully, it was at this time that one of the neurologists making occasional visits took it upon himself to reevaluate my mother, declaring that her diagnosis was wrong. She did not have Alzheimer's, as everyone seemed to assume. She had dementia, surely, but it was not going, and would not follow, the pattern of Alzheimer's. She would not disappear; she would maintain some awareness and consciousness of her surround-ings, he said, as though this were good news.

It was Marion, my mother's aide, a woman of remarkable humor and constancy, who had shown up one day, sent by a ran-dom agency—and who has now been with my mother every day for almost eighteen months, not a day missed—who suggested just "bringing her home." The best Manhattan approximation of "home" when there is no family homestead seemed to be the stu-dio apartment where she is now, a short walk from my sister's house.

My brother could only see this as a quagmire of cost and re-sponsibility. My sister assured him, as the doctors were assuring us, that six months was a realistic outside framework. My brother did his own Google search. "Yes, yes, they're right, six months at this stage is what you can expect. But you know what they die from? They die from neglect! *Neglect*! There's no neglect here! It's unnatural!"

I signed the lease.

"Who can believe it's been a year?" said Marion when I signed the lease for another year a few weeks ago.

My sister comes over every morning. She brings the groceries, plans the menu, and has a daily routine for stretching my mother's limbs (this in addition to the administration and paying of caregivers, and the collecting of monies from the always recalcitrant John Hancock). I'm here a few times a week (for exactly thirty minutes—no more, no less). Her grandchildren, with an unalloyed combination of devotion and horror, come on a diligent basis. And we have our family events: holiday meals eaten around her bed. Her eighty-four-year-old brother and his wife visit regularly, and so does her eighty-nine-year-old cousin and her daughter. She even has one friend left who still calls her every day (all the other friends fell away a long time ago), conducting an extremely one-sided conversation over the speaker phone.

An occasional letter arrives from retired friends in sunny climes who have somehow missed or have been unwilling to register my mother's condition. They take up in mid-conversation, proposing lunch the next time they are in the area, and recounting details of lives still going on. They continue to regard my mother as a woman who chats, cooks, reads, gossips, and commands attention. Always, suddenly, shatteringly, reading these letters, I see her this way too.

The absurdity of where we are, here on death row, measured not just in our heartache but nationally in hundreds of billions of dollars, can only be missed by the people who have no experience with the true nature and far-flung extremes of quality of life.

A few weeks ago, my sister and I called a meeting with my mother's doctor. As others had fallen to the wayside, the head of gerontology at St. Luke's, Dr. Brenda Matti-Orozco, a patient, long-suffering woman, had stepped up to this job.

The doctor eased into our meeting with tales of health-care-administration woes, of cuts in Medicaid, of fewer beds in fewer facilities around town—did we know, she asked, that Cabrini had closed? Some people, she said, just upped and left their old relatives in the hospital. So much for the small talk.

"It's been a year," I began, groping for what needed to be said: Let's do this, close it down, end it, wanting to murder the euphemisms as much as my mom. "We've seen a series of incremental but marked declines."

My sister chimed in with some vivid details.

The doctor seemed at first alarmed that we might be trying to foist my mother back on her and the hospital and relieved when we said, frankly, we planned never to return to a hospital. We just wanted to help her go where she's going. (Was that too much? Was that too specific?)

She does seem, the doctor allowed, to have entered another stage. (These half-life stages of death, such that you never reach it.)

"Perhaps more palliative care. This can ease her suffering, but the side effect can be to depress her functions. But maybe it is time to err on the side of ease."

Another advance of sorts in our grim descent: Over uncertain weeks or months, her functions will depress even further in this ultimate, excruciating winding down.

"Your mom, like a lot of people, is what we call a dwindler," said the doctor.

•   •   •

I do not know how death panels ever got such a bad name. Perhaps they should have been called deliverance panels. What I would not do for a fair-minded body to whom I might plead for my mother's end.

The alternative is nuts: to look forward to paying trillions and to bankrupting the nation as well as our souls as we endure the suffering of our parents and our inability to help them get where they're going. The single greatest pressure on health care is the disproportionate resources devoted to the elderly, to not just the old, but to the *old* old, and yet no one says what all old children of old parents know: This is not just wrongheaded but steals the life from everyone involved.

And it seems all the more savage because there is such a simple fix: Give us the right to make provisions for when we want to go. Give families the ability to make a fair case of enough being enough, of the end's, de facto, having come.

Not long after visiting my insurance man those few weeks ago, I sent an "eyes wide open" e-mail to my children, all in their twenties, saying this was a decision, to buy long-term-care insurance or not, they should be in on: When push came to shove, my care would be their logistical and financial problem; they needed to think about what they wanted me to do and, too, what I wanted them to do. But none of them responded—I suppose it was that kind of e-mail.

Anyway, after due consideration, I decided on my own that I plainly would never want what LTC insurance buys, and, too, that this would be a bad deal. My bet is that, even in America, even as screwed up as our health care is, we baby-boomers watching our parents' long and agonizing deaths won't do this to ourselves. We will surely, we must surely, find a better, cheaper, quicker, kinder way out.

Meanwhile, since, like my mother, I can't count on someone putting a pillow over my head, I'll be trying to work out the timing and details of a do-it-yourself exit strategy. As should we all.

Texas Monthly

Texas Monthly *calls itself "the national magazine of Texas"— which sounds pretty big until you take a look at the record. Then you might think the editors there are thinking too small. After all, this year* Texas Monthly *received three National Magazine Award nominations for long-form journalism and won two awards (go back and read "The Innocent Man" right after you finish this story), and it was only three years ago that the magazine won the Feature Writing award for Skip Hollandsworth's "Still Life." In fact, this is the fourth Mimi Swartz story to be nominated for an award and the second to win Public Interest. Little wonder. The judges called this look at the impact of anti-abortion legislation "a public-policy epic written by a master storyteller."*

Mimi Swartz

Mothers, Sisters, Daughters, Wives

There are things about women that most men would just as soon never discuss. The stirrups in a gynecologist's office, for one; the tampon aisle at the grocery store, for another; and pretty much any matter involving words like "cervix," "uterus," and "vagina." At least, that's how it was until March 2, 2011. Back in January of the same year, at the start of that legislative session, Governor Rick Perry had pushed as an emergency item a bill requiring all women seeking an abortion to have an ultrasound twenty-four hours beforehand. As Sid Miller, the legislator who sponsored the bill in the House, put it, "We want to make sure she knows what she is doing."

At a public hearing on the bill the following month, Tyler representative Leo Berman took the mike and insisted that 55 million fetuses had been aborted since *Roe v. Wade*—or, as he called it, "a Holocaust times nine." The author of a book on abortion rights gave a somewhat overwrought speech about the differences between "a zygote and a baby." A woman named Darlene Harken described herself as "a victim of abortion" because, she maintained, she wasn't warned about the mental and physical fallout from the procedure; Patricia Harless, a representative from Spring, thanked her for her "bravery" and "strength." Alpine's Pete Gallego countered by expressing his resentment of "people who stop caring after the child is born."

In March the bill reached the House floor, where debate raged for three days, as much as ten hours a day. Tensions ran high in the chamber, which was lit by a benevolent winter sun that glinted off the manly oak desks and super-sized leather chairs. On the first day, March 2, Miller, a burly man with white hair and a sun-lined face that wrinkles into a bright, inviting smile, explained the legislation. A former school-board member from Stephenville, he has a loamy Texas accent and favors a spotless white Stetson. If you stare at him long enough, you might easily forget that it's the twenty-first century.

Miller described his bill in a matter-of-fact tone, as if he were pushing a new municipal utility district. "What we're attempting to do is to provide women all available information while considering abortion and allow them adequate time to digest this information and review the sonogram and carefully weigh the impact of this life-changing decision," he began. Miller then listed everything his bill would require before an abortion could be performed. A woman would have to review with her doctor the printed materials required under the 2003 Woman's Right to Know Act. While the sonogram image was displayed live on a screen, the doctor would have to "make audible the heartbeat, if it's present, to the woman." There was also a script to recite, about the location of the head, hands, and heart. Affidavits swearing that all of this had been properly carried out according to Texas law would have to be signed and filed away in case of audits. A doctor who refused could lose his or her license.

As soon as Miller finished, Houston representative Carol Alvarado strode up to the podium. There could have been no clearer contrast: her pink knit suit evoked all those Houston ladies who lunch, its black piping setting off her raven hair. Her lipstick was a cheery shade of fuchsia, but her disgust was of the I-thought-we'd-settled-this-in-the-seventies variety.

"I do not believe that we fully understand the level of government intrusion this bill advocates," she said tersely. The type of ultrasound necessary for women who are less than eight weeks pregnant is, she explained, "a transvaginal sonogram."

Abruptly, many of the mostly male legislators turned their attention to a fascinating squiggle pattern on the carpet, and for a rare moment, the few female legislators on the floor commanded the debate. Representative Ana Hernandez Luna approached the back mike and sweetly asked Alvarado to explain what would happen to a woman undergoing a transvaginal sonogram.

"Well," Alvarado answered helpfully, "she would be asked by the sonographer to undress completely from the waist down and asked to lie on the exam table and cover herself with a light paper sheet. She would then put her feet in stirrups, so that her legs are spread at a very wide angle, and asked to scoot down the table so that the pelvis is just under the edge."

At this point, if there had been thought bubbles floating over the heads of the male legislators, they almost certainly would have been filled with expletives of embarrassment or further commentary on the carpet design.

"What does this vaginal sonogram look like?" Luna asked, ever curious.

"Well, I'm glad you asked," Alvarado answered, "because instead of just describing it, I can show you."

And so the state representative from Houston's District 145 put both elbows on the lectern and held up in her clenched fist a long, narrow plastic probe with a tiny wheel at its tip. It looked like some futuristic instrument of torture. "This is the transvaginal probe," Alvarado explained, pointing it at her colleagues as she spoke, her finger on what looked like a trigger. "Colleagues, this is what we're talking about. . . . This is government intrusion at its best. We've reached a"—she searched for the word—"climax in government intrusion."

Those who could still focus gaped at Alvarado. No one spoke. The silence seemed to confirm for Alvarado something she had long suspected: most of the men in the House chamber didn't know the difference between a typical ultrasound—the kind where a technician presses a wand against a pregnant belly and sends the happy couple home with a photo for their fridge— and this. She locked Miller in her sights. "What would a woman undergo in your bill?" she asked.

Miller seemed confused. "It could be an ultrasound, it could be a sonogram," he began. "Actually, I have never had a sonogram done on me, so I'm not familiar with the exact procedure— on the medical procedure, how that proceeds."

"There are two different kinds of sonograms," Alvarado said, trying again to explain. "The abdominal, which most of our colleagues may think [of as] 'jelly on the belly'—that is not what would be done here. A woman that is eight to ten weeks pregnant would have a transvaginal procedure." Miller stammered a response, but Alvarado was not done with him. She continued the grilling for several more minutes, keeping Miller on the ropes with a sustained barrage of icky female anatomy talk. Ultimately, however, the room was stacked against her.

On March 7 Miller's bill passed 107–42.

Over the next few months, as the Senate passed its version of the bill, which was sponsored by Houston senator Dan Patrick, and as Governor Perry signed the legislation into law at a solemnly triumphant ceremony, the exchange between Alvarado and Miller stood as a glaring reminder of the peculiar way in which women could be largely boxed out of decisions that were primarily concerning them. (A number of female Republican legislators supported the bill too, but the overwhelming majority of the votes cast in its favor were from men.) Of course, women have rarely held the reins of power in Texas, but there has also seldom been a season as combative on the subject of women's health as the one we have experienced in the past eighteen months.

Miller's bill was only the beginning of what turned out to be the most aggressively anti-abortion and anti-contraception session in history. In the words of one female reporter who covered the Legislature, "It was brutal." Not only did the sonogram law pass, but drastic cuts were made to statewide family planning funds, and a Medicaid fund known as the Women's Health Program was sent back to Washington, stamped with a big "No thanks." When the dust settled, Texas had turned down a $9-to-$1 match of federal dollars, and the health care of 280,000 women had been placed in jeopardy. And that wasn't all. Earlier this year, around the time that the new laws began to take effect, an epic, if short-lived, fight broke out between Planned Parenthood and the Susan G. Komen Foundation, pitting two of Texas's most powerful women against each other and highlighting the agonizing, divisive nature of the debate over women's health. No sooner had this conflict subsided than the Legislature's decision to kill the Women's Health Program was dragged into the courts for a series of reversals and counter-reversals that is still not resolved.

These conflicts could all be seen as the latest in a long struggle, as women in Texas try to gain control over not just their own health-care decisions but their own economic futures and those of their families. This is the state, after all, from which the modern abortion wars originated in 1973 with *Roe v. Wade,* a case, let's not forget, that pitted a twenty-one-year-old Houston woman and two upstart lady lawyers from Austin against formidable Dallas County district attorney Henry Wade. It's a decades-old battle between the sexes over who knows best and, more importantly, who's in charge. And over the past year, the fighting has intensified. On the one side are the Carol Alvarados of the world; on the other, the Sid Millers. The outcome will determine nothing less than the fate of Texas itself.

·   ·   ·

For most of Texas history, even during the seemingly halcyon period that was Ann Richards's governorship, the goal of Texas women to achieve parity with Texas men has been out of reach.

The men who settled the state were a tough bunch. They had to survive a harsh, unforgiving climate; murderous Comanche; soil that was in many places relentlessly resistant to cultivation; rattlesnakes; bandits; long, lonely cattle drives; and more. But women— to paraphrase Richards—had to do most of that barefoot and pregnant and without any of the liberties or rights that men enjoyed. As the saying goes, "Texas is heaven for men and dogs, but it's hell for women and horses."

Many frontier women learned quickly that they were effectively on their own—the downside to hooking up with a rugged individualist far more comfortable with his cattle than with his wife. They bore, raised, and, too often, buried their kids. They figured out how to make do in the face of cruel poverty. Women had to contend with a challenging contradiction: on the one hand, the clearly defined sex roles of the nineteenth century dictated a courtliness and paternal protectiveness on the part of Texas men that survives to this day. On the other hand, the state was settled in most cases by force, fostering a worship of physical strength and a visceral contempt for anyone too weak to make it on his or her own.

Modern Texas history is filled with stories of women who were held down by what academics like to call "the patriarchy" and the rest of us might simply call "macho white guys." When trailblazing federal judge and legislator Sarah Hughes ran for reelection to the House in 1932, for instance, her opponent suggested that her colleagues "oughta slap her face and send her back to the kitchen."

Governor John Connally's Commission on the Status of Women, established in 1967, found numerous inequities in education and the workforce—but also noted that "overly enthusiastic soapboxing oratory can do the feminine cause more harm than good." It has been frequently pointed out that Kay Bailey Hutchison, one of the most successful females in recent Texas history, became a television reporter in the sixties because, after finishing law school, she couldn't find work as an attorney. During Barbara Jordan's entire term in the Legislature, which lasted from 1967 to 1973, she was the only woman in the Senate; across the hall, there was only one female in the House: Sue Hairgrove, followed by Sissy Farenthold.

What their male counterparts seemed slow to grasp was that, having endured the same adverse frontier environment as their husbands, fathers, and brothers, Texas women developed many of the same characteristics: the indomitable independent streak, the persistent optimism in the face of lousy odds. But instead of speculating in cotton or oil or real estate, women focused on sneaking power from men.

The pseudonymous Pauline Periwinkle campaigned for improved food inspections in 1905 by suggesting that a woman lobby her otherwise uninterested husband after he "has broken open one of those flaky biscuits for which your cuisine is justly famous." During the Depression, when contraceptives were among the obscene materials the Comstock law deemed illegal to send through the mail, one Kate Ripley, from Dallas, used boxes from her husband's shirt company to disguise the contents of illicit packages that she shipped to women all over Texas.

As the twentieth century advanced and women began to win seats at more influential tables, several distinct types emerged. For many years, before it was considered politically incorrect, a woman in the political arena was known as a good ol' girl or a man's woman. This complimentary description meant she could drink, cuss, and cut a deal and probably never cried in public. Many of these women were what today we'd call liberals, people like Jordan, Farenthold, Sarah Weddington, Richards, and Molly Ivins. They may have endured the hollow loneliness of public scorn, but they managed to get the Equal Rights Amendment ratified in Texas in 1972. It's probably no accident that these particular heroines came from the liberal tradition—it's the one that has been most likely to let women talk, even if they weren't always heard.

But conservative women made their presence felt as well. The most successful ones, like Hutchison or Harriet Miers, played an inside game, making nice—or at least appearing to make nice—while quietly accumulating power. Beauty helped, especially when combined with a rich husband, as Joanne Herring has demonstrated. Barbara Bush took a page from sturdy Republican club women and made herself a commonsense heroine in low heels and pearls. In other words, there were various ways to get around men and grab the steering wheel, and over the years Texas women used them all.

Regardless of their politics, both Democratic and Republican women used their power to advance the cause of family planning. During the time when abortion was both dangerous and illegal—before 1973—volunteering for Planned Parenthood was a socially acceptable, even admirable, thing for many middle- and upper-middle-class women to do. It isn't surprising that Farenthold and Richards were big family-planning advocates, but so were the very social Sakowitz and Marcus families, the arch-conservative Hunt family, and George and Barbara Bush (at least until he joined the anti-abortion Reagan team in 1980). Partisanship just wasn't in the picture.

"Over the years, everyone wrote a check," said Peggy Romberg, who worked for Planned Parenthood in Austin for seventeen years. The issues seemed very different in the sixties and seventies: women had husbands who made them remove their IUDs, or who made them quit school to tend to their babies. A woman's sexual history was allowed to be admitted in court during rape cases. Married women who wanted credit cards in their own name needed their husbands to cosign for them.

Then came that landmark moment in the history of women all over the United States. The story of *Roe v. Wade* is, in many ways, the story of Texas women. Norma McCorvey (a.k.a. Jane Roe), raised in poverty in Houston, a high school dropout at fourteen, beaten by her husband, and pregnant with her third child in 1969, tried first to lie in order to get a legal abortion—she claimed she had been raped, which would have permitted the procedure in Texas—and then she tried to get an illegal abortion, but her clinic of choice had been shut down by the authorities. Eventually, two Austin attorneys, Weddington and Linda Coffee, filed suit on her behalf, arguing that her right to privacy included her right to have an abortion. (A San Antonio oil heiress, Ruth McLean Bowers, underwrote the legal costs of the case.) In 1973 the U.S. Supreme Court agreed that state laws banning abortion were unconstitutional. The vote was 7–2.

Nearly forty years of legal abortion have followed, along with an endless stream of bitter arguments and toxic political strife. McCorvey, who wound up having her baby as the case progressed through the courts, later did an about-face, becoming an activist with the pro-life group Operation Rescue. Weddington went on to become an icon of the women's movement. In time, the case they launched emerged as one of the most divisive and politically expedient issues in American politics. Maneuvering from the governor's mansion to the White House, George W. Bush used it to successfully solidify conservative Republicans around his candidacy. Though Bush said he was against overturning *Roe v. Wade,* he talked about promoting a "culture of life," signed the Abortion Ban Act, in 2003, and campaigned vigorously on the issue, using it to draw a sharp distinction between himself and both Al Gore and John Kerry.

In Texas the past decade has seen a sharp turn in the rhetoric of the issue. Some of it is the result of the ferocious GOP primary wars that are now a fixture in what has essentially become a one-party state. Since there is only one election that matters anymore, it has tended to become a contest over who can move furthest to the right. Being labeled a RINO—a "Republican in

Name Only"—is a fate worse than death, and what better way to establish one's conservative bona fides than by passing laws limiting abortion?

A parental notification law for minors seeking abortions passed in 1999 (later, legislators passed a law requiring that minors get permission from their parents before getting the procedure). The 2003 Woman's Right to Know Act, sponsored by Representative Frank Corte, of San Antonio, required doctors to give pregnant women a booklet—tinted pink with a daisy on the cover—that includes information about the growth and development of "the unborn child" and color photos of the fetus from 4 to 38 weeks of gestation. (This booklet is also infamous for erroneously linking abortion with difficulties during future pregnancies and higher rates of breast cancer.)

By far the most important change came as a result of a 2005 lawsuit called *Planned Parenthood of Houston and Southeast Texas v. Sanchez,* which required the separation of all family-planning facilities into two entities: one would distribute birth control and perform women's wellness checkups and cancer screenings while the other would provide abortions exclusively. Government audits were mandated annually to make sure that no state money—no tax dollars—could ever be used to fund abortions.

"I think we all thought this was harassment—it wasn't going to improve public health. But we said okay, we'll get through this too," said Peter Durkin, who was the president and CEO of Planned Parenthood Gulf Coast for twenty-seven years. Still, despite all the conflict over abortion, there remained some restraint in the Legislature over family planning. It was a given that reasonable people could differ over abortion, but most lawmakers believed that funding birth-control programs was just good policy; not only did it reduce the number of abortions, but it reduced the burden on the state to care for more children.

That changed dramatically after 2010, when Republicans won twenty-five seats in the House, giving them a supermajority of

101 to 49 and total control over the law-making process. (The male-female split is 118 men to 32 women.) As the Eighty-second Legislature began, a freshman class of right-wing legislators arrived in Austin, determined to cut government spending—a.k.a. "waste"—and push a deeply conservative social agenda. At the same time, Governor Perry was preparing to launch his presidential bid, burnishing his résumé for a national conservative audience. It wasn't a good time to be a Democrat, but it wasn't a great time to be a moderate Republican either. Conservative organizations turned out to be as skilled at social media as your average sixteen-year-old, using Twitter and Facebook to chronicle and broadcast every move of the supposed RINOs. A climate of fear descended on the Capitol. "Most people in the House think we should allow poor women to have Pap smears and prenatal care and contraception," an aide to a top House Republican told me. "But they are worried about primary opponents."

The result, in Texas and beyond, was a full-scale assault on the existing system of women's health care, with a bull's-eye on the back of Planned Parenthood, the major provider of both abortions and family planning in Texas and the country. As Representative Wayne Christian told the *Texas Tribune,* in May 2011, "Of course it's a war on birth control, abortion, everything. That's what family planning is supposed to be about."

·　　·　　·

For those with institutional memory, the most striking thing about Cecile Richards is how unlike her mother she is. The president of the Planned Parenthood Action Fund possesses none of the folksiness and none of the bite that helped make Ann Richards an icon, maybe because neither quality is really necessary or useful anymore (and could actually be considered a hindrance for the head of a national women's organization in 2012). In fact, on the rainy day I met with Richards at Planned Parenthood's headquarters in Manhattan, she looked like someone who had come into her own. Long gone was the awkward perm she once sported. Tall and willowy, she wore a deep-purple sheath with matching peep-toe heels, a combination of chic understatement with just a hint of flash.

Clearly, she had learned her political skills not just from her mother but also from her father, labor lawyer David Richards. Before coming to Planned Parenthood, in 2006, Cecile was a labor organizer and the founder of two progressive groups: America Votes, a nonprofit designed to promote liberal causes, and the Texas Freedom Network, an organization designed to combat the Christian Right. In other words, to Planned Parenthood's opposition, she's the Antichrist.

Richards long ago learned to modulate her anger for public consumption. But when she gets to talking, she can be extremely frank. "The equity that women have now in education and wages is because of family planning," she told me, leaning forward, her voice hardening just a little. "For women, it's not a social issue. It's not political. It's fundamental—fundamental to their economic well-being." She went on, seemingly unable to believe that she was being forced to restate the obvious: birth control enables women to stay in school instead of dropping out, and to get a degree that boosts their economic status for life. It allows them to control the size of their families so that they can afford the kinds of futures they envision for themselves and for their children. A woman who once had five kids might now only have two—and send them both to college. And so on.

But why, I asked, should taxpayers be on the hook to pay for it?

"Why should we pay for Viagra?" she responded. "Why should men be treated differently? We pay for all other medications. Birth control is the most normative prescription in America. Ninety-nine percent of women use birth control. It's 2012, for God's sake!"

As for the changes in Texas, she was deeply disappointed. She had worked on the border with women who have since lost access to cancer screenings. She didn't think Governor Perry was taking the majority of Texans where they wanted to go. "It's hard to go back home," she told me. "That heartlessness does not track with the Texas I grew up in."

Indeed, in the Texas of Richards's youth (she was born in 1958), lieutenant governors like Bill Hobby and Bob Bullock worked with Planned Parenthood to set up a network of clinics all over Texas, in both small towns and big cities. Texas Health and Human Services offered funding through a federal grant for communities willing to open new clinics for the underserved, and Planned Parenthood provided everything from breast and cervical cancer screenings to abortions. "We were encouraged to open new locations," Durkin recalled, "and the state sat right next to us when the extremist furor erupted—and it always died down."

One reason for the tolerance, Durkin said, was that twenty-five years ago there was a greater tendency to "keep out of a lady's business." "In the good old days," he explained, "the Texas Department of Health was managed by retired military doctors who focused more on afternoon golf than reproductive health care issues. And the governor's office didn't interfere either."

The expansion of family planning was crucial to the general health and future of the state itself. Texas has the second-highest birthrate in the nation, behind California. Historically, it has also had one of the highest rates of uninsured women in the country. Today, more than half the babies born each year are to mothers on Medicaid. Since the cost differential between a Medicaid birth plus postnatal care and a year of birth control pills is huge (around $16,000 for the former versus $350 for the latter), the notion that publicly funded birth control was good public policy had never been a subject of debate in the past. Prior to the last legislative session, the state's family-planning program was serving close to 130,000 clients who had no form of health insurance, the poorest of the poor. And according to the nonpartisan Legislative Budget Board, the state's investment in family planning saved $21 million a year by averting more pregnancies. Ironically, before the last session began the LBB advocated for more money to be spent on family planning in order to save on the cost of pregnancies and births, which last year totaled $2.7 billion.

But that's not exactly what happened.

•　　　•　　　•

"We're going to be making bad decisions all day." It was the morning of April Fool's 2011, a day of important debate in the House over HB 1, the budget bill, and Wayne Christian was just getting started. Christian, from Center, is one of the more ebullient House members, and despite his grim prediction, his mood seemed upbeat. He knew that, thanks to his party's supermajority, power would continue to rest in the heart of the Republican caucus, a place he felt very much at home. A past president of the Texas Conservative Coalition and a successful gospel singer, Christian qualified as a true believer, and on this day he was calm. He was, after all, a man with a plan.

The plan had emerged from several years of strategizing by Texas pro-life groups, and it had as its central goal the demise of Planned Parenthood. To those who oppose abortion, the separation of health-care clinics and abortion clinics that the Legislature mandated in 2005 had not gone far enough. Even though organizations like Planned Parenthood are audited annually by the state to ensure that no taxpayer dollars go to pay for abortions, this arrangement remains suspect to pro-lifers.

"The separation agreement is not really enforceable," said Elizabeth Graham, an attractive, sharp-tongued brunette who is the director of Texas Right to Life. "The Legislature has never been comfortable with giving money to 1200 Main Street and 1201 Main Street isn't getting that money. The funds are fungible." So Graham's organization had been working with legislators like Christian, diligently preparing, waiting for the right opportunity. It had finally come. The tactic was to eviscerate Planned Parenthood through the family-planning budget. Lawmakers, Graham later told me, "were prepared and understood where funds could go. They had assistance from agencies and information that helped them to redirect funds."

House Republicans also had a clever procedural maneuver up their sleeves. Ordinarily, budget amendments are vetted by the Appropriations Committee, which may hold public hearings on controversial issues. This time, however, the GOP legislators kept mum, intending to present these amendments from the floor, circumventing the traditional vetting process. (Unlike his iron-fisted predecessor, Tom Craddick, current House speaker Joe Straus has proved less inclined to prevent such tactics.) This meant the amendments would come with no advice from Appropriations, so members were left without guidelines on how to vote.

Indeed, on April 1, when the family-planning section of the budget came up for review, conservative legislators began attaching a blizzard of new amendments, each one designed to shrink the size of the $111.5 million budget from which Planned Parenthood drew support. First up was Representative Randy Weber, who wanted to move $7.3 million out of family planning and allocate it to an organization that seeks alternatives to abortion.

In support of his amendment, Weber, a conservative Republican from Pearland, cited a journal article from 2002 that asserted that in addition to contraception not eliminating pregnancies, it also correlated to a higher rate of pregnancy among women who use it. (In fact, the article stated the opposite.) Representative Mike Villarreal, a Democrat from San Antonio, asked Weber if he thought that birth control simply didn't work.

"Not for those that get pregnant," Weber quipped.

"Have you ever used contraceptives yourself?" Villarreal shot back.

"Well, you know, I don't think I know you well enough to go down this road," Weber cracked.

Villarreal shifted tactics, insisting that Weber's plan would do nothing to reduce abortions. Further, if they did what Weber asked, members would be moving money from programs that would save the state around $60 million into one that would not save it a cent.

Weber's amendment passed 100–44. Next up was Christian, who proposed an amendment that would move $6.6 million from family planning into a program to help autistic children. After consideration of additional proposals, Christian's amendment passed 106–34. Two more Republican representatives came forward and laid out amendments to move $20 million into early-childhood intervention programs and the Texas Department of Aging and Disability Services. Those passed too. Representative Bill Zedler asked to move funding from "the abortion industry" to services for the deaf and blind and those with mobile disabilities. Representative Jim Murphy wanted to move money to EMS and trauma care, which was operating with a $450 million surplus at the time. Representative Warren Chisum followed with an amendment to move family-planning money to more-generalized medical clinics.

As the night wore on, tempers flared; sometimes it was hard to hear over the members' shouting at one another. Even a staunch Republican like Beverly Woolley found herself moving to the microphone in solidarity with the Democrats. But on and on it went. By one in the morning, the House had slashed the family planning budget from $111.5 million to $37.9 million. The final vote passed with 104 ayes. On May 3, the Senate passed its budget, with the same cuts in place—partly because House Republicans had threatened to hold up the entire budget process if they did not.

By this point, the tenor of the session was clear. As the chair of the Senate Democratic Caucus Leticia Van de Putte said, "Texas is going to shrink government until it fits in a woman's uterus." A little over a month later the sonogram bill went to the governor's desk. "This will be one of the strongest sonogram bills in the nation," declared an exultant Sid Miller. "This is a great day for women's health. This is a great day for Texas," said Dan Patrick, who had tried twice before to get such a bill passed.

Needless to say, not everyone agreed. "I went to an event with Senator [Kevin] Eltife," Patrick told me some months later, "and I parked and a car pulled up behind me and a woman started screaming at me. I've never had that happen. I've had some interesting e-mails too. Just amazing. But I'm a big guy. I can take criticism, because this is the right thing to do to save a life."

By his account, over time the sonogram bill will save up to 15,000 lives. "There will be people alive in ten to twenty years who wouldn't be alive without this bill," he told me. To Patrick, the legally mandated ultrasound isn't an invasive procedure. Critics of the bill further contend that its ultimate purpose is to limit access to abortion, especially for low-income women who may not be able to take off more than one day of work to accommodate the twenty-four-hour waiting period. Patrick rejects this argument too. As he puts it, "The purpose in sponsoring this bill was to improve women's health care." His political opponents, he says, "don't know the facts. They are dealing from emotion." He thinks the claim that most women have made up their minds long before they reach the door of an abortion clinic is "nonsense."

"Most of these women don't know," he said. "No one is trying to embarrass them, but we are trying to save a life. You want the woman to have a choice to have a baby or not, but you don't want them to have a choice to look at a sonogram? That makes no sense to me." (In fact, prior to the sonogram bill, women seeking an abortion at Planned Parenthood could elect to look at a sonogram.)

As the session reached its halfway point, many female legislators grappled with the magnitude of what had happened. Democratic women could at least enjoy the full-throated support of their male colleagues, but moderate Republican women frequently found themselves all alone, treated to a front-row seat from which to view their own powerlessness. To speak up was to be targeted for defeat in the next primary, after all. They dragged through the Capitol with heads down, making apologies to staffers and colleagues for their votes. Ultimately, both Beverly Woolley and Florence Shapiro announced their retirements. The latter told a lobbyist, "These are no longer the people who elected me."

. . .

Shapiro and Woolley weren't the only veteran Republicans to find themselves in an awkward position. Take the case of Robert Deuell and the Women's Health Program. Senator Deuell, a physician from Greenville who has held office since 2003, was known to be both pragmatic and conservative when it came to public health. He supported programs like needle exchange for addicts, but he was strongly opposed to abortion. In fact, he had worked tirelessly since 2007 to toss Planned Parenthood from the network of providers included in the Women's Health Program, a Medicaid fund for poor women started in Texas in 2006. Yet unlike many of his new comrades-in-arms, Deuell favored taxpayer-supported birth control.

If the state doesn't make birth control available, he told me, "we are going to be providing prenatal care. It's the lesser of two undesirables, and that's the point I've tried to make. Do I wish women waited? Yes, but they don't."

Deuell has always favored shifting the services provided through the WHP from Planned Parenthood to community-based health organizations and clinics known as Federally

Qualified Health Centers. There were some obstacles to this, among them the question of whether the FQHCs could deliver the same quality of care. Many FQHCs were already overrun with very sick people. Jose Camacho, the head of the Texas Association of Community Health Centers, which oversees FQHCs in Texas, had insisted that, despite what Deuell wished, the FQHCs could not absorb the overflow, given Texas's soaring birth and poverty rates along with the vast number of uninsured. "We served one million patients this year, at least," he told me. "To think that any health system can ramp up to take, in effect, 20 percent more patients is not realistic."

Deuell didn't give up. The rules of the WHP had been written to exclude providers affiliated with organizations that perform abortions. This was in conflict with federal law, so in 2008, a waiver was granted that allowed Planned Parenthood to participate. In 2010 Deuell asked Attorney General Greg Abbott, who also fervently opposes abortion, to check on the constitutionality of the waiver, and when the Eighty-Second Legislature rolled around, Deuell was prepared with a rider to the budget bill that would reauthorize the WHP while explicitly preventing Planned Parenthood from ever taking part in it. But by May, he had a problem. He could see a disaster looming—the health care of 130,000 women was already at risk because of cuts to the state's family-planning budget, and now, as a result of the political climate, he saw that he didn't have the votes in the Senate to get his version of the WHP reauthorized.

"I guess what took me by the most surprise was an overall opposition to family planning," Deuell told me. The fact that such programs were statistically proven to save money by the Legislative Budget Board was not enough to change hearts and minds, even in a budget-slashing session. "My feeling is that ['the program will save money'] is what you hear every time they want to increase the size of government," said Representative Kelly Hancock, the policy chairman of the Republican caucus. He added that the caucus's opposition to such programs "had nothing to do with the women's health issue."

With time running out, Deuell found himself in the surreal position of joining forces with ultraliberal Garnet Coleman, who was trying to push a bill to save the Women's Health Program in the House. (Back in 2001, it was Coleman, the son of a prominent Houston doctor, who first carried legislation to create the WHP, which Governor Perry vetoed.) This did not go over well, especially with the folks at Texas Right to Life. After a particularly nasty budget committee hearing, Elizabeth Graham compared Deuell to Margaret Sanger, the founder of Planned Parenthood.

Finally, the bill was saved at the end of May by some last-minute politicking—it was attached as an eleventh-hour budget rider. But the victory for women was a hollow one: Planned Parenthood was no longer allowed to participate. It promptly filed suit, as many who had kept their frightened silence in the Legislature had hoped it would. By then, nearly 300,000 Texas women were facing the loss of birth control, wellness checkups, and cancer screenings.

And Deuell, for his part, was still stinging from Elizabeth Graham's attack. "For her to compare me to Margaret Sanger," he told me, "it's beyond the pale."

·　　·　　·

This past January, one year after the start of the Eighty-Second Legislature, the U.S. Fifth Circuit Court of Appeals ruled that the sonogram bill was legal and could stand. (The opinion was written by Edith Jones, a female judge from Texas who has never made her opposition to abortion a secret.) Many women in Texas who had perhaps not been closely following the moves of the Legislature were now discovering the fruits of their representatives' labors. Others were beginning to realize that, because of the cuts to health care, they couldn't even get in to see a doctor for annual pelvic exams. Clinics were already closing, or cutting hours, or charging fees for services that had previously been covered.

The session had made it clear that Republican legislators and pro-life groups were intensifying their fight against Planned Parenthood not just in Texas but across the country. If there was anyone who still didn't get it, the news of January 31 made it impossible to miss. That was the day that the Associated Press reported that Susan G. Komen for the Cure, originator of the pink ribbon, had decided to cancel the $700,000 annual grant it had been contributing to Planned Parenthood since 2005 for breast cancer screenings. (None of Komen's money ever went to abortion services.)

The news erupted nationwide, but in Texas it detonated like an atomic bomb. Komen, after all, was based in Dallas and was worshipped there in almost cultlike fashion. What's more, the organization's founder, Nancy Brinker, was a role model for many Texas women, a radical reformer who back in the early eighties had, as one of her oldest friends put it, "brought breast cancer out of the closet." Before she took on the cause, promising her dying sister in 1982 she'd find a cure, most people wouldn't even say the word "breast," much less "breast cancer," in polite conversation. Brinker, a former PR woman originally from Peoria, Illinois, who had married well, to the late Dallas restaurateur Norman Brinker, built Komen into a $1.9 billion philanthropic powerhouse in a relentless, but very feminine, way. She was also a highly visible moderate Republican woman, and a friend of George and Laura's who was rewarded with an ambassadorship to Hungary in 2001 and a position as White House chief of protocol in 2007.

What happened, in brief, was this: anti-abortion groups had been harassing Komen (and the Girl Scouts of America and Walmart) for years over its support of Planned Parenthood. A very vocal if small faction was alarming affiliates with threats to disrupt the footraces that have long been Komen's major source of funds. John Hammarley, Komen's senior communications adviser, found himself fielding more and more phone and e-mail inquiries about the relationship between the two organizations. "It took up a sizable amount of my time," he told me.

A few years earlier, Brinker, who is sixty-five, began to step away from running the organization. She brought in a new president, who in turn brought in former Georgia secretary of state Karen Handel. Handel, who is strongly opposed to abortion, was hired as chief lobbyist and asked to work on the problem of the protestors. Along with Hammarley, she came up with several options that included everything from doing nothing to defunding Planned Parenthood in perpetuity. Hammarley warned Komen that doing the latter would cause severe problems, so the board elected to cancel funding for one year and then reevaluate.

Komen notified Planned Parenthood, who issued a press release decrying the decision. Immediately, social media exploded with anti-Komen messages—1.3 million on Twitter alone—that ranged from irreverent to near homicidal. Komen seemed utterly gobsmacked by the response. A campaign called "Komen Kan Kiss My Mammogram" sprang up, designed to raise $1 million for Planned Parenthood to replace (and then some) what Komen had withdrawn. Someone hacked a Komen online ad and changed a fund-raising request to say "Help us run over poor women on our way to the bank." What may have been worse were all the blog posts and mainstream media reports that exhumed negative stories about Komen's business practices—how much it spent to aggressively protect its For the Cure trademark, how much of its money actually went to research, whether the organization was supporting the right kind of scientific research, whether its pink nail polish might contain carcinogens, and so on.

There was something very retro about Komen's response—as if they didn't know how to fight like modern women. First, they hid, shutting down all interview requests. Then they tried to cover their tracks, issuing a press release that claimed their decision regarding Planned Parenthood was part of their new "more stringent eligibility and performance criteria" that eliminated any group that was the focus of a congressional investigation. (At the time, Planned Parenthood was the only Komen beneficiary to have such a problem; it had been the focus of a trumped-up investigation, spearheaded by anti-abortion forces, that had come to nothing.) On February 2, a glamorous if somewhat stressed-out Brinker appeared in a video posted on YouTube. Even though stories of internal discord and resignations were already leaking to the press, she reiterated that her decision to end the funding for breast cancer screenings for Planned Parenthood was not political but simply a way of maintaining their standards. "We will never bow to political pressure," she insisted. "We will never turn our backs on the women who need us the most."

In this particular fight, however, another Texas woman, Cecile Richards, would get the upper hand. As the head of an organization under constant attack, Richards was adept at keeping her emotions in check. At every press conference, she was the picture of empathy and calm. "Until really recently, the Komen Foundation had been praising our breast health programs as essential," Richards told the *New York Times*. "This abrupt about-face was very surprising. I think that the Komen Foundation has been bullied by right-wing groups." Meanwhile, Planned Parenthood was churning out fund-raising e-mails, eventually raising $3 million, far more than it usually got from Komen.

Just four days after it all began, Komen reversed itself, and Brinker, looking even more drawn, appeared before the cameras again, this time to apologize and say that the funding to Planned Parenthood would be reinstated. Handel subsequently resigned, berating Planned Parenthood for its "betrayal" in making public Komen's decision to remove their funding. Both organizations now say they are very happy to be working together again.

Other battles have not turned out the same way. In February the Texas Health and Human Services commissioner—who works at the behest of the governor—signed a rule banning from the Women's Health Program any organizations that provided abortions themselves or through affiliates. Perry declared that if the federal government didn't like it, he would find the spare $30 million for poor women elsewhere, regardless of the state's budget shortfall. In March Kathleen Sebelius, U.S. secretary of Health and Human Services, stood among Houston's poor at Ben Taub General Hospital and announced that unless Texas relented, the WHP would not be renewed. Federal law required that women have the right to choose their own providers.

The Perry administration was still determined to stop women from being treated by abortion providers, however, so the Health and Human Services Commission distributed a flyer to clients in the WHP, saying they might have to find new places to go—even though there was an injunction in place at the time allowing Planned Parenthood to continue as a provider while the organization's case against the state made its way through the courts.*

In May district judge Lee Yeakel blocked Texas from keeping Planned Parenthood out of any women's health program receiving federal funds. "The record demonstrates that plaintiffs currently provide a critical component of Texas's family planning services to low-income women," he noted in his twenty-five-page opinion. "The court is unconvinced that Texas will be able to find substitute providers for these women in the immediate future, despite its stated intention to do so." The state is currently appealing.

·　　·　　·

In June I went to a Planned Parenthood clinic in the Gulfton section of southwest Houston. Like most of the organization's ten local affiliates, the Gulfton Planned Parenthood is a modest place.

It sits in a strip shopping center near a ninety-nine-cent store, a pawn shop, and an appropriately bicultural restaurant offering "Sushi Latino." Which is to say, it's about as far removed from the clubby halls of the Legislature or the plush headquarters of the Komen Foundation as possible.

For more than a year, Planned Parenthood, and women's health generally, had been the subject of withering attacks and intense controversies, but the scene inside the clinic was mundane. A television on a wall of the sun-streaked waiting room played some kind of *Judge Judy* variation. By eleven in the morning, the place was filled with people of all backgrounds—African, Guatemalan, Vietnamese, browns, blacks, and whites—as well as both sexes and multiple generations, not only mothers and their teenage daughters with toddlers, but mothers and their teenage sons. Almost everyone was wearing T-shirts and jeans and staring at their smart phones.

With its encouraging posters depicting happy couples and happy families, the clinic is supposed to be a cheerful place, but the atmosphere was like any doctor's office where bad news might have to be delivered about an HIV test, breast exam, or pregnancy test. And lately, the information that clinic director Maria Naranjo has to share with her patients includes the fact that, because of the drastic cuts to the family-planning budget, the clinic has had to raise its fees. The tab for a wellness checkup, formerly covered by state and federal funds, now costs $133—a prohibitive amount for someone having to choose between paying that or an electric bill. She explained to me that most people think the family-planning funds have just run out until the next fiscal year, something they are accustomed to. Most do not understand they are gone for the foreseeable future.

Naranjo, who has worked for Planned Parenthood and other family planning agencies for twenty-seven years, is a bustling, efficient woman with soulful eyes and a lined face. She is the child of migrant workers and was a mother at seventeen. "This is where I can do the best service," she told me. "I know where they are coming from, and I know how difficult it is."

Naranjo has established, on her own, a pay-as-you-go program to keep the clients from staying away entirely. But some do anyway. Those are the ones who keep her up at night—the young immigrant who wanted to get birth control for the first time after having her third child, and another, not yet thirty, who couldn't afford to see a doctor about the growing cancer in her breast. "She doesn't have anyone," Naranjo said of the woman, who is also an immigrant. (Every patient has to present proof of legal status.) Naranjo found a private organization willing to provide treatment, but she doesn't know for how long—or how many more she can continue to impose on their goodwill.

And, of course, there are all the teenagers who no longer have access to free birth control: they now have to come up with $94 for an initial visit and a month's supply of pills. "That's where we are seeing a higher incidence of pregnancy," Naranjo said. She tries to work her sliding scale. She offers condoms, which are cheaper than pills, and then, she said, "you cross your fingers that their partners use them. You know they are going to be sexually active, no matter what you say."

The cycle Naranjo predicts is this: the state government prevents poor women from getting affordable health care and birth control, so there will be more abortions, more Medicaid births, more expensive complications, and more illnesses caught too late. This doesn't seem like a good outcome for anyone, much less fiscal conservatives or those who oppose abortion.

"We are going backward instead of forward," Naranjo said with a pained shrug. And then, like generations of Texas women before her, she got back to work.

Rolling Stone

FINALIST—PUBLIC INTEREST

Never call it a music magazine. Since it was founded nearly half a century ago, Rolling Stone *has prided itself on its long-form journalism. The magazine received its first National Magazine Award in 1971 for a prison interview with Charles Manson. In the ensuing years the magazine has earned more than sixty nominations and has won four awards for Reporting and two for Features (including one story by and one story about David Foster Wallace). But Sabrina Rubin Erdely's "School of Hate" is only the third* Rolling Stone *story to be nominated in the Public Interest category. The publication of this story forced the Anoka-Hennepin, Minnesota, School board to reverse homophobic policies that had led to the suicides of as many as nine children.*

Sabrina Rubin Erdely

School of Hate

Every morning, Brittany Geldert stepped off the bus and bolted through the double doors of Fred Moore Middle School, her nerves already on high alert, bracing for the inevitable.

"Dyke."

Pretending not to hear, Brittany would walk briskly to her locker, past the sixth-, seventh- and eighth-graders who loitered in menacing packs.

"Whore."

Like many thirteen-year-olds, Brittany knew seventh grade was a living hell. But what she didn't know was that she was caught in the crossfire of a culture war being waged by local evangelicals inspired by their high-profile congressional representative, Michele Bachmann, who graduated from Anoka High School and, until recently, was a member of one of the most conservative churches in the area. When Christian activists who considered gays an abomination forced a measure through the school board forbidding the discussion of homosexuality in the district's public schools, kids like Brittany were unknowingly thrust into the heart of a clash that was about to become intertwined with tragedy.

Brittany didn't look like most girls in blue-collar Anoka, Minnesota, a former logging town on the Rum River, a conventional place that takes pride in its annual Halloween parade—it bills itself the "Halloween Capital of the World." Brittany was a low-voiced, stocky girl who dressed in baggy jeans and her dad's Marine Corps sweatshirts. By age thirteen, she'd been taunted as a "cunt" and "cock muncher" long before such words had made much sense. When she told administrators about the abuse, they were strangely unresponsive, even though bullying was a subject often discussed in school-board meetings. The district maintained a comprehensive five-page anti-bullying policy, and held diversity trainings on racial and gender sensitivity. Yet when it came to Brittany's harassment, school officials usually told her to ignore it, always glossing over the sexually charged insults. Like the time Brittany had complained about being called a "fat dyke": The school's principal, looking pained, had suggested Brittany prepare herself for the next round of teasing with snappy comebacks— "I can lose the weight, but you're stuck with your ugly face"—never acknowledging she had been called a "dyke." As though that part was OK. As though the fact that Brittany was bisexual made her fair game.

So maybe she *was* a fat dyke, Brittany thought morosely; maybe she deserved the teasing. She would have been shocked to know the truth behind the adults' inaction: No one would come to her aid for fear of violating the districtwide policy requiring school personnel to stay "neutral" on issues of homosexuality. All Brittany knew was that she was on her own, vulnerable and ashamed, and needed to find her best friend, Samantha, fast.

Like Brittany, eighth-grader Samantha Johnson was a husky tomboy, too, outgoing with a big smile and a silly streak to match Brittany's own. Sam was also bullied for her look—short hair, dark clothing, lack of girly affect—but she merrily shrugged off the abuse. When Sam's volleyball teammates' taunting got rough—barring her from the girls' locker room, yelling, "You're a guy!"—she simply stopped going to practice. After school, Sam would encourage Brittany to join her in privately mocking their tormentors, and the girls would parade around Brittany's house speaking in Valley Girl squeals, wearing bras over their shirts, collapsing in laughter. They'd become as close as sisters in the year since Sam had moved from North Dakota following her parents' divorce, and Sam had quickly become Brittany's beacon. Sam was even helping to start a Gay Straight Alliance club, as a safe haven for misfits like them, although the club's progress was stalled by the school district that, among other things, was queasy about the club's flagrant use of the word "gay." Religious conservatives have called GSAs "sex clubs," and sure enough, the local religious right loudly objected to them. "This is an assault on moral standards," read one recent letter to the community paper. "Let's stop this dangerous nonsense before it's too late and more young boys and girls are encouraged to 'come out' and practice their 'gayness' right in their own school's homosexual club."

Brittany admired Sam's courage, and tried to mimic her insouciance and stoicism. So Brittany was bewildered when one day in November 2009, on the school bus home, a sixth-grade boy slid in next to her and asked quaveringly, "Did you hear Sam said she's going to kill herself?"

Brittany considered the question. No way. How many times had she seen Sam roll her eyes and announce, "Ugh, I'm gonna kill myself" over some insignificant thing? "Don't worry, you'll see Sam tomorrow," Brittany reassured her friend as they got off the bus. But as she trudged toward her house, she couldn't stop turning it over in her mind. A boy in the district had already committed suicide just days into the school year—TJ Hayes, a sixteen-year-old at Blaine High School—so she knew such things were possible. But *Sam Johnson*? Brittany tried to keep the thought at bay. Finally, she confided in her mother.

"This isn't something you kid about, Brittany," her mom scolded, snatching the kitchen cordless and taking it down the hall to call the Johnsons. A minute later she returned, her face a mask of shock and terror. "Honey, I'm so sorry. We're too late," she said tonelessly as Brittany's knees buckled; thirteen-year-old Sam had climbed into the bathtub after school and shot herself in the mouth with her own hunting rifle. No one at school had seen her suicide coming.

No one saw the rest of them coming, either.

•   •   •

Sam's death lit the fuse of a suicide epidemic that would take the lives of nine local students in under two years, a rate so high that child psychologist Dan Reidenberg, executive director of the Minnesota-based Suicide Awareness Voices of Education, declared the Anoka-Hennepin school district the site of a "suicide cluster," adding that the crisis might hold an element of contagion; suicidal thoughts had become catchy, like a lethal virus. "Here you had a large number of suicides that are really closely connected, all within one school district, in a small amount of time," explains Reidenberg. "Kids started to feel that the normal response to stress was to take your life."

There was another common thread: Four of the nine dead were either gay or perceived as such by other kids, and were reportedly bullied. The tragedies come at a national moment when bullying is on everyone's lips, and a devastating number of gay teens across the country are in the news for killing themselves. Suicide rates among gay and lesbian kids are frighteningly high, with attempt rates four times that of their straight counterparts; studies show that one-third of all gay youth have attempted suicide at some point (versus 13 percent of hetero kids), and that internalized homophobia contributes to suicide risk.

Against this supercharged backdrop, the Anoka-Hennepin school district finds itself in the spotlight not only for the sheer number of suicides but because it is accused of having contributed to the death toll by cultivating an extreme antigay climate. "LGBTQ students don't feel safe at school," says Anoka Middle

School for the Arts teacher Jefferson Fietek, using the acronym for lesbian, gay, bisexual, transgender and questioning. "They're made to feel ashamed of who they are. They're bullied. And there's no one to stand up for them, because teachers are afraid of being fired."

The Southern Poverty Law Center and the National Center for Lesbian Rights have filed a lawsuit on behalf of five students, alleging the school district's policies on gays are not only discriminatory but also foster an environment of unchecked antigay bullying. The Department of Justice has begun a civil rights investigation as well. The Anoka-Hennepin school district declined to comment on any specific incidences but denies any discrimination, maintaining that its broad anti-bullying policy is meant to protect all students. "We are not a homophobic district, and to be vilified for this is very frustrating," says superintendent Dennis Carlson, who blames right-wingers and gay activists for choosing the area as a battleground, describing the district as the victim in this fracas. "People are using kids as pawns in this political debate," he says. "I find that abhorrent."

Ironically, that's exactly the charge that students, teachers, and grieving parents are hurling at the school district. "Samantha got caught up in a political battle that I didn't know about," says Sam Johnson's mother, Michele. "And you know whose fault it is? The people who make their living off of saying they're going to take care of our kids."

Located a half-hour north of Minneapolis, the thirteen sprawling towns that make up the Anoka-Hennepin school district—Minnesota's largest, with 39,000 kids—seem an unlikely place for such a battle. It's a soothingly flat, 172-square-mile expanse sliced by the Mississippi River, where woodlands abruptly give way to strip malls and then fall back to placid woodlands again, and the landscape is dotted with churches. The district, which spans two counties, is so geographically huge as to be a sort of cross-section of America itself, with its small minority population clustered at its southern tip, white suburban sprawl in its center, and sparsely populated farmland in the north. It also offers a snapshot of America in economic crisis: In an area where just 20 percent of adults have college educations, the recession hit hard, and foreclosures and unemployment have become the norm.

For years, the area has also bred a deep strain of religious conservatism. At churches like First Baptist Church of Anoka, parishioners believe that homosexuality is a form of mental illness caused by family dysfunction, childhood trauma, and exposure to pornography—a perversion curable through intensive therapy. It's a point of view shared by their congresswoman, Michele Bachmann, who has called homosexuality a form of "sexual dysfunction" that amounts to "personal enslavement." In 1993, Bachmann, a proponent of school prayer and creationism, co-founded the New Heights charter school in the town of Stillwater, only to flee the board amid an outcry that the school was promoting a religious curriculum. Bachmann also is affiliated with the ultraright Minnesota Family Council, headlining a fundraiser for them last spring alongside Newt Gingrich.

Though Bachmann doesn't live within Anoka-Hennepin's boundaries anymore, she has a dowdier doppelgänger there in the form of antigay crusader Barb Anderson. A bespectacled grandmother with lemony-blond hair she curls in severely toward her face, Anderson is a former district Spanish teacher and a longtime researcher for the MFC who's been fighting gay influence in local schools for two decades, ever since she discovered that her nephew's health class was teaching homosexuality as normal. "That really got me on a journey," she said in a radio interview. When the Anoka-Hennepin district's sex-ed curriculum came up for reevaluation in 1994, Anderson and four like-minded parents managed to get on the review committee. They argued that any form of gay tolerance in school is actually an insidious means of promoting homosexuality—that openly discussing the matter would encourage kids to try it, turning straight kids gay.

"Open your eyes, people," Anderson recently wrote to the local newspaper. "What if a 15-year-old is seduced into homosexual behavior and then contracts AIDS?" Her agenda mimics that of Focus on the Family, the national evangelical Christian organization founded by James Dobson; Family Councils, though technically independent of Focus on the Family, work on the state level to accomplish Focus's core goals, including promoting prayer in public spaces, "defending marriage" by lobbying for antigay legislation, and fighting gay tolerance in public schools under the guise of preserving parental authority—reasoning that government-mandated acceptance of gays undermines the traditional values taught in Christian homes.

At the close of the seven-month-long sex-ed review, Anderson and her colleagues wrote a memo to the Anoka-Hennepin school board, concluding, "The majority of parents do not wish to have there [*sic*] children taught that the gay lifestyle is a normal acceptable alternative." Surprisingly, the six-member board voted to adopt the measure by a four-to-two majority, even borrowing the memo's language to fashion the resulting district-wide policy, which pronounced that within the health curriculum, "homosexuality not be taught/addressed as a normal, valid lifestyle."

The policy became unofficially known as "No Homo Promo" and passed unannounced to parents and unpublished in the policy handbooks; most teachers were told about it by their principals. Teachers say it had a chilling effect and they became concerned about mentioning gays in any context. Discussion of homosexuality gradually disappeared from classes. "If you can't talk about it in any context, which is how teachers interpret district policies, kids internalize that to mean that being gay must be so shameful and wrong," says Anoka High School teacher Mary Jo Merrick-Lockett. "And that has created a climate of fear and repression and harassment."

Suicide is a complex phenomenon; there's never any one pat reason to explain why anyone kills themselves. Michele Johnson acknowledges that her daughter, Sam, likely had many issues that combined to push her over the edge, but feels strongly that bullying was one of those factors. "I'm sure that Samantha's decision to take her life had a lot to do with what was going on in school," Johnson says tearfully. "I'm sure things weren't perfect in other areas, but nothing was as bad as what was going on in that school."

.   .   .

The summer before Justin Aaberg started at Anoka High School, his mother asked, "So, are you sure you're gay?"

Justin, a slim, shy fourteen-year-old who carefully swept his blond bangs to the side like his namesake, Bieber, studied his mom's face. "I'm pretty sure I'm gay," he answered softly, then abruptly changed his mind. "*Whoa, whoa, whoa, wait!*" he shouted—out of character for the quiet boy—"I'm positive. I am gay," Justin proclaimed.

"OK." Tammy Aaberg nodded. "So. Just because you can't get him pregnant doesn't mean you don't use protection." She proceeded to lecture her son about safe sex while Justin turned bright red and beamed. Embarrassing as it was to get a sex talk from his mom, her easy affirmation of Justin's orientation seemed like a promising sign as he stood on the brink of high school. Justin was more than ready to turn the corner on the horrors of middle school—especially on his just-finished eighth-grade year, when Justin had come out as gay to a few friends, yet word had instantly spread, making him a pariah. In the hall one day, a popular jock had grabbed Justin by the balls and squeezed, sneering, "You like that, don't you?" That assault had so humiliated and

frightened Justin that he'd burst out crying, but he never reported any of his harassment. The last thing he wanted to do was
draw more attention to his sexuality. Plus, he didn't want his
parents worrying. Justin's folks were already overwhelmed with
stresses of their own: swamped with debt, they'd declared bank-
ruptcy and lost their home to foreclosure. So Justin had kept his
problems to himself; he felt hopeful things would get better in
high school, where kids were bound to be more mature.

"There'll always be bullies," he reasoned to a friend. "But we'll
be older, so maybe they'll be better about it."

But Justin's start of ninth grade in 2009 began as a disappoint-
ment. In the halls of Anoka High School, he was bullied, called
a "faggot," and shoved into lockers. Then, a couple of months into
the school year, he was stunned to hear about Sam Johnson's suicide. Though Justin hadn't known her personally, he'd known
of her, and of the way she'd been taunted for being butch. Justin
tried to keep smiling. In his room at home, Justin made a brightly
colored paper banner and taped it to his wall: "Love the life you
live, live the life you love."

· · ·

Brittany couldn't stop thinking about Sam, a reel that looped
endlessly in her head. Sam dancing to one of their favorite metal
bands, Drowning Pool. Sam dead in the tub with the back of her
head blown off. Sam's ashes in an urn, her coffin empty at
her wake.

She couldn't sleep. Her grades fell. Her daily harassment at
school continued, but now without her best friend to help her
cope. At home, Brittany played the good daughter, cleaning the
house and performing her brother's chores unasked, all in a val-
iant attempt to maintain some family peace after the bank took
their house and both parents lost their jobs in quick succession.
Then Brittany started cutting herself.

Just eleven days after Sam's death, on November 22, 2009, came yet another suicide: a Blaine High School student, fifteen-year-old Aaron Jurek—the district's third suicide in just three months. After Christmas break, an Andover High School senior, Nick Lockwood, became the district's fourth casualty: a boy who had never publicly identified as gay, but had nonetheless been teased as such. Suicide number five followed, that of recent Blaine High School grad Kevin Buchman, who had no apparent LGBT connection. Before the end of the school year there would be a sixth suicide, fifteen-year-old July Barrick of Champlin Park High School, who was also bullied for being perceived as gay, and who'd complained to her mother that classmates had started an "I Hate July Barrick" Facebook page. As mental-health counselors were hurriedly dispatched to each affected school, the district was blanketed by a sense of mourning and frightened shock.

"It has taken a collective toll," says Northdale Middle School psychologist Colleen Cashen. "Everyone has just been reeling—students, teachers. There's been just a profound sadness."

In the wake of Sam's suicide, Brittany couldn't seem to stop crying. She'd disappear for hours with her cell phone turned off, taking long walks by Elk Creek or hiding in a nearby cemetery. "Promise me you won't take your life," her father begged. "Promise you'll come to me before anything." Brittany couldn't promise. In March 2010, she was hospitalized for a week.

. . .

In April, Justin came home from school and found his mother at the top of the stairs, tending to the saltwater fish tank. "Mom," he said tentatively, "a kid told me at school today I'm gonna go to hell because I'm gay."

"That's not true. God loves everybody," his mom replied. "That kid needs to go home and read his Bible."

Justin shrugged and smiled, then retreated to his room. It had been a hard day: the annual "Day of Truth" had been held at school, an evangelical event then sponsored by the antigay ministry Exodus International, whose mission is to usher gays back to wholeness and "victory in Christ" by converting them to heterosexuality. Day of Truth has been a font of controversy that has bounced in and out of the courts; its legality was affirmed last March, when a federal appeals court ruled that two Naperville, Illinois, high school students' Day of Truth T-shirts reading BE HAPPY, NOT GAY were protected by their First Amendment rights. (However, the event, now sponsored by Focus on the Family, has been renamed "Day of Dialogue.") Local churches had been touting the program, and students had obediently shown up at Anoka High School wearing day of truth T-shirts, preaching in the halls about the sin of homosexuality. Justin wanted to brush them off, but was troubled by their proselytizing. Secretly, he had begun to worry that maybe he was an abomination, like the Bible said.

Justin was trying not to care what anyone else thought and be true to himself. He surrounded himself with a bevy of girlfriends who cherished him for his sweet, sunny disposition. He played cello in the orchestra, practicing for hours up in his room, where he'd covered one wall with mementos of good times: taped-up movie-ticket stubs, gum wrappers, Christmas cards. Justin had even briefly dated a boy, a seventeen-year-old he'd met online who attended a nearby high school. The relationship didn't end well: The boyfriend had cheated on him, and compounding Justin's hurt, his coming out had earned Justin hateful Facebook messages from other teens—some from those he didn't even know—telling him he was a fag who didn't deserve to live. At least his freshman year of high school was nearly done. Only three more years to go. He wondered how he would ever make it.

•   •   •

Though some members of the Anoka-Hennepin school board had been appalled by "No Homo Promo" since its passage fourteen years earlier, it wasn't until 2009 that the board brought the policy up for review, after a student named Alex Merritt filed a complaint with the state Department of Human Rights claiming he'd been gay-bashed by two of his teachers during high school; according to the complaint, the teachers had announced in front of students that Merritt, who is straight, "swings both ways," speculated that he wore women's clothing, and compared him to a Wisconsin man who had sex with a dead deer. The teachers denied the charges, but the school district paid $25,000 to settle the complaint. Soon representatives from the gay-rights group Outfront Minnesota began making inquiries at board meetings. "No Homo Promo" was starting to look like a risky policy.

"The lawyers said, 'You'd have a hard time defending it,'" remembers Scott Wenzel, a board member who for years had pushed colleagues to abolish the policy. "It was clear that it might risk a lawsuit." But while board members agreed that such an overtly antigay policy needed to be scrapped, they also agreed that some guideline was needed to not only help teachers navigate a topic as inflammatory as homosexuality but to appease the area's evangelical activists. So the legal department wrote a broad new course of action with language intended to give a respectful nod to the topic—but also an equal measure of respect to the antigay contingent. The new policy was circulated to staff without a word of introduction. (Parents were not alerted at all, unless they happened to be diligent online readers of board-meeting minutes.) And while "No Homo Promo" had at least been clear, the new Sexual Orientation Curriculum Policy mostly just puzzled the teachers who'd be responsible for enforcing it. It read:

> Anoka-Hennepin staff, in the course of their professional duties, shall remain neutral on matters regarding sexual orientation including but not limited to student-led discussions.

It quickly became known as the "neutrality" policy. No one could figure out what it meant. "What is 'neutral'?" asks instructor Merrick-Lockett. "Teachers are constantly asking, 'Do you think I could get in trouble for this? Could I get fired for that?' So a lot of teachers sidestep it. They don't want to deal with district backlash."

English teachers worried they'd get in trouble for teaching books by gay authors or books with gay characters. Social-studies teachers wondered what to do if a student wrote a term paper on gay rights or how to address current events like "don't ask, don't tell." Health teachers were faced with the impossible task of teaching about AIDS awareness and safe sex without mentioning homosexuality. Many teachers decided once again to keep gay issues from the curriculum altogether, rather than chance saying something that could be interpreted as anything other than neutral.

"There has been widespread confusion," says Anoka-Hennepin teachers' union president Julie Blaha. "You ask five people how to interpret the policy and you get five different answers." Silenced by fear, gay teachers became more vigilant than ever to avoid mention of their personal lives, and in closeting themselves, they inadvertently ensured that many students had no real-life gay role models. "I was told by teachers, 'You have to be careful, it's really not safe for you to come out,'" says the psychologist Cashen, who is a lesbian. "I felt like I couldn't have a picture of my family on my desk." When teacher Jefferson Fietek was outed in the community paper, which referred to him as an "open homosexual," he didn't feel he could address the situation with his students even as they passed the newspaper around, tittering. When one finally asked, "Are you gay?" he panicked. "I was terrified to answer that question," Fietek says. "I thought, 'If I violate the policy, what's going to happen to me?'"

The silence of adults was deafening. At Blaine High School, says alum Justin Anderson, "I would hear people calling people 'fags' all the time without it being addressed. Teachers just didn't respond." In Andover High School, when tenth-grader Sam Pinilla was pushed to the ground by three kids calling him a "faggot," he saw a teacher nearby who did nothing to stop the assault. At Anoka High School, a tenth-grade girl became so upset at being mocked as a "lesbo" and a "sinner"—in earshot of teachers—that she complained to an associate principal, who counseled her to "lay low"; the girl would later attempt suicide. At Anoka Middle School for the Arts, after Kyle Rooker was urinated upon from above in a boys' bathroom stall, an associate principal told him, "It was probably water." Jackson Middle School seventh-grader Dylon Frei was passed notes saying, "Get out of this town, fag"; when a teacher intercepted one such note, she simply threw it away.

"You feel horrible about yourself," remembers Dylon. "Like, why do these kids hate me so much? And why won't anybody help me?" The following year, after Dylon was hit in the head with a binder and called "fag," the associate principal told Dylon that since there was no proof of the incident she could take no action. By contrast, Dylon and others saw how the same teachers who ignored antigay insults were quick to reprimand kids who uttered racial slurs. It further reinforced the message resonating throughout the district: Gay kids simply didn't deserve protection.

•   •   •

"Justin?" Tammy Aaberg rapped on her son's locked bedroom door again. It was past noon, and not a peep from inside, unusual for Justin.

"Justin?" She could hear her own voice rising as she pounded harder, suddenly overtaken by a wild terror she couldn't name. *"Justin!"* she yelled. Tammy grabbed a screwdriver and loosened the doorknob. She pushed open the door. He was wearing his Anoka High School sweatpants and an old soccer shirt. His feet were dangling off the ground. Justin was hanging from the frame of his futon, which he'd taken out from under his mattress and stood upright in the corner of his room. Screaming, Tammy ran to hold him and recoiled at his cold skin. His limp body was grotesquely bloated—her baby—eyes closed, head lolling to the right, a dried smear of saliva trailing from the corner of his mouth. His cheeks were strafed with scratch marks, as though in his final moments he'd tried to claw his noose loose. He'd cinched the woven belt so tight that the mortician would have a hard time masking the imprint it left in the flesh above Justin's collar.

Still screaming, Tammy ran to call 911. She didn't notice the cell phone on the floor below Justin's feet, containing his last words, a text in the wee hours:

:-(he had typed to a girlfriend.

What's wrong
Nothing
I can come over
No I'm fine
Are you sure you'll be ok
No it's ok I'll be fine, I promise

.   .   .

Seeking relief from bullying, Brittany transferred to Jackson Middle School. Her very first day of eighth grade, eight boys crowded around her on the bus home. "Hey, Brittany, I heard your friend Sam shot herself," one began.

"Did you see her blow her brains out?"

"Did you pull the trigger for her?"

"What did it look like?"

"Was there brain all over the wall?"

"You should do it too. You should go blow your head off."

Sobbing, Brittany ran from the bus stop and into her mother's arms. Her mom called Jackson's guidance office to report the incident, but as before, nothing ever seemed to come of their complaints. Not after the Gelderts' Halloween lawn decorations were destroyed, and the boys on the bus asked, "How was the mess last night?" Not after Brittany told the associate principal about the mob of kids who pushed her down the hall and nearly into a trash can. Her name became Dyke, Queer, Faggot, Guy, Freak, Transvestite, Bitch, Cunt, Slut, Whore, Skank, Prostitute, Hooker. Brittany felt worn to a nub, exhausted from scanning for threat, stripped of emotional armor. In her journal, she wrote, "Brittany is dead."

As Brittany vainly cried out for help, the school board was busy trying to figure out how to continue tactfully ignoring the existence of LGBT kids like her. Justin Aaberg's suicide, Anoka-Hennepin's seventh, had sent the district into damage-control mode. "Everything changed after Justin," remembers teacher Fietek. "The rage at his funeral, students were storming up to me saying, 'Why the hell did the school let this happen? They let it happen to Sam and they let it happen to Justin!'" Individual teachers quietly began taking small risks, overstepping the bounds of neutrality to offer solace to gay students in crisis. "My job is just a job; these children are losing their lives," says Fietek. "The story I hear repeatedly is 'Nobody else is like me, nobody else is going through what I'm going through.' That's the lie they've been fed, but they're buying into it based on the fear we have about open and honest conversations about sexual orientation."

LGBT students were stunned to be told for the first time about the existence of the neutrality policy that had been responsible for their teachers' behavior. But no one was more outraged to hear of it than Tammy Aaberg. Six weeks after her son's death, Aaberg became the first to publicly confront the Anoka-Hennepin school board about the link between the policy, antigay bullying and suicide. She demanded the policy be revoked. "What about my parental rights to have my gay son go to school and learn without being bullied?" Aaberg asked, weeping, as the board stared back impassively from behind a raised dais.

Antigay backlash was instant. Minnesota Family Council president Tom Prichard blogged that Justin's suicide could only be blamed upon one thing: his gayness. "Youth who embrace homosexuality are at greater risk [of suicide], because they've embraced an unhealthy sexual identity and lifestyle," Prichard wrote. Anoka-Hennepin conservatives formally organized into the Parents Action League, declaring opposition to the "radical homosexual" agenda in schools. Its stated goals, advertised on its website, included promoting Day of Truth, providing resources for students "seeking to leave the homosexual lifestyle," supporting the neutrality policy and targeting "pro-gay activist teachers who fail to abide by district policies."

Asked on a radio program whether the antigay agenda of her ilk bore any responsibility for the bullying and suicides, Barb Anderson, coauthor of the original "No Homo Promo," held fast to her principles, blaming *pro-gay* groups for the tragedies. She explained that such "child corruption" agencies allow "quote-unquote gay kids" to wrongly feel legitimized. "And then these kids are locked into a lifestyle with their choices limited, and many times this can be disastrous to them as they get into the behavior which leads to disease and death," Anderson said. She added that if LGBT kids weren't encouraged to come out of the closet in the first place, they wouldn't be in a position to be bullied.

Yet while everyone in the district was buzzing about the neutrality policy, the board simply refused to discuss it, not even when students began appearing before them to detail their experiences with LGBT harassment. "The board stated quite clearly that they were standing behind that policy and were not willing to take another look," recalls board member Wenzel. Further insulating itself from reality, the district launched an investigation into the suicides and unsurprisingly, absolved itself of any responsibility. "Based on all the information we've been able to gather," read a statement from the superintendent's office, "none of the suicides were connected to incidents of bullying or harassment."

Just to be on the safe side, however, the district held Power-Point presentations in a handful of schools to train teachers how to defend gay students from harassment while also remaining neutral on homosexuality. One slide instructed teachers that if they hear gay slurs—say, the word "fag"—the best response is a tepid "That language is unacceptable in this school." ("If a more authoritative response is needed," the slide added, the teacher could continue with the stilted, almost apologetic explanation, "In this school we are required to welcome all people and to make them feel safe.") But teachers were, of course, reminded to never show "personal support for GLBT people" in the classroom.

Teachers left the training sessions more confused than ever about how to interpret the rules. And the board, it turned out, was equally confused. When a local advocacy group, Gay Equity Team, met with the school board, the vice chair thought the policy applied only to health classes, while the chair asserted it applied to all curricula; and when the district legal counsel commented that some discussions about homosexuality were allowed, yet another board member expressed surprise, saying he thought any discussion on the topic was forbidden. "How can the district ever train on a policy they do not understand themselves?" GET officials asked in a follow-up letter. "Is there any doubt that teachers and staff are confused? The board is confused!"

With the adults thus distracted by endless policy discussions, the entire district became a place of dread for students. Every time a loudspeaker crackled in class, kids braced themselves for the feared preamble, "We've had a tragic loss." Students spoke in hushed tones; some wept openly in the halls. "It had that feeling of a horror movie—everyone was talking about death," says one sixteen-year-old student who broke down at Anoka High School one day and was carted off to a psychiatric hospital for suicidal ideation. Over the course of the 2010–2011 school year, 700 students were evaluated for serious mental-health issues, including hospitalizations for depression and suicide attempts. Kids flooded school counselors' offices, which reported an explosion of children engaging in dangerous behaviors like cutting or asphyxiating each other in the "choking game."

Amid the pandemonium, the district's eighth suicide landed like a bomb: Cole Wilson, an Anoka High School senior with no apparent LGBT connection. The news was frightening, but also horrifyingly familiar. "People were dying one after another," remembers former district student Katie MacDonald, sixteen, who struggled with suicidal thoughts. "Every time you said goodbye to a friend, you felt like, 'Is this the last time I'm going to see you?'"

· · ·

As a late-afternoon storm beats against the windows, fifteen-year-old Brittany Geldert sits in her living room. Her layered auburn hair falls into her face. Her ears are lined with piercings; her nail polish is black. "They said I had anger, depression, suicidal ideation, anxiety, an eating disorder," she recites, speaking of the month she spent at a psychiatric hospital last year, at the end of eighth grade. "Mentally being degraded like that, I translated that to 'I don't deserve to be happy,'" she says, barely holding back tears, as both parents look on with wet eyes. "Like I deserved the punishment—I've been earning the punishment I've been getting."

She's fighting hard to rebuild her decimated sense of self. It's a far darker self than before, a guarded, distant teenager who bears little resemblance to the openhearted young girl she was not long ago. But Brittany is also finding a reserve of strength she never realized she had, having stepped up as one of five plaintiffs in the civil rights lawsuit against her school district. The road to the federal lawsuit was paved shortly after Justin Aaberg's suicide, when a district teacher contacted the Southern Poverty Law Center to report the antigay climate and the startling proportion of LGBT-related suicide victims. After months of fact finding, lawyers built a case based on the harrowing stories of antigay harassment in order to legally dispute Anoka-Hennepin's neutrality policy. The lawsuit accuses the district of violating the kids' constitutional rights to equal access to education. In addition to making financial demands, the lawsuit seeks to repeal the neutrality policy, implement LGBT-sensitivity training for students and staff, and provide guidance for teachers on how to respond to antigay bullying.

The school district hasn't been anxious for a legal brawl, and the two parties have been in settlement talks practically since the papers were filed. Yet the district still stubbornly clung to the neutrality policy until, at a mid-December school-board meeting, it proposed finally eliminating the policy—claiming the move has nothing to do with the discrimination lawsuit—and, bizarrely, replacing it with the Controversial Topics Curriculum Policy, which requires teachers to not reveal their personal opinions when discussing "controversial topics." The proposal was loudly rejected both by conservatives, who blasted the board for retreating ("The gay activists now have it all," proclaimed one Parents Action League member) and by LGBT advocates, who understood "controversial topics" to mean gays. Faced with such overwhelming disapproval, the board withdrew its proposed policy in January—and suggested a new policy in its place: the Respectful Learning Environment Curriculum Policy, which the board is expected to swiftly approve.

The school district insists it has been portrayed unfairly. Superintendent Carlson points out it has been working hard to address the mental-health needs of its students by hiring more counselors and staff—everything, it seems, but admit that its policy has created problems for its LGBT community. "We understand that gay kids are bullied and harassed on a daily basis," and that that can lead to suicide, Carlson says. "But that was not the case here. If you're looking for a cause, look in the area of mental health." In that sense, the district is in step with PAL. "How could not discussing homosexuality in the public-school classrooms cause a teen to take his or her own life?" PAL asked *Rolling Stone* in an e-mail, calling the idea "absurd," going on to say, "Because homosexual activists have hijacked and exploited teen suicides for their moral and political utility, much of society seems not to be looking closely and openly at all the possible causes of the tragedies," including mental illness. Arguably, however, it is members of PAL who have hijacked this entire discussion from the very start: Though they've claimed to represent the "majority" opinion on gay issues, and say they have 1,200 supporters, one PAL parent reported that they have less than two dozen members.

Teachers' union president Blaha, who calls the district's behavior throughout this ordeal "irrational," speculates that the district's stupefying denial is a reaction to the terrible notion that they might have played a part in children's suffering, or even their deaths: "I think your mind just reels in the face of that stress and that horror. They just lost their way."

That denial reaches right up to the pinnacle of the local political food chain: Michele Bachmann, who stayed silent on the suicide cluster in her congressional district for months—until Justin's mom, Tammy Aaberg, forced her to comment. In September, while Bachmann was running for the GOP presidential nomination, Aaberg delivered a petition of 141,000 signatures to Bachmann's office, asking her to address the Anoka-Hennepin suicides and publicly denounce antigay bullying. Bachmann has publicly stated her opposition to anti-bullying legislation, asking in a 2006 state Senate committee hearing, "What will be our definition of bullying? Will it get to the point where we are completely stifling free speech and expression? . . . Will we be expecting boys to be girls?" Bachmann responded to the petition with a generic letter to constituents telling them that "bullying is wrong," and "all human lives have undeniable value." Tammy Aaberg found out about the letter secondhand. "I never got a letter," says Tammy, seated in the finished basement of the Aabergs' new home in Champlin; the family couldn't bear to remain in the old house where Justin hanged himself. "My kid died in her district. And I'm the one that presented the dang petition!" In a closed room a few feet away are Justin's remaining possessions: his cello, in a closet; his soccer equipment, still packed in his Adidas bag. Tammy's suffering hasn't ended. In mid-December, her nine-year-old son was hospitalized for suicidal tendencies; he'd tried to drown himself in the bathtub, wanting to see his big brother again.

Justin's suicide has left Tammy on a mission, transforming her into an LGBT activist and a den mother for gay teens, intent upon turning her own tragedy into others' salvation. She knows too well the price of indifference, or hostility, or denial. Because there's one group of kids who can't afford to live in denial, a group for whom the usual raw teenage struggles over identity, peer acceptance and controlling one's own impulsivity are matters of extreme urgency—quite possibly matters of life or death.

Which brings us to Anoka Middle School for the Arts' first Gay Straight Alliance meeting of the school year, where nineteen kids seated on the linoleum floor try to explain to me what the GSA has meant to them. "It's a place of freedom, where I can just be myself," a preppy boy in basketball shorts says. This GSA, Sam Johnson's legacy, held its first meeting shortly after her death under the tutelage of teacher Fietek, and has been a crucial place for LGBT kids and their friends to find support and learn coping skills. Though still a source of local controversy, there is now a student-initiated GSA in every Anoka-Hennepin middle and high school. As three advisers look on, the kids gush about how affirming the club is—and how necessary, in light of how unsafe they continue to feel at school. "I'll still get bullied to the point where—" begins a skinny eighth-grade girl, then takes a breath. "I actually had to go to the hospital for suicide," she continues, looking at the floor. "I just recently stopped cutting because of bullying."

I ask for a show of hands: How many of you feel safe at school? Of the nineteen kids assembled, two raise their hands. The feeling of insecurity continues to reverberate particularly through the Anoka-Hennepin middle schools these days, in the wake of the district's ninth suicide. In May, Northdale Middle School's Jordan Yenor, a fourteen-year-old with no evident LGBT connection, took his life. Psychologist Cashen says that at Northdale Middle alone this school year, several students have been hospitalized for mental-health issues, and at least fourteen more assessed for suicidal ideation; for a quarter of them, she says, "Sexual orientation was in the mix."

A slight boy with an asymmetrical haircut speaks in a soft voice. "What this GSA means to me, is: in sixth grade my, my only friend here, committed suicide." The room goes still. He's talking about Samantha. The boy starts to cry. "She was the one who reached out to me." He doubles over in tears, and everyone collapses on top of him in a group hug. From somewhere in the pile, he continues to speak in a trembling voice: "I joined the GSA 'cause I wanted to be just like her. I wanted to be nice and—loved."

The New Yorker

FINALIST—FEATURE
WRITING INCORPORATING
PROFILE WRITING

Much of what we know about the wars in Iraq and Afghanistan we learned from Dexter Filkins. In 2002, he was a Pulitzer Prize finalist for his reporting in Afghanistan for the New York Times. In 2009, he won the Pulitzer as a member of a team of Times reporters covering Afghanistan and Pakistan. The same year his story "Right at the Edge" won the National Magazine Award. Two years later he wrote the essay that accompanied Ashley Gilbertson's National Magazine Award–winning photo portfolio "The Shrine Down the Hall." In "Atonement," Filkins revisits the war in Iraq—and reminds us of the price paid for a decade of combat—by bringing together a marine who participated in the killing of innocent civilians with Iraqis who survived that bloody day.

Dexter Filkins

Atonement

I n the early hours one morning last September, Lu Lobello rose from his bed, switched on a light, and stared into the video camera on his computer. It was two-thirty. The light cast a yellow pall on Lobello's unshaven face. Almost every night was like this. Lobello couldn't sleep, couldn't stop thinking about his time in Iraq. Around San Diego, he'd see a baby—in a grocery store, in a parking lot—and the image would come back to him: the blood-soaked Iraqi infant, his mother holding him aloft by one foot. "Why did you shoot us?" the woman demanded over and over. Other times, Lobello would see a Mercedes—a blue or white one, especially—and he'd recall the bullet-riddled sedan in the Baghdad intersection, the dead man alongside it in the street, the elderly woman crying in broken English, "We are the peace people! We are the peace people!" He'd remember that the barrel of his machine gun was hot to the touch.

Once a wild teenager in Las Vegas—"I was a crazy bastard!"—Lobello had become, at thirty-one, a tormented veteran. When he came home from Iraq, he bought an AR-15 semiautomatic rifle, the weapon most like the one he had in combat, and two pistols, and kept them close at night. "You lay them on the bed, like it's your girlfriend, and go to sleep," he said. That had helped a little, but then he moved to California, where the gun laws were stricter, and he'd left them behind.

The marines had shot a terrible number of Iraqis that day—maybe two dozen in all. At times, as Lobello lay awake, he wondered, Whom had he killed? Who had survived? He combed the Internet for names, dates, and addresses; he pestered the members of his Marine company for details and consulted a cousin who had traveled in the region. He piled up documents. At last, the clues led him to the Facebook page of a young woman named Nora: maybe, he thought, it was the young woman he'd seen in the back seat of the Mercedes, with the bloody shoulder. And so, at two-thirty that morning, eight years after he had sprayed bullets into cars filled with Iraqi civilians, Lobello turned on his video recorder.

"It's very hard for me to say this, Nora, but we met on April 8, 2003," Lobello said. "I was with Fox Company, Second Battalion, Twenty-Third Marine Regiment, and our fate crossed that night. I'm not sure if you remember, because it was so long ago now. Almost a decade."

He turned the camera to show the documents he'd gathered. "I have been trying to learn what happened that day, I think, since that day ended," he said. For nearly ten minutes, he spoke about his family and his plans for the future. He asked about Nora's mother, whether she was alive. He talked about other marines. "Lots of the people I was with that day," he said, "they don't do too good sometimes." At one point, he started to cry. "I'm so sorry for your loss," he said, composing himself. "I just think that talking to you guys will help me out so much. I know it seems really selfish. I hope it helps you, too, but really I can't—I can't go on not trying to say hello to you.

"I need to talk to you, if you let me," Lobello said. "I have so much to say to you. I have so much to say."

Lobello switched off the camera and attached the video to the Facebook message. He pressed send and went back to bed.

·   ·   ·

On April 16, 2003, I was driving a rented SUV through the streets of Baghdad when I spotted a crowd rushing the doors of an Iraqi hospital. Saddam's regime had collapsed a week before, and the Iraqi capital, like most of the country, had disintegrated into bloody anarchy. Baghdad was burning; mobs were swarming government buildings; ordinary Iraqis were robbing and killing one another. I drove up to the hospital, Al Wasati, just as a doctor walked out the front door and fired a Kalashnikov into the air. The crowd backed off, but only a little.

Inside, wailing patients wandered around, clutching ravaged limbs. Doctors were treating wounded people in the hallways. There were no lights, no medicine. In the lobby, a doctor introduced himself as Yasir al-Masawi. "There is a very tragic case here, one that sticks in my mind," he said. "Come, I will show you." I followed him down a hallway, into a ward reeking of old bandages and festering wounds. In a corner, seated on the edge of a bed, was a young woman with blond hair, which was rare in Iraq. Her left shoulder was heavily bandaged; blood and pus had seeped through and dried in a dark-red stain. She was semicoherent, talking one second, murmuring in a deep voice the next. In a lucid moment, she said that her name was Nora Kachadoorian.

Two women stood next to the bed: her mother, Margaret, and her aunt, Dina. They told me that, as the American forces closed in, the Kachadoorian family was living in eastern Baghdad, in a neighborhood called Baladiyat. As ethnic Armenians and Christians, they had quietly prospered on the fringes of Iraqi society, running a business that sold machinery. They did not welcome the war. "We thought of leaving Baghdad, but where would we go?" Margaret said.

Just down the road from where they lived was a secret-police compound that was one of the invasion's big targets. As the Americans began bombing, the Kachadoorians drove to a relative's house in Zayouna, the next neighborhood over. Then a shell destroyed the relative's house, and the Kachadoorians decided to make a dash back home. There were nine of them, piled into three vehicles: Margaret and her husband, James; their two sons, Nicolas and Edmund; Edmund's wife, Anna, and their infant son, Sam; Nora; Dina; and a young cousin, Freddy. The Kachadoorians drove quickly, even though the explosion had shattered the windshield of one of their cars, a blue Mercedes. They'd heard shooting, but as they turned onto Baladiyat Street, they decided to keep going. "Our home was just around the corner," Margaret said. It seemed too risky to turn back.

In their neighborhood, a company of marines was engaged in a furious gun battle with Iraqi forces in the State Security building. As the Kachadoorians turned into the intersection, the Americans opened fire. Bullets ripped through the cars, and the three drivers—James, Edmund, and Nicolas—were killed. Nora's shoulder was shattered, and Anna and her baby were covered in blood. Nicolas, seated next to Margaret, tumbled out of the car and into the street. "Nicky is dead!" she screamed. She improvised a surrender flag, she told me, by pulling off the baby's white undershirt and waving it above her head.

In Nora's hospital room, an Iraqi doctor showed us an X-ray of her shoulder. On the film was a cluster of dots where shrapnel was lodged. The bone had been splintered, the shoulder dislocated. "She will be crippled, I think," he said. Nora rolled her head and called out, "Mike!" It was the name of an American navy corpsman who had bandaged her shoulder and shielded her from gunfire. For days, she'd been calling out to him. A second Iraqi doctor appeared, flanked by two orderlies, to change Nora's bandages. The orderlies began to snip the dressings and pull them away from the skin. Nora shrieked. The doctor said he could give her something for the pain, but the wait would be long. "Please give me an anesthetic," Nora pleaded, as the orderlies kept tugging. Then she shrieked again, a long, high-pitched scream that frightened everyone. The doctor winced and left the room. Not long afterward, I left, too.

Margaret had described the unit whose members shot them: Fox Company, Second Battalion of the Twenty-Third Regiment of the U.S. Marines. A few hours later, I found the men camped in a field near Baladiyat Street. During the war, I sometimes asked American soldiers about dead civilians, and the reaction was almost always defensive, even angry. But these marines spoke in somber tones about what had happened. The firefight had been intense—they'd shot five thousand rounds and seen eleven of their comrades wounded. When the Kachadoorians came barreling through the intersection, the marines thought they were under attack. They called to the Kachadoorians to stop, and then they opened fire. When they realized what they had done, they ran into the middle of the intersection—with the firefight still going on—to rescue the survivors. "I still have nightmares about that day," their commander, Staff Sergeant John Liles, said.

I found the medic whom Nora had called for: Mike DiGaetano, a navy corpsman from Las Vegas. He had asked for a helicopter to take the wounded Iraqis to an American field hospital, and his request was denied—the hospital wasn't taking Iraqi civilians. The marines screamed and screamed into the radio, but the answer was no. So they patched up Nora and Anna and the others, and then sent them away. DiGaetano seemed relieved to hear that Nora was alive.

In the days that followed, I saw Margaret at her home in Baladiyat and visited the graves of James, Nicolas, and Edmund in the cemetery at St. Gregory's Armenian Church. Margaret fed me *lahmajun*, a kind of Armenian pizza, and told me she'd majored in English literature at Al Mustansiriya University, in Baghdad. She had read Dickens, Melville, Faulkner, and Hemingway, she said; her favorite book was *A Farewell to Arms*. When Margaret told me that she had a sister-in-law in Canada, I let her use my satellite phone to call. I wrote a story for the *Times*, which ran under the headline "For Family in Iraq, Three Deaths from a Moment of Confusion."

After that, I tried to stay in touch with the Kachadoorians, but our connection was lost in the violence that engulfed the country. Whenever I went to Baladiyat, I asked about them, about Nora, the Armenian Christian with the blond hair and the bad shoulder. When I left the country, in late 2006, at the height of the civil war, I made one last try. No one knew a thing.

Then, this past March, I got a Facebook message from Lu Lobello, whom I'd never met: "I have been trying to get a hold of you for 10 years about. Ever since April 8th 2003." He said that he had been a member of Fox Company. He wanted to talk about the Kachadoorians. "You could ease my PTSD," he wrote. "Please contact me back. Please."

.　　　.　　　.

As Fox Company neared Baghdad that day, Lance Corporal Lu Lobello was one of its most dedicated members. Lobello, then twenty-two, was a machine gunner in the company's Third Platoon. He wasn't especially enthusiastic about the American invasion of Iraq, and he wasn't eager to see combat. But he took pride in his skill as a warrior, and he was determined to acquit himself well. "I was part of something big," he said.

As a teenager at Durango High School, in Las Vegas, Lobello had done just about everything he figured he could get away with. "Drinking, smoking, doing drugs, stealing shit, getting in fights, fucking around," he said. "I thought maybe I should get out of there." The marines transformed him, giving him discipline and purpose and a sense of loyalty to his fellow fighters. They gave him a very big weapon, too: an M-249 machine gun, which fired a thousand rounds a minute.

Lobello had joined a reserve company, which meant that he trained and fought largely with people from the area where he lived. Fox Company's recruits came from Salt Lake City, where many of them were members of the Church of Jesus Christ of

Latter-day Saints, and from Las Vegas, where they had grown up around casinos and night clubs. They called themselves the Sinners and the Saints. Lobello and his buddies were mobilized after the 9/11 attacks. By the time the invasion of Iraq began, they had been training for a year.

Fox Company had crossed over from Kuwait in a blind rush, following the hasty strategy of the first part of the war. At the edge of Baghdad that day, the marines decided to leave their Humvees and trucks behind; in the more populated area, their bulky vehicles seemed a burden. They planned to walk to the big intersection just before the secret-police compound and stop there. At first, everything was calm. As they walked into Baladiyat, women offered cookies and flowers, thanking the marines for getting rid of Saddam. Some of them wore dresses, instead of burkas. Lobello spotted a woman on a balcony holding a string of rosary beads. "We were in a Christian neighborhood," he said.

As the first marines of Fox Company neared the intersection, Corporal David Vidania, the radio operator, fell backward, shot in the head. There was a volley of bullets, and a rocket-propelled grenade exploded in the street. Lobello and the rest of the Third Platoon were a couple of streets behind and ran to catch up. When they arrived, an orange-and-white taxi sat just ahead, riddled with holes and smoking. Five roads met at the intersection, and bullets were coming from all around: from the street, from the secret-police compound, even from a mosque. Marines were getting hit, and the company commander's radio had failed. Lobello entered an abandoned building and ran up the stairs to the second floor. At the top, he found a marine walking around in circles and screaming: "We killed a baby, Lobello! We fucking killed a baby!"

At the time, Lobello and other marines recalled, the rules of engagement, which governed when they could fire, didn't offer much guidance about distinguishing civilians from enemy fighters. The basic rule was to spare civilians when possible, but above all to protect yourself. The way the taxi had sped across the intersection—the way it kept coming, even after the driver had been shot—led some of the marines to conclude that members of the Iraqi militia known as Fedayeen Saddam were hijacking vehicles and using them to ram the Americans' lines. There had already been a couple of suicide attacks on American positions, and the men began to think that they were next. "We decided we had to take out any car that came into the intersection," Lobello told me. He looked out the window, set up his gun, and started shooting back at the Iraqis. He saw a red Volkswagen Passat, shot through and smoldering. A Red Crescent ambulance darted across the intersection toward Fox Company's position, and the men opened fire. "We were lighting everything up," he said.

Lobello spotted a line of cars coming into the intersection a hundred yards away: a blue Mercedes sedan, a white Mercedes, a white pickup. He leveled his gun, looked down the sight. The gunfire from the Iraqi positions, Lobello recalled, was relentless. Some marines below were calling to the cars to stop, but their voices were drowned out by the shooting. No one gave an order to fire, at least not one that any of the marines could recall later. Lobello aimed at the lead car and squeezed the trigger. "I was firing at the same thing everyone else was," he said.

The bullets poured into the blue Mercedes, and the driver-side door swung open. Nicolas Kachadoorian rolled into the street. His brother, James, jumped out of the white pickup and was shot dead. Then the front passenger door of the Mercedes opened. A woman leaped out. She was waving her hands and shouting, "We are the peace people!"

A second woman emerged from the Mercedes, bleeding from the scalp, holding up a crimson baby. Lobello stopped firing, but the Iraqis kept on. A group of marines ran into the intersection. Lobello remembered seeing a third woman in the blue Mercedes, struggling to get out of the back seat. She was bleeding from the shoulder.

•   •   •

Most of Fox Company returned from Iraq in May 2003. The fire-fight on Baladiyat Street was the most intense combat the men saw there. They had been deployed a long time—more than seventeen months—and their commanders were eager to get them back to real life. Less than a week after leaving Iraq, they were with their families. They didn't get any lectures about the challenges of reintegrating into civilian life, nothing about post–traumatic stress disorder. "They wanted us off the clock so bad," one of the marines said.

At first, Lobello didn't think much about what he had done in Iraq, but soon he started to slip. In less than a year, he tested positive for marijuana and was demoted a rank. He tried to go straight and mostly did, but he was embittered by his demotion and began to quarrel with his commanding officers. "My rank was my life," he said.

In 2006, Lobello tested positive for painkillers and was stripped of the command of his squad. He snapped: he denounced his commanders, walked off his base, in Las Vegas, and never went back. "I completely broke down," he said. The marines took the opportunity to get rid of him, handing him a discharge that was "other than honorable."

Lobello is reluctant to blame his experiences in Iraq for his departure from the Marines, or for his drug use. "I was a wild guy before I joined the marines, and I was still a wild guy when I was with them," he said. But others traced his problems to Baladiyat Street. "Lobello was a good marine," Liles, now a gunnery sergeant, said. "The trouble he got into was completely and utterly due to post–traumatic stress. It's not a normal thing for a human being to take a rifle and kill another human being."

After Lobello left the marines, he enrolled in the University of Nevada, Las Vegas, and worked off anxiety by boxing at a gym outside the city. In December 2009, he was called to substitute for an instructor there, and he got in the ring with a woman in the class: Margaret Gryczon, a tall thirty-three-year-old brunette. She was impressed by him—"He's very good at boxing," she told me—and they started dating. Within a year, they had married, taken a honeymoon trip to visit Margaret's family in Poland, and moved to San Diego. Lobello told Margaret early on that he'd been in Iraq. "He told me something happened," she said. "He kind of told me it was something I would have to deal with. He would share bits and pieces with me."

Lobello told me, "She doesn't understand—how could she? No one who hasn't been in a war can understand what it's like. For men, it's like childbirth. We have no idea."

From the moment he returned from Iraq, Lobello found that he couldn't sleep, and he became more aggressive and erratic. Over time, he got worse. Margaret told me, "He loses it pretty bad. He punches walls, breaks things." She said that she didn't feel at risk, though: "He is such a loving and caring and compassionate person. I know the pain he suffers." One time, Lobello ran into the parking lot of his apartment building in his underwear, clutching his AR-15, preparing to shoot a man he believed had been following him. A few months later, he was detained by the police inside a veterans' clinic: he'd lain down on the floor and refused to leave until a doctor examined him. He was given a diagnosis of severe post–traumatic stress disorder. The Marines gave him a disability payment of a thousand dollars a month, and he started receiving treatment, mostly in the form of antidepressants. "I was a functioning fucking crazy person," he said.

Without the marines, Lobello found himself cut off from the main source of his identity. "The Marine Corps is like a church, and I felt excommunicated," he told me. His buddies who stayed in appeared far better adjusted than those who got out—not because of the counseling or medical services they were offered but because the other marines could understand what they had been through. "You're only as crazy as the people around you," Lobello said. Like the police or the FBI, the Marine Corps represented its own moral universe, an institution that gave you license to kill and absolved you of your sins. Without it, Lobello had to figure things out on his own.

A few weeks after he left, Lobello began searching the Web for stories about what his unit had done in Iraq. He imagined that he'd find a newspaper or magazine article memorializing Fox Company's deeds. Despite all that had gone wrong, he was proud of the time he had spent in Iraq, proud of his role in helping to remove Saddam. Instead, on the Web one night, he found the story I had written about the Kachadoorians. He was aghast: here were the dead and the survivors, with faces and names. "What was so weird was that the story wasn't about us," Lobello said. "It was about them—the Iraqis. It just kind of hit me: Oh, my God, these are the people we killed."

Lobello wondered about the Kachadoorians. What had become of them? What would they think of him, or of the other men in his unit? Lobello's father died when he was eight, and he imagined that he could feel at least some of Nora's pain. As time went on, he began to harbor deeper suspicions about the war. How was it that he and his buddies, all good and patriotic young men, had been thrust into a situation where they were almost certain to kill innocent people? He felt guilty, and also powerless.

One night, lying in bed, Lobello decided there was something he could do. He and his buddies may have killed a bunch of innocent Iraqis, but, now that he had the name of one of the families, he could find them. "I thought it would do them as much good as it would do me," he said.

Lobello set up a website, called Finding the Kachadoorians. He established a group page on Facebook, so that former members of Fox Company could recall the details of the day. The project made him feel part of something larger than himself again. "Finding the

Kachadoorians wasn't just simply about physically finding them," he said. "It allowed me to give meaning to this experience that all of us had shared and none of us understood."

By the summer of 2011, he had found some significant clues. Among them was a story in the *Los Angeles Daily News* that quoted a relative of the Kachadoorians, who was living in Glendale, California. As it happened, Lobello had graduated from college and was headed to law school in San Diego, a few hours' drive away. A cousin of his turned up a Facebook page of a woman named Nora Nicola. The last name was different—but it was similar to Nicolas, one of the Kachadoorians who was killed. She was the right age. And Nora Nicola was a Facebook friend of the relative who had been quoted in the *Daily News*. Though it was only a guess, Lobello said, "I figured it was her."

For weeks, Lobello tried to compose a letter to Nora, but he couldn't find the words. Finally, one night, unable to sleep, he decided to make the video instead. A week later, an answer came back. Lobello was terrified: maybe the message would be withering, a condemnation. He waited for his wife to come home from work, and he also asked a grade-school friend and fellow veteran, Richard Shehane, to come over. They opened the message together. "hi lu," the note said, "me & my mother we both forgive you, we know we will see them in the kingdom of Jesus." Then Nora quoted a passage from the Bible: "Do not marvel at this, because the hour is coming in which all those who are in their memorial tombs will hear his voice and come out."

Lobello ran to the bathroom and wept with relief. "He was so excited—I can't even explain the excitement," his wife said. But the feeling lasted only a moment. "It didn't lighten the load," he said. There was something that troubled him about Nora's note. She had left off the second part of the Bible verse, the part that consigned "those who committed the evil deeds to a resurrection of judgment."

Lobello still didn't know where the Kachadoorians lived, and he was afraid to ask. He thought about driving to Glendale to look. The city had the largest population of Armenians in the United States; if she was living there, he could ask an Armenian priest to make the introduction. But he was worried that an unannounced visit would upset the family. "I wanted to be respectful, so I wasn't going to just knock on their door," Lobello said. "I thought there was the possibility that they would not welcome my visit. " Instead, he decided to get in touch with me and ask if I would arrange a meeting.

.   .   .

In July, I flew to Los Angeles and drove down the coast to La Jolla, where Lobello lived in a densely packed apartment complex called Verano, just off Interstate 5. I recognized the man in the video: a square-faced marine with intelligent, searching eyes framed by big glasses. He and Margaret had laid out sandwiches and fruit and set up a video camera to record our conversation.

Lobello might have said "I'm sorry" in the video, but it quickly became clear that his views of his culpability were tangled. "I want to apologize, but not for my actions," he told me, between cigarettes. Under the circumstances—in a gun battle, in an urban area, fighting an unseen enemy—he and his fellow marines had done the only thing they could have done. "Our numer-one priority is to make sure—you go see your friend's mom before you ship out, and she looks at you and says, 'Don't let my son die.' You always care about the people you know the most." While he acknowledged that he had helped kill the Kachadoorian men, he did not acknowledge that he had done anything wrong: "It's not an apology for my actions. I just want to show them that I recognize the sacrifice that they put up. They gave up far more in that couple of hours than any one of us did. Whether or not one of the marines got shot that day, none of us lost our father, none of us lost our two brothers. We just decimated the whole male population of their family."

Jonathan Shay, a psychiatrist who has advised the military on psychological trauma, told me that some of the most severely affected soldiers suffer "moral injury." "It occurs when you've done something in the moment that you were told by your superiors that you had to do, and believed, truthfully and honorably, that you had to do, but which nonetheless violated your own ethical commitments," he said. "It's bad moral luck. Unfortunately, war is filled with that." Typical soldiers, Shay told me, do not regard themselves as murderers. "There is a bright line between murder and legitimate killing that means everything to them," he said. "Any civilian who says that in war there are no rules—that's bullshit." The rules of engagement are central to soldiers' well-being. "They hate it when they have killed somebody they didn't need to kill," he said. "It's a scar on their soul."

The marines on Baladiyat appear to have followed the rules they were given. But at one point Lobello suggested that the rules were far too loose. "What bothers me is that, by the time we got set up and consolidated, the understanding was: if they drive down the street, that's it—it doesn't matter, just fucking shoot them," Lobello said. "But we didn't have one single suicide bomber. And these guys that were running at our position—were they? Were they really? Or did we just shoot them while they were driving toward us?"

Lobello had only the vaguest idea how many Iraqis they had killed and wounded; he could remember only the frenzy of it, the terrifying thrill, the streams of bullets going in. "A lot of times, I think what happened was, somebody would realize, Fuck, dude, we're not shooting the right people. But it was like the beast was already going. You can't say hold on, stop, wait—no way. No way. You can *say*, 'Cease fire. Cease fucking fire!' Well, fuck, all right, man, but let me get off a couple more rounds. It's like having sex with a woman, and she's saying, 'Let's stop right now.' You can't. You're in it."

Lobello might not have felt that he needed to apologize, but he was haunted by what had happened, traumatized, maybe even ruined. He wanted to know that the survivors understood why he had done what he had, even if it was not entirely defensible. And he wanted them to know that he felt their suffering in his own. Lobello did not quite say it, but when I left his apartment I felt that what he was really looking for was absolution.

.   .   .

Driving into Glendale off Interstate 5, I started seeing signs, at restaurants and shops, in Armenian script. I turned on Glenoaks Boulevard, and it seemed like a picture of the immigrant's California dream: a wide boulevard lined with small apartment houses with big lawns and tall, thin palms. When I pulled up to the Kachadoorians' house, the front door was open. Two small children were playing in the yard, and Nora and Margaret stood in the doorway.

Nora was just as I remembered her, with her blond hair and her husky voice, except that now she spoke a little English. She was wearing a tank top, and her shoulder, but for a few scars, had healed completely. "No problems!" she said. Margaret seemed much older, her face lined and sad, but she was as gregarious as before. "Of course I remember you," she told me. The Kachadoorians lived on the bottom floor of a two-story stucco building, downstairs from another Armenian family. Nora was married to a man named Asaad Salim. The children were theirs; Asaad sat on the stoop and watched them.

The Kachadoorians' journey to Glendale had been marked by disasters and miracles, the first of which was Asaad. He'd been a cameraman for Reuters at the time of the American invasion. The day that the Kachadoorians were shot, an American tank on the other side of Baghdad had fired at the Palestine Hotel. The tank crew apparently believed they were shooting at enemy soldiers, but instead they killed two cameramen working for Western news agencies and wounded three Reuters employees. Asaad, who had been on a lower floor, took one of the wounded, a British technician, to Al Wasati hospital. After the doctors operated on Nora, they brought her to a bed in the technician's ward, where Asaad was visiting. By then, her wounds had become infected, and she moaned and cried. "It broke my heart listening to her—I couldn't take it," Asaad said. He found a nurse, gave her some money, and told her to find some painkillers and antibiotics. Asaad and Nora started to talk. A year and a half later, they were married.

The two of them, along with Margaret, stayed in Baghdad until 2006. By then, the rest of the Kachadoorian family, like many of Iraq's Christians, had scattered, moving to the United States, the United Kingdom, Canada. Asaad continued to work for Reuters, until, one day, he received an e-mail from someone in the Badr Brigade, the Shiite militia, threatening to kill him if he continued. It was the height of the civil war, and death squads were roaming Baghdad. Asaad took Nora and Joseph, the couple's newborn son, to Damascus, and eventually Margaret joined them.

For three years, the family lived among the hundreds of thousands of other Iraqi refugees, waiting for a Western country to take them in. Then, in 2009, Asaad and Nora gave staff members at the United Nations a copy of the article I had written about the Kachadoorians, six years before. (Nora's aunt in Canada had mailed it to them.) "Before that, we had no proof that our family had been killed by the Americans," Nora said. Now their application moved immediately. In November 2009, Margaret, Nora, Asaad, and their two sons—the second, Sam, was born in Syria— arrived in San Diego. Within a couple of months, the five of them were sharing the apartment on Glenoaks Boulevard.

Asaad began working as the manager for a valet-parking service, living the reduced life of the immigrant who comes to America in middle age. Margaret took antidepressants, and she spent a couple of nights a week with a Jehovah's Witnesses prayer group at the local Kingdom Hall. When I visited, her memory was flawless. Every time I asked a tricky question, she smiled and said, "You asked me that in Baghdad."

Nora brought out a tray of tea and *lahmajun*, the same Armenian dish that Margaret had served me nine years before. A framed photo of the Kachadoorian men—Nicolas, James, and Edmund—stood on a table next to the couch. "Every day when I put my head on my pillow, I remember this sight," Margaret said, "how my eldest son, Nicky, fell in the street."

When the talk turned to Lu Lobello, Margaret wondered if she had met him that day. After the Kachadoorians were shot, the marines carried the women from the street. Then they dropped off Nora, Margaret, and Sam, the baby, at the home of an Iraqi family nearby. Holding the baby, Margaret approached one of the marines, she remembered: "I said to him, 'Why did you kill my husband and my two sons? We are Christian people. We read the Bible. We do not do anything.' And his eyes just make to the ground."

It seemed possible that they would refuse to talk to Lobello. After he sent the video, he followed up with a Facebook friend request, and Nora accepted it, but a few days later she deleted him. "I think he want to kill me and kill my mother," Nora said, with a small laugh. "He want to kill the rest of the family." One of Lobello's buddies had jokingly asked him the same thing: "What are you going to do when you meet them? Finish them off?"

But when I asked the Kachadoorians if they would see Lobello, they did not hesitate. "If he is asking for forgiveness, then we will give him forgiveness," Margaret said. "God ordered us to forgive. He forgives us, so we must forgive others. Even people who killed our dears."

"I want him to come," Nora said.

As I rose to leave, Asaad pulled me aside. "They need this," he said. "They cry all the time. Every night." His face hardened. "But me, as an Iraqi? If someone do that to my family"—he made a pistol with his fingers—"I would kill him."

.   .   .

The marines in Fox Company had wounds of their own. When I called Kenneth Toone, a former lance corporal, he started sobbing the moment I mentioned the Kachadoorians, and he cried for several minutes. "I'm haunted," Toone said. "I am so glad we found them. I think a lot of us want to see them and say we are sorry. We don't get that chance. There was a different mindset back there: we deal with it when we come back. But wait a second: what were we doing over there? They gave us this power to shoot anyone we wanted and face no consequences. Well, you have to live with yourself. It destroyed me. I'm a wreck."

When Toone went to Iraq, he was nineteen, a member in good standing of the Mormon Church. He was one of the marines who fired into the intersection, and he broke his spine carrying a wounded comrade to safety. When Toone got home, he married his girlfriend, who was seventeen and still in high school. ("Kind of a Utah thing," he said.) They had two children. Right away, he started having nightmares and flashbacks. Military doctors declared him 100 percent disabled and gave him a medical retirement. They also prescribed the painkiller Oxycontin, and Toone found that it helped soothe the ache in his back and keep the memories at bay. He became addicted, and then he left the Church. Three years ago, his wife took the children and walked out. "She told me I wasn't the same anymore. I wasn't. It wasn't fair to her," he said. "There's something about killing."

According to Toone and others, half the men of Fox Company face severe psychological problems. Some are divorced;

some are addicts; some are homeless; many are unemployed. The best known of Toone's disintegrating friends is Lance Corporal Walter Smith, who also shot people in Baghdad that day. Like Toone, Smith left the church after he came back from Iraq, and turned to alcohol and drugs. One night in 2006, he drowned the mother of his two children in a bathtub. He received a sentence of one to fifteen years.

Toone was trying to get his life back together. He had completed a treatment program to get off Oxycontin, and when we spoke he was packing for a drive to Sheridan, Wyoming, to begin a six-week in-patient program for soldiers with severe psychological trauma. But he had not found a way back to the Mormon faith. "I don't believe any of it anymore," he said. "We are atheists now, several of us, because of what happened. I can't deal with the thought. Basically, it was—I think we murdered those people. We murdered them. I don't understand God—whatever, if there is a God. You don't understand how terrible it really is."

It is difficult to know exactly what happened on April 8, 2003. But, as I talked to the Kachadoorians and Lobello and half a dozen other members of Fox Company, it became clear that things were far worse than anyone had acknowledged at first. As Toone told me, "Very many people were killed and hurt that day who were innocent." DiGaetano, the navy corpsman, said that he treated twenty wounded Iraqis, and none were evacuated to receive treatment. Like the Kachadoorians, they were patched up and sent into the streets.

The marines' accounts were irregular, unprocessed, conflicting. They agreed mainly that the fight had been confusing and chaotic. Their greatest fear was that the cars coming into the intersection were filled with Iraqi soldiers. Nelson Wong, a lance corporal, told me, "We were just hearing all these things. People jacking cars. There was no way to validate anything—IEDs or suicide bombers or people stealing taxis." The entire company, facing its first real battle, was on edge. "Especially after Vidania"—the radio operator—"was shot, we were very angry and very pissed off," Toone said. The men's recollections of the shooting are a reel of hideous images: a dead teenage boy splayed out in the back seat of a car; the mother with a mangled arm holding up a baby who was red with blood.

When I asked Bruno Moya, a lance corporal, whether the rules of engagement had been adequate, he said, "Rules of engagement? I don't think I've ever thought about that." He went on, "We got a couple of briefs. They were brief. Generally, we were told that the enemy had no uniforms. Anyone could be hostile." He thought of the killings every day, and, like Lobello, he seemed to be wrestling with questions of culpability. "Of course our force was excessive—but that is how we are trained," he said. "We use maximum force. We didn't train for civilians coming out of houses."

Nick Lopez, a first sergeant who was manning a casualty-collection point near the intersection, remembered that the marines fired at a series of cars, one after another. "There was a car driving right at us," he said. "Two adult males, father and son—we killed them." During the firefight, Lopez said, Fox Company had an unexpected visitor, Brigadier General John Kelly, the deputy commander of the First Marine Division. Lopez remembered Kelly yelling at the top of his lungs, nearly hysterical with anger. "You're shooting civilians," he said. But they didn't stop. "We see another car, a four-door American sedan, and it drove right through the wire at us," Lopez said. "Everyone was thinking, This is part of the attack. We lit the car up. I put in twenty rounds."

A rear door opened, and a teenage boy fell into the street. "All I remember is this kid rolling out. Bright-red blood, lying in the road. These two corpsmen ran out to get him, they jump up and clamp his two arteries that are bleeding. There is a woman. She's screaming, and she's got this black eye makeup. Crying in Arabic, both hands out. She's pointing at her son, pointing at me. I can't communicate with her." Another woman, perhaps eighteen years old, was slumped over, dead, in the center seat. A third was on the ground behind the car, cradled by young marines. "She's shot up so bad, the whole side of her body peeled away, still alive. What do I do?" Lopez said. "I lost my marriage over this. Wonderful lady. You are not the same person when you come back."

I asked John Liles if his men had used too much force. Couldn't they have just shot the engines of the cars? "That's not a fair question," he said. "Thousands and thousands of rounds are being shot; marines are getting shot; there are vehicles literally coming at us. We had to shoot the vehicles. We thought we were going to die."

Liles acknowledged the harm that he and his men had done to the Kachadoorians: "We killed their family. What do you say to someone like that?" But he told me that his conscience was clear—the marines didn't know who was in the oncoming cars, so they had to assume that they were hostile. "I don't have a problem with what we did that day," he said. "I am not going to cry about what happened. That's what we need for closure. It's best to leave it."

And yet many of the marines said that memories of the killing dogged them. When I told Toone that Nora was married and had kids, and was living in the United States, he said, "That's really good to know. I remember that girl was shot. You think about that stuff, and you don't know that they're OK. I'm so glad. I'm so glad. You don't humanize things over there, but you do when you get back here. You realize what you did. You just destroyed so many things. They were just innocent families that day. The cars were piled up like in a junk yard."

Lobello, though, was alone in trying to find his victims. "Lu is just, like, really friendly," Wong said. "The things we do affect him more. I don't want to say I don't care. Lu connects to things more emotionally. Generally, he's more sensitive. He just dwells on it."

• • •

Lobello and I arrived at the Kachadoorians' home on a Saturday morning in July. When the front door opened, Asaad came out first, with Nora and Margaret behind him. Lobello embraced them and tried to say something, then began to sob. "Don't cry," Margaret said, and patted him on the back. They led us in, and we sat in a small, unadorned living room, Lobello on a couch against a wall, Nora and Asaad at a table by the window. Margaret walked heavily to another couch and settled into the cushions. On a table across from her sat the framed photograph of the dead Kachadoorian men.

"It's been almost ten years," Lobello said. "I just wanted to know how you were doing. You have kids. Two boys? What are their names?"

"Joseph and Sam," Asaad said.

"My dad's name is Joseph," Lobello said.

"It's an old name from the Bible," Margaret said. "You read the Bible?"

"I used to," Lobello said. "A lot more than I do now. Maybe I should start again."

As they talked, the conversation kept stalling, with everyone quiet for minutes at a time. Asaad sat impatiently, tapping his foot, answering for Nora. She sat in silence, but it was easy to see that she was as haunted as the others. Later, in an interview with a female Iraqi translator, she told her story with a sad exactitude, explaining that she had even refused to have a wedding party. "I didn't have any brothers," she said.

The Kachadoorians had always put faith before war. Nora's father, James, refused to pick up a gun when he was pressed into serving in Saddam's army; he was imprisoned twice for being a Jehovah's Witness. The same stubborn belief compelled Nora and Margaret to absolve Lobello; Corinthians says that, when someone has caused pain, "forgive and comfort him, or he may be overwhelmed by excessive sorrow." Yet excessive sorrow had overwhelmed the Kachadoorians, too, and Margaret seemed determined to make sure that Lobello didn't forget it.

"You saw us," Margaret said, from her place on the couch. "You are better now?"

"I want to make sure you guys have everything you need," Lobello said. "If there is anything I can do, I am here for you." He cleared his throat.

"You are crying," Margaret said. "You know, I cannot cry. My eyes have no tears left."

Nora stood and left the room, and I could hear her weeping in the kitchen. When she returned, she carried a tray with cakes, Iraqi candy, and glasses for tea. She set the tray between Margaret and Lobello, who were looking at each other.

"You said you are suffering," Margaret said.

"I never sleep," Lobello said.

"I, too, not sleep, every day, you know? Yesterday it was four o'clock, I not sleep. I take the Bible and go to the kitchen and began to read," Margaret said. "I have the same, this depression, you know. I think this is because you are sensitive. We are sensitive person."

"There is not a day or a week that goes by that I don't think about what we went through," Lobello said. He seemed to be posing a kind of equivalence between him and his victims. If this was self-serving, there was also an undeniable truth to it: of all the people in the world, no one else could better understand what had happened.

"When you were in Iraq, and they said the Americans were maybe going to invade, did you guys want us to?" Lobello asked. "Is it worth it? Is it worth your family?"

"Where is the freedom?" Margaret said. "It's worse over there now. More worse."

Lobello turned in his chair and straightened. He had told me that he wasn't coming to apologize—that, however much carnage he and his fellow marines had caused in Baghdad that day, they had had no choice. Now, sitting with the Kachadoorians, he seemed to waver. "We thought that any vehicle, you know, was going to try to hurt us," he said. "I don't know if it was your vehicle or one before that almost ran over one of our guys. So, once that happened, we just figured—it was just what we ended up doing."

Margaret wasn't listening. She was talking about the marine she had confronted after the shooting in Baghdad. "When I look at him, his eyes go to the ground," she said.

Lobello persisted. "We just had no idea that there were families out there," he said. "What we thought at first was, Why are they driving here? We didn't understand."

Margaret's eyes were unfocused, somewhere else. The family had been just a few feet from home when the firing started. "Our house," she said.

Lobello leaned forward, struggling to find words. For nearly a decade, he had grappled with that moment when he looked down the barrel of his M-249 and into the blue Mercedes and pulled the trigger. "We just thought you could hear the guns— that you couldn't be friendly people," he said. "It just got so confusing. When we realized what happened, everyone shut down. As soon as we realized, Look, man, what did we do? people started crying."

Lobello sank into the couch and exhaled. The cakes sat on the tray, untouched. Nora, her back to the window, looked at him and said nothing.

"Now you are comfortable that we gave you forgiveness?" Margaret said.

"I feel very good meeting you," Lobello said.

"But, you know, forgiveness is something strong—I think not everyone would say, 'I forgive you,'" Margaret said. "We forgive you, but don't think we forget our dears."

"Yeah," Lobello said. His eyes turned to the floor.

"But we want you not to be hurt," Margaret said. "It's not your fault. I am right?"

Lobello began to cry. "Asaad, I need a cigarette." He sounded as though he had come up for air.

"Let's go," Asaad said, standing up, and the two men walked together into the front yard.

In the Bible, Numbers 31 prescribes a purifying ritual for soldiers returned from war: a cleanse of fire and water. American culture has no such rituals. Instead, it has legal constructs, like the rules of engagement—printed on cards to fit in your wallet—that allow soldiers like the men in Lobello's unit to feel that they have merely done what they should. They are absolved even before they come home.

In Iraq, a tribal society, guilt is traditionally expunged by *fasil*, the payment of blood money. A man is killed, the tribes meet, a price is agreed on, and the act is, if not forgotten, then at least set aside. Life goes on. When the war began, the Americans acted without regard for Iraq's traditions and in so doing took a tiny insurgency and helped make it enormous—multiplying their enemies by obliging entire families and tribes to take revenge. Eventually, they caught on, and began making payments to the families of those they had wrongly killed. It worked. I saw Iraqis who had sworn eternal hostility put away their anger in an instant.

But in a war that killed 4,000 people on one side and 100,000 on the other, neither system—of legal delineation or of paid recompense—can suffice. What Lobello was doing was more personal: he had come before the Kachadoorians, whose sons he had killed, to beg for their forgiveness. Jonathan Shay, the psychiatrist, told me that Lobello was a supplicant, making the only plea he could: "I don't have money to give you. I am not going to take my life. I can't give my blood. All I can give you is my anguish."

Out the window, I saw Asaad and Lobello chatting as they smoked, looking like neighbors. For a moment, the two women sat quietly. I unwrapped a piece of candy. Finally, Nora spoke. "We want to help him," she said.

"Some people say, 'No, we must revenge'—they say, 'Eye for an eye,'" Margaret said. "We aren't like those people."

When the men came back in, they seemed relaxed, almost buoyant. Everyone sat for a while longer, talking about their families. The hard work, it seemed, was done.

At last, Lobello said, "Well, I guess it's time."

"I appreciate that you came," Nora said. "You are like my brother. We are brother and sister."

Margaret looked exhausted but serene. "You have done as best you can to come here and say I did it," she said. "I appreciate this."

"We have more in common, and we understand each other, more than anyone I meet," Lobello said.

Margaret looked toward the family photograph, and said, "You remind me of my older son, Nicolas"—one of the men who had died on Baladiyat Street. "Even your behavior. Your looking. Everything. Everything. Believe me."

Lobello nodded, with his hands clasped, seeming relieved.

"Everything is OK now," Margaret said. "You are welcome to our house. I thank you very much. This is good behavior, you know."

"Can I have a hug now?" Lobello asked.

Margaret pulled herself up from the couch. Lobello was waiting for her. "All us are not perfect," Margaret said, and they embraced.

．　　　．　　　．

When Lobello got back to San Diego, he told his buddies what he had done. Most of them were happy, he said, and some, like Mike DiGaetano, said that they wanted to go to Glendale, too. Lobello started to make plans—to introduce the Kachadoorians to his wife, even to speak to lawmakers about compensating Iraqis like them. "He was so happy that he met them," his wife, Margaret, said. "He seemed at peace. I can just see the relief he feels for being forgiven." He still couldn't sleep, he said, but the meeting in Glendale had helped ease his anguish, and especially because it had helped the Kachadoorians, too. Asaad sometimes calls him for advice on adapting to American life, Lobello told me. "This is just the beginning," he said.

A few days after the meeting, he got a Facebook message from Nora. It was written in the same carefree, unpunctuated English as the one she had sent a year before: "when you came i feel so happy & i feel doing grate on my life & with my family, i really changed . . . & the same time i feel i get a third brother & the third son to my mom . . . thanks to you for every thing."

Reading the message, Lobello noticed that Nora had confirmed him as a friend.

Esquire

Once a month, all year round,
Esquire *delivers a tutorial on
magazine making. Whether it's
the front-of-the-book section
"Man at His Best," service
packages like "Fatherhood for
Men" (track down the June–July
2012 issue), or the award-winning
tablet edition,* Esquire *is, in the
words of the National Magazine
Awards judges, "riotous and
energetic . . . edgy yet accessible."
But few would argue with the
notion that the best of* Esquire *is
its long-form journalism—the work
of writers like Tom Junod, Luke
Dittrich, and, of course, Chris
Jones, whose stories have won*
Esquire *National Magazine
Awards twice in the last decade. In
"The Big Book," we get the rare
opportunity to see two formidable
reporters at work—Jones and his
subject, the Pulitzer-winning
biographer of Lyndon Johnson,
Robert Caro.*

Chris Jones

The Big Book

I. The Fisk Building

On the twenty-second floor of the Fisk Building in New York—
an elegant brick giant built in 1921, stretching an entire block
of West Fifty-seventh Street between Broadway and Eighth
Avenue—the hallways are lined with doors bearing gold plaques.
The plaques reveal the professions of the people at work behind
them: lawyers, accountants, financial advisors. But one plaque
displays only a name, with no mention of the man's business:
ROBERT A. CARO.

Behind that door on this February morning, as on most
mornings for the twenty-two years he has occupied this office,
Caro is hunched over his desk. His tie is still carefully knotted;
his hair is slicked back. But his fingers are black with pencil. In
front of him is a pile of white paper: the galleys for *The Passage of
Power,* the fourth book in his enormous biography, *The Years
of Lyndon Johnson.* The seventy-six-year-old Caro has worked on
this project nearly every day since 1974; he has been working on
this particular volume for ten years. In most cases, once a book
reaches galleys—once it has been designed and typeset and a few
preliminary copies printed, unbound—it is finished, or close to
it. All that remains is one last pass. This is not true for Caro. For
him, the galleys are simply another stage of construction. Less

than three months before 300,000 copies of his book are due to be in stores on May 1, Caro has torn down and rebuilt the fifth paragraph on the 452nd page—and torn it down again. (It is, in fact, the fifth paragraph on the 2,672nd page of his work, factoring in the first three volumes of the series: *The Path to Power, Means of Ascent*, and *Master of the Senate*.) Now nearly every word of it sits dismantled in front of him like the pieces of a watch. He starts fresh. "The defeat had repercussions beyond the Court," he writes.

This was meant to be the last of the Johnson books, but it is not. *The Passage of Power* spans barely four years in 605 pages. It picks up Johnson's story with the 1960 Democratic nomination, won by a young senator from Massachusetts named John F. Kennedy, and it ends with President Lyndon Johnson passing the Civil Rights Act in 1964. There is an assassination in between. On two large rectangular bulletin boards, Caro has carefully pinned up his outline for his next volume, the fifth book, the rest of the story: Vietnam, resignation, defeat. The pages of that outline overlap the lighter rectangles where the outline for the fourth book had been pinned for so many years. "I don't feel my age," Caro says, "so it's hard for me to believe so much time has passed." He knows the last sentence of the fifth book, he says—the very last sentence. He knows what stands between him and those final few words, most immediately the fifth paragraph on page 2,672. He digs his pencil back into the paper.

This room is almost a temple to timelessness. Caro has worked with the same set of tools since 1966, when he began his first book, *The Power Broker*, his definitive 1,162-page biography of Robert Moses, the controversial New York planner and builder. For so many writers, for most of them, *The Power Broker*, which won a Pulitzer Prize in 1975, would represent their crowning achievement; for Caro, it was just the beginning. Back then, he and his wife, Ina, lived in a pretty little house in Roslyn, Long Island—he was a reporter at *Newsday*—and one of the great crumbling neighboring estates had a fire sale. Caro went. He bought a chess set, and he bought a lamp. The lamp was bronze and heavy and sculpted, a chariot rider pulled along by two rearing horses. "It cost seventy-five dollars," Caro remembers. The chess set is hidden away under a couch in their apartment on Central Park West. The lamp is here on his desk, spilling light onto his galleys. Except for a brief period when he couldn't afford an office, when Caro worked instead in the Allen Room at the New York Public Library, he has written every word of every one of his books in the same warm lamplight, millions of words under the watch of that chariot rider and his two horses.

"Nobody believes this, but I write very fast," he says.

Before he writes, however, he sits at his desk, and he looks out his window at the glass building across the street, and he thinks about what each of his books is to become. In those quiet moments, he remembers the words of one of his professors from when Caro was a young man at Princeton, studying literature. The professor was the critic and poet R. P. Blackmur, and Caro, who always wrote his assignments in a hurry, under the pressure of deadline, and who usually received good grades for his rushed work, thought he had fooled him. Blackmur was not fooled: "You're not going to achieve what you want to achieve, Mr. Caro, unless you stop thinking with your fingers," the poet said.

So Caro knits together his fingers until he knows what his book is about. Once he is certain, he will write one or two paragraphs—he aims for one, but he usually writes two, a consistent Caro math—that capture his ambitions. Those two paragraphs will be his guide for as long as he's working on the book. Whenever he feels lost, whenever he finds himself buried in his research or dropping the thread—over the course of ten years, a man can become a different man entirely—he can read those two paragraphs back to himself and find anchor again.

The Passage of Power, more than anything else, is a book of transition. Caro met Johnson only once, just shook his hand, in

1964; it was the day Ted Kennedy was in his plane crash, and Caro covered Johnson's visit to the hospital. Johnson was at his greatest height just then, and this book lifts us up there with him. The '60 election; Johnson's miserable, lonely period as vice president; his blood feud with Robert Kennedy; the assassination; the aftermath and Johnson's overwhelming assertion of political power—it feels in some ways as though each chapter could have been a book unto itself. When Caro talks about his work, about his moments of discovery, about those afternoons when the words just pour out of him, that this book is coming out at all seems like a miracle, as though a decade weren't nearly enough time.

But time is constantly falling away. Luckily, Caro has always had a second anchor. The way he knows the last line for the final volume on Johnson, he has always known the last line for each book before he writes the rest of it. "This is the way I do it," he says. "I'm not saying this is the right way to do it, but this is the right way for me to do it." He has done it this way since he sat in Flushing Meadows Park in 1967, watching Robert Moses dedicate "a huge marble bench for reflection donated by the Roman Catholic Diocese of New York," Caro later wrote. In that moment at the park, Caro found himself grasping. He had already done so much reporting, but he still couldn't see the shape of *The Power Broker*. "It was so big, so immense," he says, "I couldn't figure out what to do with the material." Then he watched Moses give his dedication. "Someday, let us sit on this bench and reflect on the gratitude of man," Moses said over loudspeakers. The builder was already being broken down by then, his legacy already starting to crumble, and his few still-loyal lieutenants in the audience nodded and began to whisper to one another: Couldn't people see what he had done? Why weren't they grateful?

Why weren't they grateful?

Caro had his last line. "All of a sudden, I knew what the book was."

He gestures at the pile of paper on his desk.

"So with every book," he says, "I have to write to the last line."

II. The Random House Tower

Standing just around the corner from the Fisk Building, the head-quarters of Random House rises fifty-two stories over Broadway; from certain angles, it looks a little like three books on a shelf. Finished in 2002, after Random House was taken over by the German publishing giant Bertelsmann AG, the tower is black and square-shouldered and enormous enough to require a tuned liquid damper to gentle its sway. Random House and its many divisions occupy the first twenty-six stories. Hidden away in the middle of them is Knopf, named for its founder, Alfred A. Knopf, who began publishing books in 1915. Although Knopf was acquired by Random House in 1960 and merged corporately with Doubleday in 2008, it has kept its name and its distinct identity, mostly because it has kept its people, too.

Its iconic editor in chief, sixty-nine-year-old Sonny Mehta, only the third in Knopf's history, arrived from England in 1987. Today he is sitting behind his desk in his corner office, a wall of books looming over his shoulders. "We need the book," Mehta says, referring to the galleys that Caro was supposed to have returned days ago. There is no panic in Mehta's voice, still with its soft English accent; there is no urgency. He is making a simple statement of fact.

He inherited Caro—"At Knopf, everything is inherited," Mehta says—from his storied predecessor, Robert Gottlieb. Now eighty years old, Gottlieb is still on the payroll; he still has an office of his own. He isn't often in it anymore, but today he's behind his own desk, surrounded by his own books. Gottlieb remains what he always has been: a charming egotist, a publishing giant, and Caro's principal editor, which he was even for the five years he left to edit *The New Yorker*, and which he is now, twenty-five years after Mehta's arrival. "We think continuity's important," Mehta says.

Neither Mehta nor Gottlieb is the most senior member of the staff here. That is a small, whispering seventy-year-old woman named Katherine Hourigan, Knopf's managing editor. She began working for Knopf in 1963, when Kennedy was still president, arriving in plenty of time to have helped Gottlieb edit every one of Caro's books, starting with *The Power Broker*. Her tiny office, stacked so high with paper that it feels like a nest, like a cocoon, also has a desk somewhere in it, and like the others, she is at it today. The three of them are each sitting in their offices, each buried in a book, trying to ignore the passage of time.

But May 1 is coming fast. They need Caro to finish. Less than three months is a finger snap in the anachronism that is modern publishing, especially at a publisher like Knopf, especially for a book so big, especially when the author is rewriting whole sections of the book in black pencil. "We should be getting the galleys back any time," Hourigan says, smiling a hopeful smile. She, like Mehta and Gottlieb, doesn't seem to have any idea that Caro is locked inside his office on the twenty-second floor of the Fisk Building, jammed hard against the fifth paragraph of page 452.

When Mehta arrived in America, he was a roaring presence, a drinker and smoker and larger-than-lifer. That could not last. There have been heart surgeries, and today there is a persistent cough. Tomorrow he leaves for four weeks of rest, in part to try to clear his lungs. Now he pulls each of Caro's books off his shelf, *The Power Broker* and the first three Johnson volumes. He stacks them on his desk like blocks, resting his hand on top of the pile, saving a place for the next one. "I can't imagine this being done or even attempted by anyone else," Mehta says, almost to himself. "He's given over so much of his life to another guy."

It's not just Caro's single-mindedness that makes repeating *The Years of Lyndon Johnson* a modern impossibility. The world outside his office has changed in the nearly four decades since he began. Publishers might like to pretend that they're different from other manufacturers, or at least that they're farms rather than factories, but they're not. Books like Caro's don't make corporate sense anymore, if they ever did. They require not just staggering investments of time but also of money, of jet fuel and paper and cloth. There will be five books now rather than four—and in the beginning, there were meant to be three—partly because they became victims of their own physical scale. Mehta remembers reading a version of what was then supposed to be the first half of the final book, most of these 605 pages, during his Christmas vacation more than a year ago, and deciding he couldn't cut a word of it. "I was just completely absorbed," he says. But he also knew that so much of Johnson's story remained. Almost by necessity, half of a book became all of one. "The alternative," Mehta says, "was producing a book that was going to make *The Power Broker* look like something portable."

Gottlieb did the same math and agreed. In an industry that survives mostly by lying to itself, he is an antiromantic, an unsentimentalist. When he edits Caro, they sit side by side at a conference table and go through the pile in front of them, page by tattered page, Gottlieb attacking anything that reads too much like writing, too much like nostalgia or indulgence. He and Caro have mellowed with age, but they have fought bitter fights, fights that have caused people to close their office doors hundreds of feet away. "Everything to him is as serious as everything else," Gottlieb says. "When we came to something like a semicolon, it was war."

In their little circle, their well-established ecosystem, Mehta is the patient patron. Hourigan is the heart; her job is to provide the warmth, the enthusiasm. (Gottlieb calls her Caro's "love slave.") "Is there a thrill?" Hourigan says when asked about the feeling she has when a fresh batch of Caro's pages lands on her desk. "Are you kidding? It's unbelievable. It's a masterpiece is what it is." Gottlieb is the taskmaster. ("I can remember when he told me, 'Not bad,'" Caro says. "Once.") Gottlieb and Caro, bound for forty years, rarely see each other socially. Theirs is a professional relationship, clear-eyed and clinical.

Yet they are also prisoners of a mutual faith. "Bob is convinced that without me, he cannot function," Gottlieb says. "I have explained to him for years that it isn't the truth. It isn't the truth. But because he believes it to be true, it is true." And Gottlieb has given over so much of his own life to Caro, has fought so hard over semicolons, because he believes something else to be true. "These books will live forever," Gottlieb says. "We all know that."

Gottlieb has questioned the veracity of Caro's reporting only once. There was a single paragraph that stood out on what would become the 214th page of *The Power Broker*. In it, Bella and Emanuel Moses, Robert's parents, were depicted at their summer lodge at Camp Madison, a camp for poor and immigrant children that Bella had helped found. There, they were leafing through the *New York Times* one morning in 1926, Caro wrote, when they learned of a $22,000 judgment against their son for illegal appropriations. Caro included a quote from Bella Moses, who was long dead: "Oh, he never earned a dollar in his life and now we'll have to pay this."

How, Gottlieb asked Caro, did he get that quote?

Caro told the story. Moses had instructed friends and close associates not to talk to him. Shut out, Caro then drew a series of concentric circles on a piece of paper. In the center, he put Moses. The first circle was his family, the second his friends, the third his acquaintances, and so on. "As the circles grew outward," Caro says, "there were people who'd only met him once. He wasn't going to be able to get to them all." Caro started with the widest circle, unearthing, among other things, the attendance rolls and employment records from Camp Madison. Now some four decades later, Caro tracked down, using mostly phone books at the New York Public Library, every now-adult child and every now-retired employee who might offer him some small detail about Robert's relationship with his parents. One of the employees he found was the camp's social worker, Israel Ben Scheiber, who also happened to deliver the *New York Times* to Bella and Emanuel Moses at their lodge each morning. Scheiber was standing there when Bella had expressed her frustration with her deadbeat son, and he remembered the moment exactly.

"So that's how," Caro told Gottlieb.

"Every step of that story is by all ordinary standards insane," Gottlieb says today. "But he didn't say any of it as though it were remarkable. We're dealing with an incredibly productive, wonderful mania."

III. The Wall of Glass

The building that fills almost the entire view from Caro's office was not always made of glass. For decades, 1775 Broadway—the old *Newsweek* building—was a wall of bricks. But in 2008, its owners decided that bricks made it look old, especially because the neighborhood was changing. Caro watched out his window while the old building was wrapped, panel by blue panel, in glass. Now, most of the time, all Caro can see is a reflection of his city in front of him. But if the light is right, he can see through that new glass and remember the bricks underneath.

It wasn't long after his third volume, *Master of the Senate*, came out to a rapturous reception in 2002, winning a Pulitzer Prize and a National Book Award, when Robert Caro nearly died. He began to feel a searing pain in his guts. "I thought I was going to lose him," Ina says. "I don't know what I would have done without him." He doesn't like to talk about his illness—what the people close to him call "the scare"—but Caro confesses that he was struck down by necrotizing pancreatitis, a painful and often fatal inflammation of the pancreas. He lost an entire year of work. That was the first time he confronted the prospect of not finishing. He has not confronted it much since. "I don't like to think about that," he says, his blackened hand waving away the air around him. "Then I might feel like I have to rush. I don't want to rush." He doesn't want four of his books to be made out of bricks and the fifth to be made out of glass. He would rather leave the fifth book unwritten than have it feel different from the rest. (Caro has requested in his will that nobody finish it for him, either.)

After Caro composes his one or two anchor paragraphs, he writes his outline, the first of his outlines. This is the one that he pins onto his bulletin boards: maybe two dozen pages, typewritten on his Smith-Corona Electra 210. ("It's like giving your fingers wings," the advertisements in *Life* magazine read in 1967. "They just kiss the keys. Never punch them." Caro has nine spares that he can cannibalize for parts, and he collects ribbon like a hoarder.) Here, he writes only the briefest sketches of scenes, entire chapters reduced to single lines: *His Depression* or *The Cuban Missile Crisis*. "Once that's done," Caro says, "I don't change it." He has his frame.

Then he writes a fuller outline that usually fills three or four notebooks, throwing himself into the filing cabinets that surround him, the yields from nearly four decades of research. Caro has spent vast stretches of his life poring over documents, mostly at the Johnson Library in Austin—it alone contains forty-five million pages, held in red and gray boxes, many of which he is the only visitor ever to have opened, rows and rows of boxes stretched across four floors—and interviewing hundreds of subjects. Some have stopped talking to him; he lost Lady Bird Johnson's ear after the first book. Some have refused to talk to him altogether; Bill Moyers, the journalist and Johnson's former press secretary, has steadfastly said no for thirty-eight years. (Awkwardly, Moyers also has an office in the Fisk Building. Moyers did not respond to requests for an interview for this story, either.)

But most people, even people who were reticent at first, ended up talking to Caro. They came to understand what his books would become. He has traveled thousands of miles to talk to them in person, even the most minor actor, always in person; he once spent three days sitting on top of a fence with former Texas governor John Connally, watching horses, discussing the trajectories of bullets.

He bristles at the word *obsessive*, his eyes flashing through his thick, dark glasses. "That implies it's something strange," he says. "This is reporting. This is what you're supposed to do. You're supposed to turn every page."

Like the occasion when Caro learned that a college classmate of Johnson's named Vernon Whiteside was living in a trailer in Florida, but Caro's source for that information could remember only that Whiteside was living in a town with *beach* in its name. He and Ina began going through Florida phone directories together, calling every trailer park in every damn Florida town with *beach* in its name: Boynton Beach, Daytona Beach, Fort Walton Beach. . . . It was Ina who made the call that found Whiteside, in Highland Beach, and she can still hear the confirmation in her ear. Caro flew to Florida unannounced—"It's harder to say no to a man's face," he says—and knocked on the door. Soon Caro found himself inside, filling notepads with scribbled secrets about Johnson's cruel collegiate rise, then returned to his hotel to type up another transcript to slip into another file to slip into another drawer.

Each of the files is labeled in blood-red ink—Busby, Horace; Jenkins, Walter; The Gulf of Tonkin—and given a code. (A particular file on the assassination of John F. Kennedy is labeled ASS. 107X, for instance.) Caro's outline contains hundreds of these codes, leading him directly to the file he will need when he is writing that particular section. "I try to have a mood or a rhythm for a chapter," he says, "and I don't want to interrupt it, searching through my files."

So many of the names on the files are of people who have died, most of them long gone, in fact. But in this room, inside those folders, it's as though they're still alive. ("It's not in a strange way," Caro says. "It's in a real way.") Many of the interviews remain vivid memories. Ted Sorensen, Kennedy's late former speechwriter and confidant, also lived on Central Park West, and Caro would sometimes stop in on his way home, after another day at the office. Sorensen had gone blind, and he and Caro would sit in his living room, talking, one of them ignoring that the sun had set, the other unaware. "We'd be sitting there in the dark," Caro says, now finding Sorensen's folder, and there the departed man is again, with so many of his quotes marked with that familiar red ink, cross-referenced to that finished outline.

Only after he has filled and annotated those notebooks does Caro begin to write, three or four drafts in longhand, on pads of legal paper. With each pass, muscle is added to the frame. Finally, Caro feels prepared to give his fingers wings. "There just comes a point you feel it's time to go to the typewriter," he says. He does write quickly; the math dictates that he must. When he finished *The Power Broker*, it was thirty-three hundred typewritten pages, more than one million words. (Gottlieb cut three hundred thousand: three normal-size books.) Caro's sentences are long, fluid, intricate. (A single sentence in *The Passage of Power* contains a parenthetical, an em dash, a colon, a comma, another two commas, a semicolon, two more commas, and a period.) There are stretches in each of his books that feel as though they rolled out of him in flurries, and they feel that way because they did. Three or four more drafts will appear out of that battered Smith-Corona Electra 210, each one hundreds of thousands of words, until he has his final draft.

Even then, Caro is far from finished, crossing out lines and rewriting them, often tearing out paragraphs along the edge of a ruler and taping them into a different place on a different page. There are single pages in his final draft that are three feet long.

"When I'm doing this, I can feel it," Caro says. "There's a feeling about it. You feel almost like a cabinetmaker, laying planks. There's a real feeling when you know you're getting it right. It's a physical feeling."

That hammered and glued final draft is delivered to a typist, Carol Shookhoff, who lives on Central Park West and has typed the last three of Caro's manuscripts. In her office, the book will become electronic for the first time. It will become a virtual rather than a physical thing, and soon it will be delivered, through the air, to that black glass tower on Broadway. There, it's turned back into something tangible, into clean white pages to be fought over for months, and finally into galleys, and those galleys are returned to an office on the twenty-second floor of the Fisk Building, where Caro now sits, refusing to turn the page until he feels in his body that it is right.

IV. The Apartment

When he is done for the night and turns off his ancient bronze lamp, Caro walks home, fifteen minutes, the same walk he makes every day, past Dino's Shoe Repair, where his autographed picture hangs on the wall, and through Columbus Circle, to the apartment he and Ina have shared since 1972 or so. (He can't remember exactly.) The apartment, near the top of an old gray stone co-op building on Central Park West, is expansive by today's standards, grand and formal, paneled with dark wood. There are many shelves lined with many books, and they open, like doors, to reveal more shelves with more books. There are also photographs. One, black-and-white, is a photo taken of Robert and Ina on the night they met. She was just sixteen; he was nineteen, a young student at Princeton. He is wearing a tuxedo, no glasses yet, his thick hair cut short; she's wearing a pretty dress. They are standing close to each other, smiling—his smile is wide; hers is shy. They had talked about books that night. "He wants his books to last because he had studied those books that had lasted," Ina says. They have been together since.

She is a writer, too—her fixation is France—and she has been the only research assistant Caro has ever had. In her high school yearbook, which she pulls off the shelf, she painted her dream life under her portrait: "research worker." She has lived her dream life: She has labored over boxes of documents, tracked down sources, made countless phone calls to places like Highland Beach to find men like Vernon Whiteside. She was her husband's emissary when they traveled into the Texas Hill Country, trying to sift Johnson's childhood out of the dust and the old women who lived there and remembered him as the man who brought them electric light. She even sold that pretty little house in Roslyn, unannounced, when they could no longer afford it, after Caro had spent so many moneyless years on *The Power Broker*, long having burned through his small advance. With their young son, they moved to an apartment in the Bronx. "We were broke," Caro says. "It was a horrible, horrible time." That's when he worked out of the library, when his key to the Allen Room, a shelter for homeless writers, "was my most prized possession." He can remember how much their rent was exactly, $362.73, because it was a figure that filled him with fear.

When Caro had signed on to write *The Power Broker*, in 1966, he thought it would take him a year. After four years, he had written 500,000 words and wasn't half done. Caro's original contract was with Simon & Schuster, which was headed by a young editor in chief named Robert Gottlieb. ("I couldn't think of anything more boring," Gottlieb says today, "but I said okay.") Caro sent his mountain of paper to his editor, a former classmate of his named Richard Kluger. He also made an appeal for more money so that his family didn't starve while he finished his work. Kluger invited Caro for dinner at a Chinese restaurant on the Upper West Side, where he delivered his answer: Simon & Schuster wasn't going to give him any more money. In fact, it didn't see much potential in this book that was so long and so many years late. It didn't even like the title.

Caro left the restaurant bone numb. Back out on the street, he pointed himself north, toward that cursed apartment in the Bronx. He began to walk. "I walked the length of Broadway," he says, "and back then, that wasn't something you really did." Block after block he walked, past 96th Street, 110th, 126th, 168th. Had he made a terrible mistake? Had he written a bad book? Caro felt trapped: in too deep to abandon his book, too far away from finishing it to continue. Ina remembers receiving her husband that night, ruined. Her anger is still in her voice today: "I was livid," she says. "I just thought they'd treated him miserably." They sat down and talked into the night. "He's such a beautiful writer," she says. "I just always felt everything would work out."

There was a single line in his contract that changed Caro's fate. If his editor left Simon & Schuster, he could leave, too. And not long after that night, Kluger left for a rival publisher, Atheneum, and Caro took his pile of paper to the open market.

A friend gave him a list of four agents; he met with each of them. "Three of them were men who looked like me," he says—dark-rimmed glasses, jackets with elbow patches. The fourth was a petite young woman from Dundee, Illinois, named Lynn Nesbit. She had, by then, a burgeoning Manhattan career (for reasons that still remain unclear to her, Tom Wolfe had agreed to become one of her early clients); the agency she helped start would become, in time, International Creative Management. But Caro didn't choose her because of that. He chose her because she wasn't him.

Nesbit, today one of the principals of Janklow & Nesbit, sits in her sunlit office, and the iconic names of her clients jump out from the shelves: Michael Crichton, Hunter S. Thompson, Joan Didion, Jeffrey Eugenides. But she can still remember sitting down to read those first 500,000 words of Robert Caro's.

"I thought, Who's Robert Moses?" she says. "I was young and hadn't been in New York City that many years. I didn't really know who he was. And then I started reading the manuscript, this incredibly compelling narrative about this man I knew nothing about. He came alive."

She turned the last page and made two phone calls. The first was to Caro. He remembers it as one of the great moments of his life. "I know you've been worried," she said. "You don't have to worry anymore."

Soon Nesbit made her second phone call. She had known immediately the man she hoped would buy *The Power Broker*: Gottlieb, now the editor in chief at Knopf. "I didn't know what we had," Gottlieb says today of his brush with Caro at Simon & Schuster. "It was just a wonderful book." Gottlieb gave Caro enough money to finish his book, and to write a second, and to move to Central Park West.

After *The Power Broker* had become a giant success, winning the Pulitzer and selling hundreds of thousands of copies, Caro visited Gottlieb. The next book was supposed to be a biography of Fiorello La Guardia, but privately, each man had been having his doubts. Caro wanted to write about power, and he had written already about urban power, about the shaping of cities and streets. He wanted to do something bigger. Gottlieb had found his mind equally untied, and now he thought for a few seconds.

"You have to understand," Gottlieb says today, "I have a megalomaniac's confidence in my instincts. You decide this, and you make the best of it. If you make the wrong decision, tough shit."

Gottlieb looked up at Caro and said, "How about Johnson?"

V. The Coliseum

For years, it loomed over Columbus Circle, on the southwest corner of Central Park. If Robert Caro stood in the second of his two office windows, he could look up Eighth Avenue and see the New York Coliseum's white-brick facade and the four cast-aluminum medallions that decorated it. Three of the medallions—each eleven feet square and weighing twelve hundred pounds—depicted the federal, state, and city seals. The fourth represented the Triborough Bridge and Tunnel Authority, which, under the chairmanship of Robert Moses, had built the Coliseum in 1956.

Moses had named it the Coliseum because he thought the exhibition hall, and its adjacent twenty-story office block, would rival Rome's for longevity. He had always believed that through his buildings he would live forever. (The authority's emblem included a bridge that Moses had built, the Bronx-Whitestone, and a tunnel that he had built, the Brooklyn-Battery.) "He used to ask me about *The Power Broker*, 'How long will it last?'" Caro says, looking out that same window today. "'In a short while, it will be yesterday's news.' That's what he would say to me." Moses had good reason to believe in his own work: The Coliseum's soaring ceiling was supported by seven massive steel trusses, each two stories high and 120 feet long. Almost from the beginning of its life, the Coliseum was regarded as an architectural blight, a cold and faceless divide between midtown and the Upper West Side. But structurally, it was faultless.

In the fall of 1999, Caro watched when the four medallions were carefully removed from the building's face and trucked away. And for much of the following year, he would get up from his desk and watch while the Coliseum was dismantled piece by piece, those seven steel trusses cut into sections, all those white bricks crumbled into piles. And then Caro would go back to his desk, working under the light of his lamp, and roll another clean sheet into his Smith-Corona.

"When they tore it down, I felt something about books," Caro says. "When they tore it down, I felt something about books."

The Power Broker, like all of Caro's books, has never been out of print.

A sixty-one-year-old man named Andy Hughes has designed and built each of Caro's books since *The Path to Power*. In one of those cosmic turns, Hughes was a child when Caro first entered his field of view: His father, also named Andy, was Caro's libel lawyer, first at *Newsday* and then for all of his books. Andy Hughes, the son, then found his way to Knopf, where he has worked since 1979 and today is its chief of production and design. He is tall, lean, with a smoker's voice and a deep understanding of the architecture of books. Typography, binding techniques, paper weights and measures—for Hughes, a book is the sum of its physical parts, of hinges and gutters and spines.

Like almost everyone else in Caro's small publishing ecosystem, Hughes keeps the books within arm's reach, and like the others, he's almost compelled to touch them when he talks about them. One by one, he pulls them off the shelf. Running his long fingers over the first volume, he marvels. "How did we survive? How did we do this?" Caro has been at his work for so long, his books span the modern history of book making. *The Path to Power*, published in 1982, was printed using hot-metal typesetting, on a Linotype machine; its handsome cover lettering was drawn meticulously by hand. *Means of Ascent*, published in 1990, was part of the computer-mainframe generation. *Master of the Senate*, published in 2002, was the easiest to create, via desktop publishing. Still, even with newer digital technology at his disposal, Hughes is anxious about *The Passage of Power*. Not only are the galleys late—"It's getting really tight," he says—but time is falling away from Hughes in other ways.

It's important to him that each of Caro's books looks and feels the same as the previous one and the next. He wants them to be built to last. Unfortunately, book building is another dying art. Bindings are glued instead of stitched; most hardcovers are made from paper rather than cloth; hinges aren't as sharp as they used to be and half rounds aren't as tight. "These are just things that have been lost in the march of time," Hughes says.

Today, he looks at books and sees weakness as often as he sees beauty.

He sees it especially in something he calls "mousetrapping," one of our invisible modern plagues. He opens the three Caro books to demonstrate: Each stays open on his desk. Each lies flat. Hughes then finds a more recent book, and no matter how much he cracks its spine, it wants to snap shut. "It's like we're asking readers to close them," he says. *The Passage of Power*, Hughes says, will lie flat. He has a printer in Berryville, Virginia, that will make this book the way the others were made. It will be wrapped with the same thick black cloth, stamped with the same gold lettering, printed with the same pleasing wide gutter and colored endpaper. Hughes rises in his chair when he imagines it—he can picture himself opening those heavy cardboard boxes when they arrive from Virginia, hopefully sometime before May. "I'll be absolutely thrilled. It's pure joy for me, and it's never gone away."

But first, Robert Caro must finish with his galleys.

A few days later, back in the Fisk Building, he has finally beaten the fifth paragraph on page 452, and now he is tearing through the rest of his book. Now he has that physical feeling again. He is soaring.

VI. The Last Line

Caro recently extended his lease at the Fisk Building. He's practically finished with this book, and then all he will have left are the notes and the index. Maybe another hundred pages. He'll be done by early March, he says. And the fifth book, the last book, is all right here, waiting for him. After *The Passage of Power* comes out, he's going to take Ina to France, but then he'll be back here, back in his office, back at his work.

His research is finished, he says. "Mostly, anyway." His outline is pinned up on the wall, and it will not change. He even has some sections of it written, first drafts—including the first of two chapters on Bill Moyers ("He wrote a lot of memos," Caro says, "so I got him")—and he knows what to do with the rest. Nobody believes it, but he writes very fast. "I think I can write the next book in two or three years," he says. He tries not to think that people are waiting, the way he tries not to think about many things, but he knows that they—Mehta and Gottlieb and Hourigan, and Andy Hughes and Lynn Nesbit and Carol Shook-hoff the typist, all the people who have touched his books from the beginning, who are touching this one now—are out there waiting all the same, just around the corner.

A few of them, like so many of the men and women frozen in Caro's files, will not see how this story ends. Nina Bourne, Knopf's legendary copywriter, died in 2010 at the age of ninety-three, having still come into the office until a few months before her death. Andy Hughes the libel lawyer is now eighty-nine and in an assisted-living facility in Florida.

The others? "Oh, I'll still be here," Andy Hughes the book builder says. "I want to see this through."

"I don't think that way," Gottlieb says. "It will be horrible and terrible if this book doesn't get finished. But people die."

"You can't worry about it," Hourigan says. "You can just go on."

She goes quiet then, thinking about what she should say next and how she should say it.

"I am so lucky to have been involved with books that are going to live forever," Hourigan finally continues in her quiet voice. "We're all this close," she says, and she holds up her hand, her finger and her thumb just a whisper apart. To what end, she doesn't say.

The last chapter of *The Passage of Power*, the twenty-sixth chapter, is called "Long Enough." It is heartbreaking, foreshadowing the tragedy of Lyndon Johnson that is to come in the final book. Johnson, Caro has just shown us, was a heroic figure in the dark days after the Kennedy assassination. In the first seven weeks of his presidency, Johnson was the embodiment of courage and industry under unimaginable circumstances. The passage of the Civil Rights Act alone was an accomplishment of singular consequence. But his gifts wouldn't last. Soon, Johnson's worst impulses would overtake him—his insecurity, his terrible self-doubt. His greatness would be temporary.

Now Caro reads over those final few pages one last time. His pencil doesn't much touch them.

> If he had held in check those forces within him, had conquered himself, for a while, he wasn't going to be able to do it for very long.
> But he had done it long enough.

Robert Caro puts down his pencil. For now, this is the last line.

The Paris Review

WINNER—GENERAL
EXCELLENCE, PRINT

*Founded in 1953—"the great
invention of George Plimpton," as
the National Magazine Award
judges put it*—The Paris Review
has long been known for its
interviews. *So it may seem natural
to include here an interview from
a recent issue. But even the most
undiscerning reader may find it
odd that the interviewee is, well,
dead—and has been for nearly
twenty years. It turns out that
this interview was conducted in
1967—the same year the subject,
Terry Southern, had a cameo on
the cover of* Sgt. Pepper's Lonely
Hearts Club Band—*but for one
reason or another never appeared
in print until now. But here is
another unmissable chance to
listen to a writer, in this case one
of the pioneers of the New
Journalism, talk about his work.*

Interview by
Maggie Paley

Terry Southern:
The Art of
Screenwriting

T erry Southern was born in 1924 in Alvarado, Texas, the son of a pharmacist and a dressmaker. He was drafted into the army during World War II and studied at the Sorbonne on the G.I. Bill. In Paris he became friends with George Plimpton, H. L. Humes, and Peter Matthiessen, who published his story "The Accident" in the first issue of *The Paris Review*. Back in the United States, Southern was often associated with Beat writers like Burroughs, Corso, and Ginsberg, some of whose attitudes he may have shared, yet the elegant clarity of his prose—which Norman Mailer characterized as "mean, coolly deliberate and murderous"—situated him, aesthetically, as a player in the "Quality Lit Game" he liked to mock.

At the time of this interview (1967), Southern was famous as the coauthor of *Candy*, the best-selling sex novel, and as the screenwriter behind Stanley Kubrick's dark antiwar, antinuke comedy, *Dr. Strangelove*. Both appeared in the United States in 1964 (a headline in *Life* magazine read "Terry Southern vs. Smugness"). By 1967 he could be spotted on the cover of *Sgt. Pepper's Lonely Hearts Club Band*, standing between Dylan Thomas and Dion. Gore Vidal called him "the most profoundly witty writer of our generation." Lenny Bruce blurbed his books.

Candy (written with Mason Hoffenberg) is loosely based on *Candide*. Its heroine is a delicious, perky, generous young woman; the joke is that she remains impregnably innocent in the face of one grotesque sexual adventure after another. The book attacks prudery, a particularly Anglo-Saxon vice, and yet, like Candy herself, its tone is appealingly sweet. The novel was first published in Paris by Maurice Girodias's Olympia Press in 1958 (even after the 1960 *Lady Chatterley* case redefined obscenity, publishers here were unsure of the novel's "redeeming social value").

For *Dr. Strangelove*, Southern was hired by Kubrick to make a satire out of a screenplay originally based on the serious novel *Red Alert*. The movie takes us into the war room of a certain President Merkin Muffley, there to reveal a military culture gone berserk, as its leaders cheerfully prepare for death, destruction, and the imminent end of the world.

Even before these blockbusters made him a household name, Southern had attracted a passionate following. His first novel, *Flash and Filigree* (1958), the tale of a persecuted dermatologist, is replete with mad inventions (among them a TV game show called *What's My Disease?*). In *The Magic Christian* (1959), his most brilliant sustained narrative, a billionaire prankster spends a fortune "making it hot for people," unearthing hypocrisy as he goes. Southern's essays and journalism were esteemed—and imitated—by other writers. "Twirling at Ole Miss," a piece of personal reportage published in *Esquire* in 1962, is especially trenchant and funny. Its nominal subject is baton twirling; it's really—or equally—about the mindlessness of racism in the South. Tom Wolfe called it the founding work of the New Journalism.

By the time this interview was conducted, Southern had also worked on Tony Richardson's film *The Loved One* (1965), based on the Evelyn Waugh novel, and *The Cincinnati Kid* (1966), a drama about high-stakes poker, starring Steve McQueen, and had published *Red-Dirt Marijuana and Other Tastes* (1967), a collection of short fiction, journalism, and occasional pieces. He would go on to write or contribute to the screenplays of *Barbarella* (1968), *Easy Rider* (1969), *End of the Road* (1969), and *The Magic Christian* (1969). His only other credited script to make it to the screen, *The Telephone* (1988), starring Whoopi Goldberg, was a disaster. By the seventies, alcohol and drug abuse had slowed Southern's productivity. He published two more novels, *Blue Movie* (1970) and *Texas Summer* (1992), and had a short stint in the eighties as a writer for *Saturday Night Live*. Later, he became a devoted and much-loved teacher of screenwriting at Columbia University. In 1995, he collapsed on his way to teach a class, and four days afterward died of respiratory failure.

On the day of our interview—meant to be the first in a series on the art of screenwriting—we met for lunch at the Russian Tea Room. The decor, then as now, was Christmas all year round, with red banquettes, green walls, chandeliers festooned with red Christmas-tree balls, and so on. Our waitress, a tiny Russian with a coronet of braids and a name tag that read "Nadia," took a motherly interest in Southern—a rumpled man, with a long, beaky nose and a generous mouth—as he squirmed in his seat, answering questions. Nadia is what I remember best about the lunch, in particular the way Southern gently put her on ("Do you really think I should have the borscht, Nadia? If that *is* your name"), thus deflecting the spotlight from himself.

After the interview was transcribed, a copy was given to Southern (according to *Paris Review* custom) for him to revise as he saw fit. He never gave it back. Every so often I would ask him, on my own or at the prompting of George Plimpton, when the interview would be ready. "I'm working on it," he would say. "It's got to be tight and bright." After a year or two, Plimpton stopped asking; I continued to question Southern about it but less and less frequently. When Southern died in 1995, his long-time companion, Gail Gerber, said to me, as a consolation of sorts, "Well, at least now that interview can come out." But the interview—complete with Southern's clarifications and

emendations—got lost in a pile of papers. It emerged without its title page and fell into the hands of a Ph.D. student, who mistakenly attributed it to the biographer Albert Goldman. Since then, short excerpts have appeared, always under Goldman's name. Thanks to the steadfast and remedial efforts of Southern's son, Nile, the finished text is available here for the first time.
    —*Maggie Paley*

INTERVIEWER: When and how did you decide to be a writer?

SOUTHERN: I never "decided" to be a writer. I used to write a lot, then show it to my friends—one or two of them anyway—with the idea, more or less, of astonishing or confounding them with the content of the pages. I knew they had never seen anything like this before—I mean, the weirdest thing they could possibly have read before was Poe or one of those little cartoon fuck-books, as they were called, whereas my stuff was much weirder and more immediate. I used the names of teachers, classmates, et cetera. These productions were well received by the two or three people—no girls—who read them, but finally I went too far and alienated one of the readers, my best friend, by using his sister in a really imaginative piece, perhaps the best of this period. That slowed me down for a while, in daring, but finally I learned not to care too much and would write wholly for an imaginary reader whose tastes were similar to my own.

    And this is, of course, is the only way to work well.

INTERVIEWER: *Life* magazine claims that you once lived on a barge hauling rocks from Poughkeepsie to Jones Beach. Is that true?

SOUTHERN: Yes, I lived on a barge. I was captain of the barge. This is the lowest form of organized labor in the country—except possibly circus roustabouts—and it comprises winos and layabouts, persons of such low account they have been kicked out of the longshoreman's union, and it pays one dollar per hour. Alex Trocchi got me the post. There was a period when these positions came into favor with young drug addicts, also persons of creative bent who needed robot-type jobs—like those people in fire towers, lighthouses, et cetera—which would not take much time from the real work in hand. There were few or no duties—just catch the line, actually a big rope, thrown from the tugboat and put it around the capstan, a stumpy post, and off you go. Later, release the rope, called "letting go the mainsail" or similar, and secure to moorings.

George Plimpton can explain barge life to you, since he used to take young girls out on Trok's barge and try, as he said, "to get them." Suffice it to say that this is a pleasant enough way to spend a summer, though I wouldn't really want to be in the position of recommending it.

INTERVIEWER: Was writing movies something you always wanted to do?

SOUTHERN: Yes, but there was never any possibility of it. They just weren't making movies I could have worked on. I did get a letter one time from Jerry Wald, saying, "I have read your story in *Harper's Bazaar*, and I think you have a very good cinematic quality, would you be interested in writing for the screen," and blah blah blah. And then it went on to say, "Too many serious writers dismiss the potential of the screen as commercial, however may I point out to you that only recently such outstanding literary personages as Mr. William Faulkner," and so on.

I showed this letter to a friend of mine, Harold Meeske, who said, "Don't even answer the letter. The thing to do is to write a screenplay and send it back, like, 'Am I interested? Dig this!'" I said, "Okay, what's the story?" and he said, "I've got it. This friend of mine is just coming out of Sing Sing. America's number-one jewel thief. He's getting out Friday, and we'll write a script based on his adventures. His name"—well, we'd better leave out his name. He's making it in Hollywood now, as a screenwriter.

Anyway, he comes to Harold and Marilyn Meeske's. So there was this guy, America's number-one jewel thief, and he moved in with them, and I moved in with them, and the four of us worked on this screenplay, and then we sent it in to Jerry Wald. No response. Nothing. Later I found out that this letter I'd gotten, although it wasn't mimeographed, was in fact a form letter he had sent, you know, to Herbert Gold and Philip Roth—everybody got one of these letters. That was my first brush with the Film Capital.

INTERVIEWER: And your next was working in London with Kubrick on *Dr. Strangelove.* What was that like?

SOUTHERN: It was the first time in my life that I'd gone anywhere with a sense of purpose. I mean, I'd always traveled, I'd made about ten trips back and forth, but just aimless, with no justification except having the G.I. Bill and using it as a means to be there. It was the first time I'd gone anywhere and been paid for it. It was very satisfying, very interesting, and almost unbelievable to be moving about like that.

Stanley himself is a strange kind of genius. I'd always had a notion that people in power positions in movies must be hacks and fools, and it was very impressive to meet someone who wasn't. He thinks of himself as a "filmmaker"—his idol is Chaplin—and so he's down on the idea of "director." He would like, and it's understandable, to have his films just say, "A Film by Stanley Kubrick." He tries to cover the whole thing from beginning to end. Including the designing of the ads.

He's probably the only American director who works on big-budget pictures who has complete control of his movies.

INTERVIEWER: *Strangelove* was originally conceived as a melodrama, not a comedy. Did you work with Kubrick to restructure the whole thing, or were you able to just insert the jokes?

SOUTHERN: I knew what he wanted. It was a question of working together, rewriting each line, and changing the tone.

INTERVIEWER: When you started the project, you'd never written movie dialogue. You presumably didn't know anything about how to write a screenplay.

SOUTHERN: Yes, I knew, because I like movies. And writing dialogue has always been easy for me.

INTERVIEWER: How much directorial description does a writer usually put into a screenplay?

SOUTHERN: It depends. If you have a natural inclination for visualizing, you see it in the way you hope it will be, and you put that in the script. The petty directors resent that—they think it's usurping their prerogative—but the better directors are more open-minded. The only way I can write is to write it as fully as possible, in as much detail, as though I were directing it myself and wanted to tell the actor how to do it.

INTERVIEWER: How do you feel about a movie you've written but somebody else has directed? Do you feel that it's yours?

SOUTHERN: Oh no, it's the director's. As the writer, you have no power except persuasion. Even a good director resents your suggestions after a while. He begins to take them too personally. He thinks he's being influenced by someone in a lower echelon. Codirecting is good, because some other guy can carry the ball—in terms of saying, "All right,

action"—and you can still be in there without embarrassing him.

INTERVIEWER: Even as codirector, wouldn't you need
experience working with actors?

SOUTHERN: I get along very well with actors. They're like
children. They need to be encouraged and reprimanded
enough to know that you're interested. You'd think that
great actors, like George C. Scott or Laurence Olivier,
would resent direction, but they all depend on it. They've
got to have the attention—it's like dope—but at the
same time the attention has to be convincing, it has to be
something that they can acknowledge as real attention,
and they get pretty discriminating, because they get lots
of broadside, blind attention. That's the thing. If you give
them that, you can enchant them into anything.

INTERVIEWER: What about other things, like camera? Can
you just rely on a cameraman to take care of that?

SOUTHERN: You have to persuade them, too. You say, What
would be interesting from your point of view as a crafts-
man, an artist? What would you like to do that you've
never done, that you haven't been allowed to do? Then
they set up the shot, and you can look at the thing and
actually see the way it's going to be, in terms of composition and in terms of movement, and then you can look
ahead and see where the cut will be possible.

I wouldn't rely on an editor to cut a movie. He might
be a great editor, but still you've got to think of it in terms
of your own cuts, just as in writing you would have an
abrupt juxtaposition, an abrupt transition, or an otherwise engaging one or a smooth one. You have to think of
the flow of it.

INTERVIEWER: Have you ever considered writing plays?

SOUTHERN: I've had to curtail my interest in the theater,
because the limitations are so appalling. I find it too

difficult to rationalize the existence of the whole thing—
the unnaturally loud voice to carry to the gallery, the
broad gestures, the clomp-clomp-clomp exits and en-
trances, the pretense of the fourth wall. I think if a thing
is so weird, so new, so original that it can't be done
cinematically at the time, like *Krapp's Last Tape*, *The
Connection*, or *Marat/Sade*, then it's justified. I can't
imagine any other reason for not doing it as a movie,
unless you're going to take advantage of the one thing
that doesn't exist in a movie, which is a live audience.

You can't have close-ups in theater, you can't have
dissolves. A play gets out of the control of the director
because it gets very much into the hands of the actor,
and the actor is grooving out there and can't be edited.
I mean, I dig great moments on the stage, but I think it
should be like that, like Gielgud's *Ages of Man*, where he
picks out the cream. Or if you could just have Olivier's
soliloquies. But to sit through a whole play is like sitting
through an entire opera just to hear one aria.

There's another aspect of it, which is the historical
moment—like seeing Nureyev doing his grandest grand
jeté, or Bird blowing his ass off—but I think the whole
mystique of the theatergoer is really sick. These first-
nighters, they go—to everything. It's just too romantic.

INTERVIEWER: Some critics seemed to think the movie of
The Loved One, which you wrote for Tony Richardson,
strayed too far from the book. How important is fidelity
to the book in a screen adaptation?

SOUTHERN: In the old sense of watering down and making
more palatable by leaving things out—well, of course,
that's terrible. That should be against the law. But in the
case of *The Loved One*, or in similar cases, where the
intent is to extend, expand, and deepen and bring up to
date, that isn't a valid criticism.

The Loved One used to be everybody's favorite book
in high school, but if you read it now, you'll see that it's
relatively limited. I'm sure that Evelyn Waugh, if he were a
young man writing it now, would write it very differently.
For example, that whole English colony, to which he
devotes about one-third of the book, doesn't exist any
more. You used to have a real group of people who felt
they'd sold out, that Hollywood was an awful place, and
they stuck together, but now the scene itself has become
diversified. It's no longer the intellectuals versus the old
guard. And the English colony has been assimilated.

INTERVIEWER: What did you think of *The Loved One*?

SOUTHERN: I thought it had great moments. By great
moments I mean moments that hadn't been done
cinematically before. As a totality, it seemed pretty
shaky and uneven and eccentric.

INTERVIEWER: Have you any idea why?

SOUTHERN: Well, whatever's good or bad in a movie is finally
the responsibility of the director, and Richardson wants
to depart completely from whatever he thinks of as the
Establishment at any given moment. He has this antislick
notion, for example. At the rushes, he would have three
takes, and he would choose the take where the camera
might shake a little, or light was coming through from the
sun or a leak in the camera, because then it makes it look
like something other than a slick Hollywood job. And then
he feels that a movie shouldn't be advertised or publicized
at all, that the viewers are bound to be disappointed
because they've been led to expect something, whereas if
they're led to expect nothing, then they think, Well, this
is a pleasant surprise!

INTERVIEWER: How were the previews of *The Loved One* in
Hollywood?

SOUTHERN: Everybody blasted it—I mean on those cards
that they fill out. But these days they don't judge so much
from what a card says as from how many people fill out
the cards. It's like *The Sandpiper*—everybody filled out
the cards, and said things like, "Liz ought to be horse-
whipped!" or "Burton is a fag!" and so on, but they were
all filled out.

Speaking of which, we had a good idea about how to
improve *The Sandpiper*, John Calley and I. You open on a
penthouse apartment at the Plaza, about eleven in the
morning. Liz is sitting there getting her nails, her hair
done, and you hear a telephone ring in the background
and Burton comes out, in pajamas, robe, shades, terribly
hung over—"Listen, Kurt wants to know what we're
going to do about this picture."

And she says, "What picture?"

And he takes a big drink and says, "You know, the one
about the bird."

And she says, "How much money is involved?"

"A million and a half," he says.

And she says, "Oh yeah?" and thinks about it for a
minute. "Is that the one set in Big Sur?"

"Yes," he says.

"And then in Paris?"

"Uh-huh."

"Well, I do have to go to Paris soon, to get some
clothes . . . Why don't we do it?"

So the movie starts. And you keep cutting back to this
principal scene with Liz and Burton talking about it. "For
God's sake," he's saying, "why did you get me into this?
Don't you realize I've got a reputation as a serious actor?"
Et cetera. And then at the very end you have a scene
where they're getting on a plane, and they've got the

money in a suitcase, and the suitcase opens, and it all blows away. Sort of *Sierra Madre* style.

INTERVIEWER: You were very lucky to have started in movies with Kubrick and Richardson.

SOUTHERN: It couldn't have happened any other way. Most directors won't hire you unless you've already done something. Faulkner and Irwin Shaw and Truman Capote could collaborate on a script, and if they submitted it cold, the producers would say, Great, there's a great idea here. We'll buy the script. But they wouldn't think of using those guys to do the second draft. They think of writers in two categories—there are idea men and plot men. They think they need a professional screenwriter who knows the format. They don't realize that the format is nothing any child couldn't do, any child with a visual sense, a visual attitude, and a basic familiarity with movies.

Most screenwriters I've met are the people least suited to their work, because they have no ear, no notion of human relationships, no notion of psychology at all. They're just scuffling in the dark, they're searching. They think it's a good racket to be in, like shingle salesmen or something—they've heard about the pay, and they fast-talk their way into a job by working in talent agencies, submitting scripts, getting personal relationships with producers, directors, actors. Finally somebody carries them in, some actor says, Let's give Joe here a credit. And then they're set, they've got a credit and are recognized as writers, but it's like pulling teeth each time they put down a word. It's a laborious, tedious process for them, because they can't write. And they'll work on anything, with absolutely no regard for material. All they ask is, How much money do I get? They never work for less than they worked for on the last one. If they do, they're finished, it's downhill all the way.

But these are movies you never hear about unless you happen to look at the newspaper on the one particular day they open. They're potboilers, like *The Cincinnati Kid*, for example. There's one big ad or a small ad, and people are aware of it for about a week, and then it doesn't exist anymore, except as a credit. That's why the most prominent writers in Hollywood are people you've never heard of. People who write, say, the Doris Day movies. Stanley Shapiro is supposed to be the highest-paid writer. At last report he was getting $350,000 a whack. He writes the Doris Day/Rock Hudson/Cary Grant movies, and he gets a producer's piece of it, too. They figure he doesn't miss. All of these pictures are made for one and gross ten— something like that. He's got a formula, a very simple formula. You have this girl, a career girl, swinging, you know. Really a ball-breaker. She likes the idea of guys wanting to make it with her, but she's not interested, and then she meets this one guy who doesn't seem to want to make it with her, he's amused by her, and so she's going to get him. Finally she does get him, but instead of becoming a housewife, she continues with her career.

It's a twist on the old thing where the guy says, I won't have my wife working, and puts her in the home and dominates her, and she's ready to be dominated. With this formula, the girl is not dominated—she gets the guy, and she goes on with her career. It's that simple.

INTERVIEWER: How much does good writing actually matter in a good screenplay? Lillian Hellman, in an interview, suggested that it might be practical to try doing screenplays that were nothing more than outlines. You'd have an outline of where the movie was going, with an ending, but no dialogue, and it would be improvised as it went along.

SOUTHERN: I'm all for improvisation, but you can take off from a better base than just an outline. Have the dialogue as good as you can, and then improvise.

INTERVIEWER: Do actors often add a lot?

SOUTHERN: No. Peter Sellers, for example, is good at improvisations, but by *improvisation* I mean making lines believable. Improving lines, no. When you have a scene, the scene has to go in a certain direction, because you've got all the setups, the locations, and everything. You can't change the story. You already know where the scene's going to go.

INTERVIEWER: Where do you work when you're in Hollywood? Do you write in a writers' building?

SOUTHERN: You get an office. They put your name on the door, and you get assigned a secretary, even though you have no use for her. You don't have to show up.

INTERVIEWER: How much of a studio is there nowadays?

SOUTHERN: The old guard has really been falling apart since television came in. Picture-making used to be a science, a formula. Their aim—they tried to get it really neat—was to produce fifty-one pictures a year, one a week, skipping Christmas week. That was it. They had it figured out and they knew exactly how much they were going to get on each picture. Now everything is changed, and they're no longer sure of what they're doing. They seem very much out of place.

INTERVIEWER: Is there any sort of fraternity of writers now?

SOUTHERN: No. Studios don't have contracts with writers anymore, there aren't any studio writers, so there's no way they would know each other. Writers out there are hit-and-run people, very transient, one studio one day, another studio the next. There's no occasion for anything to develop between them.

INTERVIEWER: You've lived in Paris, London, New York—
how does Hollywood compare?

SOUTHERN: Those three cities seem to me equally different,
and I wouldn't be inclined to compare them, with each
other or with Hollywood. Hollywood, that is to say, Los
Angeles, is not, of course, a city, and its sinister forces are
very oblique. There's no public transportation system
whatever, so the people drive around as though they were
living in Des Moines, and it has all the rest of the disad-
vantages of a small town, only filled with displaced
persons. On the other hand, life there has an engaging
surrealist quality, an almost exciting grotesqueness.

    The cultural scene there in general is sped up, sort of
concentrated. Southern California is a mecca for all
manner of freakishness, beginning on the most middle-
class level—hot-dog stands in the shape of a hot dog. If
you go there, you'll immediately see a carnival, Disney-
land aspect that is different from any other place in
America.

INTERVIEWER: Is there a noticeably large proportion of
beautiful girls there?

SOUTHERN: There are a lot of beautiful girls there because,
well, girls who want to be writers come to the Village
and girls who want to be actresses go to Hollywood.
And not necessarily to be writers or to be actresses, but
to be identified with that scene, that action. So you see
unusually attractive waitresses, and girls sort of spilled
over from the casting office.

INTERVIEWER: How does the casting office function?

SOUTHERN: The casting office is interesting. Each of the
studios has a big door saying casting. Girls arrive from
Des Moines and go to one of the studios and ask, Where's
the casting office?

    "Over there, go in that door."

They go in, and they think it's like a personnel department in a department store. They think they're applying for something, and they fill out a form and they give in their photographs, and these things are put in a file cabinet, and that's it. In the history of cinema there's never been a case of anyone being hired to work in pictures through the casting office. The people who work in the casting office have no connection with the industry. Quite Kafkaesque.

INTERVIEWER: You mean the casting office is just there to satisfy the girls?

SOUTHERN: Mainly it's something they can point out on the bus tour. All the studios now are aiming at these tours. They charge two fifty, and they sell things. They sell film clips, Technicolor, 35mm, about four pieces of film—they're transparencies, and they're perforated, and it looks as though they're cut out of a negative, which is what they're trying to simulate, but actually there are, say, four frames from different parts of different reels, put together and printed again. They sell these for two dollars or so, and various other souvenirs. At Universal, they claim now that their income from the tours pays the overhead of the studio.

In the beginning, they were authentic. They would take the tourists around to a set and say, "Quiet now, everyone, they're shooting," but people would talk and ruin the shot, so the directors and producers were flipping. Finally, Universal set up a thing, up on top of a hill—a corral, with barns and horses and about six guys, a director and an assistant director, and a camera with no film in it. The bus pulls up, and when it's at a distance of twenty-five yards or so, the guide says, "Say, we're really in luck! I think they're about to shoot a scene." And sure enough, that's what they do—but it's all fake.

The interesting thing is that these people on the fake set, since they're not working in movies, are not even in the union. They're paid something like two dollars an hour. Except for two guys who are stunt men. The tours happen every forty-five minutes, and it's the same thing each time. First they stage a fistfight, one of them knocks the other down and gets on a horse, then the other recovers and shoots the first one as he's riding away, and he falls off the horse. And of course they have this guy acting as the director, for two dollars an hour, not even connected in any way with the movies, and everybody else is just standing around, a fake makeup girl and a fake script girl—the whole thing.

INTERVIEWER: What happens to those girls, those aspiring starlets? Do they sit around in Schwab's drugstore, or the Brown Derby, or whatever?

SOUTHERN: In the beginning, they come to Hollywood, presumably, with the idea of the action. Then they find out that you can't even get into any of these buildings without an agent, that there's no possibility of getting in, that even a lot of the agents can't get in. Meanwhile a substitute life begins, and they get into the social scene, you know. They're working as parking attendants, waitresses, doing arbitrary jobs . . .

INTERVIEWER: Hoping that somebody will see them?

SOUTHERN: Finally they forget about that, but they're still making the scene. They continue to have some vague peripheral identification with films—like they go to a lot of movies, and they talk about movies and about people they've seen on the street, and they read the gossip columns and the movie magazines, but you get the feeling it's without any real aspiration any longer. It's the sort of vicariousness a polio person might feel for rodeo.

INTERVIEWER: Was there ever any attempt to put you through the publicity-department mill?

SOUTHERN: Well, they sort of gave up on me. It's very difficult for me to say no, but it's not too difficult not to show. They couldn't understand that. They'd make an appointment with one of the trade papers that they consider really important, hot stuff—and then somebody not even showing up? Shocking! That happened a few times, and then I guess they gave up.

INTERVIEWER: Is working on a screenplay different from writing a book?

SOUTHERN: Well, to begin with, you're usually working against a deadline—the standard thing for a screenplay job is ten weeks. And first they want to see an outline.

INTERVIEWER: Do they require you to stick to it once you do it?

SOUTHERN: No, no. It's just a practice that exists. I suppose it has advantages from a producer's point of view, because a producer can read a ten-page outline and get some kind of feeling for the beginning, middle, and end. It used to be that writers would submit outlines, cold, on speculation, and then, on the basis of an outline, would get a commission to do a fifty-page treatment, and if the treatment was accepted, a commission to do a first draft, and so on. Now the treatment is generally bypassed, although you do see them lying around offices.

INTERVIEWER: Would you rather do adaptations or originals?

SOUTHERN: You can't set out to do something really original in films. People who say, Let's do something original, and mean it, have no money to do it with. The ones who have the money say, Let's do this, with this beginning and this end and these characters. That means you're working within a framework. If you tried to do an "original" you wouldn't accept those limitations—it would be like a novel.

When you write a novel or a story, you don't know where it's going, and you don't do it for money, and you don't do it because someone says, We'll print it if you do it, and we'll pay for it. You may do it out of some weird principle, or when you get a surge of some inexplicable feeling, or the way certain people just fall into a habit of getting up, having breakfast, and then starting to write. But you do it because it's a kick, and so there's no telling where it will go.

INTERVIEWER: Then you don't see movies as a substitute for writing fiction?

SOUTHERN: You want to make a comparison between writing a novel and writing a screenplay, but I don't think there is any at all. As a medium, movies are obviously superior, in the sense that the strongest perceptions are sight and sound, but unless you're the producer or director you have no control over the final product. In a novel, you do. An editor or publisher can try to persuade you, but you can always say, I won't make those changes. So on the one hand you have control when you're writing prose, and on the other hand the cinema is really the greater medium, if only you could use it the way you wanted to.

INTERVIEWER: Even if you were the producer-director, if you were making a so-called commercial film, I wonder whether you could match what you do in writing.

SOUTHERN: The only excuse for writing a novel these days is if it can't be done as a movie. And there are limitations in movies—not just inherent limitations, but limitations in practice. It's very difficult to do interior monologues and first-person narratives, for instance. In a book you can have italics, or you can say, "'Au revoir,' he said, comma, thinking, 'Forget it,'" whereas in a movie, what are you going to do? Put it through an echo chamber, or have a close-up to show that, even though his lips aren't moving, there's dialogue, so "forget it" must be what he's thinking? Audiences are simply so unfamiliar with that, the very fact of it would put them off.

It's like using four-letter words—in a novel they don't distract the reader, but if you have a four-letter word in a movie, suddenly everyone thinks, Did you hear that? and they lose the thread of what's happening. Longshoremen don't talk the way they talked in *On the Waterfront*, but if you had a realistic conversation, the audience—not to mention the police—would be upset and distracted.

INTERVIEWER: Do you ever feel hampered by the pressure of deadlines on a script, or by having a plot already established before you start?

SOUTHERN: With a screenplay, you've got to deliver, because at some point the producers make other arrangements. They've rented a sound stage, and they've hired actors, and so they've got to begin on a certain date and finish on a certain date because these actors have other commitments. So they're going to start shooting, whether it's your script or not. With a novel, you never have pressure. I mean, who cares? There's no money involved. What if they've given you two thousand dollars? They're not panicked about that—you can put it off, and put it off, and put it off. They put some weird pressure on you, they try to make you feel bad, saying, Well, it's a shame you're not going to make the spring list, ha-ha. With a movie it's, Man, you're hanging us up! Everybody's standing around, waiting for the script.

So you feel a fantastic motivation, and it's not commercial, even though you may have taken the thing on for commercial reasons. Because finally there's this moment when all these people are just waiting.

INTERVIEWER: So the pressure is good for you?

SOUTHERN: Yes, assuming that it's a good situation, where you dig the people and have some kind of a rapport.

INTERVIEWER: When you write a movie, do you write with particular actors in mind, and does that help or hinder you?

SOUTHERN: That helps a great deal. You're given Marlon Brando, and you can already think of him saying a certain line. In a book you have to create the character. Sometimes a character is more inflexible than an actor, because an actor has a range. You can imagine Marlon Brando saying almost anything. Whereas if you create a character, there he is, and you think of him in a certain way—there are things he cannot say, things he might say, things he'll probably say—it's different.

INTERVIEWER: Your really serious writing—in the sense that it's noncomic—is in your short stories. Is that by design?

SOUTHERN: That's just the way it's worked out. I have a lot of longer noncomic things, too. I have this novel called *The Hipsters*, of which I've written about three hundred pages, which is a full-on *Jean-Christophe*. The idea was to take the development of a man—I mean, beginning in childhood. It's introspective, in a completely different tone. Very conventional, very simple. I don't know whether I'll get back to that. It doesn't really interest me much any more.

INTERVIEWER: You used to be identified with the Village hipster scene. How do you feel about that now? Are you still attached to it?

SOUTHERN: No. Those scenes change—like in Paris, the way it kept switching, from St. Germain to Montmartre to Montparnasse. As soon as they're invaded by tourists, the prices go up, it's impossible to get cheap places to live, and the people who know what's happening all move out. Then what you have left is a kind of deliberate bohemianism. It

seems to me that's happened in the Village. You've got to
have cheap rents, places that are completely undeveloped,
like lofts, before a real scene can emerge. Artists have to
have a place to live, cheaply. Now it's the Lower East Side.

INTERVIEWER: What's your favorite piece of work that you've
ever done?

SOUTHERN: I've never thought of it like that. I love to reread
stuff, and occasionally I read something and think, My
God, did I write that? Some of my favorites appeared in
The Realist. Then there's some stuff in *Candy* that I like.
Or maybe letters, some letters, never published, and
unpublishable, I suppose.

INTERVIEWER: Why do you sometimes sign your letters with
girls' names?

SOUTHERN: Because the letters are chatty. And obscene.
Signing "Cynthia" or "Paula" after a lot of obscenity
makes a curious juxtaposition. Letter writing is the best
writing of all, because it's the purest. It's like writing to
yourself, but you've got an excuse to do it because this
other person will dig it. And you can transmit information
in a strange way, you can sort of mix things up, so they
wonder, Well, is this true? You say something outlandish, and then you throw in, "John and Mary just ran
away to Hawaii," and they think ha-ha-ha, but in fact it's
true.

I don't know why, but I always feel a kind of necessity
to write things that are beyond acceptance, that are too
offensive or something. For people to read them and say,
Ha-ha-ha, very funny. No, we can't print that. I mean,
even *The Realist* has turned down stuff of mine. I've got a
piece there now that they turned down a couple years ago.
It's about Frank O'Hara, and it's very weird—not obscene,
but it violates a lot of taboos. That's the whole history of
writing, really, trying to emancipate images and language.

It's not just a question of four-letter words—you can get away with that—but of attitude. Great writers like Céline and Henry Miller, they affect attitudes, weird attitudes. Like Miller, dancing with a girl, and moving her up against a doorknob. He isn't really like that, of course. I mean *he* doesn't do that—he simply felt compelled to have a first-person narrator who could say, Yeah, got that doorknob up her cunt, because you couldn't print it, and he felt you've got to be able to print it, even though it's disgusting.

He's really quite finicky. He's no Greg Corso.

INTERVIEWER: Maybe he was thirty years ago.

SOUTHERN: I don't think so. The beauty of it is, he created a first-person narrator and made it very believable. What J. D. Salinger did, taking a thirteen-year-old, pre-sex kid and making him believable as a first-person narrator is relatively easy. But when you've got a *Lucky Jim*–age person, or Henry Miller, then it begins to get dicey, because you've got this sexual thing to deal with. The whole trick is frankness, candor, directness—and when grown men start being candid and frank and direct about sex, how far are you going to take it? Well, Miller tried to take it as far as he could. But this wasn't self-expression— he had an obsessive interest in the development of literature, in the idea of being able to go farther than D. H. Lawrence.

In *Candy*, I wanted to do something that hadn't been done, to go a little farther, but on a different level—to make it funny rather than disgusting. It's like a painter looking at a canvas, and he sees there's something missing in a certain area, and so he tries to put it in. No one's ever written a novel about the relationship between a girl and her father, for example. I mean, from the girl's point of view. Someone like Susan Sontag should devote herself to that.

INTERVIEWER: What about pornography on the screen, which is in one way the theme of your novel, *Blue Movie*? Would that be a next step?

SOUTHERN: Of the things that thrive unjustifiably, very salient among them are the clandestine—things that are taboo thrive, almost by definition. These dirty movies are so bad, and so expensive, because they're taboo. If you allowed them to be played freely, it would be much easier to make better ones than exist now, because the bad ones simply couldn't survive. And then, when they got better, they wouldn't be called pornographic—they'd just either be good or bad. And then you might say, Well, this is stimulating, or, This is erotic, but there's no law against eroticism. It's stock-in-trade for all filmmakers.

INTERVIEWER: If filmmakers had that freedom, do you think a movie would have to include eroticism to be considered good?

SOUTHERN: I've never seen a good erotic movie, so I really don't know. That's the exploration of *Blue Movie*. The idea is to find out at what point the erotic would become too much, aesthetically—in the view of the creator, not in the view of the audience.

For instance, in *Les Amants*, the Louis Malle film, there's that scene where the lovers are in bed—what we call a "tight two-shot"—nude, from the waist up. He's on top of her, and his head goes down, between her breasts, and horizontally out of the frame. It's supposed to be very erotic, but I just felt a kind of mischievousness on the part of the director. On the other hand, I was wondering what would happen if, instead of letting his head go out of the frame, the camera followed his head. How far would that go before it was, I don't know, embarrassing?

There may be something so personal or intimate about lovemaking that it's impossible to do that successfully. In a novel you can leave just enough to the mind's eye that the reader will construct a very personal image. In a movie, I don't know. If you do it merely "suggestively," it's a cop-out.

INTERVIEWER: How do you feel about the sudden popularity of black humor as a genre, something you were doing a long time ago?

SOUTHERN: It's a sign of the times, isn't it? Old values are crumbling.

INTERVIEWER: How does it feel, after years of being a so-called underground figure, to have "made it?" Are you afraid at all that money and fame will change your outlook? In other words, will success spoil Terry Southern?

SOUTHERN: Any feelings of success I may have experienced came much earlier—in the form of whatever readership I have had in *The Realist*, in certain literary magazines, and among friends whose reactions I valued. These few readers, and not the general public, are what give meaning to a work. In fact, it is almost axiomatic—the wider the acceptance of a work, the weaker its quality is bound to be.

As for my outlook, I would certainly welcome a change there, because it is basically one of discomfort. I'm afraid, however, that God would have to show his hand, in some way more dramatic than fame and fortune, before that could happen.

INTERVIEWER: But now you are selling a lot of books, *Life* magazine writes about you . . .

SOUTHERN: The important thing is to keep in touch with the youth of whatever culture you're in. When you lose them, you can forget it. When they're no longer surprised or astonished or engaged by what you say, the ball game is over. If they find it repulsive, or outlandish and disgusting, that's all right, or if they love it, that's all right, but if they just shrug it off, it's time to retire. Or rather, you can still write for a living if you want to, but it's suicidal if you have any relationship to the work other than that.

INTERVIEWER: People seem to like the idea of putting you down, now that you've "made it." It probably happens to everybody, but you hear them say, Terry Southern, isn't he a junkie? or, Isn't he a faggot? or a God knows what, but I wonder if it's . . .

SOUTHERN: If it's true? A junkie fag! A spade junkie commie fag!

New York writers are very suspicious of people who spend any time in Los Angeles. Most of them don't get invited, and they're sort of hurt and confused by it.

INTERVIEWER: Do you find it more difficult to attack now? If, after all, attacking comes from feeling angry?

SOUTHERN: I'm not interested in attacking, I'm interested in astonishing. Lenny Bruce was one of the great astonishers, and he was a very gentle, mild person. He didn't lead any protest marches or anything—what was funny to him was the irony of the smugness and so on, and he deflated it, because it's funny to see it deflated. Of course he was very conscious of injustices and absurdities, like any sensitive person, and that came out as an attack, but it wasn't his motivation.

It's different in Europe, where there is, or used to be, a very definite notion of class conflict. You can set about illustrating a theme in a more conscious way. Sartre writes that way. He'll pick out a subject, like religious hypocrisy, and he'll write a play to flesh it out. I think Mailer writes like that. I have never approached writing that way.

Say I were to witness a scene, some sort of fracas between a headwaiter and a Negro. There would be something grotesque, something ironic about it, and the engaging thing in writing about it would be the grotesqueness, the irony. It wouldn't be because I thought, This is a terrible social injustice that should be dramatized and brought to the attention of the public.

INTERVIEWER: What movie would you make if you could make any movie?

SOUTHERN: *Naked Lunch* and *A Clockwork Orange*.

INTERVIEWER: What about underground movies, do you think they're doing something good? If you had the opportunity, would you make them?

SOUTHERN: There are any number of things that are inherently cinematic and dramatic and that haven't yet been fully realized or exploited. Rather than go to the underground, or the so-called expanded cinema, I think these things can be done under existing conditions. It's no good if the audience just thinks, Oh yeah, this is very curious, very interesting. I'd be more inclined to work under the prevailing mechanics of moviemaking, using other people's money.

INTERVIEWER: You talk about exploring and experimenting under prevailing conditions. If the studios are in control, will they let that happen?

SOUTHERN: They're relenting all the time, because they're losing ground. Television is the thing, you see—its existence puts movies in a position of having to do something different. In five years television screens will be half the size of a movie screen, they'll occupy a whole wall. And people will just sit there. They're not going to leave the house except to see something groovy, something that they can't see at home.

The great future, not for creative writers, but for professional writers, is in television, because pay television is going to come in, and that will take the place of the art movies that exist now, and ordinary television will take the place of what now exists in movies. In twenty years, the movies that compete with TV and pay TV will have to be pretty far out. Otherwise people will simply hang with the tube.

INTERVIEWER: If you weren't a writer and could choose any job, profession, or career, what would you do and why?

SOUTHERN: If I were not a writer I would prefer being a psychiatrist-gynecologist. I'm not sure this exists—like eye, ear, nose, and throat specialist—but I personally think it is a winning combo and would like to give it a whirl.

INTERVIEWER: If you were given enough money so that you didn't have to work or make any commitments and could do whatever you wanted, where would you live and what would you do?

SOUTHERN: First I would engage a huge but clever and snakelike "Blowing Machine," and I would have it loaded with one ton of dog hair each Monday, Wednesday, and Friday. It would be brought up East Seventy-second Street to the very end, where it would poise itself outside George Plimpton's house like a great dragon. Then, exactly when Katherine the Char had finished one room, the powerful, darting snout of the machine would rise up to the third floor windows and send a terrific blast of dog hair into the room—a quarter ton per room. I would observe her reaction—I have friends opposite—with a spyglass, room by room. The entire place would be foot-deep in dog hair, most of which however has not yet settled and has the effect of an Arctic blizzard. Then I would drop in—casually, not really noticing her hysteria, or that anything at all was wrong, just sort of complaining in a vague way, occasionally brushing at my sleeve, et cetera, speaking with a kind of weary petulance: "Really, Katherine, I do think you might be more . . . uh, well, I mean to say . . ." voice trailing away, attention caught by something else, a picture on the wall: "I say, that is an amusing print—is it new?" fixing her with a deeply searching look, so there could be no doubt at all as to my interest in the print. If this didn't snap her mind I would give her several hundred thousand dollars—all in pennies. "Mr. Plimpton asked me to give you this, Katherine—each coin represents the dark seed of his desire for you."

Wired

FINALIST—FEATURE
WRITING INCORPORATING
PROFILE WRITING

If Kim Dotcom hadn't invented himself, it would have taken somebody like Terry Southern to do it for him. Charles Graeber went to New Zealand to meet the six-foot-seven, 350-pound Dotcom in his Dotcom Mansion soon after he was arrested by Kiwi authorities. The result was, in the words of its editors, "a fast-paced crime story, an adventure yarn, a legal thriller, and a tearful portrait of a troubled child prodigy who becomes an international robber baron." Plus, there's the Filipino ex-model wife, the three-year-old son, and a posse straight out of The Big Bang Theory *(or* The Hangover, *take your pick). In any case, the National Magazine Award judges were impressed, describing this as a "masterly, sometimes hilarious profile that brings its larger-than-the-web subject brilliantly to life."*

Charles Graeber

Mega

Ten Days Inside the
Mansion—and the
Mind—of Kim Dotcom,
the Most Wanted Man
on the Internet

Please Choose One of the Following Statements:

- A. **Kim Dotcom is not a pirate.** He's a hero. The savior of
  my online liberties. A visionary digital entrepreneur. His
  company Megaupload was a legitimate data-storage business used by hundreds of millions of individuals and by
  employees of NASA, U.S. Central Command, even the FBI.
  The raid on his New Zealand home was excessive and
  illegal—shock-and-awe bullshit. Hollywood is terrified by
  the digital future, and an innocent paid the price. Kim is a
  martyr. But Kim will triumph.

    You'd like him, he's cool.
- B. **Kim Dotcom is a pirate.** A megalomaniacal gangsta
  clown. An opportunistic and calculating career criminal.
  His Megaupload enterprise willfully made hundreds of millions of dollars off stolen movies, songs, videogames, books,
  and software. And, oh yeah, he couldn't be more obnoxious
  about it.

He wanted *Wired* to write a nice story about him, so he manipulated its writer by providing exclusive access, and even a few tears, in hopes of a puff piece. But Kim is a criminal. He knows he's a criminal. Like any pirate, the only freedoms he really cares about are the ones he can exploit to make himself rich. The rest is all PR.

If you think he's cool, you don't know him.

- C. **Kim Dotcom is rich enough** to work however and wherever he wants. And what he wants is to work from bed.

His bed of choice is a remarkable piece of custom Swedish craftsmanship made by a company called Hästens. Each one takes some 160 hours to produce and is signed by a master bed maker who lays out the most perfect matrix of horsehair, cotton, flax, and wool. Price after custom framing: $103,000. Kim has three such beds in his New Zealand mansion, one of which faces a series of monitors and hard drives and piles of wires and is flanked on either side by lamps that look like, and may well be, chromed AK-47s. This is Kim's "work bed" and serves as his office. It was here that he returned in the early morning of January 20, 2012, after a long night spent on his music album, one of his many side projects.

Kim had spent the previous seven hours down the road at Roundhead Studios, laying down beats with songwriter Mario "Tex" James and Black Eyed Peas producer Printz Board in a studio owned by Crowded House frontman Neil Finn. They finished around four-thirty a.m., and Kim slid into the backseat of his Mercedes S-Class for the ride back to his mansion. Soon after leaving the parking lot, Kim noticed headlights behind them. He said to his driver, "I think we're being followed."

They pulled into Kim's rented palace around dawn. His wife and children were long asleep in another wing. Kim walked to his upstairs chambers, showered and changed into his customary all-black sleeping costume, grabbed his customary chilled Fiji water from the upstairs fridge, and settled before the monitors of his work bed. Then he heard the noise.

A low, wavering bass, it seemed to be coming from outside. Kim couldn't tell—the cavernous stone labyrinth of rooms swallowed and scattered sound, and the thick velvet blackout curtains blocked out everything else. Kim guessed it was his helicopter. He didn't bother with details, he had a staff for that, but he did know that VIPs from the entertainment world were expected in from LA in celebration of his thirty-eighth birthday. Maybe they'd arrived early and Roy, his pilot, had been dispatched to meet them. A moment later the helicopter theory was confirmed by the sound of rocks from the limestone drive raining against the windows. Fucking Roy! He'd been told not to land too near—the thought was interrupted by a boom, echoing and close.

This noise was coming from the other side of his office door. It was heavy hardwood several inches thick, secured by stout metal bolts in the stone casement. Kim struggled to his feet as the door shook and heaved on its hinges. Someone or something was trying to break through. Now Kim heard other noises, shouts and bangs and the unmistakable stomping of boots on stairs. Intruders were in the house. Kim Dotcom realized he was under attack.

. . .

Across an ocean, hours before Operation Takedown began, the U.S. Department of Justice had already tipped off a select group of journalists about the raid's planned highlights. If you know nothing else about Kim Dotcom, about the federal case against him and his former online business, Megaupload, you've probably heard about the raid. The story played out like a Hollywood blockbuster. And it was a great story.

The scene: New Zealand. Lush and Green and Freaking Far Away. It's the Canada of Australia, Wales in a Hawaiian shirt, a Xanadu habitat for hobbit and emu.

And harbor home to the villain: Kim Dotcom, né Kim Schmitz, aka Tim Vestor, Kim Tim Jim Vestor, Kimble, and Dr. Evil. A classic comic-book baddie millionaire, an ex-con expatriate German ex-hacker lording over his own personal Pirate Bay just thirty minutes north of Auckland. Kim Dotcom was presented as a big, bad man, larger-than-life, larger than his 6' 7", perhaps 350-pound frame. We saw him posed with guns and yachts and fancy cars. We watched him drive his nitrox-fueled Mega Mercedes in road rallies and on golf courses, throwing fake gang signs at rap moguls and porn stars, making it rain with $175 million in illicit dotcom booty.

His alleged fifty-petabyte pirate ship was Megaupload.com, a massive vessel carrying, at its peak, 50 million passengers a day, a full 4 percent of global Internet traffic. Megaupload was a free online storage locker, a cloud warehouse for files too bulky for e-mail. It generated an estimated $25 million a year in revenue from ads and brought in another $150 million through its paid, faster, unlimited Premium service.

The DOJ maintains that the legitimate storage business was only a front, like a Mafia pork store; the real money was made out back, where Megaupload was a mega-swapmeet for some $500 million worth of pirated material, including movies, TV shows, music, books, videogames, and software. Kim, they contend, was the Jabba the Hutt–like presence running this grand bazaar of copyright criminality with impunity from his Kiwi Tatooine, protected by laser break beams and guards and guns, CCTV and infrared and even escape pods—including a helicopter and high-performance sports cars. The FBI also believed Kim possessed a special portable device that would wipe his servers all across the globe, destroying the evidence. They called this his doomsday button.

Operation Takedown was carried out by armed New Zealand special police and monitored by the FBI via video link. Descriptions of the raid varied from one news outlet to another, but most included the cops' dramatic helicopter arrival on the expansive Dotcom Mansion lawn and their struggles with a security system fit for a Mafia don.

We read that police were forced to cut their way into Dotcom's panic room, where they found him cowering near a sawed-off shotgun. That same day, similar raids were under way in eight other countries where Megaupload had servers or offices.

This was justice on an epically entertaining scale, topped by a final cherry of schadenfreude: the rich fat bad man humbled and humiliated, the boastful pirate king brought down. He was cuffed and put in jail, his booty seized, his business scuttled upon the reefs of anti-racketeering laws. If all went as planned, he and his six generals would be extradited to the United States to face a Virginia judge and up to fifty-five years each in prison. The message was, if it could happen to him, it could happen to anyone. Look upon these works, ye BitTorrenters of Dark Knight trilogies, sneak thieves of 50 Cent, and despair in your pirate bays. Justice was served, the end, roll credits. Yes, it was a great story.

The only problem was, it wasn't quite true.

•　　•　　•

Kim Dotcom's head of security is waiting for me at the Auckland airport on a gray day last July. Wayne Tempero is easy to spot. Amid the limo drivers and families with Mylar balloons is one deadly serious shave-headed New Zealander with a lantern jaw—a tattooed wall of muscle wearing a tight black hoodie. Before working "close protection" for the most famous man in New Zealand, Tempero had protected other big faces and names, from David Beckham to the royal family of Brunei. He specializes in military hand-to-hand combat and looks like a very nice person who'd be very handy with a knife.

The car is waiting just outside. Not the Lamborghini or pink Series 62 Cadillac or any of the three retrofitted Mercedes CLK DTMs with extra-wide seats—the cops had impounded those. This is just a modest black Mercedes G55 AMG Kompressor with the license plate KIMCOM. "I think I was followed on my way here," Tempero says. In fact, everyone in Kim's entourage assumes everything is monitored, including all their communications. Tempero is the one facing gun charges after the raid—the shotguns were registered in his name—and he doesn't need any more problems with the police. "Maybe we're all a little paranoid these days," he says with a grin as he edges up to the speed limit for the drive.

The Dotcom Mansion is impossible to miss, mostly because of the chromed industrial-park letters spelling out DOTCOM MANSION across the gatehouse in blue backlighting. It's said to be the island nation's most expensive home, located in the lush hills of the town of Coatesville. The limestone drive winds up to a $24 million suburban castle with ponds, a tennis court, several pools, a Vegas-style stairstep fountain, and a hedgerow labyrinth. The surrounding sixty acres of lawn are manicured and impossibly steep.

Until just two months ago, Kim couldn't live in his own home, as a condition of his house arrest following a month of jail time. For three months he was confined to the guesthouse, a prison of black lacquer and black leather, black Versace tables and wall-sized LCD flatscreens. The walls are adorned with poster-sized photographs of Kim and his beautiful twenty-four-year-old wife, Mona, but mostly just Kim: Kim in front of a helicopter, Kim on the bow of a luxury yacht, Kim reeling in a great fish or in front of a European castle holding a shotgun and a limp duck, or straddling a mountaintop, eyes pinned on the distant future. The effect is more Kim Jong-Il than Kim Dotcom. Dotcom—or the iconic character of Dotcom—is everywhere here, but most of the fifty-three members of the household staff that once maintained the larger estate are gone with his seized fortune.

Outside the windows there are no humans to be seen or things to do. The grounds are gray and cold, winter in the southern hemisphere. The perimeter fences warn of electrocution. Closed-circuit cameras take in every angle from stations in the trees and rooftops, sending flickering images to the panels monitored by the skeleton staff still manning the distant guardhouses. My suspicion of surveillance by the FBI or New Zealand anti-terror forces—or perhaps even by the millionaire former hacker himself—prevents me from logging onto Kim's wireless network or even making a phone call. I feel like I've been kidnapped and held as a "guest" by a Bond villain. A Bond villain who is asleep. In fact, Tempero tells me, the boss had just gone to bed shortly before I arrived at dawn. There's no telling when he'll be awake.

Kim has surrounded himself with luxury, but what he prizes above all other indulgences is pure, deep sleep. He simply doesn't always like to get up in the morning, and he doesn't always like going to bed at night, and—here's the kicker—he doesn't have to. The sun is up or down—who cares? The clock is numbers in a circle, duodecimal nonsense. It is a guilt machine, a metronome for the normal lives of normal people. But it is always dark somewhere. And it is always night in the Dotcom Mansion. Great black curtains shut out the light, thick stone walls block the sound. The $103,000 horsehair Hästens bed is waiting. In his sleeping chamber there are no electronic things, no humming or beeping devices, no leaking of LED, no sigh of capacitor or fan. For sleep of the finest quality, for epicurean, luxury slumber, total silence is required and enforced.

The gardeners do not mow, the cleaners do not clean. The cooks chop quietly in other wings, the nannies tend the children in another house. When he sleeps the mansion holds its breath. Kim can't provide a schedule. He doesn't have to. It's his house.

When Kim sleeps, he is flying. He's not sweating, he doesn't have health problems, bad knees, or a bad back. He's not on trial or fighting for recognition. He's not a kid afraid of his father coming home or more afraid that he won't. He's not being extradited to a place where jailers mark day from night with a light switch. When Kim sleeps, he is free.

"I usually just watch his Twitter," Tempero says. "That's really the only way to know when the boss is up."

It's late afternoon before Kim's tweets start pouring forth. He tweets a lot, announcing updates on the coming court hearings, plugging his new pop single—a catchy duet with his wife called "Precious"—and a music video featuring home footage of the five Dotcom kids, including hospital shots of the arrival of his new twins only five months before. Other messages in the stream address Julian Assange or Internet freedoms or the tyranny of the FBI. A few minutes later, Tempero is at my door. The boss is up.

·   ·   ·

I find Kim behind the wheel of his golf cart, layered in his usual uniform of black vest over diaphanous black shirt and three-quarter-length pants, a black scarf and heavy black leather ball cap. He is a large man and fills most of the front seat. Despite his blue-tinted Cartier sunglasses, his eyes squint against the sunlight. Spotting me, he motors over and extends a fist bump.

"Wow, you look like a Viking," he says, meaning probably that I'm blond and tall like him. His English is precise and tinged with a German-Finnish accent. "Cool!" Then he zips away on a golf cart that has been hacked to top 30 mph.

I follow along the limestone trail to what Kim calls his hill, where he can soak in a few minutes of precious winter sun.

At this time of year Kim and family would usually be based out of their floor-wide residence in the Grand Hyatt Hong Kong, or on a rented yacht off the shores of Monaco or St. Tropez. The raid has enforced a Hotel California–style house arrest: stuck in a mansion on an island paradise, but still stuck.

"We will win the extradition trial eventually," Kim says. "But what's the point of that?" They'd still be stuck in New Zealand or vulnerable in any country with an extradition treaty with the United States. The only real victory would be to face the charges in the States and win. But so far, the U.S. Department of Justice has refused to allow them to use frozen Megaupload assets to relocate to the United States and to pay lawyers. Their legal bills are already in the millions of dollars and rising.

But Kim has reason to hope that his adopted home might aid his cause. In a few days he will be in court for a much-expected showdown with prosecutors about the excesses of the raid on his home. It's a sideshow ahead of the extradition hearing in March—but a sideshow that might determine Kim's fate.

Kiwis still recall with pride their government barring American nuclear-powered warships from their harbors. Kim is not a New Zealand citizen, but many here took the FBI-instigated raid on his home quite personally, as a *COPS*-style American invasion.

In recent weeks, New Zealand Crown judges have pushed back against the DOJ, ruling that the search warrant on Kim and the removal of his personal hard drives under the guidance of the FBI were illegal. Still, the jeopardy is daunting—up to fifty-five years in jail for alleged crimes including conspiracy to commit copyright infringement, money laundering, and racketeering. "They're treating us like a mafia, man!" Kim says. "It's unbelievable. It's only because they cannot extradite us to the U.S. just for copyright violation. If they treat us as some sort of international criminal conspiracy, they can."

The "us" Kim is referring to are his six codefendants, his partners in Megaupload. Andrus Nomm, a resident of both Turkey and Estonia, was captured in Holland; Sven Echternach escaped to his home in Germany (which does not extradite its citizens); and Julius Bencko of Slovakia remains at large. The other three were, like Kim, nabbed in New Zealand. Two now arrive atop Kim's hill in golf carts, young men in jeans and untucked oxford shirts.

First Bram van der Kolk, who oversaw programming for the Mega websites and at thirty looks something like a Dutch Matt Damon. Then Finn Batato, Megaupload's chief marketing officer. Batato is a thirty-nine-year-old half-Palestinian, half-German from Munich, a mellow chain-smoking playboy with a taste for wine and watches. And finally, snaking up the hill on an all-terrain Segway, is Mathias Ortmann, Megaupload's chief technical officer, cofounder, and director, the Spock to Kim's Teutonic Kirk, and the 25 percent to Kim's 68 percent ownership of Megaupload. Ortmann is a forty-year-old German ex-hacker and looks like it, with a dark V-neck over his thin frame and square glasses.

"He's a genius, you know," Batato says, lighting a cigarette. "Not because he speaks four languages, but an Einstein-type genius."

Ortmann looks up from his iPhone and blinks.

"Mathias, please, at least admit that—it's true."

Ortmann just looks back at his screen, setting up a Skype call with his girlfriend back home in Germany.

"Please, tell the world," Batato says to me, "these are normal people here." Usually he would be in Europe, perhaps in the south of France, drinking Opus. Instead he is stuck in winter, facing jail, borrowing cigarette money, and living with van der Kolk. Batato is worried folks back home might think he is some kind of gangster.

"I mean, look at us," van der Kolk says. He's not some mafia pirate. He's a programming nerd with a Filipino ex-model wife and a three-year-old son. "It's bullshit. We seem to be an easy target with this lifestyle. But driving around with license plates that say 'mafia' and stuff—it's just our kind of humor."

In the distance, Tempero appears in a golf cart. He works his way up the steep hill and hands a fresh bottle of Fiji water to Kim.

"Everything good, boss?"

"Yeah," Kim says, wringing the cap off the bottle. The guys watch him as the dying sun signals the end of another day in their life in this island paradise. Their Elba.

At this point, all that stands between them and their fate are legal teams and Kim himself. Sure, the DOJ case cites a handful of seized e-mails that sound damning, but it was Kim who got them here. Dotcom has compared himself to Bill Gates, Steve Jobs, Julian Assange, and Martin Luther King Jr. He was the team's visionary. Now he'll need to think his team out of this jam. Kim promises he will. He has a plan.

And something even bigger and better in the works. More Mega than Megaupload. A technology nobody can touch. One that will change the world. They'll beat the Department of Justice, humiliate them. And then, Kim promises, they shall have their vengeance.

.　　　.　　　.

The sun sets early in winter. The men file back down the hill to the warmth of Kim's house-sized kitchen beside a sixteen-foot saltwater fish tank. A young Filipino maid brings Kim a fresh facecloth and water. Batato leaves for his usual spot on the back porch, to smoke and brood. The rest of the men stare silently into their iPhones, studying news blogs for hints of their fate.

Lately the news has been about donations Dotcom made to a New Zealand parliamentarian named John Banks—the deciding vote in the prime minister's majority. When cornered, Banks insisted he didn't remember the source of the donations or the ride in Kim's helicopter or other allegations that might get him indicted. There have been calls for his resignation or impeachment.

"What do you think, Mathias?" Kim asks. "Should I give them an interview about the donations?"

"Did you tell the truth, the whole truth, and nothing but?"

"Yes."

"Well then, go ahead," Mathias says. "But I think it's a sideshow."

"But it would be interesting, no?"

"What, toppling a government?"

"Yes."

"Let's focus on toppling the bigger government."

That government, of course, would be the United States. Kim and his associates are convinced that their company was targeted by the Obama administration for political rather than legal reasons. So, while twenty-eight lawyers for Megaupload fight those charges around the world, Kim is taking on the Obama administration as well.

He's starting with the music video of his single "Mr. President" and an online drive to collect promises not to reelect him.

Social media is new for Kim, but he already has more than 130,000 followers on Twitter and after only a few days has reached Facebook's 5,000-friend limit. "Oh it's stupid," he says. "The interface is terrible. I'm bombed with news from people I don't know—why does anyone put up with it?"

Kim is soliciting real friends too, inviting startled admirers to "swim at Kim's" events at his pool and hosting Apple cofounder Steve Wozniak only a few weeks earlier in a show of Electronic Freedom solidarity. He's reframing the issue: It's not the DOJ versus Dotcom, it's Hollywood versus Silicon Valley.

Kim maintains that the real issue is a lack of understanding of the Internet. He was simply operating a hard-disc drive in virtual space. There's no arguing that Megaupload wasn't a legitimate cyberlocker, storing data for millions of individuals. Megaupload server logs show addresses that trace back to Fortune 100 companies and governments around the world. It's also obvious that Megaupload was one of many Internet sites that stored, and profited from, copyright-infringing material. The only question is whether Kim and company bear criminal responsibility for that duality.

The law addressing this balance between the rights of copyright holders and Internet service providers was signed by President Clinton in 1998. The Digital Millennium Copyright Act provides ISPs with "safe harbor" from liability, so long as the provider doesn't know for certain which, if any, of its stored material is copyright-infringing and "expeditiously" removes infringing material following a takedown notice.

The act was tested in June of 2010, when a U.S. district court ruled that YouTube was protected by safe harbor against a $1 billion suit by Viacom; Google employees simply could not be expected to make tough, and often impossible, calls as to which clips of, say, Jersey Shore, had been uploaded without permission.

The DMCA was intended to clear up the gray areas of Internet law. But by making ignorance of its own business a cloud storage provider's only defense, the law created a brand-new gray area, leaving in place an Internet where piracy was blatant big business. The world still hadn't worked out how to have data storage that was both private and policed. Lawmakers attempted to tackle that issue this year with the antipiracy SOPA/PIPA measures, but millions of Internet freedom advocates shouted it down and on January 20 the legislation died; Kim was raided that same week. "The U.S. showed the world they don't need SOPA or a trial to control the Internet," Kim says. "They did it with guns."

The DOJ claims Megaupload was anything but ignorant of the pirated material on its site. In fact, the indictment claims, Megaupload's generals engaged in illegal file-sharing themselves, encouraged it with an incentive program that paid cash for popular content, and were slow and selective in complying with takedown notices, only pulling infringing content and dropping the incentive program when the company was at the peak of its power. Megaupload counters that policing the billions of files on its service would be both impossible and a violation of their customers' privacy, that they did their best to comply with takedown notices as the law required, and that they had reasonable expectations of the same DMCA safe harbor afforded to YouTube.

But unlike the Viacom versus YouTube case, the charges against Megaupload are not civil but criminal; the key players aren't being sued, they're facing jail. Not for the first time, Kim finds himself embroiled in a criminal case based on uncertain tech precedent. Does safe harbor even apply in a criminal case? It's not clear that a criminal statute against second-party copyright violation even exists. Welcome to the grayest gray zone on the Internet.

At the heart of the DOJ's case is the concept of "willfulness." It's a question of whether the Megaupload boys knew they were criminals. And for that reason, much of the focus has been on the character of Kim Dotcom himself.

Dotcom does have several criminal convictions in Germany, a history of working at the edges of the technologically possible and legally permissible, and a bad-boy reputation. What's less clear is whether this patchwork description makes Dotcom a Don Corleone or a Da Vinci.

"They probably thought, this guy's fucking crazy and illegal, and we will find so much shit on him once we open it up," Kim says. "They thought I was an easy target. They thought I was a joke. But they underestimated me, man. Everything they're saying about me is ten years old. What they didn't know is, I'm the cleanest guy out there."

Dotcom wipes the sweat from his forehead and refolds his black facecloth. "That's the funny part of all this," he says. "Everyone thinks they know me. But nobody really knows me at all."

•   •   •

Kim was nineteen the first time he was sent to jail. The charge was "handling stolen goods," but it wasn't as simple as that; the German court simply didn't have a word for this new crime of hacking.

Growing up in the northern German city of Kiel with his mother and alcoholic father, Kim was in trouble before he even discovered computers. As he sits with me at the table long after the maids have cleared the plates and his wife and business partners have gone to bed, Kim speaks haltingly of a childhood "filled with fear" and a father who would beat his mother while drunk or dangle young Kim over the balcony, Michael Jackson–style. "I wanted to be the one who would fix everything," Kim says. "I thought if I tried hard enough, I could reengineer my father or, later, convince my mother to get back with him." His stratagems didn't work, but the trauma imprinted on his personality. "I had all the fear I could handle by the time I was six," Kim says. "It made me strong."

The kid who emerged from this childhood was smart and willful, unafraid of adults and unimpressed with their authority. He didn't have much interest in their schools either, the arbitrary courses or the magic supposedly conferred by a degree. Kim preferred to sleep late and skip class; his inattentiveness got him sent from high school back to middle school. He says his difficult behavior landed him in a psychiatrist's office. The man gave him some tests; Kim stole the doctor's wallet and took his friends out for ice cream.

He was around eleven when he saw his first Commodore C-16 in a shop window, running a demo of some pixelated game. He hectored his mother until she finally bought it for him. It sat on his desk, a puzzle asking for his solution in BASIC, interesting in a way school never could be. A friend in school had a tool called ICE on a floppy disk. It allowed him to make copies of games, simply by removing a line of code.

Nobody called that piracy. The point was unfettered access. The point was the possible. One of Kim's schoolmates had described an online Shangri-La called X.25—basically a pre-Internet closed network. Kim bought himself a 2400-baud modem, the kind where you stick a phone handset into a rubber coupler. "I was in my new world." He didn't want to be anywhere else.

"X.25 was quite hard to get into—you needed the code—but once you got in, the people there were very open about how to hack various things, sharing access numbers, speaking freely." Kim sat silently lurking, absorbing the information. But before long he started his own attacks.

One of the recurring hacks was a backdoor attack on corporate PBX systems—a company's internal phone and data exchange. "Back then, there really was no concept of a system administrator," he says. "Very few admins even knew how to change the default passwords. It never occurred to them that a kid might try to break in. It was like moving to some little Swedish village with no locks on the doors. You got in, became a super-user, and basically owned the network. It was a bonanza."

Most of the early PBXs were across the ocean, in Manhattan's 212 area code, and required an expensive long-distance call. Luckily Kim had access to a hacker BBS forum for exchanging stolen calling-card numbers too.

He loved crawling through a new company's data, paying special attention to outgoing modem calls, which would lead him to even more PBXs. Kim wrote a little script and set it running at night, dialing up numbers, jiggling the knobs of the back doors; the next day he'd have access to 800 accounts, complete with usernames and passwords. He was building an army. "You find this world as a teenager, fourteen, fifteen years old? You don't even think about going to school now, man. Who gives a shit about that?" Kim just wanted to stay inside, controlling a virtual world as he'd never been able to control his own. His exploits made him seem dangerous and cool to his friends, a hero. And the hacker scene fed perfectly into his sense of the world as being us-versus-them.

The scam that got him arrested focused on the pay-by-the-minute phone chat lines popular in the early nineties. These were the German equivalent of 1-900 party lines that the phone company charged as a long-distance call, usually at around $1.20 a minute. The operator of the line received a percentage from the local telecom, about 15 cents a minute per caller; the more callers, the more money the party line owner made. So Kim set up his own party line in the Netherland Antilles. Then he generated massive caller traffic using stolen calling-card numbers from the hacker bulletin boards.

"It worked really well," Kim says. He says he made more than 75,000 Deutschmarks (or about $195,000 today)—"which at the time was a huge amount of money, because I was a kid. I wanted to buy more modems for my BBS, a better computer—nice stuff to advance my capacity."

In 1993, three years into the scam, Kim got caught. He was arrested and spent four weeks in jail as a juvenile. Kim says he was "scared to shit" in jail but found it interesting too. "I had all these visitors, grown-ups from MCI and AT&T, coming just to talk to me." He was shocked that these so-called experts from major corporations had no idea how a PBX operated, much less how it could be hacked. "It was like I was speaking Chinese," Kim says. "It was unbelievable." It was also a potential business.

He partnered with fellow hacker and coding genius Mathias Ortmann to form Data Protect, one of the world's first white-hat consultancies, charging hundreds of dollars an hour to tell businesses how to protect against people like themselves. Their former colleagues in the hacker community thought of them as traitors. Kim and Ortmann thought they were growing up.

The German media quickly discovered the teenage wunderkind, and Kim discovered he enjoyed the spotlight. "The hacker was the new magician," Kim remembers. "They treated you like you must be a fucking genius, man. But all I did, I scanned message boards. I got passwords. Any monkey could do that. There was nothing genius about it. But you get addicted to the head-lines, people saying nice things, telling you you're smart."

The gun was loaded: Kim had the needs of an outsider and the cred of a rock star. He had contempt for the system and the tools to beat it. He felt powerful and reckless and was being told he was smarter than the rest of the world. He was in his early twenties and getting paid, buying expensive custom cars and fine suits, renting yachts, throwing money around nightclubs, swaggering. Growing up he'd never felt particularly special. Now he had girls. He had a posse. He was featured in German magazine spreads.

By 1997 Kim took it upon himself to make his own headlines, launching a website about his life and philosophy. He called it Kimble.org, for his hacker name, Kimble—as in *The Fugitive*'s Richard Kimble. Kim liked that his real name was inside it, and he identified with the movie about a good guy misunderstood and persecuted.

A decade before Facebook made online oversharing the norm, Kim used Kimble.org to showcase his life. It was also one of the first websites to incorporate Flash. "The Internet was just ugly fonts with underlined blue links," Kim says. "People would come to my site, see it moving and animated and colorful, and think—what is this? They'd never seen anything like it."

There were videos of Kim, photos of Kim. Kim as an icon of success, an inspiration. Kim with women. Kim on a mountaintop. Kim in a black suit. Kim in a white suit. Kim on a jet. He rounded out the site with motivational lists like "10 Rules of Success."

"People thought I started the site to promote my ego," Kim says. "But it was to motivate people." He knows it sounds silly, but that's what he was, or wanted to be anyway—a motivational figure, a Gates, a Jobs, a Branson, Tony Robbins, and Donald Trump. The photos and videos, the posing and bragging and clowning—these were a clarion call for nerd confidence, an en-ticement to take a risk and achieve. As he was doing.

By 2000, Kim had sold most of his stake in Data Protect and started a private capital investment fund. He had particular interest in a company called LetsBuyIt.com—a sort of proto-Groupon, ten years too early. Kim invested in shares of the company, believing that he could simplify its interface and make it a success. Then he announced his plan to raise another $50 million to fund it. The company stock jumped 220 percent, and Kim sold some shares at a profit.

"I was chilling in Bangkok when I heard the news," he says. He was being accused of insider trading. He says he didn't consider acting on his own plans to be insider trading and was committed to the company; apparently, the securities regulators were less sure. The story of yet another crazy caper by the flamboyant Kim Schmitz created a media frenzy, and a German TV station sent a team to interview the famous genius in his presidential suite at the Bangkok Grand Hyatt. "I was really angry and a little cocky," Kim concedes. "I told them that if this is how Germany treats their entrepreneurs, I don't know if I ever want to be in Germany again. And that was a mistake."

German television replayed the images of the rich young troublemaker talking smack from a luxury suite in Thailand, acting like he was beyond the reach of German laws. A German prosecutor set out to prove him wrong and asked for Kim's arrest; the German embassy in Bangkok revoked his passport. Now Kim was in Thailand as an illegal alien. Thai police cuffed him in his suite and led him to an immigration prison. "This wasn't a normal jail," Kim says. "This was fucking crazy. I'm wearing a custom suit. I'm thrown into a place, eighteen guys sleeping on a concrete floor, everyone in sweaty shirts, it's forty degrees Celsius and smells like shit. I've got mosquitoes eating me, the food comes in a bucket."

Kim's lawyer told him he could fight in court and win—he'd be out in a month. Kim hoped he was kidding. Germany was offering a two-day travel document if he'd agree to come home.

Kim said, "Let's go." He was escorted onto a plane by two German policemen. The press were waiting.

This was big news in Germany—the biggest insider trader in history, accused of violating a law that was only a few years old. "The headlines all said something about me being fat, 'the downfall of the loudmouth,' like that," Kim says. "My lifestyle and Kimble.org had painted a target on my back." They called him a megalomaniac, a swindler, the "hacker king."

Kim was considered a flight risk and spent five months in jail before being offered probation and a small fine if he'd plead guilty. "I was just tired," Kim says. "I knew I was finished in Germany anyway." And he knew Kimble.org was finished as well—there was no chance of his being an inspiration to anyone now. "So I took the deal. And there's nothing I regret more. Because if I hadn't pled, I wouldn't have had that 'career criminal' label. And I wouldn't be here today."

.   .   .

There is only one area in which Kim embraces an illicit identity: He has a rabid need for speed. He doesn't drink or do drugs, but he drives unapologetically fast. Driving is his vice, an addiction to the rush of velocity and control of a graceful machine. Kim says that before he left Germany he tried to set a record for points against his license, "speeding past red-light cameras, flashing thumbs-up, getting off the exit, and doing it again." In road rallies, he's been known to bump cars or use the sidewalk to take the lead. His style is described by some as fearless, by others as reckless, and by all his competitors as truly good.

Beginning in 2001 he and his computerized Mercedes "mega-Car" were a regular in the Gumball 3000 rally, a quasi-legal rich man's Cannonball Run. Videos from the time show an outrageous Kim, often in the company of scantily clad women and sometimes sporting a replica Nazi helmet and the trophy. In 2004 he wanted to start his own rally, at a more mega-ultimate level.

"The Ultimate Rally was supposed to be Gumball on steroids," Kim says. He'd host it somewhere like North Korea and attract professional drivers from Formula One with a million dollars cash awaiting the winner. Kim saw a business based on video rights, films, and sponsorship.

Kim and his new partner, Bram van der Kolk, drummed up interest by sending out videos of Kim's racing exploits, often by e-mail. The problem was, the video attachments were too big, and the e-mails kept bouncing. Clearly, there had to be a better way to share large files online.

They called their solution Megaupload. The charges against the company describe their technology concisely: "Once that user has selected a file on their computer and clicks the 'upload' button, Megaupload.com reproduces the file on at least one computer server it controls and provides the uploading user with a unique Uniform Resource Locator ('URL') link that allows anyone with the link to download the file."

"It was a little idea," Kim says. "At that point we honestly never expected to do anything more with it."

At first Kim used Megaupload to generate buzz around the Ultimate Rally, offering $5,000 for the best street-racing videos. "All of a sudden you have all these car people uploading videos and linking to them to share with friends," Kim says. Soon they were pushing the limits of their servers.

This had potential beyond racing videos, he began to realize. File sizes were getting bigger; HD had gone mainstream. The future was obvious. He never would have seen it if he was still in Germany, if his old business hadn't been destroyed. The cloud was the future. "I decided, fuck Ultimate Rally," Kim says. From then on, he would be all Megaupload. But he would no longer be Kim Schmitz.

Schmitz was his father's name. The last time he'd seen the man, he was being interviewed by a German television station. He seemed to be living in a garden shed, weathered and ravaged by drink. He told the interviewers that his hotshot son never came to see him. "How could they let him just say that, man?" Kim asks. He looks away. "It wasn't right." Kim got some letters after that but never responded. "I don't know, maybe he's dead now," he says, blinking hard.

Kim had left that world behind. His new business was a fresh start that promised to rebrand him as a dotcom giant. Why shouldn't the world know him as a giant Dotcom? A URL was just a location, a phone number was too. But what was a name? He was honestly surprised nobody had thought of doing it sooner.

As Dotcom, his name was his website, his presence, business, and legacy. How stupid and inefficient to be Kim Schmitz of Megaupload whom you could find online at Kimble.org—what a mouthful, what a bulging pocket of tiny keys. Who listens that long? But "Dotcom"—it was the Megakey. The rights to the Kim.com domain cost a small fortune, but it was worth it. It would pick up where Kimble.org had left off, a source of world-wide inspiration. You might laugh when he compared himself to the great innovators, but once Kim revolutionized the way we bought and shared and thought and knew, Kim.com would be the stuff of legend. Kimble.org had made him a joke. But with Kim.com, Kim could still be a hero. All he needed now was a mega-success story.

•   •   •

The idea was simple, and the team was small. Ortmann and van der Kolk alone controlled access to the servers. To generate buzz and draw advertisers, they needed volume, high traffic. To build it, they offered cash rewards to anyone who uploaded popular content.

Megaupload users had quickly graduated from sharing racing videos to sharing everything else—including porn and copyright-infringing material. Kim says they realized early on that their service was being used that way and looked at what they needed to do to deal with it. According to their lawyers, Kim says, the answer was simple: Take it down when asked. Kim says they did; the indictment from the Department of Justice says they did so only on a "selective basis."

Kim says they did their best to comply with the law, better than most, even putting the power to take infringing material off their servers directly into the hands of the studios themselves. "All the major studios had direct access," he says. "Nobody else did that." He says they believed they had done enough. They never imagined they were risking jail time.

The truth was that by 2010, Kim and his partners had more to lose than ever. Kim had met a young woman named Mona Verga in the Philippines; they'd married and started a family. Kim said he chose New Zealand because it was clean and green and the most likely to survive an uncertain future. It was an ideal place from which to run a legal and successful Internet company with more than one hundred employees.

It's the legality of that success that will play out in the court system. The DOJ cites several Megaupload e-mails as evidence of criminal "willfulness" (van der Kolk: "We have a funny business . . . modern-day pirates :)." Ortmann: "We're not pirates, we're just providing shipping services to pirates :)."). Kim says the FBI can't take a joke and points to the 45,000 seized e-mails they didn't cite. "They've read our internal correspondence," Kim says. "They know we were good corporate citizens."

Certainly the Megaupload technology itself wasn't criminal— depending on how it was used, the service had the power to connect pirates with illegal downloaders or major artists directly with a major audience. With the site attracting some 4.9 billion annual visits by 2011, Kim was charging premium ad rates and making legit deals for the backing of premium stars like Kanye West, will.i.am, Jamie Foxx, Sean "Diddy" Combs, Alicia Keys, and Chris Brown. It was all leading up to the launch of a service called Megabox, which would allow musical artists to make money from ads attached to free downloads of their songs. Free downloads with permission wasn't piracy, it was a new media model that would kill the incentive for most illegal downloaders and get everyone paid. He had a similar product ready for Hollywood movies and TV shows. Dotcom was ready to go supermega. But by that point, though he didn't yet know it, it was too late.

On January 5, 2012, a federal grand jury filed its sealed seventy-two-page indictment of Megaupload, based on a two-year FBI-led investigation. A few days later, members of the FBI contacted officers from the New Zealand fraud and antiterror forces and began planning what they then called Operation Debut.

By January 18, two American special agents and an assistant U.S. attorney were in New Zealand. On the nineteenth, a local constable was sent into the Dotcom Mansion with a camera pen to secretly record the layout and security features. The next day, two sections of New Zealand's Special Tactics Group and four sections of the elite antiterror Armed Offenders Squad were mobilized to Coatesville. Operation Takedown was a go.

·   ·   ·

Rich men hire security for the same reason that banks do; they're where the money is. Robbery, gang attack, and kidnapping were always within the range of possibility for Kim's family. They had never imagined a raid by a tactical antiterror team.

The morning of the raid, Kim heard the noises and, remembering Tempero's security protocol, reached for the panic button at the side of his work bed. It looked like a Jeopardy buzzer in black lacquer, protected from accidental activation by a clear, hinged safety. Kim pressed the button, sending a security SMS alert across the compound.

The door behind him was cracking now. Kim moved away from it, heading toward a hub for the staircase and various wings. Ahead lay a supersized bathroom and the blue-lit atrium of a one-lane, thirty-meter swimming pool. Towels for both were stored in a closet. The shelving hid a secret door to a hidden staircase.

This was what Tempero called the Red Room. It was a simple carpeted attic following the curved roofline. Kim went to the far end and placed himself behind a pillar. He heard crashes and booms and shouts filtering through the corridors and up the stairs. One was the word "Police!"

Kim knew what was happening then. He could stop. He could head down the stairs, emerge into the noisy scene. But that seemed unsafe. He wasn't going to pop out and surprise them. He'd follow the protocol.

News reports would later claim that he was found hiding near, or even clutching, a sawed-off shotgun. There was, in fact, a shotgun stored there, but in a safe on the opposite end, about thirty feet away. And Kim wasn't hidden—his frame was easily visible behind the pillar—but at least his head was protected. He'd wait there.

Kim waited for what felt like a long time. The noises grew louder. Within minutes of the tactical team's arrival, dozens more men arrived in a second helicopter and several black-windowed vans, fanning across the gated suburb in the dawn light. A small army was combing the property now.

But the police were having a rather difficult time locating Kim. They knew there was a safe room—somewhere. But they didn't know exactly where the door was located. So the special forces men zeroed in on a dumbwaiter.

Gonglike booms echoed through the mansion as the police labored against the metal doors with sledgehammers. Finally a member of the house staff opened the dumbwaiter from the kitchen. Kim wasn't inside. The elite antiterror squad was losing a game of hide-and-seek against a giant computer nerd. The man supposedly armed with the doomsday button had been missing for a full ten minutes.

Tempero had heard the commotion when the first helicopter landed. He headed outside and was met by a guy in black tactical gear who put a gun in his face. "That's good as gold, mate," he said, and got on the ground. He was still there when the police came back to question him. Tempero was worried for his boss. He showed them the hidden Red Room door. It was still unlocked.

Kim says he was kneed in the ribs, punched in the face, and his hand was stepped on until his nails bled. (Police dispute this.) He was then laid out and briefly cuffed before being led back to the main stairwell. When he passed the windows, Kim finally grasped the full scale of the operation.

Cops were everywhere. In uniform, out of uniform, some with body armor, most with Bushmaster rifles or tactical semi-automatics. They had a dog unit and guys on the roof with binoculars. There were so many people involved in the raid that the cops had brought in chemical toilets and a craft services truck. Kim couldn't believe it. Guys were hanging around, having coffee and sandwiches, high-fiving.

The impound inventory would read like a *Robb Report* shopping list, including fifteen Mercedes worth hundreds of thousands of dollars, two Mini Coopers, a '57 El Dorado, the pink Series 62 Cadillac convertible, a Lamborghini LM002, a Rolls-Royce Phantom Drophead Coupe, Harley and Von Dutch Kustom motorcycles, eight TVs, and works of art of obvious value—including a towering Planet Hollywood–style statue of the Predator.

But the real prize would be the cash—millions from more than fifty bank accounts around the world. If the Mega-Conspirators were going to defend themselves against the might of the U.S. legal system, they'd have to do it on credit.

Police led Kim to the lawn, where most of the household was gathered. "I was so worried about Mona—she was pregnant with the twins. I kept asking where she was, where the kids were." Kim couldn't see the kids, but he saw Ortmann. He and Batato had flown in for the birthday Kim shared with his son, Kimmo. It promised to be an epic event, complete with A-list entertainers from the United States. The bouncy castle hadn't even been blown up yet.

The police found Batato by the back of the house with his laptop; he was still in his robe. Ortmann was in bed when the tactical team burst in. He looked freaked out and shattered. He wasn't the sort who pretended at the gangsta stuff. He didn't even play shooter videogames.

Kim asked a police officer, "What are the charges?" He imagined that, with more than fifty staff members from around the world, maybe one of them was mixed up in something.

The answer surprised him: "Copyright infringement."

As the cops led him to a police van, Kim passed Mona. She seemed frightened. "All this for copyright?" he said to her. "Bullshit."

In the police van, Kim was given a copy of the charges. He saw the copyright infringement and, more surprisingly, conspiracy to commit money laundering. The first charge on the list he didn't understand. "Racketeering?" he asked an officer.

"That's a criminal organization charge, like Mafia," came the reply.

That didn't sound right. Kim had a license plate that said MA-FIA—but then he had ones that said GOD and POLICE and EVIL too, and they didn't accuse him of being those. There had been some sort of mistake. They'd spent a lot of money and time to understand every facet of the business—including the DMCA. "That's why we bothered putting servers in Virginia," Batato says. "To be protected by safe harbor." They were prepared for all sorts of claims in civil court. But they'd never prepared for criminal charges, or jail.

The Megaupload boys were brought down the road to the North Shore Policing Centre for processing, then driven to the Mount Eden Corrections Facility. It was nearly dark by the time they entered the induction unit. Kim's cell had a concrete-block bed with a three-inch mattress. "Which, for me, with my weight, it's nothing," he says. Within a few days he was immobilized with back spasms. They gave him ibuprofen and a wheelchair and put him on suicide watch. "The shrink had talked to me. He asked, did I feel like killing myself, and I said no. I didn't, you know?" Kim says. "But they put me on the watch list anyway, so they could come back to my cell every two hours, see if I moved."

The Mega crew were all on the same cell block. During open cell hours, they could sit together and pore over the indictment. The more Kim read, the more bullshit it appeared.

They'd win, Kim promised. Then they'd get their lawyers to recoup every penny taken from them, every penny of lost revenue, and even more for pain and suffering. He told Ortmann, "I'm going to name my boat *Paid For by the FBI*."

The Americans were the enemy here. Hollywood had backed Obama; maybe the mega-takedown was mega-payback. Trying to make a difference in the election would be part of their comeback, but as hackers they needed something bigger. Hollywood hadn't taken the hand Kim had offered them. Now he would offer something else.

Hollywood had busted them as pirates on the grounds that they were aware of and responsible for what their Megaupload customers uploaded and downloaded. But what if they created a cloud storage locker that nobody—including themselves—could look into? That would be the ultimate safe harbor. And it would entirely change the conversation about data policing.

Once again, jail forced Kim to think creatively. He sat with Ortmann, van der Kolk, and Batato in a cell; they puzzled over the problem, building a new technology from scratch in their heads. The idea was simple: One click and a file would be encrypted and uploaded. Only the uploader had the key to unlock the file. If the uploader shared the key, that was his business. Because the data was encrypted, you couldn't search it. Even if you raided the servers, they'd be meaningless without the key. Welcome to the newest gray gray area on the planet.

They called it Mega. Like Megaupload, it would combine off-the-shelf technologies into a user-friendly app. It might not enrich them quite as much as Megaupload had, but they still believed that corporate subscriptions would make it a profitable business. More important, it promised to offer Internet citizens an unprecedented level of private data-sharing while sparing the provider most legal headaches and liabilities. In other words, Mega was beyond takedown.

Kim had been worried about Ortmann. He'd seemed so fragile when he entered jail; now he seemed energized by the challenge. The tough talk wound up all the Mega boys, and Kim was genuinely enthusiastic about their new project. But privately he feared that the larger dream was dead. He might become a dotcom millionaire again. But he'd never be a dotcom hero.

·   ·   ·

As I wait for Kim on my seventh day at the estate, Saturday morning becomes afternoon becomes evening, and frost reglazes the sweeping lawn. Finally, there is a tweet, then a text. "Come." It's nine-forty-five at night and Kim is having breakfast.

When I arrive in the kitchen, one of the Filipinas has laid out waffles, pancakes, fruit, sliced bologna of various types, as well as pickles, fruit juice, and a glass of Fiji water, which she refills from tiny plastic bottles.

"I'm going to give all this food up soon," Kim promises, smearing steak tartare across another hunk of bread. "Either I lose thirty kilos or I lose the case." This was Kim the motivator, imagining himself transformed for his American debut in a tailored black suit. It was a nice image, like being dressed well for your own funeral.

Kim is a large man, but tonight he seems as vulnerable as a child beyond rest. He's in a reflective mood and wants to talk, long into the night. He remembers so clearly how difficult it was to rise again after his takedown in Germany, the effort it had taken to emerge with a new dotcom business and a new Dotcom name. Megaupload was to be a dynasty for Kim Dotcom's children to build on; Kim.com would provide the legacy of Kim Dotcom himself. He'd rekindle the ashes of Kimble.org to debut a site that revealed Kim as a self-made Ozymandias of a digital empire, an inspirational builder of worlds. After years of work, his mega-monument was nearly complete.

"But what sort of inspiration could I be now?" Kim asks. He will win the case against him and get his money back too. And then?

His wife is young and beautiful. "And me?" Kim says. I'm . . ." He gestures to himself. If the case drags on, if they are stuck for years in this dull empty mansion, Kim worries about the strain on his marriage. He isn't so keen on his prospects either.

He's thirty-eight years old. His kneecaps are shot, his back is in spasm, and he's perhaps 150 pounds overweight. He's exhausted. It would take a decade to build another empire with the next Big Idea. He doesn't think he has it in him.

"But the mistake I made in Germany was, I gave up," Kim says. It cost him his name. He wouldn't make that mistake again. There would be no plea deals. He'll stand and fight the DOJ. Even if it costs him everything.

It is five-thirty in the morning, and Kim Dotcom is just getting started.

•   •   •

Kim sleeps through the next day, resting up for three days of hearings. By midday Monday I find him at breakfast already on his new health regimen—500 milligrams of vitamin C, fruits and berries, eggs and yogurt. His wife sits next to him looking calm and radiant, her long dark hair freshly washed. "OK," Kim says. He slips on the blue-tinted Cartiers and a scarf laid out for him on the counter. "Let's kick some ass."

The courthouse is a simple brick civic building near the park. There's a metal detector nobody is much bothering with and a few TV crews waiting with fuzzy microphones. Mona and Kim file into the benches with his American lawyer, Ira Rothken, and codefendants Ortmann, Batato, and van der Kolk. Tempero and another security man wait protectively behind them.

Kim takes the stand, telling the story of the raid. "Our beautiful home was turned into a haunted house," he says. Across the courtroom, reporters bend to their notebooks. That sets the tone. "I want to go again!" Kim says during a recess. He balls his fists like a kid at an amusement park. "That was so much fucking fun!" Over the next two days the raid will be dissected in detail, and judge Helen Winkelmann will interrupt the officers frequently. In New Zealand, police usually don't even carry guns; the raid was viewed as an unprecedented use of armed antiterror forces on a civilian home, based on a faulty search warrant and misleading intelligence. On the stand, the head of New Zealand's anti-organized-crime agency is asked whether the Dotcom Mansion was being monitored by any other agencies not yet disclosed to the public. He answers no. Unfortunately, that wasn't quite true.

In fact, the compound had been under surveillance for weeks by New Zealand's spy agency. What exactly they tapped—e-mail, phone calls, text messages—remains a secret, but there is no gray area in the law. The Government Communications Security Bureau is forbidden from spying on legal residents. In the coming weeks, Kim Dotcom will become the center of New

Zealand's own Watergate. Even New Zealand's prime minister will issue Kim Dotcom a flat-out apology.

This court will eventually give Kim some of his money back—$4.8 million for his legal defense and living expenses. But before that decision can be rendered, there is evidence to go through. Some video. A bailiff dims the lights and starts showing footage.

It's from one of the police helicopters, a beauty shot at dawn on January 20. We rise over the green New Zealand hills, over power lines, over a last hill, and, as police chatter comes crackling across the microphones, we see the Dotcom Mansion, a regal white U against the green lawn, where the helicopter lands, and we see the legs of armed men, running to the front door before the helicopter lifts again to circle.

"The media will be presented with a copy of this recording," the judge promises. But how, she wonders, will they be able to distribute multiple copies at once, so that each TV station and paper has an identical copy at the same time?

Across the courtroom, the Megaupload boys begin to giggle.

Elle

Elle *describes itself as "the definitive modern high-fashion magazine for smart women." Bear that in mind as you read these columns by Daphne Merkin, especially the words "modern" and "smart." A former book critic for magazines like* Commentary *and* The New Republic, *a movie critic at* The New Yorker *during the Tina Brown years, a novelist and an essayist (her 1997 collection was titled* Dreaming of Hitler), *Merkin generates what the National Magazine Award judges called "the Merkin effect, sometimes strange, always dazzling" when she writes. Here she gives spring fashion a feminist vetting, challenges the notion that women like living alone, and examines the sexual pratfalls of writers ranging from de Sade to Lena Dunham. In all, the judges found Merkin's work both provocative and inspiring.*

Daphne Merkin

Portrait of a Lady *and* Social Animal *and* We're All Helmut Newton Now

Portrait of a Lady

I used to read a winsome children's book to my daughter when she was young that began with the all-important question: "Jesse Bear, what will you wear? What will you wear in the morning?" I found myself thinking about Jesse and his daily dilemma while I was looking at the coverage of the spring shows and trying to envision myself dressed in peplums, floaty prints, and A-line frocks—the kind of clothes that convey unadulterated, unsubversive femininity. Could I imagine trading in my wintry leggings and big sweaters, my armed-for-urban-combat uniform, for such transformative, ladylike vestments? How would white lace and pastel ruffles hold their own in my essentialist, black-on-black wardrobe? Did the New Prettiness speak to my sense of being a woman, mired in the muck of postfeminist, postmodernist, "he pays/she pays" definitions that attach to same? What had happened, I wondered, to all the ironic, ostensibly empowering signifiers of contemporary women's fashion—whether body-parading or menswear-inspired or languidly androgynous?

One answer might be innate to the fashion system itself, whereby fashion exists to pull up the shades on an eternally new day, appearing to offer us something we haven't yet seen—or that we haven't seen recently—while simultaneously addressing relevant concerns. Although fashion designers constantly reference earlier eras, they also put their own spin on them in part by virtue of a more distanced perspective. Dior's New Look of 1947 caused as much excitement as it did not only because it introduced an overtly feminine silhouette harking all the way back to *Madame Bovary*—tiny waists, sloping shoulders, and long, full skirts—but also because it came right on the heels of World War II, when a workshirt-clad Rosie the Riveter held aloft the torch of female solidarity with our men in uniform. The New Look signaled a return to woman as a decorative object, a beautifully plumed bird in a gilded cage, rather than a practical partner in a common larger cause.

Similarly, the New Prettiness comes at a moment when the culture at large seems freshly enticed by old-fashioned values, whether served up in extreme form by the Tea Party or conveyed by the hipster embrace of everything vintage and homegrown. Nostalgia is everywhere you look, no longer self-consciously so, but fully in play as a motif, informing such theater revivals as *Porgy and Bess* and *How to Succeed in Business Without Really Trying* and (underviewed) TV shows *Pan Am* and *The Playboy Club*. Prabal Gurung, whose own clothes this season almost singularly manage to hint at racier concerns (in the form of a black leather and silk-cord harness and the use of erotic images) while also gesturing toward a softer treatment, observes that "the world is moving so fast that we are feeling a bit lost in the whirlwind."

Another answer might be that we have all, designers and customers alike, grown tired of identity politics, that we yearn for the sort of social sureties we imagine existed in the decades right before consciousness raising and bra burning. "I feel that right now is an uncertain time," says Jason Wu, "and there's something about a polished, dressed-up look that's a nice contrast. When times are challenging, the one thing you can control is the way you look." We might ridicule the gender constrictions that marked the fifties and sixties, but the success of *Mad Men*, among other backward-looking phenomena, suggests that they also speak to some part of ourselves that doesn't want to construct a working model of femaleness from scratch each day. I can't be alone in sensing a withdrawal from embattled agendas of self-definition, especially among younger women, as well as a renewed interest in traditional modes of femininity—even if it's as gestural as slipping on a skirt instead of a pair of pants. It's hard enough getting out the door in the morning in these complex, economically shaky times without having to put on a suit of armor first—and looking pretty might require less energy, conversely, than we have been taught to think.

To this end, designers, with Miuccia Prada leading the pack, seem to have studied their theme books and visual inspirations and decided to bypass the contested ideological territory of the female figure in favor of exploring a tried-and-true template of femininity, someone pristinely ladylike, not so much retro-anything as prefeminist hullabaloo. And there is indeed a certain comfort to be had, after so many years of overly exposed and overly sexed-up fashion, in clothes that flatter the feminine shape without parodying it or exploiting it. Perhaps we are feeling our way back to a period when it was possible to look pleasing without feeling insipid or obeisant to male dictates. Think of Bette Davis in *All About Eve*, a ballsy and driven dame if ever there were one, admitting toward the movie's end that being a woman is "one career all females have in common, whether we like it or not."

Of course, for some designers, such as Carolina Herrera, it has been ever thus. "The idea of getting dressed is to look more beautiful," she tells me in a phone conversation. "I want to see women dress very feminine, very soigné." Herrera goes on to ridicule the notion of fashion as a deliberate statement, a costume to be painstakingly pieced together from what we see on the runway and in magazines. She thinks the metaphysics of getting dressed is simpler than that: "Women want to be admired by men and women," Herrera observes. "They don't want to be laughed at." I listen to the note of assurance in her voice and wonder at my own resistance to the feminine mystique, my entrenched fear of Stepford Wife glossiness and insistence on comfort and informality. Even so augustly cerebral a figure as Virginia Woolf fretted about looking risible in the wrong dress and consulted with the editor of British *Vogue* about which dressmaker to see. Who am I to eschew the seductions of a nipped-in waist and prim pumps?

Then again, I can't help feeling some unease about all this reclaimed femininity and where it might lead. Does dressing like Doris Day in an A-line or pleated skirt mean that we have to go around batting our eyelashes and acting all helpless? Is it possible, that is, to go back in time without feeling railroaded into an older, discarded style of being? Gurung, who insists that "there's got to be something that cuts the sweetness, a bit of grit," sounds a cautionary note: "Femininity is good, but conflict and confrontation are not a bad thing. Are women really going to dress up in clothes that look like a rehash of vintage? It feels a little regressive."

My guess is that designers are betting on our being able to have it both ways, loosening up on power dressing while losing none of our power. One has only to look at Michelle Obama's relaxed habitation of a wife-and-mother role versus Hillary Clinton's rather strident efforts to influence policy when her husband was in the White House to realize that there has been a shift in the wind, that women no longer feel the need to roar. Wu, meanwhile, insists that the new femininity is sharper, infused with a tougher attitude and the cleaner lines that are a legacy of minimalism. And Miuccia Prada sprinkled images of cars over pleated skirts and demure white and yellow dresses as if to suggest that toughness is at best a pose you can borrow as you please. Here's hoping that they're right, that this time around the lady is neither a vamp nor a tramp but serenely in charge, not waiting for Prince Charming but confident in her ability to save herself.

Social Animal

I have lived alone on and off for much of my adult life, and, despite a recent wavelet of articles and books attesting to the wonders of the single life and what it signifies about us as a culture that so many more people are "going solo," as one book title calls it, I can safely say that I have never made my peace with it. Nor do I believe that the new statistics on single living—which are now higher than they have ever been, coming in at 28 percent of U.S. households and nearly 50 percent of Manhattan residents—indicate a profound psychological change in the way we conceive of ourselves, as some are arguing. Rather, I think they're a reflection of certain social realities, not all of them positive (accomplished women who put off marriage often find a scarcity of compatible mates), and certain adaptations (rather than compromise, women remain single). But perhaps the best place to start is not with a fresh-off-the-press "trend," based on more or less factual evidence and more or less provocative findings by sociologists and opinionmongers, but with myself, as an ostensible representative of this new singleton condition.

Looking back, I can't recall ever having harbored a deep wish to live alone. Although I grew up in a big family and shared my room for the longest time with first two brothers and then two sisters, there was a "lonely-in-a-crowd" flavor to my experience that didn't lend itself to dreams of holing up by myself so much as sharing quarters with more compatible souls. Oh, there may have been a period during my twenties when living on my own seemed like a great adventure, a deep immersion in selfhood that would stand me in good stead, even if only for the inevitable pairing up that lay ahead. I enjoyed fitting out my first apartment, a dark faux triplex on Seventy-Ninth Street, with dishes and bookshelves, and reveled in the luxury of working at my desk, writing a bimonthly book column, into the early morning hours without anyone protesting the light or the noise. There was pleasure in staking out my own turf, filling the fridge with handpicked groceries, turning on my Farberware coffeepot every morning to brew the kind of ground beans—strongly flavored but not too tannic—that I'd come to prefer. But I also recall the heaviness of the air striking me each time I returned home and unlocked the door with no one awaiting me on the other side, only an empty apartment and what the English poet Philip Larkin, a lifelong bachelor, called "the instantaneous grief of being alone."

Of course, there's nothing like the drawn-out sorrow of being part of an unhappy couple to make you wonder whether you overdramatized the burden of living on your own. To wit: I married in a state of great ambivalence at thirty-four, became a mother at thirty-five, and by forty was on my own again, sharing custody of my daughter with my ex-husband. By the end of my marriage I felt overrun, the most basic decisions—like whether to feed our girl broccoli or some other virtuous green for dinner— taken out of my hands, and the idea of having a living space to myself, without an antagonistic male presence to contend with, seemed heaven-sent. I remember the sense of spaciousness I felt toward evening, when I looked forward to getting into bed and the prospect of reading or watching TV without having to make conversation or, as was more likely, patch up an earlier argument. But it must also be said that living with a small child, as I did for some of the week, is not the same as living alone; I found a good deal of companionship in my daughter even when she was addicted to make-believe and couldn't discuss grown-up subjects. Then too, the fact of her dependence on me was a constant, space-filling one, which went a ways toward alleviating my newfound partnerless state.

The years passed, my daughter grew up and away from a focus on me, and I meanwhile became involved with two men in succession, each of whom spent a lot of time in my apartment without officially moving in. The idea of marriage came up with both of them, but I didn't feel prepared to take that conclusive a step, and they both went on to other relationships. Then, as can happen without warning, the opportunities for meeting men became ever more scanty; I was older, for one thing, and pickier, for another. My daughter lived in a dorm in the same city and came home for sleepovers, but other than that, I was back to being the sole occupant of my apartment. Given that as a writer I also work at home, and of necessity by myself, that's a lot of time to one's own.

So let me be blunt about it. These days living alone often seems closer to a sentence of solitary confinement—an advanced course in living within the boundaries of the unaccompanied, unechoed self—than it does a racy prelude to a more domesticated future. If there is a claustrophobia that comes with being in too close proximity to another person, I've discovered that there is another kind of claustrophobia that comes with being in too unmediated a relation to one's own hermetic self. For one thing, there is no one to put on your "best" self for, so you're more likely to skip brushing your teeth before bed, say, or forgo a shower. It's nothing radical, but the subtle softening of grooming standards comes to reflect a deeper laxity of self-care. For another, it's easy to fall into a pattern of inertia, of not making the effort to see the movie or exhibition everyone's talking about. Not to mention something more important that is rarely alluded to in the new paeans to the single life—the lack of physical connection with another person, be it as basic as the touch of someone else's skin next to yours or the heightening of the senses that comes with good sex.

Indeed, there's a certain hour of the night—usually right before I go to sleep, when the noise of the city has abated and I can hear the anxious whirring of my own mind—when my aloneness strikes me with renewed strength, almost as a metaphysical condition to be uneasily pondered: What am I doing adrift in a queen-size bed, with no one's snoring to grumpily ignore or leg to push out of the way? How did I get to this place, where everyone I know seems to be coupled, happily or unhappily, but coupled all the same? (Although I don't mean to suggest that I'd prefer being in just any relationship to being on my own.) And am I fated to be stuck in this condition? From here it's a hop, skip, and jump to forecasting the scene of my own death, à la Bridget Jones, with no one to find me before the dogs have finished off my remains.

·   ·   ·

I've been thinking about this issue, despite the fact that I don't fully qualify as living on my own now that my twenty-two-year-old daughter is temporarily back in her old room, because from what I can tell the single life—or "singlism," as social psychologist Bella DePaulo calls it—has suddenly acquired a new cachet. Whether it's a much-noticed article in *The Atlantic* by Kate Bolick called "All the Single Ladies" or a book called *Going Solo: The Extraordinary Rise and Surprising Appeal of Living Alone*, by Eric Klinenberg (who himself is married and a father of two), there is a growing cadre of people bent on making a case for the promise of living alone. Most recently, *New York Times* op-ed writer David Brooks penned a column addressing the multiple factors—including the more than half of adults who are single—that have led to "an amazing era of individualism," in which "people want more space to develop their own individual talents." Unlike many others, though, Brooks also points out that this more flexible approach to human connections favors people with greater "social capital"—those who have the ambition and gifts to custom-make their lives—while leaving others to "fall through the cracks" into hapless solitude.

Klinenberg, whose book has become the go-to manifesto for what looks to be a movement of cheerleaders for the single life—although earlier books, such as E. Kay Trimberger's *The New Single Woman* and DePaulo's *Singled Out* helped set the stage—believes that the rise in living alone is nothing less than "a transformative social experience." To back up his claim that "we have embarked on this massive social experiment in living alone because we believe it serves a purpose," he brings together anecdotal evidence regarding all manner of "singletons," ranging from young people who've left home and are partaking "in their city's robust social life" to women who have outlived their husbands. He invokes something called "restorative solitude" (a little of which, I'd like to suggest, goes a long way) and touts the "rich new ways" the Internet offers us "to stay connected," with little mention of the impoverishing effect it has had on old-fashioned, flesh-on-flesh contact.

To his credit, Klinenberg does address the sense of stigma that women who live alone in their thirties and forties continue to feel. "Regardless of their personal or professional accomplishments," he points out, "they see their public identity 'spoiled,' as the sociologist Erving Goffman put it—reduced from something big and complex and interesting to that of the single woman alone." Still, he insists that confidence in being a singleton comes if you work hard at it. Perhaps, but most of us are brought up with the expectation that grown-up existence entails being part of a duo of some sort. All of our cultural forces promote this image, from romantic songs to vacation resorts, and the fewest of us, I'd hazard, cultivate youthful visions of a future that features ourselves living alone by choice. Add to this the fact that in our society loneliness and aloneness are often experienced as one and the same state. "People are in this incredible panic to avoid being alone in the room with themselves," says Helen, one of the few women Klinenberg interviews who doesn't chirp about loving her domestic autonomy or remaking society. "Many people—and I'm one of them—absolutely live with loneliness all the time. It's like an illness."

I don't begrudge people who've found definition and meaning in the very fact of their being alone. I applaud their enthusiasm and satisfaction in being able to live as eccentrically as they like without worrying about being observed conversing with their cat or walking around in days-old clothes (heck, some days I barely make it out of my nightgown), but I'm not convinced that these are the signposts of a thrilling alternative to a more conventional way of being. Perhaps the real issue has less to do with whether we end up in a pair or alone than with the dramatic lack of options in how we conceive of adult living arrangements. By far the most intriguing part of *Going Solo*, tucked away in the conclusion, has to do with a description of the cooperative housing that exists in Stockholm, where people of different ages and sometimes genders live in collective dwellings, alone but not isolated. One such building, called Färdknäppen, operates like a modified kibbutz—offering different-size units, depending on family size, along with communal dining and shared services such as exercise classes and hobby rooms. To me, it sounds ideal—a way of living with others outside the usual confinement of coupledom. I can't imagine that this kind of visionary housing will be hitting our shores anytime soon, though, so in the meantime I'll have to make do with navigating my solo life as best I can, trying to ignore those lines from Bruce Springsteen's "Hungry Heart" that I can't get out of my mind: "Don't make no difference what nobody says / Ain't nobody like to be alone." Ain't that the truth.

We're All Helmut Newton Now

A group of young women—ranging in age from their early twenties to early thirties—have gathered in my apartment ostensibly to talk about fundraising for an online magazine, but along the way we segue into a discussion of *Girls*, *Fifty Shades of Grey*, Internet porn, the mandatory denuding of pubic hair, and all the rest of the phenomena that seem to characterize the present erotic moment. These young women routinely refer to men as *dudes* and appear to be at ease with casual sex—speaking dispassionately about their experiences, reducing them to amusing anecdotes—in a way that was once seen as more true of men. I find myself wondering whether this has been all to the good, whether some essential frisson has been lost along with the traditional self-consciousness about sex. I think of the film director Luis Buñuel's famous statement, "Sex without sin is like an egg without salt," which I've always taken to mean that sexual satisfaction requires an edge—that without some sort of impediment to bump up against, we risk vertigo-inducing psychological free-fall.

What strikes me as truly strange, however, is this: I'm older than these women and should by all rights be envious of their paradise of sexual opportunities, but I find myself feeling sorry for them instead—just as I winced when I watched *Girls*, finding it as sad as it was funny. I've read various defenses of the show's deflated rendering of sexual engagement, and I'm still not convinced that the pivotal scene—in which Adam (played by Adam Driver) masturbates over the awkwardly naked body of Hannah (played by Lena Dunham) to the tune of a vocalized fantasy about her being an eleven-year-old druggie—is impressive for its candor so much as dreary in its implications.

For one thing, what is so new, much less revelatory, about autoeroticism and a young man's "wanton absorption" in it? Why on earth would it engage the viewer, as Elaine Blair suggests in the *New York Review of Books*, more than Hannah's flustered attempts to connect at all costs, even if that means going along with said fantasy? "We can feel the erotic charge of the scene," writes Blair, "in spite of its limitations, qua sex, for Hannah. We can contemplate Hannah's lack of sexual confidence without condemning Adam. We can appreciate, rather than lament, Hannah's attraction to Adam despite the fact that he is wont to do things like dismiss her from his apartment with a brusque nod while she is still chatting and gathering her clothes and purse."

Can we? Perhaps, if we don't have our own identification with Hannah—and our own hopes on her behalf for something approaching sexual fulfillment (not to mention a little love). Unless we're all irretrievably jaded voyeurs by now, on the lookout for the next debased thrill, it seems to me that the erotic context is still potent with promise for many of us, remaining one of the last outposts of the unironic in a culture bent on demystifying every last experience. Or, at least, it ought to be, if we weren't so set these days on undercutting its power by holding it up to the light and examining it. What, one might ask, happened to the blissed-out dream of sex that came with the Sexual Revolution, the promise of intense intimacy and naked abandon—sex as "the long slide / To happiness, endlessly" that the British poet Philip Larkin envisioned in his poem "High Windows"? Why does it seem to have been cast aside in favor of a more banal discourse, one bleached of excitement and mystery?

· · ·

Let me make clear where I'm coming from. I'm not trying to speak for the joys of good, old-fashioned sex as against current subversions/perversions thereof. I'm not even sure I believe in such an entity as good, old-fashioned sex. Sexual arousal, to the extent that it takes place in the brain as much as in the body, is one of the most subjective of all pleasures, encoded in highly individualized scripts that contain our psychic histories in the form of charged images and fantasies. The details of these scripts—or "microdots," as the psychiatrist Robert Stoller calls them in his book *Sexual Excitement*—are designed to reproduce and, ideally, repair past traumas and humiliations that we carry with us from childhood. But as Stoller points out on the very first page of his book, the phrase "sexual excitement" is itself woefully inexact: "*Sexual* has so many uses," he observed, "that we scarcely comprehend even the outer limits of what someone else indicates with the word; does he or she refer to male and female, or masculinity and femininity, or eroticism, or intercourse, or sensual, nonerotic pleasure, or life-force?"

I should point out as well that my own tastes have historically run to the edgier end of the sexual spectrum—and, indeed, in some circles I am seen as a promoter of unsavory sexual preferences. I am referring to a lengthy essay I wrote for *The New Yorker* in 1996 called "Unlikely Obsession." This piece, which has continued to haunt me from the moment it appeared, was a graphic account of my longtime fascination with erotic spanking and my cautious flirtation with more serious S&M; it also attempted to trace the psychological origins of my interest and to envision a future less tied to this kind of scenario. "The fact is," I wrote early in the piece, "that I cannot remember a time when I didn't think about being spanked as a sexually gratifying act, didn't fantasize about being reduced to a craven object of desire by a firm male hand. . . ."

If I had ever imagined the reading public was no longer shockable, the reception to what I thought was my carefully considered and psychologically nuanced revelations cured me of that notion. The article caused an immediate stir, the likes of which was impossible to foresee but easier to understand in retrospect. I'd talked openly and in a high-toned forum about matters of the flesh—unwholesome, perhaps titter-inducing matters of the flesh, at that. I received hundreds of letters, was praised and reviled in print for my courage and my effrontery, and eventually discovered that my name had become a form of shorthand (as in "looking for a Daphne Merkin type") in personal ads. "Unlikely Obsession" was referred to in a recent *Newsweek* cover story by Katie Roiphe that explored the renewed interest in S&M among younger women, and it was then raked over the coals by Virginia Heffernan in a rebuttal to Roiphe's piece: "Did anyone read Merkin's 1996 tale of her unlikely obsession with finding men to whack her and conclude she needed a Nobel Prize for savage honesty and lapidary prose? Not as I remember it. The takeaway was, Something is wrong with Daphne Merkin." (To which I will only add that Heffernan's response put me in mind of a remark the journalist Richard Goldstein once made about an infamous sex scene in *Last Tango in Paris*: "There's no unity in people's fantasies; some of us will always think a stick of butter is for bread.")

I am dredging all this up in the interest of full disclosure but also to try to provide some perspective on the way we view contemporary manifestations of age-old sexual preferences. Sadomasochistic impulses, whether light or heavy, have been a staple of the erotic imagination at least since people started reading novels, beginning with the eighteenth century's *Fanny Hill* and the works of the Marquis de Sade. The nineteenth century saw an outpouring of fiction dealing with flagellation and enslavement—the most notable instance being *Venus in Furs*, written by Leopold von Sacher-Masoch (from whose name the term *masochism* derives). Closer to our own era are works like *Story of O*, *Nine and a Half Weeks* (my personal favorite), and the *Sleeping Beauty* trilogy, penned by Anne Rice under the pseudonym A. N. Roquelaure. *Fifty Shades of Grey*, the pros and cons of which have been widely discussed by every journalist with a blog to stand on, is the most recent entry in this genre. The runaway success of the book, which tells the story of an "innocent" college girl's introduction to S&M by a sexy corporate titan, doesn't suggest to me anything so much as the fact that, in the world outside of *Girls*, the collective sexual imagination is kept on a pretty tight leash. By which I mean that we live in postfeminist, assiduously politically correct times that don't allow for much deviation from "enlightened" behavior both in and out of the bedroom. The transgressive may be part of our daily cultural fare—a little perversion here, a little fetishism there, we've seen it all, we take it in stride, we're all Helmut Newton now—but we tend to file it away silently rather than discuss its significance. The insistence on gender equality, which is one of the legacies of women's liberation, even for younger women who are otherwise disengaged from its politics, has put the lid on the articulation of desires that don't speak to a carefully maintained balance of power within couples. This, in turn, has only whetted our appetite for expressions of love-slave desires, abject or unruly though they may be.

Then again, it's the nature of our sexual selves—no matter how see-through our amorous lives might appear—to remain impenetrable in the uniqueness of our references. In other words, the quality of a sexual experience is something known only to oneself, a reality neatly summed up by the question we've all either asked or been asked: "Was it good for you?"

It's probably easier to get a consensus on any subject other than sex. The very variableness of what we might mean when, for instance, we refer to someone as being "great in bed" is what informs the dismissively mordant German saying my mother used to be fond of citing: *Bei Nacht sind alle Katzen grau.* ("At night all cats are gray.") Your idea of a stud might be my idea of a lummox, but the point is: How am I to know other than by trying him out for myself? In "The Forbidden Realm," an essay in *The Best American Sex Writing* 2004, the subtitle of which asks, "Why Hasn't There Been a Great Movie About Sex?," Steve Erickson makes the telling observation: "Every sexual relationship is so much the calculus of two subjectivities colliding that the sex other people have is too foreign for most of us to even consider, let alone watch, no matter how great the actors look or how well posed their interplay."

The fact that our sex lives comprise a vast collection of secret histories may have suited the tenor of earlier times—the repressive 1950s, say, when women hadn't yet been liberated from the myth of vaginal orgasm, men hadn't yet been charged with understanding the complexity of female responsiveness, and everyone kept their deviant tendencies to themselves. But it's decidedly less suited to the way we live now, in a "milk-and-honey society of free-market sex," as Philip Roth characterized it in *The Dying Animal.* These days, the dominant cultural impulse is one of exposure, of uncovering what has previously been hidden from view, whether it is a Rutgers student spying on his gay roommate's sex life via a hidden camera, or journalists tracking down Anthony Weiner's show-and-tell e-mails or what exactly transpired in Dominique Strauss-Kahn's hotel room. And I'd argue that it is our unease with the intractable privacy of the erotic experience that marks the present moment. We're so used to the performance aspect of experience our digital culture fosters, so used to exhibiting our every gasp for others via tweets, pinning, etc., that we squirm under the burden of intimacy, the way it casts us back on ourselves and our own feelings without the mediation of an audience. In this erotic moment, when we imagine we can know all and communicate all about what creates desire or pleasure, throwing ourselves wholeheartedly into sexual communion, in all its unpredictable singularity, seems dangerous.

Then, too, as creatures of this great consumerist epoch, in which desire is relentlessly externalized and airbrushed, we're wedded to the notion that what is of intrinsic value can be put on display and objectively assessed. If we can only zoom in on the grainy reality of sex, enlarge the pornographic images on our computers, we'll be able to judge for ourselves, see how we stack up. Under the cover of voyeurism, we watch people we envision as being sexier than ourselves, doing sexier things to each other than we've ever chanced to try. That carnal appetites work in unfathomable ways gets largely lost in the rush to revelation.

It was at college, as an English major during the heyday of the French-influenced deconstructionist approach to literary texts, that I first became fully aware of the more twisted byways of passion, the roads less taken. In cloistered seminar rooms filled with attentive, note-taking types like myself, my eyes were opened to a hitherto undreamed-of philosophy of sex, its lawless nature, and the conviction that societal conventions, such as marriage and monogamy, are the death of sexual love. (De Rougemont: "Is there something fatal to marriage at the very heart of human longing? . . . It is obvious that Western Man is drawn to what destroys 'the happiness of the married couple' at least as much as to anything that ensures it.") I warmed to the French writer Georges Bataille's hip, truth-or-dare assertions about the wonders of transgressive eroticism ("Eroticism, it may be said, is assenting to life up to the point of death"), even if I wasn't precisely sure what they meant, and I stayed up late at night in my narrow dorm-room bed reading and rereading the iconic, galvanizing piece of contemporary erotica, *Story of O.* As much as I was elated by these writers' radical, non-white-bread approach to the implicit power play of romantic love, I wondered about the emotional consequences in the here and now. What if you wanted to do something with your life when you weren't "moaning in the darkness" à la O—being flogged or branded with a red-hot iron with your lover's initials? How did the wish to have children, much less a career, fit into this consuming vision of sexual absolutism?

In 2004, I saw a documentary called *Writer of O* about the pseudonymous author of the book, an editor at the prestigious French publishing house Gallimard. Her real name was Anne

Desclos, and the filmmaker Pola Rapaport had tracked down the disarmingly mild-looking ninety-year-old provocateur in her modest house outside Paris, where she lived alone with her cat, before she died in 1998. According to her own clipped and elliptical statements in the film, Desclos wrote this groundbreaking (and, depending on your point of view, liberating or horrifying) novel as a form of a love letter to the married man with whom she was involved for many years, the prominent French intellectual Jean Paulhan, who was a glamorous womanizer and an admirer of the work of the Marquis de Sade, and who also happened to be her colleague at Gallimard.

I remember watching the white-haired and straight-backed Desclos talk quietly but intensely, her still-blazing blue eyes seeming to look backward without so much as blinking, about her dogmatic belief in love as a kind of secular calling, demanding a complete surrender of self. What impressed me most of all about this brainy and fiercely proud woman, who lived with her parents until they died, was her desperate allegiance to a philandering eminence whose interest she was afraid of losing as she aged, having never seen herself as pretty to begin with (she was forty-six when she penned *Story of O* in a feverish period of a few weeks). How better to embrace the humiliation of trying to keep him than by insisting that there was a delirium all its own to be had in degradation.

What's most curious about this hypersexual moment, filled to the brim with Internet porn, mega-best-selling erotica, and the casual nudity of shows like *Girls*, is that the fugitive spirit of eroticism seems to have quietly escaped through the bedroom window. Where are the extramarital love affairs that were all the rage in the seventies, endlessly described in novels like John Updike's *Couples* and analyzed in the pages of women's magazines? If they exist—and undoubtedly they do—they're no longer touted as attempts to break free of stultifying marital conventions in favor of a more authentically lived existence. And why do younger women seem so rarely to be the objects of romantic pursuit or breathless seduction and much more likely to be willing partners in what one twenty-three-year-old woman I know refers to, somewhat defeatedly, as "goal-oriented sex"? This same woman muses that "the grand romantic gesture seems dead to my generation. I've never had a love letter counting the ways delivered to my doorstep. More often it's a quick e-mail or text message asking what movie time is best for me." That men are wont to compartmentalize sex and love is hardly a revelation, but now women are doing it themselves, or perhaps doing it to themselves.

Recently I saw a movie—Sarah Polley's melancholic, lovingly observed *Take This Waltz*—that reminded me of everything that seems to be missing in today's sexual climate. It stars Michelle Williams as an aspiring writer married to a cookbook author (played by Seth Rogen). She loves her husband but is bored by him, and then she meets up with a man (played by Luke Kirby) who speaks to all her buried sexual longings. The film makes a case for the elusive nature of sexual ecstasy—its way of bounding out of reach just when we think we've caught it—but it makes an even stronger case for our imagination as the authentic erotic domain, capable of lingering over the details of arousal in a way that real-life sex rarely lives up to. I'm thinking of a scene in which Kirby's character, a free-spirited artist and rickshaw driver, describes in feverish language that put me in mind of no one so much as D. H. Lawrence how he would make love to Williams if and when such a possibility came to pass. The scene is charged with eroticism precisely because it is so untainted by self-conscious irony.

Which brings me to the following suggestion: Perhaps it's time to reconsider the situation, beginning with a reconsideration of D. H. Lawrence, the high priest of antirationalist, transcendent fornication who went from an image of gross indecency to over-the-top datedness in less than thirty years. Lawrence, of course, is best known for *Lady Chatterley's Lover*, a novel characterized by overheated and androgynous insights that led T. S. Eliot to remark of its author that he "seems to me to have been a very sick man indeed." It seems to me, on the other hand, that *Lady Chatterley's Lover*, with its mix of wordlessness and sudden dips into hamstrung tenderness on the part of Oliver and expressed vulnerability and fearful excitement on the part of Lady C, speaks with more truth to the original dreams we all have of where sex—or the sensuous experience generally—might take us if the lover in question were responsive enough and the circumstances conducive.

Then again, all of Lawrence's work was marked by his peculiar, almost oracular sexual candor—"Sex is the fountain head," he wrote, "where life bubbles up"—beginning with *The Rainbow*, which was banned in Great Britain shortly after its publication in 1915. He was willing to bet his all on klutzy, breathless passion—is passion ever graceful, except in the movies?—in his writing and his life, where as a young man he went off with someone else's wife, having fallen in love within minutes of meeting her. Although he's not taught much these days and probably read even less, Lawrence almost more than any writer I can think of took sex seriously—so seriously, in fact, that it lent him a suspicious air in his time and has rendered him impossibly uncool, almost quaint, in our own. Here is one of his many fraught, decidedly unironic, and resolutely uncasual descriptions of sex, which, even in its opening steps, is viewed as a kind of erotic dance to the death: "She took him in the kiss, hard her kiss seized upon him, hard and fierce and burning corrosive as the moonlight. She seemed to be destroying him. He was reeling, summoning all his strength to keep his kiss upon her, to keep himself in the kiss." Try a little of that on for size, why don't you, Lena Dunham and Adam Driver . . .

The New Yorker

FINALIST—ESSAYS AND
CRITICISM

Roger Angell has long been associated with The New Yorker. He first began contributing to the magazine in 1944 and joined the staff in 1956 after nearly a decade at Holiday (where the editor was Ted Patrick, later the first president of ASME). For many readers, Angell is perhaps best known for his writing on baseball. Nearly thirty of his finest pieces are collected in Game Time, though any fan of magazine journalism should seek out his earlier baseball books as well as his memoir Let Me Finish. "Over the Wall" is also a memoir, a personal history of loss that records the death of his wife, Carol. The National Magazine Award judges called it a "deeply moving work by one of our most celebrated prose stylists."

Roger Angell

Over the Wall

My wife, Carol, doesn't know that President Obama won reelection last Tuesday, carrying Ohio and Pennsylvania and Colorado and compiling more than three hundred electoral votes. She doesn't know anything about Hurricane Sandy. She doesn't know that the San Francisco Giants won the World Series, in a sweep over the Tigers. More important, perhaps, she doesn't know that her granddaughter Clara is really enjoying her first weeks of nursery school and is beginning to make progress with her slight speech impediment. Carol died early last April, and almost the first thing that she wasn't aware of is that our son, John Henry, who is Clara's father, after saying goodbye to her about ten hours before her death, which was clearly coming, flew home to Portland, Oregon. Later that same night, perhaps after she'd gone, he had a dream, which he wrote about briefly and beautifully in an e-mail to the family. In the dream, she is hovering close to him, and they are on 110th Street, close to the Harlem Meer, at the northeast corner of Central Park. The park is bursting with spring blossoms. She is walking a dog that might be our fox terrier Andy. Then she falls behind John Henry. He turns to find her, and she has become an almost black shape and appears to be covered with feathers or black-and-dark-gray Post-its. She and the dog lift off the ground and go fluttering past him, and disappear over the low wall of the park.

What the dead don't know piles up, though we don't notice it at first. They don't know how we're getting along without them, of course, dealing with the hours and days that now accrue so quickly, and, unless they divined this somehow in advance, they don't know that we don't want this inexorable onslaught of breakfasts and phone calls and going to the bank, all this stepping along, because we don't want anything extraneous to get in the way of what we feel about them or the ways we want to hold them in mind. But they're in a hurry, too, or so it seems. Because nothing is happening with them, they are flying away, over that wall, while we are still chained and handcuffed to the weather and the iPhone, to the hurricane and the election and to the couple that's recently moved in downstairs, in Apartment 2-S, with a young daughter and a new baby girl, and we're flying off in the opposite direction at a million miles an hour. It would take many days now, just to fill Carol in.

There's a Kenneth Koch poem, "Proverb," that begins "*Les morts vont vite*, the dead go fast, the next day absent!"

Later, it continues:

The second after a moth's death there are one or two hundred
    other moths
The month after Einstein's death the earth is inundated with
    new theories
Biographies are written to cover up the speed with which
    we go:
No more presence in the bedroom or waiting in the hall
Greeting to say hello with mixed emotions.

Yes, but let's stay with Carol a little longer. She was seventeen years, nine months, and seventeen days younger than me (we had a different plan about dying), but now that gap is widening. Soon our marriage will look outlandish or scandalous, because of the age difference. I'm getting old, but I'm told almost every day that I'm keeping up, doing OK. What Carol doesn't know by now is shocking, let's face it, and I think even her best friends must find themselves thinking about her with a certain new softness or sweetness, as if she were a bit backward. Carol, try to keep up a little, can't you?

All right, I take that back, and I also feel bad about those moths getting in here. Carol had a serious moth and bat phobia, dating back to childhood. She was a teacher at the Brearley School, an eminent New York academy for girls, and one day one of her students got an urgent telephone call from her in algebra class. "I need you down here right away," Carol said.

"But, Mrs. Angell, I'm in math class," the girl said.

"Never mind that," Carol said. "There's a moth in my room, and I need you to come down and remove it right now."

Anecdotes sweep away time, and are there to cheer us up, but just as often they work the other way, I'm finding out. Let's get to my unstartling theory, which is that it may not be just years that make you old or young but where you stand on the treadmill. Shakespeare possessed an astounding knowledge of history and of his own times, it's agreed, but missed out on Newton and Napoleon and the Oreo sandwich. Dickens joined the conversations of his day about Darwin, but stayed mum about Freud and Cézanne and Verdun. Lincoln never understood Auden. Verdi just missed Louis Armstrong, leaving the room before the first run-through of "Mahogany Hall Stomp." Donald Barthelme's fiction was known for its flashing and ironic references to contemporary names and styles of thought; he died in 1989, however, at the age of fifty-eight, and under the regulations was forbidden ever to mention Michele Bachmann or the Geico lizard. Carol knew Donald well, and loved his writing. She was also a fan of John Donne, an even more sternly handicapped genius, and one evening got us into an extended conversation—I remember almost every word of it—about his poem "Aire and Angells" (note the spelling), which she was unraveling with an eleventh grader.

·   ·   ·

What do these people have in common: William Shawn, Nancy Stableford, Bill Rigney, Joseph Brodsky?

Well, for one thing, I knew them all, though Brodsky, the poet and Nobel Laureate, only passingly or socially: he was a fabulous conversationalist. Shawn was my boss, the decades-long editor of *The New Yorker*; Nancy Stableford was my older sister and a biology teacher; and Bill Rigney—a onetime major-league infielder and then a manager of the Angels, Twins, and Giants— my best friend in baseball. Each of them was a grownup and, in their different ways, vibrantly intelligent. What else did they have in common? Why, all of them died before September 11, 2001, which is to say that all of them, in company with many hundreds of my bygone and deceased schoolmates and office friends and relatives and summer acquaintances, and their parents and my parents, had no inkling of the world we live in today. I think of them often—my seniors, my innocents, my babies— and envy them, and believe that many others my age have had this passing thought as well, and have from time to time felt a flow of protective love for them, and even a bit of pride that we can stand in for them, or stand up for them, that rational and more hopeful old gang of ours, and so put up with this dismal flow of violence and schlock and complicated distant or very near events that makes up our daily and hourly menu. Clara and the baby downstairs in 2-S (her name is Quinn, I've learned) are scarcely aware of irony or bad news yet, but they'll catch up and be OK with it very soon. Thinking about them the other day, I remembered a poem called "Conch," written by my stepfather, E. B. White, back in the 1940s. He wrote light verse, but took it seriously. Here it is:

Hold a baby to your ear
As you would a shell:
Sounds of centuries you hear
New centuries foretell.

Who can break a baby's code?
And which is the older—
The listener or his small load?
The held or the holder?

·   ·   ·

Quite a lot of time has gone by since Carol died, and though I've forgotten many things about her, my fears about that are going away. There will always be enough of her for me to remember, and some of it, to my surprise, comes back with fresh force. I've been thinking about her hands, for instance, which are visible, of course, in the hundreds of photographs we have of her, often lightly touching someone else in a family setting. Her hands in repose were strikingly beautiful, their resting or down-angling familiar shape somehow expressing both confidence and a perfect ease that a great ballerina could envy. I go back to look at that again and again.

E. B. White—we called him Andy, and, yes, the dog is named for him—and Carol are close to each other now, in the Brooklin, Maine, cemetery. His and my mother's graves are side by side, under a tall oak tree that Andy planted there when my mother died, in 1977. Their gravestones are made of bluish gray slate, but Carol's and mine, though they have the same shape and old-fashioned narrow body, are in white Vermont marble. They carry the same lettering that Mother's and Andy's do: a suave contemporary style called Centaur that was recommended to us back then by an art-director friend of mine named Hank Brennan.

My decision to have my gravestone put in at the same time as Carol's, in early August—it only lacks the final numbers—wasn't easy, but has turned out to be comforting, not creepy. Brooklin is much too far away just now—I live in New York—but the notion that before long my familiar June trip back there will be for good is only keeping a promise.

I visited Carol's grave every day during the rest of my summer stay, often in the early morning, when the oblong shadows of my mother's and Andy's markers nearly touched hers. There's more family nearby: my brother Joel White's gray granite marker (he died in 1997) and that of my daughter Callie, who died two years ago. The two of them had their ashes put into the sea at almost the identical place: an upper sector of Jericho Bay from which you can see the steep mountains of Mount Desert, to the east, and, in the other direction the rise of Isle au Haut. Token cupfuls of their ashes were saved and went into the cemetery later. This is a currently popular option, but Carol and I passed it up. There are ten cemeteries in Brooklin, which is a lot for a population of eight hundred; many are family plots, half-hidden in fields or brush now, and the little Mount Eden Cemetery, on Naskeag Point, is probably the most beautiful. The Brooklin Cemetery is the largest, and lies right in the middle of town: across Route 175 from the Baptist Church and a couple of hundred yards down from the library and the Brooklin General Store, where the road bends.

My visits to Carol didn't last long. I'd perk up the flowers in the vase we had there, and pick deadheads off a pot of yellow daisies; if there had been rain overnight, I'd pick up any pieces of the sea glass that had fallen and replace them on the gentle curve and small shoulders of her stone. We first thought of this tribute in the family on the day of her burial. Good sea glass is getting scarce, now that everybody has learned not to throw bottles overboard, but Carol's collections were made long ago, plucked from a stone beach of ours on Eggemoggin Reach and an even better spot, just to the east, that belongs to a neighbor. There are dishes of sea glass in different sizes all over the house. Carol's favorite pieces (and mine) were small pale mauves and those smoothly rounded gray shapes, probably from old milk bottles, worn to sensual smoothness by the actions of tide and time. In recent years, when she knew that children of friends were coming over to visit us, she'd sometimes grab a small handful and secretly seed the beach in places where she'd bring the kids later.

I often took Andy along on my visits—a violation of cemetery rules, I'm sure, but we almost never saw another soul, and in any case he only wanted to rocket about in the vacant fields, away from the graves and their flags and plantings. On our way home, I sometimes stopped in the oldest part of the cemetery, closest to the road, and left the dog in the car while I walked among the graves there. These are marble or granite headstones, for the most part, but all are worn to an almost identical whiteness. Some of the lettering has been blackened by lichen, and some washed almost to invisibility. These aren't old graves, as New England cemeteries are measured—there's nothing before 1800, I believe—but their stories are familiar. Many small stones are in remembrance of infants or children who died at an early age, often three or four in the same family; there are also names of young men or old captains lost at sea. There's a low gray column bearing lowercase lines of verse in memory of a beloved wife who died in 1822, at the age of twenty-seven. Many of the names—Freethey, Eaton, Bridges, Allen—are still well represented in Brooklin today. What I noticed most, though—the same idea came over me every time—was that time had utterly taken away the histories and attachments and emotions that had once closely wrapped around these dead, leaving nothing but their families and names and dates. It was almost as if they were waiting to be born.

Harper's

WINNER—FICTION

Harper's Magazine *has been publishing fiction since its founding in 1850 (making it the second-oldest continuously published monthly in the United States, after* Scientific American*), and in recent years the short story has flourished in its pages, bringing it five National Magazine Awards for Fiction in the last two decades. Stephen King may be best known for his novels (and their various adaptations), but he has written hundreds of short stories. This, in fact, is the second time one of his pieces has earned a National Magazine Award: his story "Rest Stop" won* Esquire *the award in 2004. The judges this year were especially enthusiastic about "Batman and Robin Have an Altercation," calling it "a surprising, bittersweet lesson in filial alienation—a story for our times."*

Stephen King

Batman and Robin Have an Altercation

Sanderson sees his father twice a week. On Wednesday evenings, after he closes the jewelry store his parents opened long ago, he drives the three miles to Crackerjack Manor and sees Pop there, usually in the common room. In his "suite," if Pop is having a bad day. On most Sundays, Sanderson takes him out to lunch. The facility where Pop is living out his final foggy years is actually called the Harvest Hills Special Care Unit, but to Sanderson, Crackerjack Manor seems more accurate.

Their time together isn't so bad, and not just because Sanderson no longer has to change the old man's bed when he pisses in it or get up in the middle of the night when Pop goes wandering around the house, calling for his wife to make him some scrambled eggs or telling Sanderson those damned Fredericks boys are out in the back yard, drinking and hollering at each other. (Dory Sanderson has been dead for fifteen years and the three Fredericks boys, no longer boys, moved away long ago.) There's an old joke about Alzheimer's: The good news is that you meet new people every day. Sanderson has discovered the real good news is that the script rarely changes.

Applebee's, for instance. Although they have been having Sunday lunch at the same one for more than three years now, Pop almost always says the same thing: "This isn't so bad. We ought to come here again." He always has chopped steak, done medium rare, and when the bread pudding comes he tells Sanderson that his wife's is better. Last year, bread pudding was off the menu of the Applebee's on Commerce Way, so Pop—after having Sanderson read the dessert choices to him four times and thinking it over for an endless two minutes—ordered the apple cobbler. When it came, Pop said that Dory served hers with heavy cream. Then he simply sat, staring out the window at the highway. The next time, he made the same observation but ate the cobbler right down to the china.

He can usually be counted on to remember Sanderson's name and their relationship, but he sometimes calls him Reggie, who died forty-five years ago. When Sanderson takes his father back to Crackerjack Manor, his father invariably thanks him, and promises that next time he will be feeling better.

In his young years—before meeting Dory Levin, who civilized him—he was a roughneck in the Texas oil fields, and sometimes he reverts to that man, someone who never would have dreamed he would one day become a successful jewelry merchant in San Antonio. Then he is apt to "cut up rough," as the Manor's orderlies say (Sanderson has even seen the phrase on his father's chart), and use language not fit for the common room—or for the Applebee's on Commerce Way, for that matter. Then he is confined to his suite. On one occasion he turned his bed over and paid for his efforts with a broken wrist. When the orderly on duty—Jose, Pop's favorite—asked why he did it, Pop said it was because that fucking Gunton wouldn't turn down his radio. There is no Gunton, of course. Not now. Somewhere in the past, maybe.

Lately, all sorts of things have turned up in Pop's room: vases; silverware (actually sturdy plasticware) from the dining hall, where patients who are well enough to choose things from the steam table eat buffet breakfasts and lunches; the TV controller from the common room. Once, Jose discovered an El Producto cigar box, filled with various jigsaw-puzzle pieces and eighty or ninety playing cards, under Pop's bed. He cannot tell anyone, including his son, why he takes these things, and usually denies—with gentle puzzlement that is certainly genuine—that he has taken them at all. Once, he told Sanderson that Gunderson was trying to get him in trouble.

"Do you mean Gunton, Pop?" Sanderson asked.

Pop waved a bony driftwood hand. "All that guy ever wanted was cunt," he said. "He was the original cunthound from Cuntsville."

But the klepto phase seems to be passing—that's what Jose says, anyway—and this Sunday his father is calm enough. It's not one of his clear days, but it's not one of the really bad ones, either. It's good enough for Applebee's, and if they get through it without any accidents, all will be well. He's wearing incontinence pants, but of course there's a smell. For this reason, Sanderson always gets them a corner table. That's not a problem; they dine at two, and by then the after-church crowd is back home, watching baseball or football on TV.

"Who *are* you?" Pop asks in the car.

"I'm Dougie," Sanderson says. "Your son."

"I remember Dougie," Pop says, "but he died."

"No, Pop, huh-uh. Reggie died. He . . ." Sanderson trails off, waiting to see if Pop will finish. Pop doesn't. "He had a car accident."

"Drunk, was he?" Pop asks. This hurts, even after all the years. That's the bad news about what his father has—he is capable of random cruelties that, while unmeant, can still sting like hell.

"No," Sanderson says, "that was the kid who hit him. And then walked away with nothing but a couple of scratches."

That kid is in his fifties now, probably going silver at the temples. Sanderson hopes this grown version has prostate cancer and it hurts, he hopes the guy had a kid who died of SIDS, hopes he got mumps and went both blind and sterile, but he's probably just fine. Why not? He was sixteen. All water over the dam.

Youthful indiscretion. The records would be sealed. And Reggie? Also sealed. Bones in a suit under a headstone on Mission Hill. Some days Sanderson can't even remember what he looked like.

"Dougie and I used to play Batman and Robin," Pop says. "It was his favorite game."

Sanderson looks at his father and smiles. "Yeah, Pop, good! We even went out that way for Halloween one year, do you remember? I talked you into it. The Caped Crusader and the Boy Wonder."

Pop looks out through the windshield of Sanderson's Subaru, saying nothing. What is he thinking? Or has thought flattened to nothing but a carrier wave? Sanderson imagines what that might sound like: a flatline *mmmmmmmm*. Like the old test-pattern hum on TV.

Sanderson puts his hand on one thin topcoated arm and gives it a friendly squeeze. "You were drunk off your ass and Mom was mad, but I had fun. That was my best Halloween."

"I never drank around my wife," Pop says.

No, Sanderson thinks as the light turns green, not once she trained you out of it.

•   •   •

"Want help with the menu, Pop?"

"I can read," his father says. He no longer can, but it's bright in their corner and he can look at the pictures even with his sunglasses on. Besides, Sanderson knows what he will order.

When the waiter comes with their iced teas, Pop says he'll have the chopped steak, medium rare. "I want it pink but not red," he says. "If it's red, I'll send it back."

The waiter nods. "Your usual."

Pop looks at him suspiciously.

"Green beans or coleslaw?"

Pop snorts. "You kidding? All those beans were dead. You couldn't sell costume jewelry that year, let alone the real stuff."

"He'll have the slaw," Sanderson says. "And I'll have—"

"*All those beans were dead!*" Pop says again, and gives the waiter an emphatic look.

The waiter merely nods and says, "They *were* dead," before turning to Sanderson. "For you, sir?"

.   .   .

They eat. Pop refuses to take off his coat, so Sanderson asks for one of the plastic bibs and ties it around his father's neck. Pop makes no objection to this, may not register it at all. Some of his slaw ends up on his pants, but the bib catches most of the mushroom gravy. As they are finishing, Pop informs the mostly empty room that he has to piss so bad he can taste it.

Sanderson accompanies him to the men's room, and his father allows him to unzip his fly, but when Sanderson attempts to pull down the elasticized front of the continence pants, Pop slaps his hand away. "Never handle another man's meat, Patrick," he says, annoyed. "Don't you know that?"

This prompts an ancient memory: Dougie Sanderson standing in front of the toilet with his shorts puddled around his feet and his father kneeling beside him, giving instruction. How old was he then? Three? Only two? Yes, maybe only two, but he doesn't doubt the recollection; it's like a fleck of bright glass seen at the side of the road, one so perfectly positioned it leaves an afterimage. Memory is such a mystery.

"Unlimber, assume the position, fire when ready," he says.

Pop gives him a suspicious look, then breaks Sanderson's heart with his grin. "I used to tell my boys that when I was getting them housebroke," he says. "Dory told me it was my job, and I did it, by God."

He unleashes a torrent, and most of it goes into the urinal. The smell is sour and sugary. Diabetes. But what does that matter? Sometimes Sanderson thinks the sooner the better.

· · ·

Back at their table, still wearing the bib, Pop renders his verdict. "This place isn't so bad. We ought to come here again."

"How about some dessert, Pop?"

Pop gazes out the window, mouth hanging open, considering the idea. Or is it only the carrier wave? No, not this time. "Why not? I have room."

They both order the apple cobbler. Pop regards the scoop of vanilla on top with his eyebrows pulled together into a thicket. "My wife used to serve this with heavy cream. Her name was Dory. Short for Doreen. Like on the Mickey Mouse Club. Hey there, hi there, ho there, we're as welcome as can be."

"I know, Pop. Eat up."

"Are you Dougie?"

"Uh-huh."

"Really? Not pulling my leg?"

"No, Pop, I'm Dougie."

His father holds up a dripping spoonful of ice cream and apples. "We did, didn't we?"

"Did what?"

"Went out trick-or-treating as Batman and Robin."

Sanderson laughs, surprised. "We sure did! Ma said I was born foolish but you had no excuse. And Reggie wouldn't come near us. He was disgusted by the whole thing."

"I was drunk," Pop says, then begins eating his dessert. When he finishes, he points out the window and says, "Look at those birds. What are they again?"

Sanderson looks. The birds are clustered on a dumpster in the parking lot. Several more are on the fence behind it. "Those're crows, Pop."

"Christ, I know that," Pop says. "Crows never happened back then. We had a pellet gun. Now listen." He leans forward, all business. "Have we been here before?"

Sanderson briefly considers the metaphysical possibilities inherent in this question, then says, "Yes. We come here most Sundays."

"Well, it's a good place. But I think we ought to go back. I'm tired. I want that other thing now."

"A nap."

"That other thing," Pop says, and gives him an imperious look.

Sanderson motions for the check, and while he's paying it, Pop sails on with his hands tucked deep in his coat pockets. Sanderson grabs his change in a hurry and has to run to catch the door before Pop can wander out into the street.

.   .   .

"That was a good night," Pop says as Sanderson buckles his seatbelt.

"What night was that?"

"Halloween, you dummy. You were eight, so it was 1959. You were born in '51." Sanderson looks at his father, amazed, but the old man is staring straight ahead at the traffic. Sanderson closes the passenger door, goes around the front of his Subaru, and gets in. They say nothing for two or three blocks, and Sanderson assumes his father has forgotten the whole thing, but he hasn't.

"When we got to the Foresters' house at the bottom of the hill—you remember the hill, don't you?"

"Church Street hill, sure."

"Right! Norma Forester opened the door, and to you she says—before you could—she says, 'Trick or treat?' Then she looks at me and says, 'Trick or drink?' " Pop makes a rusty hinge sound that Sanderson hasn't heard in a year or more. He is laughing. He even slaps his thigh. " 'Trick or drink!' What a card! You remember that, don't you?"

Sanderson tries, but comes up empty. All he remembers is how happy he was to have his dad with him, even though the Batman costume was pretty lame. Gray pajamas, the bat emblem drawn on the front with Magic Marker. The cape cut out of an old bedsheet. The Batman utility belt was an old leather tool belt in which his father had stuck an assortment of screwdrivers and chisels from the toolbox in the garage. The mask was a mothy old balaclava that Pop rolled up to the nose so his mouth showed. Standing in front of the hallway mirror before going out, he pulled the top of the mask up on the sides, plucking at it to make ears, but they didn't stay.

"She offered me a bottle of Shiner's," Pop says.

"Did you take it?"

"Sure did." He falls silent. Where Commerce Way meets Airline Road, the two lanes become three. The one on the far left is a turn lane. The lights for straight-ahead traffic are red, but the one handling traffic in the left-turn lane is showing a green arrow. "That woman had tits like pillows. She was the best loving I ever had."

They hurt you. Sanderson knows this not just from his own experience but from talking to others who have relatives in Crackerjack Manor. They may not mean to, but they do. What memories remain to them are a jumble—pilfered puzzle pieces in a cigar box—and there's no governor on them, no way of separating the stuff that's okay to talk about from the stuff that isn't. Sanderson has never had a reason to think Pop was anything but faithful to his wife for the entire forty-some years of their marriage, though perhaps that's the assumption all grown children make if their parents' marriage was serene and collegial.

He takes his eyes off the road to look at his father, and that is why there is an accident instead of one of the near misses that happen all the time. Even so, it's not a terribly serious one, and though Sanderson knows his attention wandered from the road for a second or two, he also knows it still wasn't his fault.

A pickup truck with oversize tires and roof lights on the cab swerves into his lane, wanting to get all the way left in time to turn before the green arrow goes out. There's no taillight blinker; this Sanderson notes as the left front of his Subaru collides with the rear of the pickup truck. He and his father are both thrown forward into their locked seatbelts, and a ridge suddenly heaves up in the middle of his previously smooth hood, but the airbags don't deploy. There's a brisk tinkle of glass.

"Asshole!" Sanderson cries. "Jesus!" He pushes the button that lowers his window, sticks out his arm, and wags his middle finger at the truck. Later he will think he only did it because Pop was in the car with him, and Pop was on a roll.

Sanderson turns to him. "You okay?"

"What happened?" Pop says. "Why'd we quit?" He seems confused but otherwise fine.

Sanderson leans over Pop's lap, thumbs open the glove compartment, gets out his registration and insurance card. When he straightens up again, the door of the pickup truck is standing open and the driver is walking toward him, taking absolutely no notice of the cars that honk and swerve to get around them. There isn't as much traffic as there would be on a weekday, but Sanderson doesn't count this as a blessing, because he's looking at the approaching driver.

He knows this guy. Not personally, but he's a south Texas staple. He's wearing jeans and a T-shirt with the sleeves ripped off at the shoulders—not cut, ripped, so that errant strings dangle against the slabs of muscle on his upper arms. The jeans are hanging off his hip bones so the top two inches of his underwear shows. A chain runs from one beltless loop of his jeans to his back pocket. He's got tats on his arms. This is the kind of guy who, when Sanderson sees him on the sidewalk outside his jewelry shop via closed-circuit TV, causes him to push the button that locks the door. Right now he would like to push the button that locks his car door.

Instead, Sanderson opens the door and gets out, ready to placate, to apologize for what he shouldn't need to apologize for—it was the guy who cut across, for God's sake. The man's tats are crude, straggling things: chains around the biceps, thorns around the forearms, a dagger on one wrist with a drop of blood hanging from the tip of the blade. No tattoo parlor did those. That's jailhouse ink. Tat Man is at least six-two in his boots, and at least 200 pounds, maybe 220. Sanderson is five-nine and weighs 160.

"Look what you did to my truck!" Tat Man says. "Why the fuck didn't you let me in, asshole?"

"There was no time," Sanderson says. "You cut across, you never blinked—"

"I blinked!"

"Then how come it isn't on?" Sanderson points.

"Because you knocked out my fucking taillight, fucknuts! How am I supposed to tell my girlfriend about this? She fronted the fucking down payment! And get that fucking shit out of my face."

He strikes the insurance card and registration, which Sanderson is still holding out, from Sanderson's hand.

"I'm going," Tat Man says. "I'll fix my damage, you fix yours. That's how it's going to work."

The damage to the Subaru is far worse than the damage to the pickup, probably fifteen hundred or two thousand dollars more, but that isn't what makes Sanderson speak up. It's the thought of his gorked-out father sitting there in the passenger seat, not knowing what's happening, needing a nap. They should be halfway back to Crackerjack Manor by now, but no. Because this happy asshole had to cut across traffic. Just had to scoot under that green arrow before it went out, or the world would go dark.

"That's not how it's going to work," Sanderson says. "It was your fault. You cut in front of me without signaling. I didn't have time to stop. I want to see your registration, and I want to see your driver's license."

"Okay," the big man says, and punches Sanderson in the stomach. Sanderson bends over, expelling all the air in his lungs in a surprised whoosh.

"There's my registration," Tat Man says. Big streams of sweat are running down the sides of his face. "I hope you like it. As for my driver's license, I don't have one, okay? Fuckin' *don't*. I'm gonna be in a lot of trouble, and it's all your fucking fault because you were jerking off instead of looking where you were going. Fucking ringmeat!"

Then Tat Man loses it completely. Sanderson has just time enough to see the blue eyes on the guy's knuckles before a double-fisted blow drives him back against the newly distressed side of his car. Sanderson slides along it, feeling a prong of metal tear his shirt and the skin beneath. His knees buckle and he lands on the road. He stares down at his hands, not believing they are his. His cheek is hot and seems to be rising like bread dough. His right eye is watering.

Next comes a kick to his side, just above the belt. Sanderson's head hits the hubcap of his Subaru and bounces off. He tries to crawl out from under Tat Man's shadow. There's another kick, this time in the meat of his upper left thigh. He wants to raise his head—if he's going to die he would like to do it looking at something more interesting than the front of his own wounded car—but he can't. Then Tat Man gives a cry, and red drops begin to splash the composition surface of the roadway. Sanderson at first thinks it's from his own nose—or maybe his lips, from the blow to his face—but then more warmth splashes the back of his neck. He crawls a little farther, past the hood of his car, then manages to turn over and sit. He looks up, squinting against the dazzle of the sky, and sees Pop standing beside Tat Man. Tat Man is groping at the side of his neck, which has sprouted a piece of wood.

At first Sanderson can't understand what has happened, but then he gets it. The piece of wood is the handle of a knife, one he's seen before. He sees it almost every week. You don't need a steak knife to cut the kind of chopped meat Pop has at their Sunday lunches, but at Applebee's they bring you one anyway. Pop may no longer remember which son comes to visit him, or that his wife is dead—he probably no longer even remembers his middle name—but it seems he hasn't lost all the cleverness that enabled him to rise from a no-college oil-fields roughneck to an upper-middle-class jewelry merchant in San Antonio.

He got me to look at the birds, Sanderson thinks. *The crows on the dumpster.*

Tat Man has lost interest in the man sitting in the road and never looks at the older man standing beside him. Tat Man has begun coughing. One hand is on the knife in his neck, trying to pull it out. Blood pours down the side of his T-shirt and splatters his jeans. He begins walking toward the intersection, still bent over and still coughing. With his free hand he gives a jaunty little wave: *Hi, Ma!*

Sanderson gets to his feet. His legs are trembling, but they hold him. He can hear sirens approaching. Sure, now the cops come. Now that it's all over.

Sanderson puts an arm around his father's shoulders. "You all right, Pop?"

"That man was beating on you," Pop says matter-of-factly. "Who is he?"

"I don't know." Tears are coursing down Sanderson's cheeks. He wipes them away.

Tat Man falls to his knees. He has stopped coughing. Now he's making a low growling sound. Most people hang back, but a couple of brave souls go to him, wanting to help.

"Did we eat yet, Reggie?"

"Yeah, Pop, we did. And I'm Dougie."

"Reggie's dead."

"Yeah, Pop."

"That man was beating on you." Now his father also starts to cry. His face twists into the face of a child, one who is horribly tired and needs to go to bed. "I've got a headache. Let's blow this pop stand. I want to lie down."

"We have to wait for the cops."

"Why? What cops? Who *is* that guy?"

Sanderson smells shit. His father has just dropped a load.

"Let's get you in the car, Pop."

His father lets Sanderson lead him around the Subaru's crumpled snout.

He helps the eighty-three-year-old Caped Crusader into the car and closes the door to keep the cool in. The first city police car is pulling up. The sixty-one-year-old Boy Wonder, hands pressed to his aching side, shuffles back to the driver's side to wait.

Byliner

FINALIST—FEATURE
WRITING INCORPORATING
PROFILE WRITING

Byliner is a new kind of magazine—literally unbound—that publishes individual pieces of long-form journalism as apps. Some of these stories have been published elsewhere, but many have been commissioned by the editors for purchase on digital newsstands or by subscription. What makes Byliner a magazine is the vision of the editors, whose passion for storytelling is shared by a community of like-minded readers. Since leaving the U.S. Army in 2005—he served two tours of duty as an infantryman in Iraq—Brian Mockenhaupt has written widely about soldiers both at war and at home. The story of three Americans in Afghanistan, "The Living and the Dead" offers readers what the National Magazine Award judges described as "an unforgettable sense of the reality of modern combat."

Brian Mockenhaupt

The Living and the Dead

Dedicated to the men of Patrol Base Dakota and their families

1. The Last Step

Tom Whorl decided at twelve years old, the night he met his father's two friends at the Super Bowl party. They matched his physical conception—thick arms, straight backs, high-and-tight haircuts shaved short on the sides and just a little longer on top—but it was how they carried themselves that fascinated him: direct in speech but respectful, with a confidence that suggested they knew something about themselves and the world that many others did not. Leaving the party, Tom told his father he would join the Marine Corps.

He considered nothing else, and five years later he hustled off a bus in the early-morning darkness at Parris Island, South Carolina, and ran toward dozens of perfectly spaced pairs of yellow footprints painted on pavement, four abreast. He placed his feet on two footprints and willed himself to stillness as his heart hammered and men scrambled around him. Easy as that, the drill instructors had put their new recruits into neat rank and file. The recruits would soon do this on their own, moving in unison, as one organism.

Tom traded first person for the third. *I* and *me* and *my* vanished, replaced with *this recruit*, as in "Sir! This recruit does not know the answer, sir!" He picked that up quickly; those who slipped had the lesson reinforced with exercises in the sandpit that left them with trembling limbs and heaving lungs. The individual did not matter, except as an essential part of the whole. He was nothing on his own, and he knew nothing, until the Marine Corps taught him the proper way. To speak. To walk. To shower. To dress. To eat.

The specialized training came later, at the School of Infantry, where he learned the finer skills of the trade. But for thirteen weeks on Parris Island he learned how to be responsible for himself, and responsible for others. He could be punished for another recruit's actions, and others could suffer for his mistakes. If sweat trickled into his eye, he let it burn rather than wipe it away and risk a drill instructor punishing the group for his lack of discipline. He learned to fear, above all else, letting down his fellow recruits. Others depended on him to do a job, and someday men would depend on him to lead them. His fellow Marines, once they had all earned the title of Marine, would trust their lives to him, and he would trust his to them, and they would sacrifice without hesitation. If the man to his front fell, he would step into the void.

Of course, the Marine Corps could teach recruits how to behave in war, how to push aside fear and charge through an open field as bullets kicked up spouts of dirt at their feet. But the Corps couldn't tell them what war would do to them. Tom and his men would learn those lessons on their own, far from Parris Island.

· · ·

In a few months the room would be a clay oven, holding the day's heat deep into the night, and he would wake each morning lathered in sweat. But with the Afghan winter still pushing temperatures below freezing, Tom watched his breath roll out in a hazy plume when he woke. He squirmed out of his sleeping bag, swung his legs off the cot, and slipped his feet into his boots. He lit a Marlboro and worked his mind through the day ahead, patrolling the surrounding fields and villages, infested with buried bombs and Taliban fighters.

As the sergeant in charge of First Squad, Third Platoon, Fox Company, Second Battalion, Eighth Marine Regiment, he oversaw three four-man fire teams, the basic building blocks of a Marine infantry unit. His days had a simple rhythm: Wake up, patrol, come home, start over. Every day, he and his men pushed out on foot into the farmland around the patrol base, and every day the Taliban shot at them, sometimes just a few hastily fired rounds, but oftentimes accurate and sustained gunfire. The Marines shot back, and sometimes they saw fighters fall, but they never found bodies, only blood trails. The Taliban were good about taking their injured and dead with them, same as the Americans.

Thousands of Marines and Afghan soldiers had invaded the longtime Taliban stronghold of Marjah, in Helmand Province, a year earlier, in 2010, and driven out the insurgents. But progress was still tenuous, and success there was critical to any sort of lasting calm in southern Afghanistan. Third Platoon was a small piece of a security ring around Marjah, keeping the Taliban under pressure on the outskirts so a local government could take root and spread, with schools and markets and Afghan security forces capable of defending their own people.

The platoon had been split in two for the deployment, with the lieutenant and two more squads a kilometer to the east at Patrol Base Beatley. Tom's squad, the platoon sergeant, a medic, and five Afghan soldiers lived at Patrol Base Dakota, an abandoned farmer's compound with eight-foot mud walls, a foot thick, around a courtyard roughly one hundred feet square. The Marines lived in a row of small rooms along the northern wall that they had crowded with cots. From guard towers in each corner, outfitted with machine guns and bulletproof glass, they kept watch over fields and tree lines. Like cavalry troops in an Old West fort, they were surrounded on all sides by the enemy, and fought off attacks when they left the marginal safety of their outpost, while trying to win over an always wary and often hostile population.

The compound had been named for Corporal Dakota Huse, a nineteen-year-old Marine killed by a buried bomb during a foot patrol four months earlier. The Taliban had regularly attacked the building's previous tenants, from Second Battalion, Ninth Marines, with fighters creeping so close they chucked grenades over the walls and once snatched a machine gun from one of the guard posts. The Taliban kept its interest in Dakota after Tom's unit replaced them in January 2011, regularly shooting at the patrol base and lobbing a few rockets. From inside the compound, the Marines could hear the sharp rattle of machine-gun fire and the enormous *whoomp* of improvised explosive devices in the surrounding countryside, triggered by civilians, distant Marine patrols from other bases, or Taliban blowing themselves up while trying to build or plant bombs.

"Three IEDs have gone off in the last 24 hours," Tom scribbled in a six-by-nine-inch spiral notebook, the journal he kept to document his platoon's fight for northern Marjah. On the first page he had left instructions for the Marines who might one day have the grim duty of sorting through his gear: "This is to be returned to my wife, should that time come."

·   ·   ·

A few feet away, on a canvas cot set against the opposite wall, the platoon sergeant, Staff Sergeant James Malachowski, still lay cocooned in his sleeping bag, a fleece cap pulled over his eyes. He was "Staff Sergeant" to his subordinates, Jimmy to his friends.

Tom was both, and called him Jimmy in private but never in front of other Marines.

Their narrow, dirt-floored room doubled as Dakota's Combat Operations Center, the COC, which was really just a computer and two radios resting on a piece of plywood at the room's far end, everything coated in a layer of dirt as fine as talcum powder. A Marine sat there day and night, monitoring the radios and the computer's secret instant-messaging system, ready to report emergencies or relay communications from higher command.

Tom and Jimmy had given the room a few minimal decorations. An American flag hung on the wall above Tom's cot, and another above Jimmy's, alongside a black Jolly Roger—a Christmas present from Jimmy's mother, a former Marine herself, which became the platoon's flag. Jimmy's family also sent some of his favorites for relaxation: herbal tea and slender Bad Boy cigars, made in Maryland not far from his home in Westminster, outside Baltimore. He listened to classical music, and though Tom initially scoffed at that, he quickly found he enjoyed it. After watching movies on Jimmy's laptop at night—usually something light, like *Office Space* or *Old School*—they'd fall asleep to Bach or Brahms or, many nights, Samuel Barber's mournful *Adagio for Strings*, known to them from the Vietnam War movie *Platoon*.

At quick glance, they seemed two very different sorts of Marines. Tom wore his dark brown hair cut close on the sides and back, but the top flopped nearly to his eyes, far from the typical high-and-tight cut. But that was Tom, more interested in actions than appearance after a dozen years in the Marine Corps. Jimmy, though four years younger, at twenty-five, was already balding, and he kept his head shaved. And while Tom was wiry, with a welterweight's build, Jimmy was six feet and two hundred pounds of dense muscle, narrow waist, and massive chest.

But they shared a similar leadership style, very aggressive in combat, always pushing toward the enemy, and Tom respected

Jimmy deeply for his devotion to and concern for his men, qualities he counted as crucial in a good leader. Like Tom, Jimmy didn't often raise his voice. His men knew what he expected of them and knew he put their welfare first, without any blind deference to rank. As the Marines had prepared for the deployment back at Camp Lejeune, in North Carolina, the officer in charge of the platoon told the men not to worry, that everything would be okay. Jimmy knew better: he'd already served two violent tours in Iraq and had seen several friends die. He pulled the lieutenant aside afterwards. "Don't tell them that," he said. "We are not all coming back. We will take catastrophic injuries and we will have KIAs. Don't tell them that, because it's not true."

He and Tom had met briefly four years earlier at Parris Island, where they worked as marksmanship instructors for new recruits. Friendship came later, after Jimmy arrived at Lejeune as the new platoon sergeant, a few months before the deployment. They had both grown up in Maryland—Jimmy in the north, in the wooded hills of Westminster, in Carroll County, and Tom in the south, in St. Mary's County, on Chesapeake Bay. They talked about eating blue crabs down at the beach and argued over football—Tom for the Redskins, Jimmy for the Ravens. In those early conversations they learned that their families, generations deep in Maryland, had fought on opposite sides in the Civil War—Jimmy's for the Union, Tom's for the Confederacy. What that must have been like, they mused, their own state torn in two.

As a boy, Tom had visited the Gettysburg and Antietam battlefields with his father, and since then he had consumed books about the Civil War. He brought two with him to Afghanistan: *Robert E. Lee on Leadership*, by H. W. Crocker, and *Pickett's Charge—The Last Attack at Gettysburg*, by Earl J. Hess. He'd filled the Lee book with scraps of paper, on which he'd scrawled notes. *Awesome traits—tell them to my leaders: Know the ground;*

do your reconnaissance; be indefatigable; learn from your superiors; leadership is legitimatized by success under fire; leadership requires moral responsibility.

He read the Pickett book, heavy with raw accounts of battle, as a counterweight, to remind him that those theories of leadership played out with consequence. The scale of that destruction was remarkable, with hundreds of men killed in minutes, whole platoons and companies wiped out. For the foot soldier, war hadn't much changed. War was still miserable, the rain and the cold, the heat and the fear. Soldiers at Gettysburg watched cannonballs cut their friends in half; in Afghanistan, improvised explosive devices did the same gruesome work. Shrapnel still sounded the same whizzing an inch past the face, which brought the same euphoric relief of death cheated. The cries of the wounded and dying still sounded the same, too.

As the day's patrol snaked out of Dakota, through a gap in the triple stack of concertina that surrounded the compound, Tom imagined Pickett's men lined up shoulder to shoulder, ready to march toward likely death, resigned to the unknown of the next few minutes. He and his men knew some of that trepidation, waiting for the first bullet to crack overhead, heralding the start of an ambush or the sickening, deafening thunderclap of a buried bomb exploding under the patrol.

The Marines searched a few of the area's many abandoned compounds, for weapons and bomb-making materials, and chatted with the locals they passed. Most of these conversations followed a timeworn script: Tom asked if they knew anything about Taliban activity in the area; they said no. Some were no doubt Taliban sympathizers, or Taliban themselves. But many felt trapped in a vicious brawl. If they sided with one, they'd make an enemy of the other. Locals regularly found letters taped to their homes with terse warnings: "If you help the Americans, we'll kill you and burn your house."

Still, some must have figured the Marines had a chance of winning, or they'd simply grown weary of wondering whether they'd blow up while walking to their fields, like the farmer who told Tom, between nervous glances, about two bombs buried along a canal.

"So tomorrow we will be going IED hunting," Tom wrote in his journal that night. "I hate doing it, but it must be done. FML." *Fuck my life.*

.   .   .

To defeat the bombs, the Marines needed to disable the bomb-making network. This meant detaining or killing the men who transported the materials, assembled the bombs, and detonated them—rarely the same person—and searching buildings and fields for stashes of explosives, detonators, battery packs, and the low-tech electronics used for radio-controlled blasts. But if the bomb was already planted, a critical part of the fight had been lost. The best the Marines could do was find and disable the bomb before it found them.

At least two men in every patrol carried an electronic jammer, worn as a backpack, that blocked radio signals sent from the triggerman to the bomb. Another two men carried metal detectors, which they swept before them as they walked. The detectors emitted a tone that started low as they neared a metal object and rose to a high-pitched whine for larger objects and metal closer to the surface.

The Marines also had Holly, a yellow Labrador retriever trained to sniff out several types of explosives. Lance Corporal Matthew Westbrook, Holly's handler, would walk with her near the front of the patrol and send her to investigate suspicious areas or possible choke points, such as a road passing between two walled compounds. If she smelled explosives, she'd lie down next to the suspected bomb.

Finally, the Marines themselves became expert at spotting telltale signs: a slightly discolored patch of ground in the road or a thin layer of dirt sprinkled over a wire.

But each of these methods had serious flaws. The jammers only thwarted radio-controlled bombs and were useless against pressure plates or bombs detonated by wires, which sometimes ran hundreds of yards from a bomb to the triggerman's location. Set a metal detector's sensitivity too low and it could miss a bomb; set it too high and the men might move a hundred feet in an hour, investigating every tiny metal scrap. Holly could hunt explosives for only an hour or less before she became distracted, and as temperatures rose she would spend more time jumping into the cool canal water than sniffing out bombs. And while the Marines were good at spotting the out-of-place, no one was good enough to see everything, and a few minutes of hard rain could hide the signs completely.

On patrol, they often tried to walk in one another's footsteps. No sense taking chances with an untested patch of ground. But that didn't always work, either. Stories abounded of bombs exploding under the very spot where another Marine had just stood or stepped. Maybe he wasn't heavy enough, or hadn't compressed the pressure plate just right. Lucky for that first man; not so for the next.

As the Marines had prepared to leap six feet across a canal during a patrol west of Dakota in mid-February, Corporal Ian Muller, Tom's first team leader, spotted a tiny patch of yellow on the opposite embankment, next to a footbridge. Tom stepped into the canal and gently brushed away the dirt, revealing a piece of balsa wood wrapped in yellow tape. A pressure plate. Step on it and two metal contacts meet, sending electricity from a battery pack into a pressure cooker buried in the embankment, the same sort used in a kitchen, but this one packed with ten pounds of ammonium nitrate and aluminum powder, more than enough to blow a man in half. The Taliban knew the Marines would stay off the footbridge, so they put the pressure plate several feet away, at a likely crossing point.

This was a chess match: attack and counter.

The late-winter rains saturated the patrol base and the surrounding fields, turning everything to calf-deep peanut butter that could suck the boots off a Marine's feet. Moving through the fields exhausted the men and kept them exposed to rifle fire from distant tree lines, but they felt somewhat safe there, away from roads and trails, which were more likely laced with bombs. Until a farmer told the Marines that the Taliban had planted bombs in his field. The development rattled Tom. "The placement of IEDs in open fields is horrible," he wrote in his journal. "The worst feeling is not knowing when your last step will be. That's what takes a toll on your brain."

Over at Patrol Base Beatley, Sergeant Dan Clift had stepped on a land mine that raked his legs with shrapnel, but the wounds were light and he was expected back in a few days. Tom had to call in his own medevac helicopter that day, for an Afghan National Army soldier assigned to Dakota who had passed out during a foot patrol. "I hope I never have to call another medevac," he wrote in his journal that night. "So many people don't understand what it's like to be responsible for the lives of the Marines and Navy corpsman under me. Every day is so stressful and I lose so much sleep worrying about the next day, planning and going over so much in my head, every move and decision calculated."

●   ●   ●

The bullet smacked the dirt between Tom and Ian, inches from their feet, as they stepped out of the compound they'd just finished searching. A second later they heard the shot, fired from a string of houses along Route Animal, three hundred yards to the northwest.

"Let's go," Tom said.

As the patrol fanned out and jogged into the field, moving toward the buildings, more gunmen opened fire, from several spots along Route Animal and in Cocheran Village, farther north. Muzzle flashes twinkled from alleyways and darkened windows. The Marines at Dakota were terrified of buried bombs—the utter lack of control—but they loved firefights. Here they could influence the outcome. Many of them had joined the Corps with fantasies of moments like this—sprinting across open ground as bullets kick up dirt around them and snap overhead, then diving onto the ground and laying down cover fire as their comrades bound forward, leapfrogging toward the enemy. These were bread-and-butter infantry skills.

With Ian's four-man team in the lead, Tom pushed the patrol forward, an exhausting movement through muddy fields crisscrossed by irrigation canals. Ian spotted a gunman firing at them beside a pump house near a mosque along Route Animal. He had been trained at the Marine Corps's sniper school and carried an MK12 Special Purpose Rifle, a tricked-out version of the M-4 and M-16 rifles most Marines carry, fitted with a powerful scope. He could drop a man at a half-mile. He centered the crosshairs of his scope on the man's head and fired as Tom, Lance Corporal Ryan Moore, and Navy Hospitalman Jesse Deller, the platoon's medic, lobbed 40-millimeter grenades from launchers attached to their rifles.

They found the gunman later in an empty house with grenade shrapnel stitched across his back and a hole in his head, stuffed with gauze. Tom called in a medevac helicopter for the man, who would die soon, and the Marines kept searching. The other fighters had fled, but they found blood trails and a cache of three remote controls and six receivers, a little win for the day— fewer buried bombs and at least one less insurgent to fire a rifle or trigger a bomb.

But Cocheran Village had been an ongoing problem for the Marines, and killing a single Taliban fighter wouldn't fix that.

Fox Company would move into the area in force, search the buildings for weapons and bomb-making supplies, and kill or capture anyone who opposed them.

"The weather is getting warmer, and more fighters are coming in every day," Tom wrote in his journal a few days later, on March 10. "Tomorrow we are doing a company clearing operation to the north, where the worst fighting has been recently."

Jimmy's and Tom's men got the easy job: overwatch. Marines from First Platoon would sweep through and search the village while the Dakota Marines watched from a distance, to keep enemy fighters from moving into the village, and intercept or kill any insurgents trying to flee the area. Squirters, they called them.

In the compound where Tom and Ian had nearly been shot a few days earlier, Tom sent Ian onto the rooftop, where he'd have a clear view of the village, four hundred yards to the north, and the surrounding fields and roads. Jimmy climbed onto the roof with him to plot target reference points on his map, should he need to call in mortar fire. Though Jimmy outranked Tom, he didn't micromanage on patrols, and he let Tom maneuver the men. A platoon sergeant mostly stays in the background, running logistics, making sure the platoon has food, water, and ammunition, the resources to fight. On patrol, he would call in air support during firefights, or medevac helicopters, should someone get hurt; otherwise Jimmy acted like a rifleman, ready to charge an enemy position.

Tom checked the perimeter security around the compound and then joined Ian and Jimmy on the roof. This was tedious work, hours of watching, waiting. But Ian was a talker, and as they lay on the roof watching the village, he told Tom and Jimmy about growing up with five brothers and a sister in a huge old farmhouse in rural Vermont, where their mother had home-schooled all of them and where he learned to play the viola. Every child played at least one instrument, and Ian's brother Dylan made the viola and several of his siblings' violins. Ian was the most adventurous and athletic, and he had mountain-biked, rock-climbed, and snowboarded in the nearby White Mountains. Now twenty-two, he'd been in the Marines for four years and wasn't sure whether he would stay. Dylan worked for a Houston company called Canrig as a mud tester monitoring oil wells. Maybe he'd try that. Or he might go back to college, where he'd spent a year studying graphic design. A deployment offered plenty of time to plan a future.

First Platoon finished the search, and the Dakota Marines covered their withdrawal. Before Ian, Jimmy, and Tom climbed off the rooftop, Jesse, the medic, snapped a picture of the three peering down at him, then they filed out of the compound and started home, down a tree-lined dirt road, with Ian walking point, the most dangerous position.

Tom had conceded that argument weeks earlier. He had told Ian that walking point wasn't a team leader's job, that his place was farther back, directing movement. But Ian was determined: he didn't want his men put at extra risk, men who had wives and kids. Before the deployment he'd even broken up with his girlfriend of more than a year because he didn't want her saddled with the burden of constant worry, or caring for him should he come home crippled.

Matt Westbrook, the dog handler, and Ian had argued about walking point as well. Yes, Matt had a wife, but he also had a bomb-sniffing dog, and he couldn't let Ian assume the added danger on his behalf. Ian agreed to sometimes let Westbrook run point, and earlier that day Matt had said he'd lead the patrol back to Dakota. But by midafternoon Holly was tired, and a tired bomb dog is useless.

"I'll take us back," Ian said.

Matt nodded and fell in behind him on the road, with Holly between them, zigzagging down the road, sniffing.

"Sergeant Whorl," Ian called back, "do you want me to stay on the road or go through the field?"

Moving on foot through Afghanistan offered nothing but bad options. Of course the roads were dangerous. But now the fields were, too. The men were tired from being out all day, and a quick shot back to Dakota would limit their time exposed in the open.

"Stay on the road," Tom said.

Ian turned south, sweeping the mine detector before him, an olive-drab metronome. *Tick tock.*

With the mine detector, his rifle, ammunition, grenades, body armor and helmet, two radios, the bomb jammer, water, and medical supplies, Ian carried close to ninety pounds, more than any other Marine in the patrol. He could handle the load: at five foot seven, he had weighed 150 pounds when he entered the Marines in 2007, but he had since bulked up to 205. He figured carrying extra weight would increase the patrol's over-all effectiveness—a weaker and overloaded Marine falling behind put everyone at risk. Besides, that way other Marines couldn't complain about their lighter loads, or not being able jump across canals with the awkward weight.

Ian turned south, onto a tree-lined road that split two muddy fields. In a month the fields would be thick with waist-high poppy plants.

Tick tock.

Fifty yards up, the road crossed a canal just in front of a large, high-walled compound to the left.

"Muller," Tom said, "slow it up a bit." The patrol had stretched out after the Afghan soldiers, farther back, stopped to question a farmer. Tom and Matt picked up their pace and closed the distance with Ian, who worked the mine detector back and forth.

Tick tock.

Holly sniffed the air, five feet behind Ian, as he stepped onto the dirt bridge that spanned the canal.

Tick tock.

Tick.

Matt still can't figure out how Holly wasn't killed.

2. Repercussions

With a patrol outside the wire, Dakota ran on a skeleton crew: a Marine in each guard post and a team leader manning the Combat Operations Center—that little desk in Tom and Jimmy's room—to relay messages between the patrol and higher-ups. Today the job fell to Ryan Moore, at nineteen the youngest of Tom's three team leaders.

He'd grown up in Navarre, a town of maybe fifteen hundred in eastern Ohio, moved out at sixteen, and spent his high school years lifting weights, repairing cars, and smoking weed. In the Marine Corps he found his groove. He listened and he worked harder than others, and when he arrived at Camp Lejeune after boot camp and infantry training, Tom noticed and soon put him in charge of three other Marines. Ryan would rather have been outside the wire leading his men and trying to kill Taliban, but he knew the importance of his role back at Dakota, should the patrol find trouble.

Before the Marines walked out of the patrol base that morning, Ryan had hugged Ian. They'd had enough close calls and heard enough terrible stories to know that life out here was utterly unpredictable. Many of the Marines made a point of telling their friends how much they cared about them.

"I love you," Ryan said.

"I love you, too," Ian told him.

From Ian's first weekend at Camp Lejeune, five months before the deployment, Ryan drew him into his group of friends, and they spent much of their free time together, watching movies in the barracks or hitting the Jacksonville bars. Five-cent Pabst Blue Ribbon at Gus' on Wednesdays. The mechanical bull on Fridays. All of which suited Ian. As he was always telling his friends, "Live each day like it's your last."

Where Ryan could be reserved, Ian was class-clown loud, all smile and uncontained energy, like at Sergeant Clift's platoon party before they left for Afghanistan, when he ran around the house in an orange wig, slugging Jägermeister. After he'd passed out in a recliner, Ryan and the other guys posed with him for pictures.

Though Ian had been trained as an infantryman, he'd spent his first three years in the Corps with the Fleet Antiterrorism Security Team, a sort of Marine SWAT team. When he arrived at Lejeune, he was new to the role of infantry team leader, like Ryan. They traded knowledge and learned together, then taught classes for the rest of the squad on everything from the use and maintenance of machine guns to calling for medevac helicopters over the radio. They peppered Tom with questions about his job as squad leader so they'd know exactly what to do if they had to step up. They regarded their roles as young leaders with something close to sacred respect. Ryan tried to set an example for his men and could often be seen picking up trash around Dakota or fixing a broken piece of equipment—not because Tom had told him to, but because it was the right thing to do. "If I know what needs to be done every day, I'm not even going to make him waste his breath by coming over to tell me," he says. "I'm going to make sure me and my guys already have it done." Likewise, when one of Ian's men had been caught sitting in his sleeping bag during a cold night on guard, Tom left it to Ian to decide the punishment. They filled a hundred sandbags for perimeter defenses—as a team, Ian included, because they were responsible for one another, and an individual lapse in judgment could affect them all.

At Dakota, Ryan and Ian still spent much of their free time together, watching movies or lifting weights. They worked out every day at Dakota's outdoor gym, an elaborate collection of homemade equipment built from plywood and two-by-fours, with sandbags, metal stakes, and spools of concertina wire as weights. Ryan figured they might get in a good late-afternoon workout when Ian returned from the overwatch mission.

The patrol had been out for several hours, and he knew they'd be back soon. He tried to call for their current location over the radio, but transmissions could be spotty inside the building, so he climbed atop the generator in the courtyard. From there he could see over Dakota's wall and send an unbroken line-of-sight radio message. As he raised the radio to his mouth, a bomb exploded near a string of trees a couple hundred yards north, just where he figured the Marines would be. Ryan saw an eruption of dirt, like a mini-volcano, that threw debris fifty feet into the field along the road, and a second later the sound reached him, a deep crunch and rumble.

He radioed for a situation report, and after a long moment Staff Sergeant Malachowski's voice responded, calm and deliberate, with a medevac request.

"Muller's hit," Jimmy said. "Heavy lacerations, arterial bleeding, left leg and left arm."

And then Ryan understood. That wasn't debris arcing over the trees and into the field. That was Ian.

·　　　·　　　·

The blast had thrown Matt to the ground and slammed into Tom as if he'd been whacked with a giant mallet. A wave of dirt and rock washed over him, and shrapnel tore holes in his helmet cover. He staggered and caught himself and watched Ian fly through the air, over a twenty-foot tree. He heard him land in the field, a heavy thud, and he leaped across the canal and ran toward him. Even at a distance, he saw red on Ian's body, everywhere. Matt, knocked unconscious for a few seconds, sat up in the road. Holly was unscathed by the bomb. She sat beside him, waiting for direction.

The medic, Jesse, was several men back in the patrol, and running forward before Ian hit the ground. A blast that big, someone up there would be hurt. Tom was already crouched over Ian when

Jesse arrived. He threw down his aid bag, a backpack stuffed with thirty pounds of bandages, splints, IV bags, painkillers, and airway tubes.

Ian didn't move. But he was alive, and struggling to breathe, choking on blood pooling in his throat from deep cuts across his face and internal bleeding. Tom and Jesse dragged him another thirty feet from the blast site—farther from any secondary bombs, a common insurgent tactic to compound casualties by hitting Marines giving aid to their injured. Jesse ran his finger down Ian's neck and found the notch at his Adam's apple, then sliced a half-inch slit in the cartilage and inserted a plastic breathing tube. He and Tom looped two tourniquets over Ian's left arm and left leg, broken and gashed by the blast. A huge knot had already formed on his forehead, likely a sign that his skull had fractured and his brain was swelling.

On the road, Matt stood on weak legs. His tongue and face had gone numb, and his body tingled. He hadn't yet started puking from the concussion, but he would soon. He needed to sweep the area for secondary bombs, but he couldn't think clearly. He ordered Holly out to search, but she stayed beside him. Tom saw Matt standing in the road, unfocused and dazed.

"Westbrook, stop," he said. "You need to sit down."

The tourniquets had stanched the bleeding on Ian's arms, and Jesse bandaged his torn face. He and Tom talked to Ian as they worked on him, but he didn't respond. He lay motionless and pulled ragged breaths through the hole in his throat.

Several Marines pushed into the field to secure a landing zone for the medevac, which now raced toward them from the north, low over the fields, and Jimmy tossed out a green smoke grenade to mark their position. The massive twin-rotor Chinook helicopter, flown by a British crew, landed fast and hard, less than a hundred feet from Tom and Jesse, and they bent over Ian to shield him from the wave of dirt thrown up by the rotor wash. Together with the flight medics, they carried their friend onto the helicopter and watched him rise up and disappear beyond the trees.

Twenty-seven minutes after the explosion, trauma doctors received Ian in the hospital on Camp Bastion, a remarkable feat of battlefield medicine. Not that it mattered.

.   .   .

Nina Whorl knew before her husband that Ian was dead.

She was deployed, too, just thirty miles away on Camp Bastion, where she worked administration and logistics for a Marine aviation unit. From her office, she heard over the radio that medevac was delivering an "angel" from Tom's battalion, the aircrews' term for deceased service members. Fearing it was her husband, she made a phone call and learned that it was Ian, then she sent a simple e-mail, which waited for Tom back at Dakota: *I already heard. Are you okay?*

They had met on Parris Island, where, as a primary marksmanship instructor, he taught new recruits how to shoot and volunteered with the Burton Fire District in his downtime. She was a sergeant, like him, and had been in the Marine Corps since 2001. They had met briefly through a mutual friend, but when she stopped by to see him at a high school football game where he was on call with the ambulance in case of injuries, he was hooked: on the blond hair, the Tennessee accent, and the sass. "I'm not a touchy-feely guy at all," he says. "People call me emotionless, but I looked at her and I knew." It was surprising for Tom to be swayed by such whimsy, and for Nina, too. They had both had marriages end badly and leave them hardened. They had forgotten that two people can be good to each other, and good for each other.

"She no-shit saved my life," Tom says. "I was in a downward spiral." He compares his life before Nina to that of firefighter Tommy Gavin, of the television show *Rescue Me*: destructive and alcohol-fueled. Gently, she dialed him back, and she found her own release from the persistent suspicion that a man would be careless with her heart. "We have a good understanding of how life can be," Tom says. "We leaned on each other at the same time." They were soft with each other, playful. Early on, she locked the car doors while they were at a gas station and made Tom dance before she'd let him back in, and that became part of them. He's danced in the rain and in front of his Marines.

Nina had two young boys from a first marriage—Lee, four years old, and Andrew, not yet a year—and from the beginning Tom regarded them as his own. "He's very protective, of me and the kids and his Marines," she says. "He reminds me of a dog. If he could pee on stuff to own it, he would."

They married in October 2007, near her family's home in Gatlinburg, Tennessee. Tom left the Marines a few months later and became a full-time firefighter. But that put a financial pinch on the family, and by the next year he was back in the Corps. A year after that he was in Afghanistan, thirty miles south of northern Marjah in the Garmsir District.

That deployment stretched from May to November 2009, but he best remembers seven endless days in July that summed up the terror, frustration, and dark comedy of being a grunt in Afghanistan.

A convoy of thickly armored trucks called a Route Clearance Patrol had been crawling down Redskins, a road near Tom's patrol base that the Taliban sowed with bombs as fast as the Marines could find them. The first truck used heavy rollers attached to its front end to detonate pressure-activated bombs. Trucks farther back had enormous mechanical arms for digging into suspicious-looking dirt patches and sophisticated electronics to jam radio-controlled detonators. Marines inside peered from three-inch-thick windows searching for signs: an exposed bit of wire running from the embankment into a field, or a plastic baggie that might hide a radio transmitter. This was nervous, slow-motion work, and while the patrol found many bombs, many bombs found them first, announced with booms like little earthquakes.

From his patrol base more than half a mile away, Tom felt the shock wave roll through him as a plume of dirt and smoke bloomed on the horizon.

The blast had heaved a fourteen-ton armored truck into a canal along the road. While maneuvering another vehicle to pull out the damaged truck, the patrol hit another bomb. Tom's squad headed up Redskins, escorting a wrecker truck. Halfway there, the first vehicle, with Jesse in the back, rolled over a bomb. From the second vehicle, Tom watched the truck lift several feet off the ground and slam down. He ran up the road, popped his head in a blown-open door, and found Jesse and the others rattled but uninjured.

The wrecker continued to the first blast site, which left Tom with nine guys and one working truck. Sit tight, his bosses told him. They sent another wrecker the next morning, and a bomb destroyed it. Sit tight, they told him again, we'll get you tomorrow. By day three, he and his men had drank most of their water and eaten all the rations stored in the truck, single-serving MREs. They ate watermelon from a farmer's field and drank water from an irrigation ditch. Every day the Marines sent more patrols to get them, and the patrols hit more bombs. At night Tom listened to the Taliban attack other stranded patrols. On day five, a bridge collapsed, stalling another rescue. On day six, a wrecker finally reached them, but they found another IED on the drive home. Staff Sergeant David Spicer, a bomb disposal tech, crept up the road to rig it with explosives. Sergeant Michael Heede, a combat engineer who had been stranded with Tom, was walking up the road to help Spicer when the bomb detonated. Tom watched both men disappear. He and his men spent the seventh day picking up the pieces.

A month later, two men from Tom's platoon, Lance Corporals Bruce Ferrell and Patrick Schimmell, died in a bomb blast while on a foot patrol. Again, Tom and his men searched for what remained.

Yet his squad was lucky, these thirteen men who had survived so many firefights and explosions without a single wound. Like the afternoon walking home along a field's edge, in the quiet moments after another gunfight. A Talib had triggered a bomb under one of Tom's light machine gunners, and an enormous concussion punched through the patrol. The bomb, big enough to kill but buried too deep for maximum effect, tossed the Marine into the air. He tumbled to the dirt, popped onto his feet, and fired into the tree line, where the triggerman likely hid. "You missed, motherfuckers!" he screamed. "You can't kill me!"

When Tom came home, Nina greeted him with an eight-foot banner, using the nickname his company commander had given the squad: WELCOME HOME SGT. WHORL AND HIS IMMORTALS!

During the second deployment, she often thought about that nickname.

"He thought he was bulletproof," she says.

.   .   .

Tom, Jesse, and Ryan stood over Ian's cot and stared at everything that represented his life over the past two months. Cans of tuna and sardines his mother had sent. Headphones. A pair of flip-flops. The sleeping bag he had woken up in that morning.

"Start packing his gear," Tom said.

He hadn't yet read Nina's e-mail, and hadn't received official word about Ian. Maybe there was a chance. But even if Ian somehow lived, Tom knew he wouldn't be coming back to Dakota, and the longer the Marines saw their friend's gear and an empty cot, the more distracted they'd be on patrol.

This was quiet work that needed few words. They separated his Marine-issue equipment—night-vision goggles, hand grenades, GPS—which needed to be accounted for on property books. Tom had Ian's bent rifle, shattered radios, shredded gear, and bloodied clothes in a pile next to his cot in the COC, which left the most personal possessions: his journal and his cell phone, letters from his family, his uniforms, and a crocheted cross from a family friend.

While Ian's friends finished separating and packing his belongings, the Fox Company first sergeant, James Breland, sent Tom a message over the secure instant-messaging system. Tom read it and pounded his fist on the plywood desk, then called together the rest of the squad.

"Corporal Muller is dead," he told them.

Some of the men cried.

"Tomorrow we're going out," Tom said. "The next day we're going out. And we're going to keep going out until our relief is here and we go home."

Late that night, Tom walked into the darkness just outside Dakota, where no one could see or hear him, and he wept. He had trained Ian to replace him as squad leader, so sure was he that he'd be the one to die, that his time had come. He did not expect to return from the deployment, and he could accept that. But losing Ian broke his heart.

.   .   .

As Tom stood alone in the blackness of southern Afghanistan, a late-afternoon sun pushed long shadows across the streets of North Danville, Vermont, where Susanne Muller had been running errands. Groceries. Auto parts store. Library. The last stop was the post office, to mail a package to Ian. She'd sent more than a dozen already in the short time he'd been in Afghanistan, along with thirty pounds of cheddar cheese donated by Cabot and several boxes of jerky and smoked meat from Vermont Smoke and Cure. But this package could wait. Her phone battery had just died, and she couldn't bear being out of contact, should her husband, Clif, or any of her other six kids need to reach her, but mostly if Ian called.

She'd last spoken to him on Sunday, five days earlier. "It's so good to hear your voice," she had said. "I was worried about you." She'd never told him that before. Of course she felt it; worry consumed her, and she barely slept. But she didn't want to add to his stress, and she wanted him to feel he could share anything with her. Two days earlier, when Ian told them he'd gotten his first kill, during the March 3 firefight, she had tried to sound supportive, even let out a little cheer.

"They take our sweet boys from our arms and they train them to kill," she says, not meant as a criticism of the Marine Corps but as a pragmatic assessment. She wanted to prepare for what war would do to him. She read about the fight in Afghanistan, learned the Marines' lingo, and watched YouTube videos of firefights to better understand what he was experiencing. She even got her passport before Ian deployed. If he was grievously injured, he would be evacuated first to Landstuhl Regional Medical Center at Ramstein Air Base, in Germany, where he might stay for several days if his condition was unstable. The Pentagon arranges travel to Germany for the families of service members injured so badly they may not make it home, but Susanne didn't want to waste time.

Ian figured that time could be fast approaching. Talking to his dad after the March 3 firefight, he said the platoon had a big mission coming up, and that he was uneasy. In the past he'd felt he had a shield wrapped around him in battle. Now that confidence had faded. "My luck is running out," he said.

By late afternoon on March 11, Susanne was home, sitting on the living room couch reading a biography of Osama bin Laden. The Mullers were a Christian family, and around Vermont, more people opposed armed conflict than supported it. "I wanted to be able to intelligently support my son at war," she says.

"Mom, there's a cop car outside," said her youngest son, Reuben, walking down the stairs. "And there's a gray car out there, too."

That set her heart to racing. She rose and walked to the door and saw four men step from the car, all in uniform: a Navy chaplain and three Marines. For months to come, that scene would replay in slow motion, often as she cried herself to sleep.

Clif was beside her now as they stepped onto the front deck. She fell to her knees. "No. No. No," she wailed. "My sweet Ian. My sweet Ian."

"Come up and tell us what you have to tell us," Clif told the men, trying to be strong enough for both of them. But it was more than an hour before Susanne's hysteria had faded and she had stopped crying long enough for the Marines to deliver their official message: that Corporal Ian Muller had been killed by an improvised explosive device while on a foot patrol in Afghanistan.

"Did anyone else die?" Susanne asked. "Did anyone else get hurt?"

The Marines told her they weren't authorized to release that information.

When the men left that night, Clif kicked the coffee table so hard a leg snapped, and then they cried together for hours, until every muscle in Susanne's face ached.

At four a.m., Susanne looked at the casualty report the Marines had brought, which Clif had folded up and shoved in a pocket. Along with detailing Ian's injuries—massive head wound, fractured left leg and right arm—it said he'd been identified by Staff Sergeant James Malachowski and the corpsman, Jesse Deller, so Susanne knew they hadn't been killed. Through an online parents' support forum, she'd become friends with Alison Malachowski and Wendy Deller, and only learned later that they were the mothers of the platoon sergeant and medic at Patrol Base Dakota. Alison and Wendy wouldn't have heard about Ian yet, because of the communications blackouts initiated after any casualty to ensure that next of kin hear through the official notification process and not from another Marine e-mailing or calling home. So Susanne made two calls, long before dawn, when a ringing phone is often the harbinger of terrible news. She could say just a few words before she started sobbing: "Ian stepped on an IED, and he's dead."

·   ·   ·

The next morning at Dakota, the Marines made a battle cross memorial in the courtyard, the traditional farewell to a fallen comrade: a rifle stuck in the ground, bayonet first, between a pair of boots, with a helmet on the rifle buttstock. Ryan hung a pair of his own dog tags from the handgrip, because they didn't have Ian's. The men approached on their own, knelt by the display, shared a few words with their friend, then gathered for a group picture. Tom wore the same pants from the day before, smeared with Ian's blood.

A convoy of armored vehicles rolled up to Dakota and delivered Lieutenant Colonel John Harrill, the battalion commander; Sergeant Major Richard Mathern, the battalion's highest-ranking noncommissioned officer; and Captain Adam Sacchetti, Fox Company's commander. They wanted to see the blast site, so Tom and his men would take them. And because Ian was dead and Matt was still rattled and puking from the explosion, Tom needed someone to lead the patrol.

"Fazenbaker," he said, "you're on point."

Corporal Craig Fazenbaker nodded.

Tom could see the distress on his men's faces. He felt it himself. They were shaken and scared, and rage knotted their guts. "You have to keep pushing," he had told them. "You have to. There's no option. Because if you don't, then we've done nothing, we've accomplished nothing."

So they left Dakota and walked north up through the fields and onto the road where Ian had been blown up. Not far from the first blast site they found a second IED along the road, and as they waited for the bomb techs from Explosive Ordnance Disposal to come blow it up, the Taliban opened fire from a cluster of buildings to the west. The higher-ups and most of the Marines with them jumped into a canal for cover. Maybe Tom was numbed by Ian's death or had just become accustomed to being shot at, but he stood in the road, then walked into the field, rifle held casually at his side, to where Lance Corporal William Saunders and Moore lay on their bellies. Bullets kicked up bursts of dirt as the gunmen walked the rounds closer to the Marines. Saunders fired in the general direction of the incoming fire. Tom poked him with the toe of his boot. "Hey, you're wasting ammunition," he said. "You need to aim when you're shooting."

After the patrol, Tom took the satellite phone outside, sat on an ammunition can, and flipped through the notebook in which he'd written his men's next-of-kin details. He tried to prepare himself for the conversation, but he didn't know how. As he'd told Ian and his other men as they trained up for Afghanistan at Camp Lejeune, he could only give the broad strokes of what to expect and how to respond. "War is something I can't teach you or explain to you," he told them. "You can't really fathom it until you go through it." Facedown in a ditch as bullets skip off the ground around you. Or the sledgehammer force of a bomb blast. Or picking up pieces of a friend. Or calling his parents.

"Mr. Muller," he said, "this is Tom Whorl, Ian's squad leader."

Susanne ran downstairs and picked up the other phone, and Tom told them what a strong leader Ian was, that he was Tom's right-hand man. He did not tell them he'd been grooming Ian to assume his job, convinced that he'd die during this deployment. But he did tell them that their son had been unconscious the whole time and felt no pain.

Tom passed the phone to the others—Ryan, Matt, Jesse—who told her that her son was loud and funny and selfless, that he encouraged other Marines to work out at Dakota's gym by poking fun of them, and that he carried so much gear and walked point so that others wouldn't have to.

In Dakota's Combat Operations Center, Jimmy sat on his cot with a notebook propped on his leg.

Mr. and Mrs. Muller,

I know how little my words mean when it comes to losing a son such as Ian. He is one of the finest Marines I have served beside, but more than that he was my friend. Ian was the type of guy that everyone could not help but like. He could lift everyone's spirits just by coming into a room. Ian and I shared a lot of things in common. We would talk about dirt bikes and tubing down the Potomac river. Then one day I found out he had been to Westminster, MD, to visit his brother, with all of the same interests we share I was surprised we had never met before. Ian would hit the gym every day out here, and all the Marines would also do so hoping they could be in the same shape as him. He could not wait to go to the beach when he got back.

Ian would talk about his family all the time, he was very proud of his brothers, and would joke how they got all of the height in the family. One day I was listening to classical music when Ian told me all about how he played the viola his entire life, and how all of his brothers played classical instruments. He went on for a long time about how one of his brothers made second chair in the Vermont symphony orchestra. He was very proud of that.

Ian was the leader all Marines want to become and the friend everyone wants to have. Of the Marines I have fought beside, Ian is one I would choose to do so with again and again. I can remember one instance where the two of us were pinned down in a canal, with rounds impacting around him he was still directing his Marines to cover while he engaged the enemy.

On March 11th, Ian, Sgt. Tom Whorl and I were on a roof overlooking a small village. The three of us sat up there for three hours and joked and laughed about everything while we watched the village. Two pictures are enclosed of us on that roof top, taken by his friend, Doc Deller.

Your family is in the prayers of everyone at PB Dakota and we thank you for Ian. He is truly the type of man who will remain in our thoughts forever.

Staff Sergeant James Malachowski
3rd Plt., Plt. Sgt.

The letter wouldn't reach the Mullers for two weeks, until the morning after they had returned from another funeral for a Dakota Marine.

3. "Building Clear"

A week after Ian died, the Marines pushed northwest again, back toward the villages of Five Points and Cocheran. But this time they took a dozen local militiamen, known as ISCI—Interim Security for Critical Infrastructure. They were mostly untrained in military tactics, wore civilian clothes, and looked more like Taliban fighters than soldiers, but they were reshaping the battlefield in ways the Marines couldn't. The few Afghan National Army soldiers stationed at Dakota were from northern Afghanistan and could barely communicate with locals, since most of them spoke Dari rather than Pashto, the language of the south. They could sometimes read a situation better than the Marines, but they were still outsiders. The ISCI were locals. Most had lived in the area since birth and could pick up on everything the

Marines couldn't: out-of-town fighters, strange accents, and locals who were helping the Taliban.

A local elder had to vouch for them, to help ensure the Taliban didn't infiltrate the force, and they were paid $150 a month. But they were motivated by more than salary. The Afghan army was plagued with apathy and poor discipline. Dakota had one excellent Afghan soldier, a few mediocre soldiers, and another who smoked marijuana all day and was too out of shape to move quickly under fire—a decent representation of the wider Afghan army. For the ISCI, though, the fight was personal. They and their families had suffered under or been hassled by the Taliban, and with the Taliban gone, they might get a sliver when the power was redistributed.

The Marines, Afghan soldiers, a few Afghan National Police, and ten ISCI left Dakota, with the militiamen in the lead. The patrol, three dozen people altogether, stretched out in a 150-meter column and pushed through the fields toward Five Points, where the sweep would start, then up Route Animal and into Cocheran Village, with the militiamen pointing out Taliban hideouts and questioning locals. Jimmy walked in the middle of the patrol, the best position from which to direct a fight. For a young Marine leader like him, this was a heady moment, moving into contested territory with a long column of heavily armed men. Counterinsurgency could often be frustrating, full of handshakes, meetings, and mild cajoling. But sometimes counterinsurgency also meant doing the traditional and straightforward work of a Marine infantryman: closing with and destroying the enemy.

As the patrol neared Five Points, a half-dozen Taliban fighters opened fire on them from Cocheran Village. Bullets threw up splashes of dirt in the fields like fat raindrops falling in puddles.

Before Jimmy could shout an order, the ISCI ran into the gunfire, up Route Animal toward Cocheran, where Tom saw a half-dozen muzzle flashes twinkling on rooftops and in tree lines. The Taliban fired shoulder-launched rocket-propelled grenades at them, and the militiamen returned fire with their own RPGs.

More gunmen fired at the patrol from the mosque and a house directly to the west. Tom and his Marines started an assault on Five Points, and Jimmy radioed up to Battalion, reporting the patrol in heavy contact from two directions and maneuvering on the enemy.

A Marine patrol under fire in Afghanistan may feel isolated, faces buried in the dirt as rounds snap inches overhead. But they're far from alone. A radio call can bring helicopter gunships, fighter jets, and even bombers, cruising at twenty thousand feet.

As the firefight unfolded below, an unmanned aerial vehicle, a drone, slid into the airspace several miles above and peered down with its powerful cameras. In a darkened room more than 8,000 miles away, behind a doorway marked SECRET, at an Air Force base somewhere in America, a pilot and a sensor operator sat in tan leather chairs with hands on joysticks and watched the battle move across a chessboard of poppy fields and farmhouses, crisscrossed by dirt roads and canals. They saw muzzle flashes everywhere, from figures lying in the middle of fields, running down roads, crouched behind mud walls, and sprawled on rooftops, and the telltale gray puffs and smoke trails of RPGs.

The ISCI pushed into Cocheran and the drone crew watched the Taliban withdraw, into fields to the north and east. The enemy fighters moved like Marines. One group bounded back to the protection of a canal or a wall and provided cover fire for the second group. The drone's pilot and sensor operator could kill them with a Hellfire missile, but discerning friend from foe was tricky at that altitude. They knew the basic layout of the battlefield but needed to confirm the location of all the friendlies, and the ISCI didn't have radios. They'd moved up so far and so fast that the Marines didn't know their exact locations relative to the

Taliban, and they couldn't risk a missile strike killing their most effective allies.

With Corporal Justin Ramos on his heels, Jimmy ran up Route Animal, dipping behind buildings to dodge gunfire. This was elemental infantry movement. Find cover. Return fire. Sprint to the next covered position. Over and over. Faces flushed, thighs burning, and breath ragged, they reached the ISCI at the southern edge of Cocheran Village and called up the coordinates. At the drone's control station in America, the sensor operator shined an infrared laser on a group of gunmen firing at Jimmy, Ramos, and the ISCI. The pilot squeezed a trigger, and a Hellfire was released from the drone's wing and streaked toward earth at nearly a thousand miles per hour, following the laser beacon.

The drone captured the aftermath with its thermal camera, which shows warmer objects in black and cooler in white. The boiling cloud of flame and smoke cleared to reveal a man lying crumpled in the field. Two men ran toward him, and each grabbed him by a wrist. They dragged him toward a tree line, and he trailed a foot-wide ribbon of black. He had been cut in half at the waist, the rest of him scattered across the field.

Shortly after the Marines returned from the patrol, a water bottle was thrown over the concertina wire along the road outside the patrol base, a predetermined signal that their neighbor, Dr. Bahki, wanted to speak with them. He made house calls throughout the area—to militants and civilians alike, the Marines surmised—and was well respected. They didn't know why he gave them tips, but the tips were always accurate. "They tried to kill you two times last night," he had told them a few days earlier, after they'd walked to and returned from Beatley. "They kept pressing the button, but the bomb wouldn't explode." They didn't tell him it was the electronic jammer; no need for his Taliban friends to know that. But the next day they found a battery near the road, and a fresh hole where the bomb had been removed.

If Bahki wanted to talk, it was probably important. Tom and Jimmy grabbed their rifles and walked over to his house.

"You killed Makeem today," he told them.

This cheered them. They already knew the name, from other informants: Makeem had built the bomb that killed Ian, and paid the triggerman who detonated it under him.

But Makeem hadn't made just the bomb in the culvert.

•　　•　　•

Tom had hit a wall with his workouts. Even though Dakota's outdoor gym had just two proper weights—a pair of thirty-five-pound dumbbells—it had everything else in improvised form: dip bars, bench press, squat rack, even a pulley system rigged from sandbags and parachute cord for working triceps and lats. But Tom wasn't getting any stronger or bigger from the daily workouts.

Jimmy could help with this. By far the strongest, fittest Marine at Dakota, if not all of Fox Company, he'd thrown the platoon into stunned silence the first time he took off his uniform blouse and they saw his biceps, which measured seventeen inches around in high school and had only grown bigger. As they stood under a noon sun outside the mosque at Five Points, he told Tom about a weightlifting program he'd read about the night before, in a fitness magazine his mom had sent. When they returned to Dakota later that afternoon, they'd start the new workout together.

But first, just a few feet from them, perhaps the most important moment in northern Marjah's recent history was under way.

Every time the Marines neared this area, they were attacked by Taliban, who held sway over local residents less through allegiance than fear of reprisal. This was about to change. Hajji Gul Mala, a local power broker, had committed to keeping a permanent presence of his militiamen in Five Points.

Jimmy and Tom had nurtured this relationship with Gul Mala through many meetings, and they understood one another to be trustworthy. Now Lieutenant Colonel Harrill, several Marines from the battalion staff, and Gul Mala gathered with about twenty local elders and villagers near the mosque and told them over chai and a spread of food that the new security force would make the area safe and allow the villagers to stand up to the Taliban.

Gul Mala, now in his fifties, had fought the Russians with the mujahideen as a young man. But as he gained power in northern Marjah in the years afterwards, he turned against some of his former comrades, a philosophical and pragmatic shift. He owned many of the market stalls at a bazaar in northern Marjah, and as the Taliban tightened their hold on the area, they demanded taxes from Gul Mala and the shop owners, enforced with beatings. But while Gul Mala had both business and political interests to protect, he also wanted more personal and religious freedom than the Taliban espoused. One of his mentors was a Sufi mystic who had traveled extensively through India and offered Gul Mala—the name means "beautiful flower"—a broader perspective than the extreme interpretation of Sunni Islam the Taliban embraced.

Gul Mala wanted both boys and girls to be educated, and he helped build the first school in northern Marjah after the Taliban destroyed the others. When the Marines asked for his help with security, Gul Mala's six bodyguards became northern Marjah's first ISCI, and he recruited more young men from the area. He would soon have seventy ISCI under him, his own private army.

"What compound do you want to occupy?" Harrill asked Gul Mala.

They had enough to choose from. Much of the area had been abandoned because of the fighting and Taliban threats.

"Right here," Gul Mala said, and pointed toward the building next door, just south of the mosque, empty since before

Tom's unit arrived in January. The Taliban used it as a firing point, which meant it possibly had buried bombs or booby traps, a deterrent should the Marines ever try to storm it during a firefight.

Tom took Fazenbaker and Matt Westbrook to sweep the compound, half as long as Dakota and half as wide, surrounded by mud walls eight feet high and eighteen inches thick, with several small, simple rooms along the back, western wall. Holly led them through the doorway at the northeast corner. Tom and Fazenbaker worked across the weed-covered courtyard with mine detectors, the same type Ian had been using when he died. *Tick tock.* They swept in rows, back and forth, until they covered all the ground. They checked out the empty rooms in back, then swept everything again. Matt worked Holly through the rooms and around the courtyard. Nothing in her behavior betrayed danger.

"Building clear, building clear," Tom called to Jimmy over the radio.

Jimmy passed word to Lieutenant Colonel Harrill, who filed into the compound with Gul Mala, Sergeant Major Mathern, and Captain Sacchetti. Together these men represented perhaps the best chance for calm in northern Marjah. Jimmy and a couple of Marines from the colonel's security detail stepped in behind them.

Outside, Ryan Moore called Tom to the northwest corner of the building, where William Saunders had spotted a man a couple hundred yards away who seemed to be watching them. Probably just a curious farmer, Tom told him. Saunders kept watch over him and the distant tree lines through his rifle scope, and Tom and Ryan stepped back into the shade, next to Matt, just on the other side of the wall from where Jimmy stood. Tom leaned against the wall. The flag raising and meeting with Gul Mala might take another five minutes or an hour, and military service had honed their ability to wait. Smoke a cigarette, bitch about the heat, kick a toe in the dust. When it was time to move, they'd be told.

Harrill, Sacchetti, and Gul Mala stood in a cluster in the courtyard and watched Gul Mala's men scramble onto the rooftop and raise a small Afghan flag on a makeshift flagpole made from a skinny tree stripped of branches. Mathern stood five feet away, closer to the flag. Jimmy stood five feet from them on the other side, near the northern wall.

Surely they shifted their weight as they stood there, maybe took a few absentminded steps. And then, a last step. A boot pressed down with just enough pressure, in just the wrong spot, on two strips of balsa wood buried just under the surface, separated by two slender carbon rods, taken from D-cell batteries, that were invisible to metal detectors. That pressure squeezed together two thin metal contacts and made the circuit whole. Electricity raced from the battery pack, buried maybe two feet deep—beyond notice of the metal detectors—up a wispy wire, through the pressure plate, and down to a blasting cap in a plastic jug packed with ammonium nitrate and aluminum powder.

The cap exploded, just a little pop, but enough to produce a detonation wave that collided with the ammonium nitrate and put the already unstable chemical under extreme pressure. Once the explosives reached a critical density, the molecules broke apart, starting a chain reaction that transformed the ten pounds of ammonium nitrate and aluminum powder into sixteen hundred liters of gas in a sliver of a second. All that gas needed somewhere to go. The explosion pushed a supersonic shock wave through the dirt and rock and into the compound.

·　　·　　·

Of the three blasts Matt had been next to, this one hurt the most, even with the thick mud wall separating him from the bomb.

"Like you're walking across the street and a fucking truck hits you," he says.

Tom stumbled a few feet, his mind already grasping. Maybe someone had accidentally dropped a grenade, or the rocket launcher Jimmy had slung across his back had somehow detonated. No. Even in those first fragments of seconds, his rattled brain knew that couldn't be. This was a bomb, the same sickening sound as the blast that killed Ian, and every other bomb he'd heard. But how? They hadn't received a single hit from the two detectors or the bomb-sniffing dog.

As he ran back to the entryway on the northeast corner, he called up a medevac request. With an explosion that big and so many people nearby, someone would be hit. The local power broker and every important Marine in the area were inside that compound. Tom worked over the possibilities. Just about his whole chain of command could be dead.

He rounded the corner as Mathern led Harrill, Gul Mala, and Sacchetti through the doorway. Harrill and Gul Mala staggered, dazed and bleeding from their faces, necks, and backs. Sacchetti clutched his left arm, where shrapnel had ripped through his triceps.

From farther in the compound, he heard Jimmy calling for him.

"Whorl!" His voice sounded hoarse and strained.

"Whorl . . . Whorl!"

Smoke and dirt hung in the air, and Tom sucked in the pungent scent of detonated ammonium nitrate. Marines shouted—maybe inside the compound, maybe outside, but forever away. Tom heard nothing, saw nothing but Jimmy.

He lay on his back, a few feet from the wall, and writhed in the sunbaked dirt near a shallow crater, his left arm extended, hand grasping at the air. Red blooms spread across his pants. The blast had torn him nearly in half at the waist.

Tom knelt beside him and grabbed Jimmy's left hand with his hands. The grip was still strong.

"It's going to be okay," Tom said. "We already have the birds spun up."

Jesse and the Navy corpsman from the colonel's security detail dropped to their knees beside Tom and Jimmy, pulled thick bandages from their aid bag, and packed them against Jimmy's thighs and pelvis to stanch the bleeding. Tourniquets, the usual lifesaver after a Marine steps on a buried bomb, were useless. Jimmy's wounds were so high on his legs, they couldn't use the nylon straps to cinch off the femoral arteries near the crotch.

"I'll be right back," Tom said. Jimmy stared at him and nodded.

Be calm, Tom told himself. *Be calm. Be calm. Be calm.* This could get so much worse if he lost his shit, and he knew everyone was looking to him to make fast, sound decisions. He left the compound to check on the other casualties and establish a landing zone for the medevac in an empty field just across the street. Ryan and Ramos swept the field for explosives, and Tom pushed more Marines to the far perimeter for security.

He returned to Jimmy, knelt, and took his hand again. "I've already taken care of everything, everything's going to be okay," he said, and he knew it wouldn't. He unsnapped Jimmy's chinstrap and eased the helmet from his head. The color had leached from his face as his blood drained into the dirt and his body redirected the remaining blood to his main organs, a last attempt to keep the whole system from failing. He spit up bile. His eyes, alert and searching for the first few minutes, lost focus. "I'll be right back," Tom said again. "I have to go see where your helicopter is."

Standing outside, he heard Jesse call out: "Starting CPR."

The Marines lifted Jimmy onto a portable stretcher and carried him to the field's edge, where they listened for a drumming on the horizon, the first sounds of the medevac helicopter. Sergeant Major Mathern crouched over him, one hand stacked atop the other, and pumped his palm against Jimmy's chest, doing for him what his heart could not.

The helicopter landed in a swirl of dust, and left with Jimmy, Sacchetti, and a wounded Marine from Harrill's security detail. Harrill and Gul Mala, though wounded, would walk with the patrol back to Dakota. They didn't want the Taliban to know they'd nearly killed the two most important men in the area.

As the sound of the helicopter faded, Jesse wandered over to the mosque and sat down.

"Doc Deller, are you okay?" Mathern asked him.

Jesse stared at him, as though he couldn't understand the question, then he wandered off, down Five Points Road, toward Dakota.

"Doc is done," Mathern told Tom, and on Jesse's face Tom saw what he himself felt: horror and heartbreak, guilt and anguish.

The Marines walked home and were greeted with the sight of Ian's memorial in Dakota's courtyard. Within minutes they had erected another beside it. Boots. Rifle. Helmet. Dog tags.

Nina once again heard the radio transmission that a medevac helicopter was bringing in an angel from Tom's unit. She called a friend, heard the name, then sent Tom another e-mail, telling him she already knew and asking if he was okay. But he wouldn't see it yet, because there was still work to be done. Nine days after they had sorted Ian's gear, Tom and his men did it again for Jimmy.

That night, Tom lay down and stared at the empty cot across the dirt-floored room, where his friend had slept that morning. With Jimmy gone but his presence still there, the room felt haunted. A boyish fear crept through Tom, and he was afraid to sleep.

4. Maximum Fun

The next day, a convoy rolled into Dakota and delivered Navy Lieutenant Commander Nathan Solomon, the battalion's chaplain, a forty-two-year-old Southern Baptist with red hair, a warm Tennessee accent, and an earnestness that could put a man at ease.

Solomon shuttled constantly between the battalion's three main outposts and eleven small patrol bases and had already been to Dakota a few times, to give services and hang out with the Marines. He liked to stay for a day or two and tag along on a foot patrol, so they'd know he didn't think his life more valuable than theirs. He could step on a bomb just as easily as them.

He would lounge on a cot in the shade of a camo net reading on his Kindle: *Treasure Island*, or Plato's *Republic*, maybe Dostoyevsky's *Crime and Punishment*. At night he'd climb into the guard towers, smoke his pipe, and chat with Marines as they scanned the fields and tree lines. He'd talk about religion if they asked, but usually they didn't, so he'd just bullshit with them, or ask about their families. Often he just sat in silence, but that still had purpose. A ministry of presence, he called it.

Tom liked Solomon. He'd been around chaplains who didn't seem to truly care about Marines. They just wanted to talk about Jesus, or thought their job was giving sermons from the safety of well-protected bases. But Solomon tried to understand the Marines, and what the killing and death and fear could do to them.

On his first visit to Dakota, while talking to Tom in his room, Solomon had noticed a few words written in black marker over the doorway, lyrics from a favorite song by Rise Against, just below Tom's rifle, which rested on two nails: WE DON'T LIVE. WE JUST SURVIVE.

What's that all about? Solomon asked.

"Well, we're alive, but we're not really living here," Tom had said. "We just survive to go home and tell people how it was."

Solomon considered that, offered a thoughtful sigh, and nodded.

Now, with the Marines still in a fog from Jimmy's death, Solomon stayed in the background and waited for them to come to him. He didn't sweep in to ask them how they were feeling, to offer prayers for their dead friend and tell them to trust in God. That wasn't his style.

"The last thing a Marine needs to hear is this is all part of God's plan," he says. "I don't think God wanted Jimmy Malachowski to die. I don't think he wanted Ian Muller to die. I just reject that out of hand. I don't want any part of a God that's like that."

But the Marines didn't ask much about God anyway. "Most of the conversations center around the randomness of why one person dies and another doesn't," Solomon says. "Why one person becomes a double amputee and another doesn't. 'Normally I'm the third person in line on patrol; I wasn't today, and the third person got blown up; I didn't. I'm a bad person.' Or 'I walked over that spot three times. Why didn't it happen to me?' There's no answer. I can't make sense of that."

Some told him they couldn't sleep, or that they had nightmares. Others said they had bursts of rage they didn't understand. "Good," Solomon told them. "You're normal. If you were totally cool with everything you saw and did, if it didn't bother you at all, then you'd be messed up."

"War is chaos and pain and destruction at its best," he said. "We're not supposed to see people with their legs blown off, or thrown fifty meters into the air by an IED. We're not supposed to see that, and it leaves a mark."

All of the Marines at Dakota bore those scars. But Solomon reserved a special worry for the leaders, like Tom, who had succeeded in the Marine Corps because they had taken very good care of their men, which often meant they hadn't taken care of themselves.

·　　·　　·

Tom and the Dakota Marines saw Solomon again on March 27, a week after Jimmy died. They geared up that morning and walked the thousand yards to Patrol Base Beatley, a routine but dangerous movement. Imagine that, they told one another, we die walking to a memorial service. They were told to wear clean uniforms, though none of them had seen a washing machine in weeks. But this service wasn't just for them. A convoy of armored trucks would deliver the Fox Company chain of command, several higher-ups from Battalion, Solomon, and even a general.

The Marines crisscrossed the patrol base, picking up scraps of litter, then rehearsed the movements and the order of speakers, culminating with a full practice run. They couldn't quite believe it, practicing how to mourn their friends, but they knew the Corps left little to chance. "You do the whole thing once," First Sergeant Breland told them, "so you won't get choked up when you do the real thing."

Wind tore through the base and brought a sandstorm that blotted the sun behind a brown veil and grounded helicopter flights, which meant the Marines would have no air support if they made contact on the way home from Beatley.

The men formed up in neat rows, and Solomon nearly had to shout to be heard above the wind. "It is difficult to see meaning and purpose in the events of the last two weeks," he said. "Indeed to ascribe too much meaning would be to dishonor the dead and their memory. To make sense out of chaos is not our task."

Remember your friends, he said, and live your lives to honor them.

The Marines chose Ryan to speak about Ian, and Tom about Jimmy. They told of how dutiful the two men were, how selfless, how funny, and of all they had learned from them about being good Marines, and good men.

"Amazing Grace" and taps played over a loudspeaker, a squad from First Platoon fired three rifle volleys, and then the Marines from Dakota geared up and walked home, down the same road, past the very spot where the Taliban had tried to blow them up earlier that month.

They returned to the war, but Tom took a breather. His commanders ordered it, and while Tom would never have admitted that he felt nearer the edge, with the ground crumbling beneath him, he welcomed the respite.

The past decade of war had retaught the Marines a lesson learned in every bloody conflict: a person can experience only so much horror before the mind's ability to cope and carry on wavers, and a moment of distraction or hesitation on the battlefield can be disastrous. A short break from combat can have powerful restorative effects, so after the memorial, Tom's commanders sent him to Camp Leatherneck, the Marines' main camp in Helmand Province, where he could enjoy a few days without gunfire or explosions, the nauseating gamble of walking down bomb-sown roads, or the helplessness of watching another friend die. Captain Sacchetti also contacted Nina's commanders, who gave her several days off to spend with her husband. Tom hadn't seen her since his first few days in Afghanistan, before he'd been dispatched to Dakota.

They stayed in a giant air-conditioned and mostly empty tent filled with bunk beds, used as temporary housing for Marines passing through Leatherneck. They hung sheets in a back corner for a little privacy, once again able to take refuge in the other's physical presence, and for several hours Tom told her about what had happened to Ian and Jimmy. But mostly they lay on the bed and spoke sweetly to each other and remembered the world beyond Afghanistan, and Tom felt some of the tension slip free.

Leatherneck was safe. Marines walked around free of helmets and body armor. They could watch movies at the morale building, exercise in gyms better equipped than some American fitness centers, and eat their fill in chow halls with plenty of choices and decent food. Tom stuffed himself, and after dinner every night he ate mint chocolate chip ice cream.

Walking to the chow hall one afternoon, he and Nina watched a Marine stumble and fall while trying to hop across a shallow ditch, and they both doubled over laughing. It wasn't just that Tom's men could leap across six-foot-wide canals wearing full combat gear. This was just how they were together: giggling at the inappropriate, just as they might when walking hand in hand around the mall in Jacksonville.

Nina saw something else, though, as they walked around Leatherneck. Even when they were immersed in conversation, Tom never stopped scanning the area around him, his eyes fixing on people, vehicles, bits of trash. As Nina stepped over a scrap of yellow caution tape, she didn't give it a thought. But she watched Tom take a step and stop, his foot hovering over the tape. The hypervigilance was back.

After his first deployment, Tom could name the perfume his wife wore on a given day, not by the scent but because he noticed which bottle's position had subtly changed on the bathroom vanity. He did the same with cars throughout the neighborhood. *The gray van five doors down is parked on the other side of the street, facing south, same as last Thursday.* He didn't consciously search for the differences; he just couldn't help but spot the out-of-place. After weeks of this, Nina took him into the bathroom, where she had rearranged the perfume bottles. "*Now* which one, Tom?" she said. "You have to stop noticing everything. You just have to shut your brain down and stop being aware of things you don't need to be aware of."

With the deaths of Ian and Jimmy stuck in his head, she wondered how much worse his readjustment would be this time.

They hung out for an afternoon with Jesse, who'd also been given a break from Dakota, and who was so happy to see Tom that tears slipped from his eyes. They stopped by the hospital to visit Corporal Ramos, who'd been shot in the shoulder a few days after Tom left. Out in northern Marjah, far from the insulation of Leatherneck, the war was alive, with points, edges, and texture. It was time for Tom to return and take over his dead friend's job as platoon sergeant, responsible for the welfare of nearly four dozen Marines at Patrol Bases Dakota and Beatley.

.   .   .

In early May, Tom sent a patrol over to Beatley to pick up the satellite phone, and for the next couple of days he watched his men pace the courtyard at Dakota or sit in the dark, invisible but for the glow of a cigarette cherry, and talk to parents and wives, girlfriends and kids. Some hadn't spoken to their families in several weeks. Tom could chat with Nina over the military's secret e-mail network, a luxury his guys didn't have, but he missed his boys. Once the other Marines had taken their turns, Tom called Nina's parents in Tennessee, and Andrew and Lee told him how they'd been swimming every day in the backyard pool, and played soccer and baseball.

"Dad," Andrew said, "are you done killing bad guys yet so you can come home?"

"Almost," Tom told him. "Almost."

With the western sky smeared pink behind silhouetted palm trees and stars rising in the east, Battalion called down with intel gleaned from two high-level detainees: a half-dozen Taliban commanders and scores of fighters had moved into Marjah and northern Marjah with machine guns and rocket-propelled grenades. Tom strode through Dakota in his green shorts, shirtless after a sunset workout, sucked on a Marlboro, and refined his battle plan. He ordered another machine gun to one guard post and an extra grenade launcher to another. Marines stretched more concertina wire in the street, and Tom gave his men a rundown of the destruction-on-call: 60-millimeter mortars from Patrol Base Beatley and, from the larger bases, heavy mortars, HIMARS and Excalibur rockets, Cobra helicopter gunships, and F-18 jet fighters. Tom's voice left no question: If the Taliban attacked, those who lived would retreat with their dead. The Marines trusted him; they believed him. And after so many nauseating steps, waiting to be blown in half, the notion of repelling a frontal assault on their patrol base cheered them.

"I'm getting pumped up, man, like right before a football game," a Marine said from the gathering darkness.

"Fuck it, man," another said. "Let 'em come."

But the Taliban did not come, which was common. The intel from detainees and informants was often unreliable or exaggerated. Instead, the Marines continued the slow, frustrating, dangerous grind of counterinsurgency. Tom pushed patrols into the surrounding countryside and villages twice a day, to search compounds and talk to locals. This exposed his men to bullets and bombs, but the harder he pushed, Tom reasoned, and the more aggressive an image he projected, the safer his men would be. "This is our area of operations," he told his men, "not the Taliban's."

Under a searing sun, the Marines waded through fields waist-high with poppies, and the fat bulbs atop each plant oozed tar-like goo that stained their uniforms with black streaks. Around them, workers scraped the bulbs and collected the resin, which would be refined into heroin. The Marines knew they would likely be fighting some of these men in the future. Laborers from Pakistan and elsewhere in Afghanistan brought in for the harvest might stick around to take a few shots at Marines, augmenting the ranks of hard-core Taliban, flush with fresh cash to finance their operations. But for now, Tom and his men enjoyed a bizarre truce, a welcome lull.

"We'll see you in a couple weeks," Tom told the laborers as he passed.

The patrol stopped in a village near Dakota, and, in a building empty save for a few dusty mats and cushions, Tom sat with Hajji Zaire. He controlled water in the village, a position of relative power, and had been kidnapped twice in recent weeks by the

Taliban. Out in the fields, Tom was an infantryman; at the moment he was a salesman. The village still hadn't elected an elder to serve on the local district council; no one wanted the job—they were convinced they'd be killed by the Taliban.

"We can't help you if you don't have an elder," Tom said. "I can't dig you a well, build you a school, or improve your road."

He offered Zaire a cigarette, and the two men smoked.

"Many times the government has promised to help us, but they don't," Zaire told him, dancing around Tom's request. "The people in this village are honest and hardworking. They just want peace. They're tired of war."

Tom knew Zaire's position was difficult. Like many Afghans in the area, he seemed most interested in being left alone, farming and raising a family without the daily threat of traumatic death, and avoiding the ire of either the Taliban or the Marines.

"You have to understand the people," Tom said after he and his men left the village. "You don't have to like them, but you have to understand them."

The Marines pushed north, through fields not far from where Ian had landed after the bomb blast, then cut west into Five Points, the site of so many firefights, but quiet now. After Jimmy died, the ISCI picked a different patrol base, an empty house just across the street from the mosque with more rooms and better views of the surrounding area.

Inside the compound, Tom took off his helmet and pulled a long draw of water from his CamelBak. Sweat matted his hair, and his cheeks flushed pink from the hump through the fields. He inspected the fighters' machine guns and deemed them cleaner and better maintained than some Marines' weapons. They asked Tom for sandbags to reinforce their guard posts, belts of machine gun ammunition, and bottles of water.

Working logistics for the ISCI was a hassle, but these were his proxies, and if they fought the Taliban, his Marines wouldn't have to. Indeed, the turning point for the Marines at Dakota and across northern Marjah had been the day these men raised the Afghan flag over the abandoned compound. Hajji Gul Mala had cried when he saw Jimmy torn up by the bomb, and was so angered by the attack that he resolved that his men would never leave the Five Points village or let the Taliban return. Days after the bomb attack, Gul Mala opened a school just down the road for girls and boys, and in coming weeks he would help open three more. More important, he met with other elders and power brokers in surrounding areas and convinced them to work with the Marines and to encourage young men to join the new security force. Within three months of Jimmy's death, more than two dozen local police stations like the one in Five Points would be established, pushing the Taliban into retreat. But the ISCI at Five Points had another problem, bigger than resupply: the homeowner wanted to move back in, which was actually a good sign: locals felt safe enough to return to the village. But they needed a new patrol base.

"Where do you want to go?" Tom asked.

A militiaman gestured across the street, to the building beyond the mosque.

"Where Staff Sergeant was blown up?" Disbelief and anger tinged Tom's voice, then gave way to resignation.

"We'll sweep it for you, but this is the last time," he said. "You'll have to have your guys guard it until you move in, because we're not coming back to sweep it again."

And so, for the second time, Tom took his Marines to clear the compound. They zigzagged back and forth, sweeping mine detectors before them. *Tick tock.* The courtyard had sprouted knee-high weeds in the weeks since the Marines had last been there, but the Afghan flag still flew from the skinny flagpole on the roof.

Tom kicked a piece of trash, then squatted and carefully brushed his gloved hand across a darkened swath of dirt. Nothing. He walked deeper into the courtyard, along the northern wall, then stopped, eyes fixed on the ground. He did not speak or move. He held his rifle absently at his side and stared at the shallow crater, the once loose dirt beaten flat by rain and hardened by sun. The hole seemed so small for the damage it had done. Birds flitted through the compound, a breeze swayed the little Afghan flag, and the mine detectors whined and chirped. Tom stared at the hole, and his heart drummed faster.

"We're good, Sergeant Whorl," Ryan called out.

Just like last time, the sweep had turned up nothing suspicious.

"Okay," Tom said. "Let's go."

The patrol snaked back to Dakota through the poppy fields, past the men who might soon trade their sickles for rifles, maybe the same men who would detonate an enormous bomb under the truck behind Tom's during a vehicle convoy from Dakota to Beatley, when Tom would again feel the sledgehammer blast wave as a giant fountain of dirt shot into the air. Fearing he'd just lost five men, he'd run to the truck, stuck in a deep crater, and find them bleeding, with battered brains and broken backs, but alive. He would dream about that moment often once he had returned to America—running up to the truck, smoking in the blast crater—but in the dream his men weren't just injured. They were dead, in pieces.

That was all to come. For now, he and his men walked home, sweat-soaked and tired and forever anxious. On the front of his body armor, clipped to an ammunition pouch, Tom wore a white button labeled FUN METER, with a black needle that could be moved between blue, yellow, and red: minimum fun, medium fun, maximum fun. His dad had sent it to him in a care package. If Tom was in a good mood, he'd slide the needle down into the blue; such was his sense of humor. Now the needle surged into the red: maximum fun.

．　　　．　　　．

Tom barely slept that night, like every night. He'd lie on his cot and watch movies or listen to music on Jimmy's laptop, and often he'd cry, quietly, rolling onto his right side, face tucked beside the mud wall, so the Marine on radio guard at the desk ten feet away wouldn't hear him. He'd usually fall asleep sometime before dawn and sleep into midmorning. He'd wake bathed in sweat, swing his feet over the edge of the cot, prop his elbows on his knees, and prepare himself for another day. Ryan now slept on Jimmy's cot, but that hardly made the room feel less empty. Tom only saw Jimmy, and felt his absence. On the wall above Jimmy's old cot, he'd hung Ian's and Jimmy's pictures, from the Beatley memorial service programs, and beneath them scrawled an inscription: GREATER LOVE HATH NO MAN THAN TO LAY DOWN HIS LIFE FOR HIS BROTHER.

In the heat of the day, after the morning patrol or before an afternoon patrol, when the farmers had retreated from their fields to lounge in the shade, Tom would unroll his foam sleeping pad in Dakota's courtyard and sprawl in the sun, listening to music on a set of portable speakers. For that one hour every day, he was home, lying in the sand at Myrtle Beach. He and Jimmy had planned a beach trip to celebrate their August birthdays when they'd returned. He imagined waves breaking and his kids' voices just beyond the music, a daydream occasionally interrupted by air strikes or roadside bombs in the distance, or fighter jets screaming overhead.

He wrote in his journal less and less after Jimmy died, then stopped, with a final, half-page entry: "I have been fighting a lot of demons. I feel so responsible and guilty for the deaths of Staff Sergeant and Ian. It's going to be a long fight for me. Have been emailing and calling both families as much as I can. They are all amazing people. I can't wait to meet them soon. This has been a nightmare of a deployment. I miss Jimmy and Ian so much."

5. Home

On a steamy morning in late July, as Tom and his Marines finished their last patrols at Dakota, Alison Malachowski left her house on the wooded hilltop in Westminster and drove south, toward an office building in Rockville, Maryland. She had been planning this day for weeks. Her husband and daughter knew her destination and wanted none of it. A friend had offered to drive with her, and Alison declined. This was far too personal to share with anyone else. Her stomach turned from the nerves, and she talked to him as she drove. *I don't want to do this. I don't want to do this. Jimmy, I'm not that strong.* But she felt him pushing her.

Before a service member killed in Afghanistan is prepared for burial by a mortuary team at Dover Air Force Base, a pathologist performs an autopsy, which has helped and maybe saved thousands of other service members: details about battlefield trauma gleaned in the exams have highlighted deficiencies in body armor and spurred improvements in bomb-resistant vehicles and frontline medical equipment. Family members can read the autopsy reports and talk to those who perform the exams, but few ever do. Bullets, buried bombs, exploding cars: no mysteries there.

Army Major Dori Franco, who worked as a forensic pathologist out of the Armed Forces Medical Examiner's office, in Rockville, had performed more than three hundred autopsies. But this was her first time meeting a parent to explain her work. "I've never done this before," she told Alison, and Alison hadn't imagined she'd want to know these details, until she spoke to Susanne Muller.

When Ian came home, the Mullers had met him at Dover, but he'd been hidden in a flag-draped transfer case as a Marine honor guard carried him from the plane. And though the family had an open-casket viewing before the closed-casket wake, they still didn't see Ian. He lay in a perfectly arranged uniform, every ribbon straight, every button polished, white gloves on his hands and his entire head wrapped in white gauze, like a mummy.

A Vermont woman who works as a grief counselor for sudden traumatic death—car wrecks, homicides, workplace accidents—had told Susanne that viewing the body could be cathartic, especially when a loved one had died so far away. Susanne asked Dover for the autopsy pictures and viewed them with the counselor, who first described each photo, asked if Susanne was ready to see it, and then showed her as they sat in Susanne's living room. Yes, his body was broken and torn. But the right side of his face was perfect. Were it possible, she would have been with him in that field and held his hand as he lay dying, but at least she could have stroked his cheek once he'd come home, one last time. Susanne told Alison that seeing the pictures had helped her.

Alison needed a different sort of closure. Jimmy's wake had been open-casket, and the Malachowskis could see him, touch him. But she wanted to know exactly how her son had died, and whether anything could have been different. For three hours, with reports and photos, Major Franco told Alison what had happened to her boy, how the blast had ripped through him, crushing and splintering bones, puncturing organs, severing arteries, and shredding muscle.

Her curious boy, who had learned so much about insects that he won first place in entomology at the Maryland State Fair at nine years old, with exquisite collections that still hung in glass-covered frames on the living-room walls. Butterflies and crickets, ants, dragonflies and spiders.

Her boy, who had called from Iraq during his first tour, frustrated and furious that he'd been told to go count enemy dead, of whom nothing but pieces remained, telling her this as two women walked past Alison griping about the terrible selection at Lord & Taylor.

Her boy, who cooked and gardened and built furniture, who studied martial arts, loathed personal failure, and always seemed older than his years, a father figure to his Marines. She told Jimmy that if any of his men died during the deployment, she and James would attend the funeral in his behalf. So they had driven ten hours to Vermont, mourned with the Mullers, and driven home, and the next morning, as Alison worked in her garden, prepping flowerbeds that would be in bloom for Jimmy's homecoming, a white van with government plates pulled into the driveway.

Here he was now, her only son, in two dimensions, pictures and diagrams. Alison asked questions and Franco answered. The pile of wadded-up tissues grew. They sat side by side in chairs, their knees almost touching. Close enough, Alison figured, that Franco must feel the pain and grief radiating from her body.

Franco walked her outside, and the wet heat swallowed them. "Are you going to be okay to drive home alone?" she asked. Alison nodded, but she wasn't sure. She sat for several minutes in her stifling black Volkswagen Jetta with the broken air conditioner, then rolled down the windows and left. Maybe she was in shock, after hearing so many horrible details, but she felt fine as she poked along with the building rush-hour traffic, unburdened even. *Thank you, Jimmy,* she said. *Thank you so much.*

Three weeks after Tom and his men came home from Afghanistan, the Marines of 2/8 held a memorial service for Jimmy, Ian, and the six other men they'd lost around northern Marjah, and Alison drove down the coast to Camp Lejeune to deliver Jimmy's absolution to the men of Third Platoon. Many of them gathered at Whorl's house after the memorial to toast their dead friends, take shelter among the living, and let liquor dull the constant ache. Alison pulled a few of them aside, one at a time, those who were with Jimmy that day in the compound, and told them what she'd learned: Jimmy's death wasn't their fault. "There wasn't anything anybody could have done, and he wouldn't have wanted to survive with what was left of him," she says. "I didn't want them thinking if they'd just been faster, or tried harder, or been stronger . . . all those things that would have held them back and destroyed them."

It wasn't his fault. Tom heard that a lot. He didn't kill Jimmy and couldn't have done anything to save him. The Mullers told him the same about Ian, and so did everyone else. Nina told her husband that their deaths were in God's plan. "The instant you're born, the day you're going to die is already set out for you," she says. "That's your destiny, and there's no changing it." The chaplain told him just the opposite, that God doesn't pick and choose who dies and when; the randomness of war decides. Lieutenant Colonel Harrill told him that this job is bloody and terrible and friends will die, and that nothing can change the nature of war. Tom's father told him that had he made different choices, things could have turned out far worse. Tom listened, and he tried to let their words help him. He knew his suffering tore at them, and he could see the truth in some of what they said. And he wanted to believe them—how easy that would have been, how quick the relief.

But Tom saw things differently. He had called the building clear. Just like he had sent Ian down that road. Simple as that. He made the decisions, and he failed them, and they died. If only. If only he had made different decisions. The guilt was obstinate and bullying. It rotted his thinking and wove roots into his days like weeds choking a garden, until it was everywhere, wrapping itself around him, squeezing, in quiet moments with Nina or during family dinners or driving across base, as he waited for sleep, while he slept, and when he woke.

·   ·   ·

Tom watched the videos of Jimmy's and Ian's funerals every day, maybe once, maybe a half-dozen times, to split the skin anew, to pull the wound open and expose the nerves. He figured he deserved that pain, since he had killed his friends, but he craved the pain, too. Better to feel something than nothing. "I looked at my wife and I didn't feel love," he says. "I'd think about Jimmy and Ian and I didn't feel sad. I never felt happy. I just did not feel shit."

He wasn't alone in this. All of the guys were struggling, falling apart.

Jesse, who had always been so mellow, now snapped at superiors, in bright flashes of anger.

Ryan still couldn't sleep. He'd lie in bed, not meaning to think about Ian, but sometimes unable to think about anything else, wondering how things might have turned out differently. When he did sleep, the dreams were bad. Some were of war and blown-up friends, but worse were the mundane dreams, bench-pressing at the gym with Ian, or drinking nickel Pabst Blue Ribbon with him down at Gus' on Wednesday nights. And then he'd wake, and as his mind cleared he'd remember anew that Ian was gone.

Since the day Ian died, Matt hadn't dreamed about anything else. Except Jimmy, of course, once he was dead, too. Some dreams were thorough, taking him through a whole day; others were just highlight reels, picking up right before the blasts. Three, four, five times a night. "It's pretty much just reliving those two days over, and over, and over," he says. "And no matter how many times I dream it, the outcome is going to be the same. And that's what drives mental health crazy, because most of the time your dreams will fluctuate. In some of them things will be different, like Ian would have lived. But mine are consistent. They're the same every time, just reliving the day."

The doctors gave him sleep meds, but more sleep just meant more nightmares, and the pills to stop the nightmares didn't work.

"Everyone keeps asking, 'Are you okay? Is there anything we can do?'" Matt says. "And you know they mean well, but it gets so irritating and so taxing because you don't want to involve them, because no matter how you explain it, they'll never understand. When you sit up for three or four months watching movies with a guy every night, you consider him your best friend, and he dies ten feet in front of you, it's going to fuck you up. When you search a building and call it clear, and then somebody who you looked to like a father figure dies, it's going to fuck you up."

The Marines sent Matt home from Afghanistan after Jimmy's bomb—his third major blast—and now he was being medically retired, because of the nightmares and headaches and memory loss, symptoms of post-traumatic stress and traumatic brain injury. Even if he could stay in, he'd never deploy again, and he couldn't imagine not being allowed to do his job. The Marines were all he'd known since he left Pike County, Georgia, after high school.

He still wasn't old enough to drink a beer legally, but he'd aged terribly, and he knew he couldn't handle seeing another friend die. "Transitioning back to civilian life scares the hell out of me," he says. "You only have this handful of people you can turn to and talk to, who you know will be there for you no matter what, and will understand if you call them at three in the morning crying because you just had the worst nightmare yet. I'm scared to death to be away from them. They keep me sane."

He told his wife about the three bomb blasts, and how his platoon had lost two men, but none of the details. He didn't want to lay on her any of the weight that was crushing him. Ryan and Jesse and Craig Fazenbaker knew. They'd been right there. They could be wounded and broken around each other. They could tell each other about their terrible dreams, or say nothing at all and know that the others understood their withdrawal, anger, and frustration.

Except for Tom. He wouldn't allow himself the vulnerability. As the pressure built, he didn't tell his guys that he had the very same thoughts and struggles. He was their leader. They looked to him for support and answers. How could they trust him if they knew he was just as fucked in the head as them? He would have failed them. He didn't tell anyone that he needed help, that he couldn't navigate the emotional wreckage by himself.

While at Dakota and when he came home, Tom spoke to or e-mailed the Mullers and Malachowskis several times a week. Initially he did this as a duty to Ian and Jimmy, looking after their families the same as he would his Marines. The families wanted to know about their sons' last weeks, hours, minutes. Their lives at Dakota. Their friendships. Their last words. Tom felt he had no right to deny them that. But he soon came to rely on the phone calls and texts, a friendly voice and shared history when few others could understand. "I had an escape," he says. "When I talked to them, even though it brought back memories, that boulder was off my chest. That's why it became so addictive—because of the feeling I had after talking to them. They were my outlet, and I was their outlet. I felt like I couldn't talk to anyone else."

Nina included.

Life had seemed good for a while. When Tom and Nina came home in early August 2011, they drove to Tennessee to pick up their three children and settled into being a family again. For the first two months, the Marine Corps eased them back into life off the battlefield, with short workdays and plenty of three- and four-day weekends. Tom lost himself in the old rhythms of home, everything he'd longed for while he baked in the Afghan sun, worried about his men, and stared at Jimmy's old cot. Many nights he grilled out, Sam Adams in hand, in the fenced-off oasis Nina had built for him during his first deployment, and nearly every weekend they drove to Myrtle Beach with the kids. They careened down slides at the water park, lounged on the beach, and ate out at night, dipping into the thousands they'd saved during their deployments, between the extra combat pay, no taxes, and neither of them being home to spend money.

But the relief of home wore off, and Tom's nerves frayed. Nina felt he was annoyed with her and the kids more and more, quick to lose patience as the kids raced through the house, banging doors. *Don't do that, she told them. Your dad doesn't like it.* She understood, far better than most spouses, the effects of a deployment. Of course loud noises might bother him, or the hassles of home life after the bizarre simplicity of war, and she knew how much he loved Jimmy and Ian. But this wasn't just anxiety or grief. This felt different. He seemed so far away, beyond reach. She'd asked what was wrong and he'd say, "Nothing." He sometimes told her he was thinking of Jimmy or Ian, but didn't go deeper.

He didn't tell her how the rest of the world fell away as Afghanistan came into focus, until he was both places at once—at home and over there, the two scenes playing on top of each other. The feel of Jimmy's dirtied hand in his. The smell of Jimmy's souring breath in his nostrils. His skin color draining to a waxy greenish yellow. His eyes pulling back, losing focus. Or the sound of blood gurgling in Ian's throat as he and Jesse sliced an airway into his trachea, as the smashed bomb jammer strapped to Ian's back beeped and its cooling fan whirred. *Beep. Beep. Beep.* "That's the shit that doesn't leave your head," Tom says. "Ever."

•　　•　　•

Tom swung open his bedroom door and bashed it against the wall, over and over, punching a jagged hole in the hallway wall with the doorknob. Andrew and Lee ran from their room into the hallway, screaming. Through the open doorway, Nina sat on the bed, an arm wrapped around little Gia, who'd been born a few months before Tom and Nina left for the deployment.

"Get out of here!" she yelled. "You're not going to terrorize us. We didn't do anything to you."

Tom charged from the house, and Nina locked the front door behind him and phoned Jesse. "You need to get your ass over here. He's flipping out."

They had argued more often in the months since their home-coming. Sometimes Tom blamed her for what he'd been through. If he'd just stayed with the fire department instead of rejoining the Marines, Ian and Jimmy might still be alive, and his own life wouldn't be falling apart. But the argument on this late November night hadn't been anything, just a mundane spat, when a few words over taking out the garbage spins into a storm.

As Nina stood in the living room and talked to Jesse on the phone, Tom circled around to the open back door and walked into the living room, with a look she'd never seen, out-of-his-head crazy. Their marriage could run hot—for better, for worse. They fought and cooled down and made up. But now she was frightened of him, for the first time since she'd known him. The boys retreated to their room, and Nina ran into Gia's room and locked herself and the baby inside. The house fell quiet. Tom stood outside the door. When he spoke, the anger had drained from his voice. "You're not going to have to worry about me any-more," he said. "I'm not going to be your problem."

Nina heard the front door close, and she followed him out-side. Tom sat in their blue Pontiac G6, parked at the curb. Nina called to him to get out of the car and talk to her, but she stayed close to the garage, figuring he might try to run her over if she neared the car. He pulled forward and back in the street several times, then backed up three hundred feet to the intersection and disappeared. Nina ran into the kitchen and opened the far right cabinet, where Tom kept his mini-pharmacy of prescription medications for insomnia, nightmares, anxiety, and pain. Gone, every bottle. She called the police, then Tom's father, who left within minutes for the six-hour drive south from Maryland to Camp Lejeune.

Jesse showed up first, then Ryan and Craig Fazenbaker and his wife. None of them seemed overly concerned. They'd all been there recently, needing a little time alone to catch their footing. Ryan told her he'd talked to Tom for ten minutes the day before and he'd seemed fine. "He's probably just going somewhere to cool off," he said.

"No," Nina said. "I know him. This isn't normal."

The Whorls use an iPhone application called Loopt that allows them to see the other's location when they're logged onto Facebook. In a dual-military household, with plenty of schedule changes and times when phones can't be used, it's an easy way for Nina to know that Tom is still out in Camp Lejeune's vast training area at the rifle range, so she should wait on starting dinner. For two hours, she checked her phone every few minutes, but Loopt hadn't updated, and still showed him at their house. She hoped he was a hundred miles away by now. Tom needed time, distance, and solitude when he was angry, so he usually would drive. After an argument in South Carolina, he drove to Florida. After another at Camp Lejeune, he drove to Virginia. He might drive for hours, but then he'd mellow, and she'd mellow, and they'd talk it through.

At ten p.m., his location finally changed on her phone, and she knew that he had gone to kill himself.

She left Jesse, Ryan, and Fazenbaker with her kids and sped toward the Jacksonville Mall, six miles away. There was the Pontiac, lights off, in front of the Ulta cosmetics store, which was Nina's favorite, always their first stop on trips to the mall. And there was Tom, slumped against the window.

"I found him!" she shouted to the 911 operator.

She opened the door and Tom pitched forward, his shirt front covered in vomit. He moaned and mumbled, barely conscious. Nina screamed at him to stand up. She worked her arms under his arms, bloodied from knife slices on his wrists, and half dragged him to the Jeep as a police car raced toward her.

He lay unconscious in the intensive care unit at Onslow Memorial Hospital, a breathing tube snaked down his throat because his body was too weak to breathe for itself. On the sixth day, he woke up, puzzled and disoriented. He tried to lift his arms, which had been restrained at his side.

"Tom, do you know why you're in here?" Nina asked him.

He shook his head. She showed him his bandaged wrists and the understanding washed over him, and he cried. Later he told her he thought it had been one more terrible dream.

Being home from Afghanistan hadn't been easy for Nina, either, as she watched her husband fall apart and tried to keep the family upright. They had always been each other's support—them against the world—but he'd retreated somewhere so dark that she couldn't find the path to bring him home. To see him so distraught that he'd choose death broke her heart, but she flushed with anger, too. "It was the biggest betrayal," she says. "It was selfish, and it was going to relieve his pain by giving me pain. I would have blamed myself for the rest of my life had I not found him.

"I just want to shake him and make it go away, make it stop and have my old husband back," she says. "I have to learn to love him this way. If he'd gotten his leg blown off, I'd learn to love him that way. I have to realize that he's not going to be like he was."

•　　　•　　　•

The Marine Corps celebrated Tom as a hero for the moment that weighed on him most heavily.

On a cool January morning, nearly eight hundred men of Second Battalion, Eighth Marines gathered beside their redbrick headquarters at Camp Lejeune, arranged by company, in perfect rows. Tom stood before them, at the position of attention: back rigid, chest out, arms at his sides with his fingers curled against his palms. He'd been promoted to staff sergeant three months earlier, and he wore on his collar the metal rank insignia he had taken from Jimmy's uniform that day in the compound.

His battalion commander, Lieutenant Colonel Harrill, who still had debris in his face from the blast that killed Jimmy, walked up to him in sharp, measured steps, stood nearly toe to toe, and pinned a red-white-and-blue ribbon to the left chest pocket of Tom's uniform. From the ribbon dangled a Bronze Star, over his heart. A Marine read from the citation for the Bronze Star with Valor over the loudspeaker: "His leadership directly led to the defeat of the insurgency in the vast majority of his battle space. By his extraordinary guidance, zealous initiative, and total dedication to duty, Sergeant Whorl reflected great credit upon himself and upheld the highest traditions of the Marine Corps."

The award references two days specifically: the running gunfight in Cocheran Village, in which they mortally wounded a Taliban fighter and recovered a cache of IED components, and the day Jimmy died. "His mental agility and ability to remain focused in a chaotic environment enabled him to rapidly coordinate a medical evacuation while simultaneously directing his squad into a security cordon. With disregard for his own safety, he repeatedly entered the blast site to treat a mortally wounded Marine and remain with him during his final moments."

Tom's father drove down from Maryland for the ceremony, and afterwards he took a picture of Tom, with the medal pinned to his chest. In the picture Tom is smiling, a rarity in the months since he'd come home. Yes, the medal reminded him—shouted to him—that Jimmy and Ian were dead, but it also made him proud of what the Third Platoon Marines, the living and the dead, had accomplished in northern Marjah.

In the weeks since he'd tried to kill himself, he had slowly started reframing the story of his time in Afghanistan, a messy, stumbling exploration that had begun as he lay in the hospital bed, wrists still bandaged, and his doctors asked if he'd like to speak with mental health.

His psychologist at Camp Lejeune hadn't been in combat, which Tom counted as an immediate mark against him, but he didn't say he knew how Tom was feeling, and that made up for plenty, because Tom was certain that almost no one could know that. The psychiatrist did tell him this: Yes, you lost two men. But you brought home forty-six, the result of thousands of good decisions. Of everything anyone had told him, the condolences and absolutions, the tough-love talks and the tips for coping, this made the most sense. "It's a small thing, but for me, that's what I needed to tell myself," he says. "Every time I think of the two I lost, I think of the forty-six I brought home, who have babies now, who have gotten married, who are doing great things with their lives."

That helped assuage the guilt, although Tom reached another conclusion, too: he may have brought home forty-six, but he couldn't stand losing another. He was done. "I can't do it anymore," he told the psychologist. "I can't lead eighteen- and nineteen-year-old guys into combat and not bring back one or two. I can't perform the job. I can't watch these kids get fucked up in the worst ways. I'm tapped out. And it's a hard thing to admit."

In June, Tom spent a month in Texas at an inpatient clinic for post-traumatic stress, where he learned how to better cope with the guilt and the sadness and how to pull himself back when he started obsessing over details, like the smell of Jimmy's last breaths or the gurgle of blood in Ian's throat.

Before he left for Texas, he told the Marines Corps he was finished, after thirteen years of service. He wanted a medical retirement. Upon his return, he moved to Camp Lejeune's Wounded Warrior Battalion, a unit full of men with shot-off faces, missing legs, and rattled brains, where the whole mission is getting better. He sometimes had three appointments a day, with neurologists, psychiatrists and psychologists, chiropractors for a back wrecked by too many years as a grunt, and counselors who helped him plan for life after the military. He worked out five times a week, with elective sports like surfing and kayaking twice a week, and he spent more time with his family.

For the first time in his Marine career, Tom didn't feel responsible for everyone else, and that was okay.

.   .   .

With Lee riding his bicycle outside on a warm Camp Lejeune evening, Andrew busy on the couch with a monster-truck video game, and Nina in the kitchen with Gia on her hip, Tom opens the closet door in his bedroom and drops to his knees. He slides out a scarred wooden toolbox, two feet wide, with three drawers and a hinged lid, passed down from his great-grandfather. He lifts the lid and his eyes flit across the contents, a story of origins and evolution, told through accumulated treasures and fierce heartache.

Great-Grandfather Mason's ivory-handled butcher knives from his days in the slaughterhouse. Grandfather Whorl's belt buckle, with its raised image of the USS *Nimitz* aircraft carrier, aboard which he'd served. A wooden checkerboard his grandfather Whorl had given his dad when he was a boy. Two musket balls from Gettysburg. A bag of sand, black and gravelly, that Tom collected on Iwo Jima in 2000. A ragged sliver of shrapnel Tom pulled from his own neck in 2009, and a black-and-white-checkered kaffiyeh scarf from that first deployment, given to him by an interpreter after Tom used his own to carry a Marine's severed arm.

He unpacks the box, fingers caressing these pieces of himself. The Velcro patch with Jimmy's name, rank, and unit that he stripped from Jimmy's uniform before they loaded him onto the medevac bird, and the dog tags Jimmy wore that day. His Bronze Star with Valor. A wad of Afghan money. The pirate flag that hung above Jimmy's cot from the first day of the deployment to the last, and the American flag that hung over Tom's cot.

In time, he'll drive up to Vermont and see Ian, out on the hillside in Danville Cemetery, with the White Mountains in the distance, and he'll visit Jimmy in Arlington National Cemetery. He knows he won't have any lasting peace until he does. But for now they meet here.

He flips through his journal, reminded of dates and names already grown foggy, his words pulling him back to Afghanistan. He unfolds a laminated satellite map from Third Platoon's sector and traces a finger across the patchwork of fields, crisscrossed with roads and canals and sprinkled with buildings, which appear as tiny squares. There's Patrol Base Dakota. The road where Ian was blown up. The building where Jimmy stepped on the bomb.

He sets aside the map and, with a reverence reserved for sacred artifacts, picks up the most cherished item, the picture of Ian, Jimmy, and Tom taken by Jesse an hour before Ian died, the picture that so disturbed Alison Malachowski when she first saw it because she feared Tom would be next, death moving down the line. Tom had figured the same, and the thought didn't trouble him; he knew he would die in Afghanistan. After all the bombs, and the bullets that passed so close he could feel them slice through the air, he still can't make sense of how he survived, or why.

When his boys are older, maybe when they have children of their own, he'll give them the box. "I'll tell them I served honorably," he says, "and the men I led served honorably." His boys can sift through the treasures, feel the jagged splinter of shrapnel pulled from their father's neck, run a fingertip over the raised lettering on Jimmy's dog tags, unfurl the Jolly Roger that hung above Jimmy's cot, still washed in the dust of Dakota. Their ears won't ring from the rifle fire. They won't smell the pungent bite of explosives hanging in the air, or hear Jimmy cry out for their father. And perhaps by then the sharpest edges will have dulled for Tom as well.

Orion

FINALIST—ESSAYS AND
CRITICISM

*This anthology closes with an
essay the National Magazine
Award judges described as both
"rich in suspense" and "cautiously
optimistic." The subject is nothing
less than the fate of humanity.
Charles C. Mann argues that
although other species have been
rewarded for their success with
extinction, our plasticity—our
ability not merely to adapt but to
change for the better—may earn
us survival. Mann is the author of
1491 and 1493, about the New
World before and after Christopher
Columbus. Mann's work has been
nominated for National Magazine
Awards twice before. Founded in
1982,* Orion *describes its mission
as hosting a conversation about
"the relationship between human
culture and the natural world."
Another* Orion *essay, Joe Wilkins's
scarifying "Out West," was an
award finalist in 2010.*

Charles C. Mann

State of the Species

The problem with environmentalists, Lynn Margulis used to say, is that they think conservation has something to do with biological reality. A researcher who specialized in cells and microorganisms, Margulis was one of the most important biologists in the last half century—she literally helped to reorder the tree of life, convincing her colleagues that it did not consist of two kingdoms (plants and animals), but five or even six (plants, animals, fungi, protists, and two types of bacteria).

Until Margulis's death last year, she lived in my town, and I would bump into her on the street from time to time. She knew I was interested in ecology, and she liked to needle me. Hey, *Charles*, she would call out, are you still all worked up about protecting endangered *species*?

Margulis was no apologist for unthinking destruction. Still, she couldn't help regarding conservationists' preoccupation with the fate of birds, mammals, and plants as evidence of their ignorance about the greatest source of evolutionary creativity: the microworld of bacteria, fungi, and protists. More than 90 percent of the living matter on earth consists of microorganisms and viruses, she liked to point out. Heck, the number of bacterial cells in our body is ten times more than the number of human cells!

Bacteria and protists can do things undreamed of by clumsy mammals like us: form giant supercolonies, reproduce either asexually or by swapping genes with others, routinely incorporate DNA from entirely unrelated species, merge into symbiotic beings—the list is as endless as it is amazing. Microorganisms have changed the face of the earth, crumbling stone and even giving rise to the oxygen we breathe. Compared to this power and diversity, Margulis liked to tell me, pandas and polar bears were biological epiphenomena—interesting and fun, perhaps, but not actually *significant.*

Does that apply to human beings, too? I once asked her, feeling like someone whining to Copernicus about why he couldn't move the earth a little closer to the center of the universe. Aren't we special *at all*?

This was just chitchat on the street, so I didn't write anything down. But as I recall it, she answered that *Homo sapiens* actually might be interesting—for a mammal, anyway. For one thing, she said, we're unusually successful.

Seeing my face brighten, she added: Of course, the fate of every successful species is to wipe itself out.

Of Lice and Men

Why and how did humankind become "unusually successful"? And what, to an evolutionary biologist, does "success" mean, if self-destruction is part of the definition? Does that self-destruction include the rest of the biosphere? What are human beings in the grand scheme of things anyway, and where are we headed? What is human nature, if there is such a thing, and how did we acquire it? What does that nature portend for our interactions with the environment? With 7 billion of us crowding the planet, it's hard to imagine more vital questions.

One way to begin answering them came to Mark Stoneking in 1999, when he received a notice from his son's school warning of a potential lice outbreak in the classroom. Stoneking is a researcher at the Max Planck Institute for Evolutionary Biology in Leipzig, Germany. He didn't know much about lice. As a biologist, it was natural for him to noodle around for information about them. The most common louse found on human bodies, he discovered, is *Pediculus humanus*. *P. humanus* has two subspecies: *P. humanus capitis*—head lice, which feed and live on the scalp—and *P. humanus corporis*—body lice, which feed on skin but live in clothing. In fact, Stoneking learned, body lice are so dependent on the protection of clothing that they cannot survive more than a few hours away from it.

It occurred to him that the two louse subspecies could be used as an evolutionary probe. *P. humanus capitis*, the head louse, could be an ancient annoyance, because human beings have always had hair for it to infest. But *P. humanus corporis*, the body louse, must not be especially old, because its need for clothing meant that it could not have existed while humans went naked. Humankind's great cover-up had created a new ecological niche, and some head lice had rushed to fill it. Evolution then worked its magic; a new subspecies, *P. humanus corporis*, arose. Stoneking couldn't be sure that this scenario had taken place, though it seemed likely. But if his idea were correct, discovering when the body louse diverged from the head louse would provide a rough date for when people first invented and wore clothing.

The subject was anything but frivolous: donning a garment is a complicated act. Clothing has practical uses—warming the body in cold places, shielding it from the sun in hot places—but it also transforms the appearance of the wearer, something that has proven to be of inescapable interest to *Homo sapiens*. Clothing is ornament and emblem; it separates human beings from their earlier, un-self-conscious state. (Animals run, swim, and fly without clothing, but only people can be *naked*.) The invention of clothing was a sign that a mental shift had occurred.

The human world had become a realm of complex, symbolic artifacts.

With two colleagues, Stoneking measured the difference between snippets of DNA in the two louse subspecies. Because DNA is thought to pick up small, random mutations at a roughly constant rate, scientists use the number of differences between two populations to tell how long ago they diverged from a common ancestor—the greater the number of differences, the longer the separation. In this case, the body louse had separated from the head louse about 70,000 years ago. Which meant, Stoneking hypothesized, that clothing also dated from about 70,000 years ago.

And not just clothing. As scientists have established, a host of remarkable things occurred to our species at about that time. It marked a dividing line in our history, one that made us who we are, and pointed us, for better and worse, toward the world we now have created for ourselves.

Homo sapiens emerged on the planet about 200,000 years ago, researchers believe. From the beginning, our species looked much as it does today. If some of those long-ago people walked by us on the street now, we would think they looked and acted somewhat oddly, but not that they weren't *people*. But those *anatomically* modern humans were not, as anthropologists say, *behaviorally* modern. Those first people had no language, no clothing, no art, no religion, nothing but the simplest, unspecialized tools. They were little more advanced, technologically speaking, than their predecessors—or, for that matter, modern chimpanzees. (The big exception was fire, but that was first controlled by *Homo erectus*, one of our ancestors, a million years ago or more.) Our species had so little capacity for innovation that archaeologists have found almost no evidence of cultural or social change during our first 100,000 years of existence. Equally important, for almost all that time these early humans were confined to a single, small area in the hot, dry savanna of East Africa (and possibly a second, still smaller area in southern Africa).

But now jump forward 50,000 years. East Africa looks much the same. So do the humans in it—but suddenly they are drawing and carving images, weaving ropes and baskets, shaping and wielding specialized tools, burying the dead in formal ceremonies, and perhaps worshipping supernatural beings. They are wearing clothes—lice-filled clothes, to be sure, but clothes nonetheless. Momentously, they are using language. And they are dramatically increasing their range. *Homo sapiens* is exploding across the planet.

What caused this remarkable change? By geologists' standards, 50,000 years is an instant, a finger snap, a rounding error. Nonetheless, most researchers believe that in that flicker of time, favorable mutations swept through our species, transforming anatomically modern humans into behaviorally modern humans. The idea is not absurd: in the last 400 years, dog breeders converted village dogs into creatures that act as differently as foxhounds, border collies, and Labrador retrievers. Fifty millennia, researchers say, is more than enough to make over a species.

Homo sapiens lacks claws, fangs, or exoskeletal plates. Rather, our unique survival skill is our ability to innovate, which originates with our species' singular brain—a three-pound universe of hyperconnected neural tissue, constantly aswirl with schemes and notions. Hence every hypothesized cause for the transformation of humankind from anatomically modern to behaviorally modern involves a physical alteration of the wet gray matter within our skulls. One candidate explanation is that in this period people developed hybrid mental abilities by interbreeding with Neanderthals. (Some Neanderthal genes indeed appear to be in our genome, though nobody is yet certain of their function.) Another putative cause is symbolic language—an invention that may have tapped latent creativity and aggressiveness in our species. A third is that a mutation might have enabled our brains to alternate between spacing out on imaginative chains of association and focusing our attention narrowly on the physical world around us. The former, in this view, allows us to come up with creative new strategies to achieve a goal, whereas the latter enables us to execute the concrete tactics required by those strategies.

Each of these ideas is fervently advocated by some researchers and fervently attacked by others. What is clear is that something made over our species between 100,000 and 50,000 years ago—and right in the middle of that period was Toba.

Children of Toba

About 75,000 years ago, a huge volcano exploded on the island of Sumatra. The biggest blast for several million years, the eruption created Lake Toba, the world's biggest crater lake, and ejected the equivalent of as much as 3,000 cubic kilometers of rock, enough to cover the District of Columbia in a layer of magma and ash that would reach to the stratosphere. A gigantic plume spread west, enveloping southern Asia in tephra (rock, ash, and dust). Drifts in Pakistan and India reached as high as six meters. Smaller tephra beds blanketed the Middle East and East Africa. Great rafts of pumice filled the sea and drifted almost to Antarctica.

In the long run, the eruption raised Asian soil fertility. In the short term, it was catastrophic. Dust hid the sun for as much as a decade, plunging the earth into a years-long winter accompanied by widespread drought. A vegetation collapse was followed by a collapse in the species that depended on vegetation, followed by a collapse in the species that depended on the species that depended on vegetation. Temperatures may have remained colder than normal for a thousand years. Orangutans, tigers, chimpanzees, cheetahs—all were pushed to the verge of extinction.

At about this time, many geneticists believe, *Homo sapiens'* numbers shrank dramatically, perhaps to a few thousand people—the size of a big urban high school. The clearest evidence of this bottleneck is also its main legacy: humankind's remarkable genetic uniformity. Countless people have viewed the differences between races as worth killing for, but compared to other primates—even compared to most other mammals—human beings are almost indistinguishable, genetically speaking. DNA is made from exceedingly long chains of "bases." Typically, about one out of every 2,000 of these "bases" differs between one person and the next. The equivalent figure from two *E. coli* (human gut bacteria) might be about one out of twenty. The bacteria in our intestines, that is, have a hundredfold more innate variability than their hosts—evidence, researchers say, that our species is descended from a small group of founders.

Uniformity is hardly the only effect of a bottleneck. When a species shrinks in number, mutations can spread through the entire population with astonishing rapidity. Or genetic variants that may have already been in existence—arrays of genes that confer better planning skills, for example—can suddenly become more common, effectively reshaping the species within a few generations as once-unusual traits become widespread.

Did Toba, as theorists like Richard Dawkins have argued, cause an evolutionary bottleneck that set off the creation of behaviorally modern people, perhaps by helping previously rare genes—Neanderthal DNA or an opportune mutation—spread through our species? Or did the volcanic blast simply clear away other human species that had previously blocked *H. sapiens*' expansion? Or was the volcano irrelevant to the deeper story of human change?

For now, the answers are the subject of careful back-and-forth in refereed journals and heated argument in faculty lounges. All that is clear is that about the time of Toba, new, behaviorally modern people charged so fast into the tephra that human footprints appeared in Australia within as few as 10,000 years, perhaps within 4,000 or 5,000. Stay-at-home *Homo sapiens* 1.0, a wallflower that would never have interested Lynn Margulis, had been replaced by aggressively expansive *Homo sapiens* 2.0. Something happened, for better and worse, and we were born.

One way to illustrate what this upgrade looked like is to consider *Solenopsis invicta*, the red imported fire ant. Geneticists believe that *S. invicta* originated in northern Argentina, an area with many rivers and frequent floods. The floods wipe out ant nests. Over the millennia, these small, furiously active creatures have acquired the ability to respond to rising water by coalescing into huge, floating, pullulating balls—workers on the outside, queen in the center—that drift to the edge of the flood. Once the waters recede, colonies swarm back into previously flooded land so rapidly that *S. invicta* actually can use the devastation to increase its range.

In the 1930s, *Solenopsis invicta* was transported to the United States, probably in ship ballast, which often consists of haphazardly loaded soil and gravel. As a teenaged bug enthusiast, Edward O. Wilson, the famed biologist, spotted the first colonies in the port of Mobile, Alabama. He saw some very happy fire ants. From the ant's point of view, it had been dumped into an empty, recently flooded expanse. *S. invicta* took off, never looking back.

The initial incursion watched by Wilson was likely just a few thousand individuals—a number small enough to suggest that random, bottleneck-style genetic change played a role in the species' subsequent history in this country. In their Argentine birthplace, fire-ant colonies constantly fight each other, reducing their numbers and creating space for other types of ant. In the United States, by contrast, the species forms cooperative supercolonies, linked clusters of nests that can spread for hundreds of miles. Systematically exploiting the landscape, these supercolonies monopolize every useful resource, wiping out other ant species along the way—models of zeal and rapacity. Transformed by chance and opportunity, new-model *S. invictus* needed just a few decades to conquer most of the southern United States.

Homo sapiens did something similar in the wake of Toba. For hundreds of thousands of years, our species had been restricted to East Africa (and, possibly, a similar area in the south). Now, abruptly, new-model *Homo sapiens* were racing across the continents like so many imported fire ants. The difference between humans and fire ants is that fire ants specialize in disturbed habitats. Humans, too, specialize in disturbed habitats—but we do the disturbing.

The World Is a Petri Dish

As a student at the University of Moscow in the 1920s, Georgii Gause spent years trying—and failing—to drum up support from the Rockefeller Foundation, then the most prominent funding source for non-American scientists who wished to work in the United States. Hoping to dazzle the foundation, Gause decided to perform some nifty experiments and describe the results in his grant application.

By today's standards, his methodology was simplicity itself. Gause placed half a gram of oatmeal in one hundred cubic centimeters of water, boiled the results for ten minutes to create a broth, strained the liquid portion of the broth into a container, diluted the mixture by adding water, and then decanted the contents into small, flat-bottomed test tubes. Into each he dripped five *Paramecium caudatum* or *Stylonychia mytilus*, both single-celled protozoans, one species per tube. Each of Gause's test tubes was a pocket ecosystem, a food web with a single node. He stored the tubes in warm places for a week and observed the results. He set down his conclusions in a 163-page book, *The Struggle for Existence*, published in 1934.

Today *The Struggle for Existence* is recognized as a scientific landmark, one of the first successful marriages of theory and experiment in ecology. But the book was not enough to get Gause a fellowship; the Rockefeller Foundation turned down the twenty-four-year-old Soviet student as insufficiently eminent. Gause could not visit the United States for another twenty years, by which time he had indeed become eminent, but as an antibiotics researcher.

What Gause saw in his test tubes is often depicted in a graph, time on the horizontal axis, the number of protozoa on the vertical. The line on the graph is a distorted bell curve, with its left side twisted and stretched into a kind of flattened S. At first the number of protozoans grows slowly, and the graph line slowly ascends to the right. But then the line hits an inflection point, and suddenly rockets upward—a frenzy of exponential growth. The mad rise continues until the organism begins to run out of food, at which point there is a second inflection point, and the growth curve levels off again as bacteria begin to die. Eventually the line descends, and the population falls toward zero.

Years ago I watched Lynn Margulis, one of Gause's successors, demonstrate these conclusions to a class at the University of Massachusetts with a time-lapse video of *Proteus vulgaris*, a bacterium that lives in the gastrointestinal tract. To humans, she said, *P. vulgaris* is mainly notable as a cause of urinary-tract infections. Left alone, it divides about every fifteen minutes. Margulis switched on the projector. Onscreen was a small, wobbly bubble—*P. vulgaris*—in a shallow, circular glass container: a petri dish. The class gasped. The cells in the time-lapse video seemed to shiver and boil, doubling in number every few seconds, colonies exploding out until the mass of bacteria filled the screen. In just thirty-six hours, she said, this single bacterium could cover the entire planet in a foot-deep layer of single-celled ooze. Twelve hours after that, it would create a living ball of bacteria the size of the earth.

Such a calamity never happens, because competing organisms and lack of resources prevent the overwhelming majority of *P. vulgaris* from reproducing. This, Margulis said, is natural selection, Darwin's great insight. All living creatures have the same purpose: to make more of themselves, ensuring their biological future by the only means available. Natural selection stands in the way of this goal. It prunes back almost all species, restricting their numbers and confining their range. In the human body, *P. vulgaris* is checked by the size of its habitat (portions of the human gut), the limits to its supply of nourishment (food proteins), and other, competing organisms. Thus constrained, its population remains roughly steady.

In the petri dish, by contrast, competition is absent; nutrients and habitat seem limitless, at least at first. The bacterium hits the first inflection point and rockets up the left side of the curve, swamping the petri dish in a reproductive frenzy. But then its colonies slam into the second inflection point: the edge of the dish. When the dish's nutrient supply is exhausted, *P. vulgaris* experiences a miniapocalypse.

By luck or superior adaptation, a few species manage to escape their limits, at least for a while. Nature's success stories, they are like Gause's protozoans; the world is their petri dish. Their populations grow exponentially; they take over large areas, overwhelming their environment as if no force opposed them. Then they annihilate themselves, drowning in their own wastes or starving from lack of food.

To someone like Margulis, *Homo sapiens* looks like one of these briefly fortunate species.

The Whip Hand

No more than a few hundred people initially migrated from Africa, if geneticists are correct. But they emerged into landscapes that by today's standards were as rich as Eden. Cool mountains, tropical wetlands, lush forests—all were teeming with food. Fish in the sea, birds in the air, fruit on the trees: breakfast was everywhere. People moved in.

Despite our territorial expansion, though, humans were still only in the initial stages of Gause's oddly shaped curve. Ten thousand years ago, most demographers believe, we numbered barely 5 million, about one human being for every hundred square kilometers of the earth's land surface. *Homo sapiens* was a scarcely noticeable dusting on the surface of a planet dominated by microbes. Nevertheless, at about this time—10,000 years ago, give or take a millennium—humankind finally began to approach the first inflection point. Our species was inventing agriculture.

The wild ancestors of cereal crops like wheat, barley, rice, and sorghum have been part of the human diet for almost as long as there have been humans to eat them. (The earliest evidence comes from Mozambique, where researchers found tiny bits of 105,000-year-old sorghum on ancient scrapers and grinders.) In some cases people may have watched over patches of wild grain, returning to them year after year. Yet despite the effort and care the plants were not domesticated. As botanists say, wild cereals "shatter"—individual grain kernels fall off as they ripen, scattering grain haphazardly, making it impossible to harvest the plants systematically. Only when unknown geniuses discovered naturally mutated grain plants that did not shatter—and purposefully selected, protected, and cultivated them—did true agriculture begin. Planting great expanses of those mutated crops, first in southern Turkey, later in half a dozen other places, early farmers created landscapes that, so to speak, waited for hands to harvest them.

Farming converted most of the habitable world into a petri dish. Foragers manipulated their environment with fire, burning areas to kill insects and encourage the growth of useful species—plants we liked to eat, plants that attracted the other creatures we liked to eat. Nonetheless, their diets were largely restricted to what nature happened to provide in any given time and season. Agriculture gave humanity the whip hand. Instead of natural ecosystems with their haphazard mix of species (so many useless organisms guzzling up resources!), farms are taut, disciplined communities conceived and dedicated to the maintenance of a single species: us.

Before agriculture, the Ukraine, American Midwest, and lower Yangzi were barely hospitable food deserts, sparsely inhabited landscapes of insects and grass; they became breadbaskets as people scythed away suites of species that used soil and water we wanted to dominate and replaced them with wheat, rice, and maize (corn). To one of Margulis's beloved bacteria, a petri dish is a uniform expanse of nutrients, all of which it can seize and consume. For *Homo sapiens*, agriculture transformed the planet into something similar.

As in a time-lapse movie, we divided and multiplied across the newly opened land. It had taken *Homo sapiens* 2.0, behaviorally modern humans, not even 50,000 years to reach the farthest corners of the globe. *Homo sapiens* 2.0.A—A for agriculture— took a tenth of that time to conquer the planet.

As any biologist would predict, success led to an increase in human numbers. *Homo sapiens* rocketed around the elbow of the first inflection point in the seventeenth and eighteenth centuries, when American crops like potatoes, sweet potatoes, and maize were introduced to the rest of the world. Traditional Eurasian and African cereals—wheat, rice, millet, and sorghum, for example—produce their grain atop thin stalks. Basic physics suggests that plants with this design will fatally topple if the grain gets too heavy, which means that farmers can actually be punished if they have an extra-bounteous harvest. By contrast, potatoes and sweet potatoes grow underground, which means that yields are not limited by the plant's architecture. Wheat farmers in Edinburgh and rice farmers in Edo alike discovered they could harvest four times as much dry food matter from an acre of tubers than they could from an acre of cereals. Maize, too, was a winner. Compared to other cereals, it has an extra-thick stalk and a different, more productive type of photosynthesis. Taken together, these immigrant crops vastly increased the food supply in Europe, Asia, and Africa, which in turn helped increase the supply of Europeans, Asians, and Africans. The population boom had begun.

Numbers kept rising in the nineteenth and twentieth centuries, after a German chemist, Justus von Liebig, discovered that plant growth was limited by the supply of nitrogen. Without nitrogen, neither plants nor the mammals that eat plants can create proteins, or for that matter the DNA and RNA that direct their production. Pure nitrogen gas ($N2$) is plentiful in the air but plants are unable to absorb it, because the two nitrogen atoms in $N2$ are welded so tightly together that plants cannot split them apart for use. Instead, plants take in nitrogen only when it is combined with hydrogen, oxygen, and other elements. To restore exhausted soil, traditional farmers grew peas, beans, lentils, and other pulses. (They never knew why these "green manures" replenished the land. Today we know that their roots contain special bacteria that convert useless $N2$ into "bio-available" nitrogen compounds.) After Liebig, European and American growers replaced those crops with high-intensity fertilizer—nitrogen-rich guano from Peru at first, then nitrates from mines in Chile. Yields soared. But supplies were much more limited than farmers liked. So intense was the competition for fertilizer that a guano war erupted in 1879, engulfing much of western South America. Almost 3,000 people died.

Two more German chemists, Fritz Haber and Carl Bosch, came to the rescue, discovering the key steps to making synthetic fertilizer from fossil fuels. (The process involves combining nitrogen gas and hydrogen from natural gas into ammonia, which is then used to create nitrogenous compounds usable by plants.) Haber and Bosch are not nearly as well known as they should be; their discovery, the Haber-Bosch process, has literally changed the chemical composition of the earth, a feat previously reserved for microorganisms. Farmers have injected so much synthetic fertilizer into the soil that soil and groundwater nitrogen levels have risen worldwide. Today, roughly a third of all the protein (animal and vegetable) consumed by humankind is derived from synthetic nitrogen fertilizer. Another way of putting this is to say that Haber and Bosch enabled *Homo sapiens* to extract about 2 billion people's worth of food from the same amount of available land.

The improved wheat, rice, and (to a lesser extent) maize varieties developed by plant breeders in the 1950s and 1960s are often said to have prevented another billion deaths. Antibiotics, vaccines, and water-treatment plants also saved lives by pushing back humankind's bacterial, viral, and fungal enemies. With almost no surviving biological competition, humankind had ever more unhindered access to the planetary petri dish: in the past two hundred years, the number of humans walking the planet ballooned from 1 to 7 billion, with a few billion more expected in coming decades.

Rocketing up the growth curve, human beings "now appropriate nearly 40% . . . of potential terrestrial productivity." This figure dates from 1986—a famous estimate by a team of Stanford biologists. Ten years later, a second Stanford team calculated that the "fraction of the land's biological production that is used or dominated" by our species had risen to as much as 50 percent. In 2000, the chemist Paul Crutzen gave a name to our time: the "Anthropocene," the era in which *Homo sapiens* became a force operating on a planetary scale. That year, half of the world's accessible fresh water was consumed by human beings.

Lynn Margulis, it seems safe to say, would have scoffed at these assessments of human domination over the natural world, which, in every case I know of, do not take into account the enormous impact of the microworld. But she would not have disputed the central idea: *Homo sapiens* has become a successful species, and is growing accordingly.

If we follow Gause's pattern, growth will continue at a delirious speed until we hit the second inflection point. At that time we will have exhausted the resources of the global petri dish, or effectively made the atmosphere toxic with our carbon-dioxide waste, or both. After that, human life will be, briefly, a Hobbesian nightmare, the living overwhelmed by the dead. When the king falls, so do his minions; it is possible that our fall might also take down most mammals and many plants. Possibly sooner, quite likely later, in this scenario, the earth will again be a choir of bacteria, fungi, and insects, as it has been through most of its history.

It would be foolish to expect anything else, Margulis thought. More than that, it would be unnatural.

As Plastic as Canby

In *The Phantom Tollbooth*, Norton Juster's classic, pun-filled adventure tale, the young Milo and his faithful companions unexpectedly find themselves transported to a bleak, mysterious island. Encountering a man in a tweed jacket and beanie, Milo asks him where they are. The man replies by asking if they know who he is—the man is, apparently, confused on the subject. Milo and his friends confer, then ask if he can describe himself.

> "Yes, indeed," the man replied happily. "I'm as tall as can be"—and he grew straight up until all that could be seen of him were his shoes and stockings—"and I'm as short as can be"—and he shrank down to the size of a pebble. "I'm as generous as can be," he said, handing each of them a large red apple, "and I'm as selfish as can be," he snarled, grabbing them back again.

In short order, the companions learn that the man is as strong as can be, weak as can be, smart as can be, stupid as can be, graceful as can be, clumsy as—you get the picture. "Is that any help to you?" he asks. Again, Milo and his friends confer, and realize that the answer is actually quite simple:

"Without a doubt," Milo concluded brightly, "you must be Canby."

"Of course, yes, of course," the man shouted. "Why didn't I think of that? I'm as happy as can be."

With Canby, Juster presumably meant to mock a certain kind of babyish, uncommitted man-child. But I can't help thinking of poor old Canby as exemplifying one of humankind's greatest attributes: *behavioral plasticity.* The term was coined in 1890 by the pioneering psychologist William James, who defined it as "the possession of a structure weak enough to yield to an influence, but strong enough not to yield all at once." Behavioral plasticity, a defining feature of *Homo sapiens'* big brain, means that humans can change their habits; almost as a matter of course, people change careers, quit smoking or take up vegetarianism, convert to new religions, and migrate to distant lands where they must learn strange languages. This plasticity, this Canby-hood, is the hallmark of our transformation from anatomically modern *Homo sapiens* to behaviorally modern *Homo sapiens*—and the reason, perhaps, we were able to survive when Toba reconfigured the landscape.

Other creatures are much less flexible. Like apartment-dwelling cats that compulsively hide in the closet when visitors arrive, they have limited capacity to welcome new phenomena and change in response. Human beings, by contrast, are so exceptionally plastic that vast swaths of neuroscience are devoted to trying to explain how this could come about. (Nobody knows for certain, but some researchers now think that particular genes give their possessors a heightened, inborn awareness of their environment, which can lead both to useless, neurotic sensitivity and greater ability to detect and adapt to new situations.)

Plasticity in individuals is mirrored by plasticity on a societal level. The caste system in social species like honeybees is elaborate and finely tuned but fixed, as if in amber, in the loops of their DNA. Some leafcutter ants are said to have, next to human beings, the biggest and most complex societies on earth, with elaborately coded behavior that reaches from disposal of the dead to complex agricultural systems. Housing millions of individuals in inconceivably ramose subterranean networks, leafcutter colonies are "Earth's ultimate superorganisms," Edward O. Wilson has written. But they are incapable of fundamental change. The centrality and authority of the queen cannot be challenged; the tiny minority of males, used only to inseminate queens, will never acquire new responsibilities.

Human societies are far more varied than their insect cousins, of course. But the true difference is their plasticity. It is why humankind, a species of Canbys, has been able to move into every corner of the earth, and to control what we find there. Our ability to change ourselves to extract resources from our surroundings with ever-increasing efficiency is what has made *Homo sapiens* a successful species. It is our greatest blessing.

Or *was* our greatest blessing, anyway.

Discount Rates

By 2050, demographers predict, as many as 10 billion human beings will walk the earth, 3 billion more than today. Not only will more people exist than ever before, they will be richer than ever before. In the last three decades hundreds of millions in China, India, and other formerly poor places have lifted themselves from destitution—arguably the most important, and certainly the most heartening, accomplishment of our time. Yet, like all human enterprises, this great success will pose great difficulties.

In the past, rising incomes have invariably prompted rising demand for goods and services. Billions more jobs, homes, cars, fancy electronics—these are things the newly prosperous will want. (Why shouldn't they?) But the greatest challenge may be the most basic of all: feeding these extra mouths. To agronomists, the prospect is sobering. The newly affluent will not want their ancestors' gruel. Instead they will ask for pork and beef and lamb. Salmon will sizzle on their outdoor grills. In winter, they will want strawberries, like people in New York and London, and clean bibb lettuce from hydroponic gardens.

All of these, each and every one, require vastly more resources to produce than simple peasant agriculture. Already 35 percent of the world's grain harvest is used to feed livestock. The process is terribly inefficient: between seven and ten kilograms of grain are required to produce one kilogram of beef. Not only will the world's farmers have to produce enough wheat and maize to feed 3 billion more people, they will have to produce enough to give them all hamburgers and steaks. Given present patterns of food consumption, economists believe, we will need to produce about 40 percent more grain in 2050 than we do today.

How can we provide these things for all these new people? That is only part of the question. The full question is: How can we provide them without wrecking the natural systems on which all depend?

Scientists, activists, and politicians have proposed many solutions, each from a different ideological and moral perspective. Some argue that we must drastically throttle industrial civilization. (Stop energy-intensive, chemical-based farming today! Eliminate fossil fuels to halt climate change!) Others claim that only intense exploitation of scientific knowledge can save us. (Plant super-productive, genetically modified crops now! Switch to nuclear power to halt climate change!) No matter which course is chosen, though, it will require radical, large-scale transformations in the human enterprise—a daunting, hideously expensive task.

Worse, the ship is too large to turn quickly. The world's food supply cannot be decoupled rapidly from industrial agriculture, if that is seen as the answer. Aquifers cannot be recharged with a snap of the fingers. If the high-tech route is chosen, genetically modified crops cannot be bred and tested overnight. Similarly,

520
Charles C. Mann

carbon-sequestration techniques and nuclear power plants cannot be deployed instantly. Changes must be planned and executed decades in advance of the usual signals of crisis, but that's like asking healthy, happy sixteen-year-olds to write living wills.

Not only is the task daunting, it's *strange*. In the name of nature, we are asking human beings to do something deeply unnatural, something no other species has ever done or could ever do: constrain its own growth (at least in some ways). Zebra mussels in the Great Lakes, brown tree snakes in Guam, water hyacinth in African rivers, gypsy moths in the northeastern United States, rabbits in Australia, Burmese pythons in Florida—all these successful species have overrun their environments, heedlessly wiping out other creatures. Like Gause's protozoans, they are racing to find the edges of their petri dish. Not one has voluntarily turned back. Now we are asking *Homo sapiens* to fence itself in.

What a peculiar thing to ask! Economists like to talk about the "discount rate," which is their term for preferring a bird in hand today over two in the bush tomorrow. The term sums up part of our human nature as well. Evolving in small, constantly moving bands, we are as hard-wired to focus on the immediate and local over the long-term and faraway as we are to prefer park-like savannas to deep dark forests. Thus, we care more about the broken stoplight up the street today than conditions next year in Croatia, Cambodia, or the Congo. Rightly so, evolutionists point out: Americans are far more likely to be killed at that stoplight today than in the Congo next year. Yet here we are asking governments to focus on potential planetary boundaries that may not be reached for decades. Given the discount rate, nothing could be more understandable than the U.S. Congress's failure to grapple with, say, climate change. From this perspective, is there any reason to imagine that *Homo sapiens*, unlike mussels, snakes, and moths, can exempt itself from the natural fate of all successful species?

To biologists like Margulis, who spend their careers arguing that humans are simply part of the natural order, the answer should be clear. All life is similar at base. All species seek without pause to make more of themselves—that is their goal. By multiplying till we reach our maximum possible numbers, even as we take out much of the planet, we are fulfilling our destiny.

From this vantage, the answer to the question whether we are doomed to destroy ourselves is yes. It should be obvious.

Should be—but perhaps is not.

Hara Hachi Bu

When I imagine the profound social transformation necessary to avoid calamity, I think about Robinson Crusoe, hero of Daniel Defoe's famous novel. Defoe clearly intended his hero to be an exemplary man. Shipwrecked on an uninhabited island off Venezuela in 1659, Crusoe is an impressive example of behavioral plasticity. During his twenty-seven-year exile he learns to catch fish, hunt rabbits and turtles, tame and pasture island goats, prune and support local citrus trees, and create "plantations" of barley and rice from seeds that he salvaged from the wreck. (Defoe apparently didn't know that citrus and goats were not native to the Americas and thus Crusoe probably wouldn't have found them there.) Rescue comes at last in the form of a shipful of ragged mutineers, who plan to maroon their captain on the supposedly empty island. Crusoe helps the captain recapture his ship and offers the defeated mutineers a choice: trial in England or permanent banishment to the island. All choose the latter. Crusoe has harnessed so much of the island's productive power to human use that even a gaggle of inept seamen can survive there in comfort.

To get Crusoe on his unlucky voyage, Defoe made him an officer on a slave ship, transporting captured Africans to South America. Today, no writer would make a slave seller the admirable hero of a novel. But in 1720, when Defoe published *Robinson Crusoe*, no readers said boo about Crusoe's occupation, because slavery was the norm from one end of the world to another. Rules and names differed from place to place, but coerced labor was everywhere, building roads, serving aristocrats, and fighting wars. Slaves teemed in the Ottoman Empire, Mughal India, and Ming China. Unfree hands were less common in continental Europe, but Portugal, Spain, France, England, and the Netherlands happily exploited slaves by the million in their American colonies. Few protests were heard; slavery had been part of the fabric of life since the code of Hammurabi.

Then, in the space of a few decades in the nineteenth century, slavery, one of humankind's most enduring institutions, almost vanished.

The sheer implausibility of this change is staggering. In 1860, slaves were, collectively, the single most valuable economic asset in the United States, worth an estimated $3 billion, a vast sum in those days (and about $10 trillion in today's money). Rather than investing in factories like northern entrepreneurs, southern businessmen had sunk their capital into slaves. And from their perspective, correctly so—masses of enchained men and women had made the region politically powerful, and gave social status to an entire class of poor whites. Slavery was the foundation of the social order. It was, thundered John C. Calhoun, a former senator, secretary of state, and vice president, "instead of an evil, a good—a positive good." Yet just a few years after Calhoun spoke, part of the United States set out to destroy this institution, wrecking much of the national economy and killing half a million citizens along the way.

Incredibly, the turn against slavery was as universal as slavery itself. Great Britain, the world's biggest human trafficker, closed down its slave operations in 1808, though they were among the nation's most profitable industries. The Netherlands, France,

Spain, and Portugal soon followed. Like stars winking out at the approach of dawn, cultures across the globe removed themselves from the previously universal exchange of human cargo. Slavery still exists here and there, but in no society anywhere is it formally accepted as part of the social fabric.

Historians have provided many reasons for this extraordinary transition. But one of the most important is that abolitionists had convinced huge numbers of ordinary people around the world that slavery was a moral disaster. An institution fundamental to human society for millennia was swiftly dismantled by ideas and a call to action, loudly repeated.

In the last few centuries, such profound changes have occurred repeatedly. Since the beginning of our species, for instance, every known society has been based on the domination of women by men. (Rumors of past matriarchal societies abound, but few archaeologists believe them.) In the long view, women's lack of liberty has been as central to the human enterprise as gravitation is to the celestial order. The degree of suppression varied from time to time and place to place, but women never had an equal voice; indeed, some evidence exists that the penalty for possession of two X chromosomes *increased* with technological progress. Even as the industrial North and agricultural South warred over the treatment of Africans, they regarded women identically: in neither half of the nation could they attend college, have a bank account, or own property. Equally confining were women's lives in Europe, Asia, and Africa. Nowadays women are the majority of U.S. college students, the majority of the workforce, and the majority of voters. Again, historians assign multiple causes to this shift in the human condition, rapid in time, staggering in scope. But one of the most important was the power of ideas—the voices, actions, and examples of suffragists, who through decades of ridicule and harassment pressed their case. In recent years something similar seems to have occurred with gay rights: first a few lonely advocates, censured and mocked; then victories in the social and legal sphere; finally, perhaps, a slow movement to equality.

Less well known, but equally profound: the decline in violence. Foraging societies waged war less brutally than industrial societies, but more frequently. Typically, archaeologists believe, about a quarter of all hunters and gatherers were killed by their fellows. Violence declined somewhat as humans gathered themselves into states and empires, but was still a constant presence. When Athens was at its height in the fourth and fifth centuries BC, it was ever at war: against Sparta (First and Second Peloponnesian Wars, Corinthian War); against Persia (Greco-Persian Wars, Wars of the Delian League); against Aegina (Aeginetan War); against Macedon (Olynthian War); against Samos (Samian War); against Chios, Rhodes, and Cos (Social War).

In this respect, classical Greece was nothing special—look at the ghastly histories of China, sub-Saharan Africa, or Mesoamerica. Similarly, early modern Europe's wars were so fast and furious that historians simply gather them into catchall titles like the Hundred Years' War, followed by the shorter but even more destructive Thirty Years' War. And even as Europeans and their descendants paved the way toward today's concept of universal human rights by creating documents like the Bill of Rights and the Declaration of the Rights of Man and of the Citizen, Europe remained so mired in combat that it fought two conflicts of such massive scale and reach they became known as "world" wars.

Since the Second World War, however, rates of violent death have fallen to the lowest levels in known history. Today, the average person is far less likely to be slain by another member of the species than ever before—an extraordinary transformation that has occurred, almost unheralded, in the lifetime of many of the people reading this article. As the political scientist Joshua Goldstein has written, "we are winning the war on war." Again, there are multiple causes. But Goldstein, probably the leading scholar in this field, argues that the most important is the emergence of the United Nations and other transnational bodies, an expression of the ideas of peace activists earlier in the last century.

As a relatively young species, we have an adolescent propensity to make a mess: we pollute the air we breathe and the water we drink, and appear stalled in an age of carbon dumping and nuclear experimentation that is putting countless species at risk including our own. But we are making undeniable progress nonetheless. No European in 1800 could have imagined that in 2000 Europe would have no legal slavery, women would be able to vote, and gay people would be able to marry. No one could have guessed a continent that had been tearing itself apart for centuries would be free of armed conflict, even amid terrible economic times. Given this record, even Lynn Margulis might pause (maybe).

Preventing *Homo sapiens* from destroying itself à la Gause would require a still greater transformation—behavioral plasticity of the highest order—because we would be pushing against biological nature itself. The Japanese have an expression, *hara hachi bu*, which means, roughly speaking, "belly 80 percent full." *Hara hachi bu* is shorthand for an ancient injunction to stop eating before feeling full. Nutritionally, the command makes a great deal of sense. When people eat, their stomachs produce peptides that signal fullness to the nervous system. Unfortunately, the mechanism is so slow that eaters frequently perceive satiety only after they have consumed too much—hence the all-too-common condition of feeling bloated or sick from overeating. Japan—actually, the Japanese island of Okinawa—is the only place on earth where large numbers of people are known to restrict their own calorie intake systematically and routinely. Some researchers claim that *hara hachi bu* is responsible for Okinawans' notoriously long life spans. But I think of it as a metaphor for stopping before the second inflection point, voluntarily forswearing short-term consumption to obtain a long-term benefit.

Evolutionarily speaking, a species-wide adoption of *hara hachi bu* would be unprecedented. Thinking about it, I can picture Lynn Margulis rolling her eyes. But is it so unlikely that our species, Canbys one and all, would be able to do exactly that before we round that fateful curve of the second inflection point and nature does it for us?

I can imagine Margulis's response: You're imagining our species as some sort of big-brained, hyperrational, benefit-cost-calculating computer! A better analogy is the bacteria at our feet! Still, Margulis would be the first to agree that removing the shackles from women and slaves has begun to unleash the suppressed talents of two-thirds of the human race. Drastically reducing violence has prevented the waste of countless lives and staggering amounts of resources. Is it really impossible to believe that we wouldn't use those talents and those resources to draw back before the abyss?

Our record of success is not that long. In any case, past successes are no guarantee of the future. But it is terrible to suppose that we could get so many other things right and get this one wrong. To have the imagination to see our potential end, but not have the imagination to avoid it. To send humankind to the moon but fail to pay attention to the earth. To have the potential but to be unable to use it—to be, in the end, no different from the protozoa in the petri dish. It would be evidence that Lynn Margulis's most dismissive beliefs had been right after all. For all our speed and voraciousness, our changeable sparkle and flash, we would be, at last count, not an especially interesting species.

Permissions

Contributors

ROGER ANGELL has been a contributor to *The New Yorker* since 1944. He became a fiction editor in 1956 and is now a senior editor and staff writer at the magazine. His first contribution to the magazine was a piece of fiction titled "Three Ladies in the Morning." While stationed in the Central Pacific during the Second World War, where he was the managing editor of the air force enlisted-man's weekly *TIG Brief*, he wrote an article for *The New Yorker* about a bombing mission to Iwo Jima. After his work on *Brief*, he became a senior editor at *Holiday* magazine, where he remained from 1947 to 1956. Once on the *New Yorker* staff, he continued to contribute stories, casuals, and Notes and Comment pieces to the magazine and began reporting on sports. Since 1962 he has written more than a hundred Sporting Scene pieces, mostly about baseball but also on tennis, hockey, football, rowing, and horse racing. In addition, he has written film reviews and, for many years, the magazine's Christmas verse, "Greetings, Friends!" He continues as one of *The New Yorker*'s fiction editors, editing the stories of John Updike, William Trevor, and Woody Allen.

Angell's writing has appeared in many anthologies and has been collected in nine of his own books. The first, *The Stone Arbor and Other Stories* (1960), is a selection of short stories. *A Day in the Life of Roger Angell* (1970) is a book of casuals and parodies. His most recent, *Let Me Finish* (2006), is a collection of his memoir writing. His baseball books include *The Summer Game* (1972), *Five Seasons* (1977), *Late Innings* (1982), *Season Ticket* (1988), *Once More Around the Park* (1991), *A Pitcher's Story* (2001), and *Game Time* (2003). In February 1997, Random House published *Nothing But You: Love Stories from* The New Yorker, an anthology of fiction selected by Angell.

Angell has won a number of awards for his writing, including a George Polk Award for Commentary. In 2011 he was the inaugural winner of the PEN/ESPN Lifetime Achievement Award for Literary Sports Writing. He is a longtime ex officio member of the council of the Authors Guild.

Angell lives in Manhattan.

TA-NEHISI COATES is a senior editor at *The Atlantic* and the author of the memoir *The Beautiful Struggle*. He lives in New York with his wife and son.

PAMELA COLLOFF is an executive editor at *Texas Monthly* and has been writing for the magazine since 1997. Her work has also appeared in *The New Yorker* and has been anthologized in three editions of *Best American Crime Reporting* as well as the e-book collection *Next Wave: America's New Generation of Great Literary Journalists*. Colloff is a four-time National Magazine Award finalist. She was nominated in 2001 for her article on school prayer and then again in 2011 for her two-part series, "Innocence Lost" and "Innocence Found," about wrongly convicted death row inmate Anthony Graves. One month after the publication of "Innocence Lost," the Burleson County district attorney's office dropped all charges against Graves and released him from jail, where he had been awaiting retrial. Colloff's article—an exhaustive examination of Graves' case—was credited with helping Graves win his freedom after eighteen years behind bars.

In 2013 she was nominated twice more, for "Hannah and Andrew" and "The Innocent Man," a two-part series about Michael Morton, a man who spent twenty-five years wrongfully imprisoned for the brutal murder of his wife, Christine. The latter earned Colloff her first National Magazine Award.

Colloff holds a bachelor's degree in English literature from Brown University and was raised in New York City. She lives in Austin with her husband and their two children.

SABRINA RUBIN ERDELY is an award-winning feature writer and investigative journalist based in Philadelphia. Her work has appeared in *Glamour, GQ, Men's Health, Mother Jones, The New Yorker, Rolling Stone*, and *Self*, among other national magazines. Her articles have been anthologized in *Best American Crime Reporting* and have received a number of awards, including a National Magazine Award nomination.

Erdely specializes in long-form narrative writing, especially about crime and health. She has written about con artists, murder investigations, vicious divorces, power brokers, lovable eccentrics, bioweapons, cults, sexual violence, medical ethics, forgotten artists, and teachers who have affairs with students—among other subjects.

DEXTER FILKINS joined *The New Yorker* in January 2011 and has since written about a bank heist in Afghanistan and the democratic protests in the Middle East. Before coming to *The New Yorker*, Filkins had been with the *New York Times* since 2000, reporting from Afghanistan, Pakistan, New York, and Iraq, where he was based from 2003 to 2006. He has also worked for the *Miami Herald* and the *Los Angeles Times*, where he was chief of the paper's New Delhi bureau. In 2009, he won a Pulitzer Prize as part of a team of *New York Times* reporters in Pakistan and Afghanistan. He was a Nieman Fellow at Harvard University in 2006–07 and a fellow at the Carr Center for Human Rights Policy at Harvard's Kennedy School of Government in 2007–08. He has received numerous prizes, including two George Polk Awards and three Overseas Press Club Awards. His 2008 book *The Forever War* won the National Book Critics Circle Award for

Best Nonfiction Book and was named a best book of the year by the *New York Times*, the *Washington Post*, *Time*, and the *Boston Globe*.

A teenage finalist for the American Poet's Prize and former medical student and researcher, **CHARLES GRAEBER** is an award-winning journalist and contributor to publications including *GQ*, *The New Yorker*, *New York*, *Vogue*, *Outside*, Bloomberg *Businessweek*, the *New York Times Magazine*, and *Wired*, for which he is a contributing editor. His journalism has received honors such as the Overseas Press Club Award for Outstanding International Journalism and the New York Press Club Prize for Spot News Reportage and has been anthologized in *The Best American Business Writing*, *The Best American Crime Writing*, *The Best American Science Writing*, *The Best of Ten Years of National Geographic Adventure*, and *The Best of Twenty Years of Wired*. Born in Iowa, he is now a resident of Nantucket, Massachusetts, but spends his summers in Brooklyn, New York.

CHRIS HEATH has been working since 2004 as a correspondent at *GQ*, where he has written countless cover stories as well as reported features on Iraqi refugees, post-Katrina New Orleans, and the devastating Japanese tsunami. In 2006, he was nominated for a National Magazine Award in the Profile Writing category for his story about country legend Merle Haggard. He has previously written for *Rolling Stone*, *Details*, *Telegraph Magazine*, and *The Face*. He is also the author of *Feel: Robbie Williams*, the best-selling 2004 book about the British pop superstar.

CHRIS JONES is a writer at large at *Esquire* and the back-page columnist for *ESPN The Magazine*. He has won two National Magazine Awards for his feature writing, but Robert Caro is much better at writing than he.

STEPHEN KING was born in Portland, Maine, in 1947. He made his first professional short story sale in 1967 to *Startling Mystery Stories*. In 1973 Doubleday accepted his novel *Carrie* for publication. In the years since he has written more than fifty worldwide best-sellers, most recently *Doctor Sleep* (2013), *Joyland* (2013), *The Wind Through the Keyhole* (2012), and *11/22/63* (2011). In 2000 he published *On Writing: A Memoir of the Craft*. He and his wife, novelist Tabitha King, live in Maine and Florida.

DAHLIA LITHWICK is a senior editor at *Slate*. She writes "Supreme Court Dispatches" and has covered the Microsoft trial and other legal issues for *Slate*. Before joining *Slate* as a freelancer in 1999, she worked for a family law firm in Reno, Nevada. Her work has appeared in *Elle*, *The New Republic*, the *Ottawa Citizen*, and the *Washington Post*. She is coauthor of *Me v. Everybody: Absurd Contracts for an Absurd World*, a legal humor book. She is a graduate of Yale University and Stanford Law School.

CHARLES C. MANN'S first feature for *Orion*, "The Dawn of the Homogenocene," appeared in the May/June 2011 issue. His book *1493* is now out in paperback.

DAPHNE MERKIN is a cultural critic and a contributing writer to *Bookforum*, *Elle*, the *New York Times Magazine*, *T*, *Tablet*, and *Travel + Leisure*. Formerly a staff writer for *The New Yorker*, where she wrote about film, books, and figures as varied as Sigmund Freud, Marilyn Monroe, and Kurt Cobain, her current work continues to span topics both high and low—including, most recently, living with regrets, Kim Kardashian, her love of Cornwall, and designer Jason Wu. Daphne is the author of a novel, *Enchantment*, and a collection of essays, *Dreaming of Hitler*. She lives with her daughter in New York City and is at work on a memoir, *The Dark Season*.

BRIAN MOCKENHAUPT is a contributing editor at *Esquire* and *Reader's Digest* and is the nonfiction editor at the *Journal of Military Experience*. Since leaving the U.S. Army in 2005, he has written extensively on military and veteran affairs, reporting from Afghanistan and Iraq, hometowns and hospitals. "The Living and the Dead" won the 2013 Michael Kelly Award.

MAGGIE PALEY is a writer, editor, and editorial associate of *The Paris Review*.

FRANK RICH joined *New York* in June 2011 as writer at large, writing monthly on politics and culture and editing a special monthly section anchored by his essay. He is also a commentator on nymag.com, engaging in regular dialogues on the news of the week.

Rich joined the magazine following a distinguished career at the *New York Times*, where he had been an op-ed columnist since 1994. He was previously the paper's chief drama critic from 1980 to 1993. His weekly 1,500-word essay helped inaugurate the expanded opinion pages that the *Times* introduced in the Sunday "Week in Review" section in 2005. From 2003 to 2005, Rich had been the front-page columnist for the Sunday "Arts and Leisure" section as part of that section's redesign and expansion. He also served as senior adviser to the *Times*'s culture editor on the paper's overall cultural-news report. From 1999 to 2003 he was also senior writer for the *New York Times Magazine*. The dual title was a first for the *Times*.

He has written about culture and politics for many national publications. His books include *Ghost Light: A Memoir* and, most recently, *The Greatest Story Ever Sold: The Decline and Fall of Truth from 9/11 to Katrina*. Rich is also a creative consultant to

HBO, where he is an executive producer of two projects, *Veep*, a comedy series written and directed by Armando Iannucci and starring Julia Louis-Dreyfus, and a documentary on Stephen Sondheim.

A native of Washington, D.C., and graduate of Harvard, he lives in New York City with his wife, the novelist and journalist Alex Witchel.

MIMI SWARTZ, the author, with Sherron Watkins, of *Power Failue: The Inside Story of the Collapse of Enron*, is an executive editor of *Texas Monthly*. Previously, she was a staff writer at *Talk* from April 1999 to April 2001 and a staff writer at *The New Yorker* from 1997 to 2001. Before joining *The New Yorker*, she worked at *Texas Monthly* for thirteen years. In 1996 Swartz was a finalist for two National Magazine Awards and won in the Public Interest category for "Not What the Doctor Ordered." She was also a National Magazine Award finalist for her November 2005 issue story on tort reform, titled "Hurt? Injured? Need a Lawyer? Too Bad!" and won the 2006 John Bartlow Martin Award for Public Interest, Magazine Journalism, for the same story. In 2013 she won her second National Magazine Award (again in the category of Public Interest), for "Mothers, Sisters, Daughters, Wives," a compelling look at the state of women's health care in Texas.

Over the years, Swartz's work has appeared in *Esquire*, *Slate*, *National Geographic*, *Vanity Fair*, and the *New York Times* op-ed page and Sunday magazine. It has also been collected in *Best American Political Writing 2006* and *Best American Sportswriting 2007*. She has been a member of the Texas Institute of Letters since 1994. Swartz grew up in San Antonio and graduated from Hampshire College, in Amherst, Massachusetts. She now lives in Houston with her husband, John Wilburn, and son, Sam.

MICHAEL WOLFF is the author of five books, including *The Man Who Owns the News* and *Burn Rate*. He is a long-time writer for *New York* and *Vanity Fair* as well as numerous other publications. His work has won many awards and is widely anthologized. He lives in New York City.

ROBERT F. WORTH is a staff writer for the *New York Times Magazine*. He first moved to the Middle East in 2003 to cover the Iraq war and remained in Baghdad until 2006. He then became the paper's Beirut bureau chief, reporting from across the region. Since 2011, he has written narrative accounts of the ongoing upheavals in Egypt, Libya, and Yemen for the *Times Magazine* and the *New York Review of Books*. He was born and raised in New York City and now lives in Washington, D.C., with his wife and two sons.